What Color Is
Your Parachute?

Other Books by Richard N. Bolles

The What Color Is Your Parachute? Workbook

Job-Hunting on the Internet,
    Fourth edition, revised and enlarged
    (with Mark E. Bolles as co-author)

The Career Counselor's Handbook
    (with Howard Figler as co-author)

The Three Boxes of Life,
    And How to Get Out of Them

How to Find Your Mission in Life

Job-Hunting for the So-Called Handicapped
    (with Dale Brown as co-author)

2006 Edition

What Color Is Your Parachute?

A Practical Manual for Job-Hunters and Career-Changers

by
Richard Nelson Bolles

TEN SPEED PRESS
Berkeley | Toronto

This is an annual. That is to say, it is substantially revised each year, the new edition appearing each October. Those wishing to submit additions, corrections, or suggestions for the 2007 edition must *submit them prior to February 1, 2006, using the form provided in the back of this book. (Forms reaching us after that date will, unfortunately, have to wait for the 2008 edition.)*

NEW LEAF PAPER
ENVIRONMENTAL BENEFITS STATEMENT

What Color is Your Parachute? is printed on New Leaf EcoBook50, made with 50% post-consumer waste, processed chlorine free. By using this environmental paper, Ten Speed Press saved the following resources:

trees	water	energy	solid waste	greenhouse gases
1,116 fully grown	395,422 gallons	703 million BTUs	51,567 pounds	88,446 pounds

Calculated based on research done by Environmental Defense and other members of the Paper Task Force.
© New Leaf Paper   www.newleafpaper.com   888.989.5323

PUBLISHER'S NOTE

This publication is designed to provide accurate and authoritative information in regard to the subject matter covered. It is sold with the understanding that the publisher is not engaged in rendering professional career services. If expert assistance is required, the service of the appropriate professional should be sought.

The drawings on pages 84–85, 159, and 236–237 are by Steven M. Johnson, author of *What the World Needs Now.*

Distributed in Australia by Simon and Schuster Australia, in Canada by Ten Speed Press Canada, in New Zealand by Southern Publishers Group, in South Africa by Real Books, and in the United Kingdom and Europe by Airlift Book Company.

Library of Congress Catalog Card Information on file with the publisher.
ISBN-13 : 978-1-58008-727-8 (paper)
ISBN-10 : 1-58008-727-2 (paper)
ISBN-13 : 978-1-58008-728-5 (cloth)
ISBN-10 : 1-58008-728-0 (cloth)

Published by 1☉ Ten Speed Press, P.O. Box 7123, Berkeley, California 94707
www.tenspeed.com

Typesetting by Star Type, Berkeley
Cover design by Betsy Stromberg
Printed in Canada

The wonderful actress
Anne Bancroft (1931–2005) was once
loosely quoted as saying
about her husband, Mel Brooks,
My heart flutters whenever I hear his key
Turning in the door, and I think to myself,
Oh goody, the party is about to begin.

That is exactly how I feel
about my wife,
Marci Garcia Mendoza Bolles,
God's angel from the Philippines,
whom I fell deeply in love with, and married
on August 22, 2004.

What a gift, such a marriage is!

Contents

Acknowledgments   x

Grammar and Language Note   xiv

The Problem

CHAPTER 1   Teach Me to Fish   1

The ten most fundamental truths about the job-hunt. How often we go job-hunting. How often we change careers. How many are unemployed currently. Teach me to fish. "Mastering the job-hunt": what it means.

CHAPTER 2   How to Master the Job-Hunt   11
or Career-Change, Once and for All, for the Rest of Your Life

Who gets hired, and why. What to do when things go wrong. When what worked in the past doesn't work anymore. Length of the average job-hunt. Data smog. What it takes to be "an information specialist." The importance of key words. The key word in job-hunting.

CHAPTER 3   There Are Always Vacancies Out There   18

What to do if there are no jobs "out there." Losing your keys. Finding a lost friend. Percentage of the population who don't have a phone. Number of people currently in the U.S. workforce. Number of people who have found jobs. When resumes fail. Who will come to save you from unemployment.

CHAPTER 4   Best and Worst Ways   23
to Hunt for a Job

Alternatives are the key. Not all alternatives were created equal. What experts don't know. The five worst ways to hunt for a job. The five best ways to hunt for a job. What works five times as well as resumes. Seven times as well. Ten times as well. Twelve times as well. The secret: what, where, and how. Approaching an employer by telephone. How many alternative job-hunting methods should you use? And why.

CHAPTER 5 How Do Employers Go Hunting? 35

There are always two actors on the stage, in job-hunting. What alternatives are open to employers? Comparison with job-hunters' alternatives. Q-letters. How to transform lists. Importance of prioritizing, how that changes everything. Sample of an excellent resume. Where to start: with what the job-market "wants," or what You want. Job-hunting is exactly like a game. When it is that you determine the rules of the game.

The Playing Field

CHAPTER 6 The Playing Field 47

Nature as the playing field. Nature on the rampage. The tsunami of December 2004. The result: the death of distance. History of people's movements around the world. History of information's movements. Rethinking how jobs are done: career coaching as one example. The coming of our fears. China. Outsourcing. Wages here vs. wages abroad. Effect of outsourcing on U.S. employees' morale. The Polish Plumber. Churning. How to build a philosophy of Work. The mortality of jobs. Actual number of job vacancies. How to transform any job. Who are your brothers and sisters?

CHAPTER 7 Where on Earth Do You Want to Live? 61

How many move each year. The fourteen reasons why you might want to move. Katrina. States with lowest unemployment rates. States with the highest. *1000 Places to See Before You Die.* The four issues you must solve. The power of a picture. Ratio of prayer to work. Websites to help you explore places. Going rural. How to work while roaming. How to get a job overseas. What to beware of. *The Rip-Off Report.* Bad counseling firms. Moving far: how to research that town or city at a distance. When "contacts" can harm your job-hunt. How hard should you expect to work, at this? The detailed story of a sixty-six-year-old man, and how he made his move.

CHAPTER 8 Choosing or Changing Careers 87

A map of how many options you have. How many paths you can take. Four "exercises" to help you refine and flesh out your vision of what you seek. The helpfulness of drawing. A list of 300 jobs or careers you can pick from (updated as of 3/29/05) and their requirements. My favorite search engine: Metacrawler, and its virtues for you. The D.O.T. and O*NET. Hot jobs. Figuring out who you most admire. Career tests, assessment instruments. List of tests on the Web. The Six Essential Warnings about career tests. Warnings about degrees and jobs. How to use the Internet to find out information you want. Additional help for the job-hunter: megal-portals. Google. *Job-Hunting on the Internet,* companion book to *Parachute.* My site: www.jobhuntersbible.com (free). Viktor Frankl: What we can always hold on to.

CHAPTER 9 How to Start Your Own Business   117

Basic tools for a home business. The three major problems of
home businesses. The perpetual job-hunt. How to choose a
home business. Your options: Mail order. Telecommuting.
Franchises: virtues and defects. Where to put your home
business. How to succeed: The A - B = C Method. What to do
when nobody has ever done what you're thinking of doing.
The five ways in which the Internet can help the self-employed,
or any job-hunter or career-changer. Helpful websites. What to
do when you just can't make your business succeed. Stop-gap
jobs: how to find them. Temp work: how to find. Job-sharing.
The three rules about taking risks.

The Creative Approach to Finding Meaning for Your Life:

What, Where, and How

CHAPTER 10 The Secret to Finding Your Dream Job 145

The Isle of You. How one sentence can change your life. What are
you trying to accomplish with your life? What did you come into
the world to do? The road to a dream job is a road that passes
first of all through you. How well do you already know yourself? A
simple exercise to test your self-knowledge. Who am I? Example
of how to fill it out. Barbara Brown's secret to finding out who you
are. The three rules. "That One Piece of Paper": *The Flower
Diagram.* Example of how to fill it out. Rich Feller's flower. The
handicapped seventeen-year-old who wanted to be a pilot. How
he figured out what else he could do. What pieces of information
are more valuable than others. Competencies. Behavioral interviews. The Nine Basic Steps to identifying your dream job. The
three main parts to the creative approach.

Part I **WHAT** skills do you most enjoy using?   159

A crash course on transferable skills. A diagram of your career.
The 3 objects of all skills: People, Things, and Data/Information/Ideas.
Skills vs. Traits: what's the difference? Personality "TYPE" Tests.
Where on the Web? Write a story; find a skill. The five essential
parts of a good story. A chart to help. How to analyze. A list of
your physical, mental, and interpersonal skills: a series of keyboard keys. Six more stories. How to prioritize your list of *anything.* Prioritizing Grid for use with 10 Items. Prioritizing Grid for
use with 24 Items. Building blocks of skills you most enjoy using.
"That One Piece of Paper." A list of your favorite traits. Some
problems you may run into, in doing skill-identification. How to do
"trioing." Shortcuts to all of this.

Part II **WHERE** do you want to use your skills?   190

Your favorite environments, or "geographies." Your favorite
fields, interests, subjects, words, or vocabulary. Go visit fields
that fascinate you. How to find "leads." Petal #1: Fields of
Fascination. Definition of fields. "The Subjects Chart." Fields

dealing with people's needs. "The People List," "The Things Phone Book." Petal #2: Your Favorite Places to Live. What to do when your partner and you can't agree. A way out of the thicket. Backup plan: Throwing darts. Petal #3: Your Favorite People. John Holland's Six People Environments. The Parachute Party Exercise. Your Holland "code." Petal #4. Your Favorite Values. The Testimonial Dinner exercise. Arthur Miller's list of values, and rewards. Petal #5: Your Favorite Working Conditions. Chart to analyze your past distasteful working conditions. Petal #6: Level and Salary. Minimum vs. maximum salary desired. Making out a budget. Getting help. Other rewards. The Flower is done!

Part III **HOW** Do You Find the Person Who Has the Power to Hire You for the Job that You Are Looking For? 228

Now, what does "That One Piece of Paper" tell you? The virtue of passion, or enthusiasm. Puzzled? Put your top three skills and your top three fields of fascination on one piece of paper. What to do with that. The 19 Job Families chart. Giving the Flower a name. Ten Possible Targets. How to cut down the territory. Career, organization, particular place. How to combine three fields to define your one ideal career target. Chart: How to Understand Your Relationships with Others. Informational interviewing: what it is, how to do it, questions to ask. Always question what you're told: look for the exception. Have a Plan B. Five ways to research places before you approach them for an interview. The Crucialness of Thank You Notes. What to do if you're shy: Daniel Porot's PIE System.

CHAPTER 11 Identifying Who Has the Power to Hire You 263

How large is the organization? The key is contacts. What (or who) is a contact? How to cultivate contacts. How to get in, the place. The interview as "rescuing the employer."

CHAPTER 12 Ten Interviewing Tips 275

The most important things to remember, going in. Behavioral interviews: goal, obstacles, solution, numbers. The ten tips about successful interviewing. The employer's fears behind the questions: chart. Mosquitos vs. dragons. Ask for the job. Thank you notes — again (and again, and again). Keep a weekly diary of your accomplishments.

CHAPTER 13 The Six Secrets of Salary Negotiation 313

Researching salaries first, offline and online. When to discuss salary matters. How to negotiate. Greatest secret of all.

Epilogue How to Find Your Mission in Life 335

Appendix A How to Choose a Career Coach or Counselor 359

Appendix B Career Counselors Guide: A Sampler 371

Index 395

Acknowledgments

This edition represents the thirty-fifth anniversary of this book, as of December 1, 2005. *Parachute* first came out on December 1, 1970, and has been revised every year, but one, since. It is my individual labor of love.

Phil Wood, my publisher and friend for all these years, has mercifully given me wide latitude all this time in the whole design of the book, the titling of the book, the cover artwork, etc. Each year he also lets me paste-up every single page of the book, as I choose, by hand—with Lectrostik hot paste-up wax, rather than doing it on the computer. (I'm very tactile, and love to use my hands.)

Bev Anderson, my layout artist for the past thirty-five years, is now retired, but joins me each year to help me with the design of the book. Thank God! And just to ensure that, in the end, I get the Good Computer-Keeping seal of approval, the folks over at Ten Speed, plus my long-suffering typesetter, Linda Davis, then pour Bev's and my own finished paste-up into the computer at the last.

Phil let me choose the title of the book (*I always recall his comment in an interview many years ago: "Had this book died, it would have been the title that killed it. Now that this book lives, it is the title that saves it.")* The meaning of the title? Since so many of you have asked, I will tell you. My friends, long ago, fed up with their jobs, would say to me, "Well, I'm gonna have to bail out." And I would reply with a smile: "What color is your parachute?"

Other people, by the hundreds, have told me that this book has helped literally millions of people around the world. I am always bumping into grateful readers from ten, twenty years back, who say, "Your book changed my whole life." What a lovely reward for any life!

I owe some heartfelt thank you's that I must express here—inasmuch as gratitude never grows old. And gratitude must always be expressed.

- My great thanks first of all to two dear friends, one living, one now dead—the late John Crystal who was my original mentor in this field, beginning back in 1969, until he died in 1988; and Daniel Porot in Geneva, Switzerland, my friend, co-teacher (for twenty-five years), pal, brilliant job-hunting strategist, and the best teacher I have ever seen.

- My thanks also to the many other leaders in this field, all of whom are friends of mine, and whose ideas have meant a lot to me, wisdom shared over numerous lunches and dinners: Sidney Fine, Arthur Miller, Tom Jackson, Dick Lathrop, Bill Bridges, Dick Knowdell, Howard Figler, Dick Leider, Beverly Kaye, David Swanson, Bob Rosner, Martin Yate, Paul Tieger, Donna Dunning, Joel Garfinkle, Marty Nemko, Susan Whitcomb, Paul Stevens in Australia, Marie-Carmelle Roy in Canada, plus many former students of mine: Brian McIvor from Ireland; Pete Hawkins from Liverpool, England; BJ Chobju from Korea; Debra Angel from England and Australia; Madeleine Leitner and John Webb from Germany; Jim Kell and Sue Cullen from Texas; Dick Gaither from Indiana; Rich Feller from Colorado. These people are some of the brightest, most generous, and wonderful souls you could ever hope to meet, on this earth.

- Regarding the Internet, I want to single out my son Mark, the brilliant writer and researcher of much of my book, *Job-Hunting on the Internet,* 4th edition; my son Gary who is a leader in every aspect of the computer field; my own webmaster, Louis Manges; plus Susan Joyce of JobHunt.org, Mary Ellen Mort of JobStar.org, Margaret Riley Dikel of the rileyguide.com, and Pete Weddle of weddles.com—for their continual friendship, counsel, and advice about the Internet and the job-hunt. Needless to say, ultimately none of them are responsible for the *opinions* I express, or the *statistics* that I use; if any of those grieve you, it is I alone who am responsible.

- More thanks—this time to all the folks over at Ten Speed Press in Berkeley, California. Some people think I have my own publishing company; I do not. Ten Speed has published almost all of my books for the past thirty-five years, and they labor very hard to get each new edition of this book out, each year: Phil Wood who has been my friend and publisher there for all of these years, Bev Anderson has been my brilliant friend and layout artist for the same period of time; she was the genius behind this book's design and readability from the beginning. Thanks to Holly Taines White, patient Holly, my eagle-eyed proofreader/editor; Erika Bradfield, my foreign rights colleague at Ten Speed; Hal Hershey, my production manager over there in Berkeley; Linda Davis, my expert type-setter; and Kristin Casemore, now of New Orleans, my wonderful publicist.

- I am not by nature a hermit. I enjoy being part of a living community. My thanks therefore to the career groups that make up that community: the ICDC, NCDA, Parachute Associates, JobDig, and the CMI, among others.

- My thanks to my extended family, near and far: to my devoted wife, Marci, who is the Lord's greatest gift to me, ever, and whom I truly adore. With her, every day is a circus of laughter, love, and joy. Also my thanks to my four grown children, Stephen, Mark, Gary and Sharon, with their spouses and families—they have all been wonderful to me; as has my dear stepdaughter, Dr. Serena Brewer, my dear sister, Ann Johnson, of Hainesport, New Jersey; my one remaining living cousin, Elizabeth Ann (Ban) Dreyer, in Janesville, Wisconsin. There are also my part-time office staff: Suzanne Anderson and Loretta Walsh. I thank God for their devotion and dedication to helping people.

- My thanks to all my readers, all eight million of you, and most especially to the two thousand or so who write me each year. I still read every one of the letters that come in, whether they come by e-mail (RNB25@aol.com) or by fax (925 837 5120) or through the postal service (P.O. Box 379, Walnut Creek, CA 94597-0379). I have to say, no author could possibly have more loving, and appreciative readers—not in a million years. So if you write me about how this book changed your life, or whatever, you can be absolutely sure that I will read whatever you have to say, and ponder it well, though I cannot acknowledge or answer your kind letter. The mail has gotten just overwhelming.

- Incidentally, if you have a job-hunting or life-changing question that needs answering, you would do better to directly e-mail my devoted friend and job-expert, Jim Kell *(a saint if ever there was one)* at jkell@texas.net; he has volunteered to answer as many such letters as he possibly can, so long as he draws mortal breath. The praise he has received from grateful job-hunters, would make a book in and of itself. (There is no charge for his service; it is his way of giving Thanks for his life here on Earth.) Alternatively, you can contact any of the career coaches or counselors who live near you, that are listed on pages 374 to 393 in the back of this book.

- In closing, since I'm giving out thanks, I'd have to be an ingrate not to mention my profound thanks to The Great Lord God, Father of our Lord Jesus Christ, and source of all grace, wisdom, and compassion, Who all my life has been as real to me as breathing, and Who has been my Rock through every trial, tragedy, and misfortune in my life (such as the assassination of my only brother), giving me strength, and keeping me in excellent health to this day; Who I believe has given me this charge to help as many people as I can with their job-hunt *(regardless of their background, income, education, orientation, faith, tongue, or nationality)*, to help them find meaning for their lives. I am grateful beyond measure for such a life, such a mission, and such a privilege.

Dick Bolles
September 30, 2005

Grammar and Language Note

I want to explain four points of grammar, in this book of mine: pronouns, commas, italics, and spelling. My unorthodox use of them invariably offends unemployed English teachers so much that they write me to apply for a job as my editor.

To save us unnecessary correspondence, let me explain. Throughout this book, I often use the apparently plural pronouns "they," "them," and "their" after *singular* antecedents—such as, "You must approach *someone* for a job and tell *them* what you can do." This sounds strange and even *wrong* to those who know English well. To be sure, we all know there is another pronoun—"you"—that may be either singular or plural, but few of us realize that the pronouns "they," "them," and "their" were also once treated as both plural and singular in the English language. This changed, at a time in English history when agreement in *number* became more important than agreement as to sexual *gender*. Today, however, our priorities have shifted once again. Now, the distinguishing of sexual *gender* is considered by many to be more important than agreement in *number*.

The common artifices used for this new priority, such as "s/he," or "he and she," are—to my mind—tortured and inelegant. Casey Miller and Kate Swift, in their classic, *The Handbook of Nonsexist Writing*, agree, and argue that it is time to bring back the earlier usage of "they," "them," and "their" as both singular and plural—just as "you" is/are. They further argue that this return to the earlier historical usage has already become quite common *out on the street*—witness a typical sign by the ocean which reads "*Anyone* using this beach after 5 P.M. does so at *their* own risk." I have followed Casey and Kate's wise recommendations in all of this.

As for my commas, they are deliberately used according to my own rules—rather than according to the rules of historic grammar (which I did learn—I hastily add, to reassure my old Harvard professors, who despaired of me weekly, during English class). In spite of those rules, I follow my own, which are: to write conversationally, and put in a comma wherever I would normally stop for a breath, were I *speaking* the same line.

The same conversational rule applies to my use of *italics*. I use *italics* wherever, were I speaking the sentence, I would put *emphasis* on that word or phrase. I also use italics where there is a digression of thought, and I want to maintain the main thought and flow of the sentence. All in all, I write as I speak. Hence the dashes (—) to indicate a break in thought.

Finally, some of my spelling (and capitalization) is *weird.* (Well, some might say "weird"; I prefer just "playful.") I happen to like writing it "e-mail," for example, instead of "email." Fortunately, since this is my own book, I get to play in my own way; I'm so grateful that eight million readers have *gone along*. Nothing delights a child (at heart) more, than being allowed to play.

P.S. Speaking of "playful," over the last thirty-five years a few critics (very few) have claimed that *Parachute* is not serious enough (they object to the cartoons, which find fun in almost *everything*). A few have claimed that the book is *too* serious, and too complicated in its vocabulary and grammar for anyone except a college graduate. Two readers, however, have written me with a different view.

The first one, from England, said there is an index that analyzes a book to tell you what grade in school you must have finished, in order to be able to understand it. My book's index, he said, turned out to be 6.1, which means you need only have finished sixth grade in a U.S. school in order to understand it.

Here in the U.S., a college instructor came up with a similar finding. He phoned me to tell me that my book was rejected by the authorities as a proposed text for his college course, because the book's language/grammar was not up to college level. "What level was it?" I asked. "Well," he replied, "when they analyzed it, it turned out to be written on an eighth grade level."

Sixth or eighth grade—that seems just about right to me. Why make job-hunting complicated, when it can be expressed so simply even a child could understand it?

R.N.B.

News
Bureau of Labor Statistics

**United States
Department of Labor**
Washington, D.C. 20212

**BLS Home | Programs & Surveys | Get Detailed Statistics | Glossary | What's New
CPS Home | CES Home**

Employment Situation Summary

Table A. Major indicators of labor market activity, seasonally adjusted
(Numbers in thousands)

Category	Quarterly averages 2004 IV	Quarterly averages 2005 I	Monthly data 2005 Mar.	Monthly data 2005 Apr.	Monthly data 2005 May	Apr.-May change
HOUSEHOLD DATA	Labor force status					
Civilian labor force	148,136	148,089	148,157	148,762	149,122	360
Employment	140,092	140,296	140,501	141,099	141,475	376
Unemployment	8,044	7,794	7,656	7,663	7,647	-16
Not in labor force	76,282	`76,949	77,079	76,679	76,547	-132
	Unemployment rates					
All workers	5.4	5.3	5.2	5.2	5.1	-0.1
Adult man	4.9	4.7	4.6	4.4	4.4	.0
Adult women	4.7	4.6	4.5	4.6	4.6	.0
Teenagers	17.1	16.9	16.9	17.7	17.9	.2
White	4.6	4.5	4.4	4.4	4.4	.0
Black or African American..............	10.8	10.6	10.3	10.4	10.1	-.3
Hispanic or Latino ethnicity	6.7	6.1	5.7	6.4	6.0	-.4
ESTABLISHMENT DATA	Employment					
Nonfarm employment	132,302	132,814	132,995	p133,269	p133,347	p78
Goods-producing(1)	22,000	22,054	22,093	p22,135	p22,149	p14
Construction..........	7,063	7,127	7,159	p7,207	p7,227	p20
Manufacturing	14,338	14,314	14,315	p14,306	p14,299	p-7
Service-providing(1)	110,302	110,759	110,902	p111,134	p111,198	p64
Retail trade(2)	15,072	15,112	15,129	15,155	p15,166	p11
Professional and business services....	16,633	16,755	16,796	p16,829	p16,828	p-1
Education and health services	17,110	17,191	17,210	p17,244	p17,284	p40
Leisure and hospitality..........	12,569	12,641	12,662	p12,725	p12,719	p-6
Government	21,702	21,725	21,731	p21,744	p21,749	p5
	Hours of work(3)					
Total private	33.7	33.7	33.7	p33.8	p33.8	p0.0
Manufacturing	40.6	40.6	40.4	p40.5	p40.4	p-.1
Overtime	4.5	4.5	4.5	4.4	p4.4	p.0
	Indexes of aggregate weekly hours (2002=100)(3)					
Total private	101.2	101.7	101.9	p102.5	p102.6	p0.1
	Earnings(3)					
Avg. hourly earnings, total private	$15.83	$15.92	$15.95	p$16.00	p$16.03	p$0.03
Avg. weekly earnings, total private	533.89	536.51	537.52	p540.80	p541.81	p1.01

1 includes other industries, not shown separately.
2 Quarterly averages and the over-the-month change are calculated using unrounded data.
3 Data relate to private production or nonsupervisory workers.
p = preliminary

The
Problem

CHAPTER ONE

Teach Me to Fish

The problem is
that you need a job.
The problem is
that you need to pay
for your medical plan,
Or for your pension plan.
The problem is that your
job just disappeared, one morning,
While you were looking
The other way.
The problem is that you're tired
of doing the thing
you've always done,
You want to find more meaning
for your life.

In solving any problem
the way to begin is
with The Truth.

So, here are the most
fundamental truths I can think of,
concerning the problem
Called "The Job-Hunt."

1

The Truth

1. *Job-hunting is not a science; it is an art.* Some job-hunters know instinctively how to do it; in some cases, they were born knowing how to do it. Others of us sometimes have a harder time with it, but fortunately for us in the U.S. and elsewhere, there is help, coaching, counseling, and advice—online and off.

2. *Mastering the job-hunt this time, and for the rest of your life, is a lot of hard work and takes some hard thinking.* The more work, the more thinking, you put into pursuing your job-hunt, and doing the homework on yourself, the more successful your job-hunt is likely to be. Caution: Are you lazy, day by day? Uh, oh! Most people do their job-hunt or career change the same way they do Life.

3. *Job-hunting is always mysterious.* Sometimes *mind-bogglingly mysterious.* You may *never* understand why things sometimes work, and sometimes do not.

4. *There is no **always wrong** way to hunt for a job or to change careers.* Anything *may* work under certain circumstances, or at certain times, or with certain employers. There are only *degrees of likelihood* of certain job-hunting techniques working or not working. But it is crucial to know that likelihood.

5. *There is no **always right** way to hunt for a job or to change careers.* Anything *may* fail to work under certain circumstances, or at certain times, or with certain employers. There are only *degrees of likelihood* of certain job-hunting techniques working or not working. But it is crucial to know that likelihood.

6. *Regarding what kind of information you are going to need, consider the rule that some travel experts teach about traveling:*

Before you go, they say, lay out on your bed, in one pile, all the clothes and stuff that you intend to pack; and in another pile, all the money you think you'll need to take. Then pack only half those clothes, but twice the money.

By coincidence, the same kind of ratio occurs in job-hunting. That is: you will need only half the information you thought you would need *about the job-market*, but twice the information you thought you would need *about yourself*. With regard to the latter, you need to figure out **what** you most enjoy doing, **where** you'd most like to do it, and **how** to identify the-person-who-has-the-power-to-hire-you-for-the-job-you-want, in the place you want.

7. *Job-hunting is more like dating than any other human activity we might compare it to.* That is to say, job-hunting is basically a protracted conversation between two people, which we can summarize as: *Do I like you? Do you like me? Do we want to take a chance on going steady?*

8. *One employer differs from another, as night from day.* Don't generalize about employers you will be approaching, with phrases like: *I just know that employers would never hire me.* You can't interpret rejection from some employers as evidence that all employers will reject you. Maybe some will, but believe me, there are others who won't. Keep going, until you find them.

9. *Job-hunting always depends on some amount of luck.* Mastering the job-hunt doesn't mean absolutely, positively, you will always be able to find a job. It does mean that you can get good at reducing the amount that depends on luck, to as small a proportion as possible.

10. *With coaching or without, the ultimate responsibility for keeping at your job-hunt is yours, yours, yours.* Under God, of course. You must keep on going. Don't give up!

You write down the most honest
things you can think of
to say, about the problem
at hand. No matter how sobering,
No matter how depressing,
You start with the truth.
For if you begin at an honest
place, there's just no telling
How much you can achieve.

Here is the overwhelming, overarching truth: you
Are going to have to go job-hunting
Many times in your life.
Lucky you, if that is not the case!
But the odds are overwhelming that it will be.
According to *experts*,
The average worker, *under* 35 years of age,
Will go job-hunting every one to three years,
And the average worker *over* 35 will go
Job-hunting every five to eight years!
And, in this process, so the experts say,
We will each of us probably change careers
Three to five times, as we go.

Yes, the job-hunt is not a one-time occurrence
In our lives.
For the 140 million of us
Who are presently in
The U.S. workforce,
It will likely keep happening
Again and again and again.
Because, you see, the economy
Is a barometer,
Measuring the rise and fall
Of what is going on, in the world.
Wars and rumors of wars occur,
And that affects jobs.
Tsunamis occur, and other natural disasters.

Nations such as India and China
Rouse from their economic sleep,
Outsourcing occurs,
Mergers occur,
And that affects jobs.
Factories, stores, and restaurants
Close,
Oil prices rise,
Downsizings occur
Our individual lives get shaken
Both by illness and by handicap.
Rising health-care costs,
New technologies—
The litany is endless
Of all the things that can occur
To shred our plans,
Or tear the fabric of our dreams,
And make us
Unemployed
Again.

Our society has taken pity
On the job-hunter and career-changer,
And invented all kinds of helps
For you,
In your plight:
You know the list: *resumes, agencies,* and *ads,*
Postings on the Internet,
Job clubs, local, federal, state
Well-meaning programs.
But,
None of these are dependable, none of these
Work very well; in fact
The number of people who turn to
One or another of these avenues
But never find a job thereby,
Is both mind-boggling and
Depressing.

9,256,000 as I write.
That's the figure.
Nine million two hundred fifty-six thousand souls
In the U.S. alone
Are hunting for a job
Or have come up continually empty-handed.

"Give me a fish, and I will eat for today;
Teach me to fish, and I will eat
For the rest of my life."
So it has been said,
For centuries.

But,
Even when this country's
(And the world's) Neanderthal
Job-hunting methods *do* work,
After a fashion,
They only
At best *give you a fish.*
They rescue you from your present
Financial
Predicament (maybe),
But often in jobs that are below
Your gifts, your skills, and experience.
They rescue you with jobs that either
Diminish you, or
Bore you, out of your mind.
Some fish!

Of course, you know,
You can sometimes *get lucky;*
Blunder your way through,
Successfully.
To just the kind of job
Or new career,
That you were hoping for.
And if so, *lucky you!* this time.

Remember: hunting for a job
Is a repetitive experience
In Life—and luck won't cut it
Every time. Luck
Runs out, eventually,
And you, once rescued,
Are bereft, this time,
Of any clue
As to what on earth you should do. You press
The same "buttons"
As you pressed
Last time. But they don't work,
This time around.
The resume which last time
Dazzled everyone who saw it,
Now hangs motionless
In outer cyberspace.
The employers who *died* to hire you
Just two, three, years ago,
Now show no interest in you.

The friends who rescued you
Last time, well, they are quiet too.
Job-hunting *was* easy, just last time around.
But now nothing works the same
As it did then.
It feels like somebody changed the locks,
And none of the old keys work
Anymore. Well, so much for *the fish!*
And close the door behind you,
As you go.

It is time,
In our society,
When we thought it a worthwhile
Experiment, to try
Not just to rescue you
One job-hunt at a time

Teach Me to Fish   **7**

But seek a longer-lasting
Goal: That each of us should aim
To *master*, now, all job-hunts,
Job-change, career-choice, career-change
That wait for us in the years ahead;
And, teach us now just *how to fish*
Hereafter, evermore.

Therefore, this book is not
Just a lot of tips, or hints, or secrets,
To be devoured (say) the night before
You go in for an interview
With a prospective employer.
Although you can use it for that, if you want to.
But the book has a higher and nobler goal.

This book is an attempt
To teach you *how to fish*,
With respect to the most difficult task
Any of us faces
In our life: namely, the job-hunt—
Whether it be your hunt for a new place,
To work; or for a new career,
Or for a first career
Whether it be a hunt for just
A job to feed your body,
Or for a real dream job

That will forever
Feed your soul.
Therefore, my plea to you,
Dear reader:
Do not simply *skim* this book,
Looking for a fish,
A hint, a tip, a secret.
No. Read and use it with but one intent:
That this time you want to learn
How to fish, and master
The job-hunt.
You have, in you, divinity,
And the job-hunt is the time for You
To find out who
You really are,
And with this Vision in your grasp, go
Make your life at last into what
It was always meant to be.

> What does *"mastering"* the job-hunt mean?
> Well, it means trying to understand *the
> nature of the beast* (the job-hunt)—its
> laws, its behavior, what you don't have
> any control over, and—much more
> importantly—what you do have control
> over, even when you think you don't;
> what works, what doesn't work, the odds,
> what best pays off an investment of your
> time, what doesn't pay off very well, or
> not at all; how to build up your self-
> esteem, how to find out why you're here;
> and how to triumph in life.

Work is Love made visible.
And if you can't work with love but only with distaste,
It is better that you should leave your work
and sit at the gate of the temple and
take alms of the people who work with joy.

Kahlil Gibran, *The Prophet*

CHAPTER TWO

How to Master the Job-Hunt or Career-Change, Once and for All, for the Rest of Your Life

H e or she who gets hired is not necessarily the one who can do that job best; but, the one who knows the most about how to get hired.

Richard Lathrop
in his classic *Who's Hiring Who?*

Oh, how true! Depressing, but true! If you're out of work, then mastering the job-hunt is even more important than mastering your job. At least when times are tough. Or when the single largest employer in your town has just closed its gates, after forty-five years. Or when your job has been *outsourced* to some overseas place.

11

There is an art to looking for a job, and you must master it. Such a mastery once was just an optional activity for dilettantes.[1] But, in this twenty-first century, it has become a necessary survival skill for everyone.

Like Lambs to the Slaughter

Now, the trouble is: many, if not most of us, think we already have mastered the job-hunt. And if someone tells us that "mastering the job-hunt" means absorbing a ton of new information—reading, studying, memorizing—our response is very likely to be: *Forget it! I'll take my chances with what I know.*

And so, when it is our time, we skim a few job-hunting books, articles, Internet essays, or whatever, just to check ourselves out. The concepts there look pretty familiar to us: resumes, contacts, networking, interviewing, salary negotiation, etc. *"Piece of cake,"* we think to ourselves. We are brimming with confidence.

So, out the door we go, job-hunting just with what we presently know, job-hunting just with "what has worked for me before." Out the door we go *like lambs to the slaughter.*

And sometimes it works—perfectly. We get a job. And we are ready for the next time.

But sometimes things go wrong. Sometimes things go horribly wrong. **And that's what *mastery* is all about: knowing what to do when and if things go wrong.**

After nineteen weeks *(that's the length of the average job-hunt in the U.S., as I write)* we often haven't found a job. And we are terribly, terribly, depressed.

Blame time! We invoke the bad economy, as the reason. We invoke overseas outsourcing, as the reason. We invoke the lack of government jobs-programs, as the reason. We invoke the heartlessness and greediness of our former bosses, as the reason. We invoke the political party that is currently in power, as the reason.

No one ever told us that mastery, or lack of mastery, of the job-hunt is the reason.

---

1. A person who dabbles in an art, science, etc. in a superficial way. (*Webster's New World Dictionary and Thesaurus*, 2nd edition)

The Information Age, Run Amok

We need to recall that this is the twenty-first century. It's called the Information Age. It's not called that, for nothing. There is a ton of information *out there*. About anything. And everything. And, at our fingertips. Especially since the advent of the Internet and its World Wide Web. We are all wandering in what David Shenk calls *Data Smog*.

So, when we are told that we must *master* some *new* subject, in this twenty-first century, like *the job-hunt* or *career-change*, a chill runs up and down our spine. We suppose this means we are going to have to bury ourself in a room for a month, and study another ton of new stuff. We are overwhelmed. We already know way too much.

But we are wrong. It is time for us to sit down and re-think what it means to be a citizen of this "Information Age." We all need to re-think what it means to be *an information specialist* in this new age. For *an information specialist* is what we all need to be, to survive, these days.

Okay, let's start with this: being *an information specialist* in the twenty-first century doesn't mean just becoming good at *gathering* information.

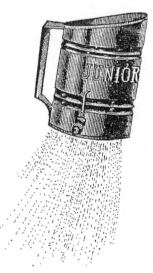

How to Master the Job-Hunt or Career-Change

Anybody who claims to be *an information specialist* must, equally importantly, become good at *cutting down* on information, throwing away information we really don't need.

Cutting down on information begins with boiling a subject down to its essence; that is, to its key concepts, and key words.

Mastering the Job-Hunt, by Simplifying the Job-Hunt

In order to master any subject, you need to decide what its key word, i.e., its most important concept, is.

In the matter of job-hunting, most people would guess that that key word is **Resumes**. Nope. Not even close! The key concept is Alternatives.

Why so? Well, let us suppose you believed in a job-hunt that had no alternatives. You believed there was only one way to hunt for a job, and that way was what you might call *"the parachute way." (Yech!!!)* Or that way was, say, resumes. You would then conduct your job-hunt depending only on resumes.

And if, by chance, that didn't work, and you completely struck out, then what would you do? Without alternatives, the answer would be: *Nada. Nothing. Nowhere.* There would be no next step. You would be left in a state of job-hunting paralysis.

This is where *mastery* comes in. Mastery is a decision, a decision that you make, for yourself. Let us say you have decided to acquaint yourself with only *one way:* only one job-hunting process, only one way to figure out what your skills are, only one skill, one field, one job, one target employer, and so forth—then you have set yourself up for depression, despair, and failure in your hunt. You have opted for *lack of mastery.*

Fortunately, there are in actual fact at least ten other ways of hunting for a job than depending solely on resumes. And, fortunately, if you know what they are, and if you know the odds of each one working or not working, *then* you will have mastered the job-hunt.

Alternatives. That's the key word. That's the most important concept, in the job-hunt.

Examples of Alternatives

You're out of work. You're job-hunting, or contemplating a change in careers. But suppose you know:

At least two alternative ways of finding out what your skills are.

At least two alternative ways of describing each skill.

At least two alternative ways of deciding which skills are most important.

At least two alternative fields that you would enjoy using these skills, in.

At least two alternative ways of uncovering any vacancies that may exist.

At least two alternative ways of constructing your resume, if you decide to use one.

At least two alternative *target* organizations that you can go after.

At least two alternative ways of going after those prospective employers.

At least two alternative people you could approach within each *target* organization, to get hired.

At least two ways you can get in to see them.

At least two alternative job titles for the kind of work that you are looking for.

At least two alternative ways of conducting the interview with them.

At least two alternative ways of negotiating salary, once they make clear they like you—and you decide that you like them.

And so forth. And so on.

The above list isn't a *Wouldn't it be nice, if* . . . list.

These alternatives do exist. If you want to survive in the twenty-first century, your job is to know them, thoroughly, so that you will have an alternative "up your sleeve" for every step of the way. That way, you will have a delicious freedom. That way you also have hope. And in the job-hunt, as in Life, hope is everything. It is the one factor that keeps you going, when all else fails. That's what this book is all about.

You can only keep hope alive if you make it your business to always have alternatives.

Finding Hope

The importance of having alternative ways of hunting for *those jobs that are always out there*, is illustrated by some interesting studies: in one, it was discovered that one-third to one-half of all U.S. job-hunters simply *give up*, by the second month of their job-hunt. Yikes!

Why is this? Well, it turns out the *why* is related to the number of job-hunting methods they used. In a study of 100 job-hunters who were using *only one* method of job-search, it was found that typically 51 of them abandoned their search, by the second month. That's over *half*.

Chapter Two

On the other hand, of 100 job-hunters who were using *several* job-search methods, typically only 31 abandoned their search, by the second month.[2] That's less than one-third. It's not hard to figure out *why these results.* If you have alternatives, your hope tends to stay alive—because, when one method doesn't work for you, you think to yourself, *well surely one of these other methods will pay off*—and so, you keep on going.

Having coached thousands and thousands of job-hunters over the past thirty-five years, I have discovered that the successful ones almost always had alternatives at their command— at every step along the way. **Alternatives.** Maybe it's the key to Life; certainly it's the key word in a successful job-hunt.

---

2. Steven M. Bortnick and Michelle Harrison Ports, "Job search methods and results: tracking the unemployed, 1991," *Monthly Labor Review, December 1992,* p. 33. (Fifteen years ago; still true today, I'm sure.)

CHAPTER THREE

There Are Always Vacancies Out There

What If There Are No Jobs Out There?

Most of us set out to job-hunt with but one job-hunting strategy in mind: *resumes.* We send our resumes to employers we would like to work for. Or we post them on the Internet, either on employers' own websites, or on Monster.com, or HotJobs.com, or Career-Builder.com and the like—and when, as is so often the case, we don't get even a nibble, we say (we *all* say) the same thing:

"Well, there are no jobs out there. I've looked."

Ho boy! Think about that statement for a moment! Just because you can't find them, doesn't mean they don't exist. You know this, instinctively, in other arenas of your life, besides *jobs.* Take *keys* for example; just because you can't find them one morning, as you're about to leave the house, doesn't mean they don't exist. Right? *Right!*

Or, let's take *friends* as another example. I had a friend who moved to another city. We lost touch with each other. But three years later I found myself in that city, and I decided to look him up. The big question: how to find him?

"The telephone book," I thought to myself. I assumed everyone had to have a telephone, so I went to the phone book, and looked him up. No listing. *Well, no problem,* I thought. He must have an unlisted number. So I called "Information" and asked. Nope, not even an unlisted number.

I assumed that everyone who existed in that city must have a telephone number. Since I couldn't find one for him, I concluded he didn't exist—at least not in that city.

To my mind, "I can't find him" equaled "Therefore he doesn't exist."

I was wrong, of course. He did still exist, and in that city; I had just picked a faulty way of finding him. Faulty, because—as I later discovered—only 94 percent of all households in the U.S. have telephones. The other 6 percent don't. He was among that 6 percent.

Eventually I located him—by adopting *an alternative* strategy for finding him. I contacted his former church back in my home town, and found friends of his there who knew exactly where he had moved to. They gave me his new address. Bingo!

As with friends, so with jobs: they may exist, but everything depends upon your using the right search method to try and find them.

Write This on Your Forehead:
There Are Always Vacancies Out There

And why is that? Simple math. In the U.S. workforce there are currently about 140,000,000 people who have found jobs. So far, so good.

But it is inevitable that some among these job-holders will become the victim of mergers, downsizing, outsourcing. Many will be let go, made redundant, fired—suddenly, and without warning.

Many could still have jobs but for the fact that they will become restless, and voluntarily quit, move, change jobs, change careers, decide to start their own business, get married, get divorced, become seriously ill, become handicapped, retire, or die.

The mere size of the *employed* workforce guarantees that in the U.S., at least, there will always be turnovers, and vacancies out there.

That's why we can affirm with confidence: there are vacancies out there. There are *always* vacancies.

The trick is, to find them. Or have them found, for us.

Ah, but by whom?

We have the conviction, all too many of us, that in a well-run society it shouldn't be our responsibility to go find them. We are owed a job, surely. We are entitled. Someone will come to our rescue, and hook us up with a proper job, surely. Voila! Our troubles will be over.

We are, of course, unclear about who that someone will be: maybe the government, or private agencies, or newspapers, or a union, or God—but we believe it will be someone.

Alas, when our time comes, and we are out of a job, instead of someone coming to save us, there is only the long, dark, deep sound of silence.

One job-hunter told me he did nothing for four months, because he was sitting at home, waiting for God to prove He loved him, by dropping a job in his lap.

It does happen. *Jobs just dropping into our lap,* I mean. But not often enough for you to ever count on it. Nope, there will always be vacancies out there, but . . . it is *your* job to go find them.

A job-hunter once came to me in deep despair. She felt she had been faithful and disciplined in her job-hunt, but was now convinced there were no jobs to be found. I pointed out that much of her despair was due to the fact that she had failed to keep in mind the crucial distinction between *existing* and *finding.* "Just because your resumes didn't find a job for you," I said, "doesn't mean no jobs exist out there. All you have so far demonstrated is that in bad times, resumes are a lousy way to try to find the kind of jobs you want to find, in the geographical area you are concentrating on."

I continued, "There are many other ways for finding the kind of job you are looking for." I enumerated what those alternatives were.

So, she chose an alternative job-hunting strategy, and found a new job in three weeks!

There are always vacancies out there!

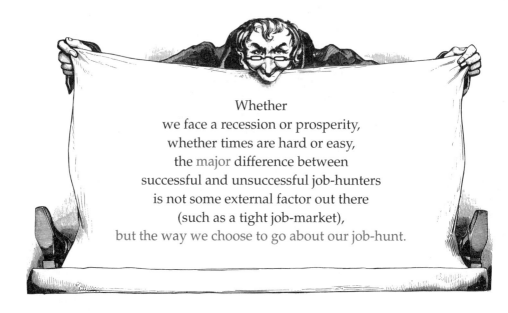

Whether
we face a recession or prosperity,
whether times are hard or easy,
the major difference between
successful and unsuccessful job-hunters
is not some external factor out there
(such as a tight job-market),
but the way we choose to go about our job-hunt.

Best and Worst Ways to Hunt for a Job

Not All Alternatives Were Created Equal

Okay, now if your resume is turning up attractive job offers, and the Internet is working for you, and working very well, then you don't need any more advice from me.

Except, of course, since you're trying to master the job-hunt process once and for all, in your lifetime, you will need to know what to do in those next times when your resume isn't turning up any job offers, and the Internet is leaving you high and dry.

At such a time, then or now, you will ultimately have to master an alternative search method. Or methods.

But, which ones? There are lots of them out there, as you no doubt know.

We would hope, at this point, that experts would be able to come up with a compelling list, backed by studies and statistics, to guide us as to which job-search methods are most likely to repay our investment of time, and which ones aren't. But, experts don't always have accurate statistics or anything other than anecdotal stories, to guide us. Studies—if there are any—are often of questionable value, because they were done too long ago, or with too small a sample, or before new technological developments arrived, or *whatever*.

All we've got are hunches. But that is not to be sneezed at, because if experts work in this field long enough, they begin to get a definite sense of how things are going. Hence, they know "ballpark" figures and can make very helpful and dependable guesses. Here, then, are experts' best guesses, expressed as percentages.

The Least Effective and Most Effective Ways to Look for a Job

Many job-hunters are astonished when they find out their favorite job-hunting strategy is on the "least effective" list.

Still, facts are facts. Some alternatives are more ineffective than others—sometimes *much more* ineffective. So, the experiences of experts can sometimes be very useful.

The five worst ways to try to find those jobs that *are* out there, are listed here, in order, from those with the least dependable payoff, to those with the most. Here they are:

The Five Worst Ways to Look for a Job

4 to 10%

1. **Using the Internet.** In this twenty-first century, the Internet has seemed a natural place to turn to. It makes access and availability between job-hunter and employer seem so easy. Of course, it doesn't always work. But maybe you'll get lucky, and find a job in 24 hours! Some have! (Some have won the lottery, too!) Unfortunately, the success rate of trying to find a job through the Internet turns out to be only 4 percent (yikes!). Yes, according to Forrester Research, in a research-finding oft-repeated since 2002, out of every 100 job-hunters who use the Internet as their search method for finding jobs, 4 of them will get lucky (well, 4.1 actually) and find a job thereby, while 96 job-hunters out of the 100 will not—if they use only the Internet to search for a job.

Exception: if you are seeking a technical or computer-related job, an IT job, or a job in engineering, finances, or healthcare, the success rate rises, to somewhere around 10 percent. But for the other 20,000 job titles that are out there in the job-market, the success rate remains at 4 percent only.

7%

2. **Mailing out resumes to employers at random.** This search method is reported to have about a 7 percent success rate. That is, out of every 100 job-hunters who use only this search method, 7 will get lucky, and find a job thereby. Ninety-three job-hunters out of 100 will not—if they use only this method to search for them.

I'm being generous here with my percentages for success. One study suggested that outside the Internet only 1 out of 1,470 resumes actually resulted in a job. Another study put the figure even higher: one job offer for every 1,700 resumes floating around out there. We do not know what the odds are if you post your resume on the Internet. We do know that there are reportedly at least 40,000,000 resumes floating around out there on the Internet, like lost ships on the Sargasso Sea.[1] No one's bothered to try to count how many of these actually found a job for the job-hunter.

---

1. Some put the estimate way higher.

7%

3. Answering ads in professional or trade journals, appropriate to your field. This search method, like the one above, has just a 7 percent success rate. That is, out of every 100 job-hunters who use only this search method, 7 will get lucky and find a job thereby. Ninety-three job-hunters out of 100 will not—if they use only this method to search for them.

5 to 24%

4. Answering local newspaper ads. This search method has a 5 to 24 percent success rate. That is, out of every 100 job-hunters who use only this search method, between 5 and 24 will get lucky and find a job thereby. Seventy-six to 95 job-hunters out of 100 will not—if they use only this method to search for them.

(The fluctuation between 5 percent and 24 percent is due to the level of salary that is being sought; the higher the salary being sought, the fewer job-hunters who are able to find a job—using only this search method.)

5 to 28%

5. Going to private employment agencies or search firms for help. This method has a 5 to 28 percent success rate, again depending on the level of salary that is being sought. Which is to say, out of every 100 job-hunters who use only this method, between 5 and 28 will get lucky and find a job thereby. Seventy-two to 95 job-hunters out of 100 will not—if they use only this method to search for them.

(The range *is for the same reason as noted in #4. It is of interest that the success rate of this method has risen slightly in recent years, in the case of women but not of men: in a comparatively recent study, 27.8 percent of female job-hunters found a job within two months, by going to private employment agencies.)*

Others in the Least Effective *category:* For the sake of completeness we should note that there are at least four other methods for trying to find jobs, that technically fall into this category of Worst Ways. Those four are:

Going to places where employers pick out workers, such as union halls. This has an 8 percent success rate.

(Less than 15 percent of U.S. workers are union members anyway, but it is claimed that those among them who do have access to a union hiring hall, have a 22 percent success rate. What is not stated, however, is how long it takes to get a job at the hall, and how temporary and short-lived such a job may be; in the trades it's often just a few days.)

Taking a civil service examination. This has a 12 percent success rate.

Asking a former teacher or professor for job-leads. This also has a 12 percent success rate.

Going to the state/federal employment service office. This has a 14 percent success rate.

Okay, so much for the Worst Ways to hunt for a job, if you have limited time and energy to give to your job-hunt, you'll probably be wise to give these only the time they merit.

But now, let's look at the other side of the coin. What are the job-hunting methods that will pay off better, for the time and energy you have to invest in your job-hunt?

The Five Best Ways to Hunt for a Job

What does "best ways" mean? Well, one useful way to think about this is in terms of your personal energy. During your job-hunt, your energies are limited (especially if the job-hunt stretches on for weeks or even months); so, it's important to know which are the best strategies *that you should start with*, in case your energy runs out before you've finished working your way through all the alternatives.

33%

1. **Asking for job-leads from: family members, friends, people in the community, staff at career centers— especially at your local community college or the high school or college where you graduated.** You ask them one simple question: do you know of any jobs at the place where you work—or elsewhere? This search method has a 33 percent

success rate. That is, out of every 100 people who use only this search method, 33 will get lucky, and find a job thereby. Sixty-seven job-hunters will not—if they use only this method to search for work. This is one of the five best ways to look for a job, but it's all relative. "'The fifth best' out of those that are out there" isn't necessarily saying much. Sixty-seven job-hunters out of 100 will still not find the jobs that are out there—if they use this so-called one-of-the-best methods.

> It should be noted that this method's success rate is almost 5 times higher than the success rate for re-sumes. *In other words, by asking for job leads from your family and friends, you have an almost five times better chance of finding a job, than if you had just sent out your resume.*

"I'm hoping to find something in a meaningful, humanist, outreach kind of bag, with flexible hours, non-sexist bosses, and fabulous fringes."

Chapter Four

47%

2. Knocking on the door of any employer, factory, or office that interests you, whether they are known to have a vacancy or not. This search method has anywhere up to a 47 percent success rate. That is, out of every 100 people who use only this search method, 47 will get lucky, and find a job thereby. Fifty-three job-hunters out of 100 will not—if they use only this one method to search for work. This is one of the five best ways to look for a job, but even so . . .

> It should be noted that this method's success rate is almost 7 times higher than the success rate for resumes. *In other words, by going face-to-face you have an almost seven times better chance of finding a job, than if you had just sent out your resume.*

69%

3. By yourself, using the phone book's yellow pages to identify subjects or fields of interest to you in the town or city where you want to work, and then calling up the employers listed in that field, to ask if they are hiring for the type of position you can do, and do well. This method has a 69 percent success rate. That is, out of every 100 job-hunters or career-changers who use only this search method, 69 will get lucky and find a job thereby. Thirty-one job-hunters out of 100 will not—if they use only this one method to search for them. This is one of the five best ways to look for a job, but even so . . .

> It should be noted that this method's success rate is almost 10 times higher than the success rate for resumes. *In other words, by doing targeted phone calls by yourself, you have an almost ten times better chance of finding a job, than if you had just sent out your resume.*

84%

4. In a group with other job-hunters, using the phone book's yellow pages to identify subjects or fields of interest to you in the town or city where you are, and then calling up the employers listed in that field, to ask if they are hiring for the type of position you can do, and do well. This method has an 84 percent success rate. That is, out of every 100 people who use only this method, 84 will get lucky and find a job thereby. This is one of the five best ways to look for a job, but even so . . . 16 job-hunters out of 100 will not find a job—if they use only this one method to search for them.

> It should be noted that this method's success rate is almost 12 times higher than the success rate for resumes. *In other words, by doing targeted phone calls in a group you have an almost twelve times better chance of finding a job, than if you had just sent out your resume.*

86%

5. Doing a Life-Changing Job-Hunt. This method, invented by the late John Crystal and myself, depends upon your doing extensive homework on *yourself* before you go out there pounding the pavements. This homework always has three parts to it:

1. WHAT. This has to do with your skills. You need to inventory and identify what skills you have *that you most enjoy using.* These are called transferable skills, because they are transferable to any field/career that you choose, regardless of where you first picked them up.

2. WHERE. This has to do with job environments. Think of yourself as a flower. You know that a flower which blooms in the desert will not do well at 10,000 feet up—and vice versa. Every flower has an environment where it does best. So with

you. You are like a flower. You need to decide where you want to use your skills, where you would thrive, and where you do your most effective work.

3. HOW. You need to decide how to get where you want to go. This has to do with finding out the names of the jobs you would be most interested in, **and** the names of organizations (in your preferred geographical area) which have such jobs to offer, **and** the names of the people or person there who actually has the power to hire you. And, how you can best approach that person to show him or her how your skills can help them with their problems. How, if you were hired there, you would not be part of the problem, but part of the solution.

This method has an 86 percent success rate. That is, out of every 100 job-hunters or career-changers who use only this search method, 86 will get lucky and find a job or new career thereby.

Such an effectiveness-rate—86 percent—is astronomically higher than most traditional job-hunting methods.[2] That's why when nothing else is working for you, this is the method that you will thank your lucky stars for.

---

2. I speak of individual job-hunting strategies. Group strategies, such as Nathan Azrin's "job-club" concept, Chuck Hoffman's Self-Directed Job-Search, Dean Curtis' Group Job Search program, etc., used to achieve success-rates in the 84 percent range, fifteen years ago or so, using telephone approaches to employers.

I GOT MY JOB THROUGH THE INTERNET — MY PREDECESSOR WAS FIRED FOR SURFING THE WEB AT WORK.

As usual, it does not work for everyone—specifically. Fourteen job-hunters out of 100 will still not find the jobs that are out there—if they use only this one method to search for them.

> It should be noted that this method's success rate is 12 times higher than the success rate for resumes. In other words, by putting in the hard time that this method requires, you have a 1200 percent better chance of finding a job than if you just send out resumes!

What If You Use More Than One of These Alternatives?

Sure. In spite of what the experts advise, you're probably going to be sending out your resume, all over the place. Force of habit. Human nature. You'll almost certainly want to try the Internet as well. From the perspective of the last fifteen years, it's new; and everyone *wants* to believe in it. (Until proven otherwise.)

And you know what? Maybe they will work for you. In which case, hallelujah!

But at least now you know what to do *if they don't* work, for you. And you will avoid *job-hunting insanity.* That's the type of thinking that says: *500 resumes didn't work? Let's try 1,000.*

The cure for this kind of insanity is alternatives.

Wise job-hunters know from the beginning that when they are out of work, they are hunting *second* for a job but *first* of all for Hope. Alternatives keep hope alive. And to someone out of work, that is everything.

So, if you answer ads in the newspapers, or if you answer job-postings on the Internet, or send out your resume everywhere, or sign up with agencies, and so far it has turned out to be all in vain, don't just do more of it. Change your tactics. Try a new strategy.

CHAPTER FIVE

How Do Employers Go Hunting?

What Are an Employer's Alternatives When Hunting?

Strange question! Hunting for what? Why, for employees, of course!

We must always remember that there are two actors on the stage, in any job-hunt: You, and Employers.

And both of you are hunting. You are hunting for Them—or someone *like* Them. And they are hunting for You—or someone *like* You.

Therefore, no discussion about the job-hunt is complete until we have asked not one question, but two. And they are: what alternatives do **you** have, in your hunt? And, what alternatives do **employers** have, in their hunt?

Let's make a list. Or two lists. And hope that the two lists will come out, looking similar.

As it turns out, they do. At first glance. Viz:

Your Alternatives	The Employer's Alternatives
Resumes[1] Using a resume to get invited in, for an interview	**Resumes[1]** Reading resumes, in order to decide who to invite in, for an interview
Colleagues Asking friends about job vacancies where they work	**Colleagues** Asking colleagues about employees, past or present, where those colleagues work
Referrals Asking friends about job vacancies they may know of, at *other* workplaces	**Referrals** Asking colleagues about employees they might know of, at *other* workplaces
Ads Answering an ad in a newspaper, or a posting on the Internet	**Ads** Placing an ad in a newspaper, or posting it on the Internet
Agencies Using an agency—private *(executive search firms, college placement offices, etc.)* or public, federal, state, or local employment gencies, to find a vacancy	**Agencies** Using an agency—private *(executive search firms, college placement offices, etc.)* or public, federal, state, or local employment agencies, to list a vacancy
Contacts Using a friend or business colleague for a direct introduction to employers (specifically, the person-who-has-the-power-to-hire)	**Contacts** Using a friend or business colleague for a direct introduction to prospective employees
Drop-Ins with Proof In an interview, initiated by the job-hunter, showing proof of what that job-hunter can do	**Drop-Ins with Proof** In an interview, initiated by the job-hunter, asking for proof of what the job-hunter can do
Inside the Company Getting inside a company as a temp worker, short-term contract worker, volunteer, or whatever, and hoping you will then be "hired from within" because you are already working there	**Inside the Company** "Hiring or promoting from within"—inside their company, either a present employee or a temp worker, or short-term contract worker, or volunteer, who is already working there

Sounds like both parties go hunting, in exactly the same way. Ah, if only it were so!

What's the problem? Well, it has to do with the nature of lists.

LISTS

By themselves, lists are pretty useless. They're mostly just a hodgepodge of information bits, in no particular order, like grains of sand on the beach. A list is only really useful when it has been prioritized in some order: let us say of importance to you, or time it takes, or money it costs, or meaning, or frequency of use, or whatever.

Here, the above two lists don't mean a thing until we ask the crucial question, *"And in what order of preference?"*

So, let's reprint these two columns (next page), but now in order of *preference*—job-hunters' or career-changers' preference. And then employers' preference. It all comes out looking like this:

Many If Not Most Employers Hunt for Employees in the Exact Opposite Way from How Job-Hunters Hunt for Them

---

1. Resumes here is a broad umbrella term, under which is included all paper or electronic forms of approaches to employers: e.g., resumes, electronic keyword or cyber resumes, cover letters, a mailed career profile, and/or a Q (for qualifications) letter, wherein you list the qualifications a company's ad said they were looking for, and in a parallel column, side by side, the matching qualification you have.

Job-Hunter's Alternatives **In order of preference** *When looking for someone*	The Employer's Alternatives **In order of preference** *When looking for someone*
1. Resumes Using a resume to get invited in, for an interview	**1. Inside the Company** "Hiring or promoting from within"—inside their company, either a present employee or a temp worker, or short-term contract worker, or volunteer, who is already working there
2. Ads Answering an ad in a newspaper, or a posting on the Internet	**2. Colleagues** Asking colleagues about employees, past or present, where those colleagues work
3. Agencies Using an agency—private *(executive search firms, college placement offices, etc.)* or public, federal, state, or local employment agencies, to find a vacancy	**3. Referrals** Asking colleagues about employees they might know of, at *other* workplaces
4. Colleagues Asking friends about job vacancies where they work	**4. Drop-Ins with Proof** In an interview, initiated by the job-hunter, asking for proof of what the job-hunter can do
5. Referrals Asking friends about job vacancies they may know of, at *other* workplaces	**5. Contacts** Using a friend or business colleague for a direct introduction to prospective employees
6. Contacts Using a friend or business colleague for a direct introduction to employers (specifically, the person-who-has-the-power-to-hire-you-for-the-job-you-want)	**6. Agencies** Using an agency—private *(executive search firms, college placement offices, etc.)* or public, federal, state, or local employment agencies, to list a vacancy
7. Drop-Ins with Proof In an interview, initiated by the job-hunter, showing proof of what that job-hunter can do	**7. Ads** Placing an ad in a newspaper, or posting it on the Internet
8. Inside the Company Getting inside a company as a temp worker, short-term contract worker, volunteer, or whatever, and hoping you will eventually be "hired from within" because you are already working there	**8. Resumes** Reading resumes, in order to decide who to invite in, for an interview

"Two Different Worlds,
We Live in Two Different Worlds . . ."

The job-hunt is a strange world. *Two* different worlds, in fact—that of the employer, and that of the job-hunter. To illustrate:

You want it to be a hiring game; but the employer regards it as an elimination game—until the very last phase.

You want the employer to at least acknowledge receipt of your resume; but the employer feels too inundated and under-staffed to find time to do that.

You want your resume to be *all that gets weighed;* but the employer studies your whole job-hunting behavior to get clues as to what kind of employee you would be.

You want the employer to be taking lots of initiative toward you; but the employer prefers that it be you who takes the initiative. For example, some employers have time to go looking for your resume on the Internet when they have a vacancy, but most don't. If you haven't posted your resume right on their site, where they can find it with a minimum expenditure of energy, you're dead.

You want the employer to tell you all about their organization *during* the upcoming hoped-for interview with them; but the employer wants you to do an impressive amount of research on them *before* you ever come in for an interview. They expect you to know what the organization does, what its product or services are, its history, its challenges *(or the whole industry's challenges)*, etc.

Final Notes on
How Employers Hunt
for Job-Hunters

The way employers absolutely prefer that you approach them is through a mutual friend. This is called "through contacts" or "through networking." They want someone to vouch for you, before they decide to give you some of their precious time.

Next preferred method: they want to get some impression of you, most likely through your resume or (if you have one—artists do) your portfolio. *What kind of resume?* is the big question. Some so-called experts will tell you there is a standard format for the resume, that employers want to see. Don't you believe them! I used to have a hobby of collecting "winning" resumes—that is, resumes that had actually gotten someone a job-interview and, ultimately, a job. I'm kind of playful by nature, so I would show these without comment, to employer friends of mine, over lunch. Many of them didn't like these winning resumes at all. "That resume will never get anyone a job," they would say. Then I would reply, "Sorry, you're wrong. It already has. I think what you mean is that it wouldn't get them a job *with you*."

The resume reproduced on the next page is a good example of what I mean; you did want an example, didn't you?

Jim Dyer, who had been in the U.S. Marines for twenty years, wanted a job as a salesman for heavy construction and mining equipment, thousands of miles from where he was then living. He devised the resume you see, and had just fifteen copies made. He mailed them out, he said, "to a grand total of seven before I got the job in the place I wanted!"

Like the employer who hired him, I loved this resume. Yet some of the employers I showed it to *(over lunch, as I said)* criticized it for using a picture or for being too long, or for being too short, etc. In other words, had Jim sent that resume to *them*, they wouldn't have even invited him in for an interview.

So, don't believe any so-called expert who tells you there's one right format for a resume, or one style that's guaranteed to win over the heart of any employer. All employers are different, and let me say that after four thousand years, we've gotten no further to date than the *ink-blot* stage of resume-writing, where each employer reads a different thing into each resume he or she holds in their hands.

And let's not forget that to some employers, *all* resumes are death. They hate them. They break out into a rash, if they even see one in their mailbox, incoming mail, or e-mails. For such employers, you would be far better off to just send them a brief individual letter, summarizing the salient facts about yourself, that make you the most attractive, and makes them the most curious about your talents and gifts. "Let's get this guy (or gal) in here, and take a look at 'em" is what you want them to say.

E. J. DYER   Street, City, Zip   Telephone No.

I SPEAK

THE LANGUAGE

OF

MEN

MACHINERY

AND

MANAGEMENT

. . .

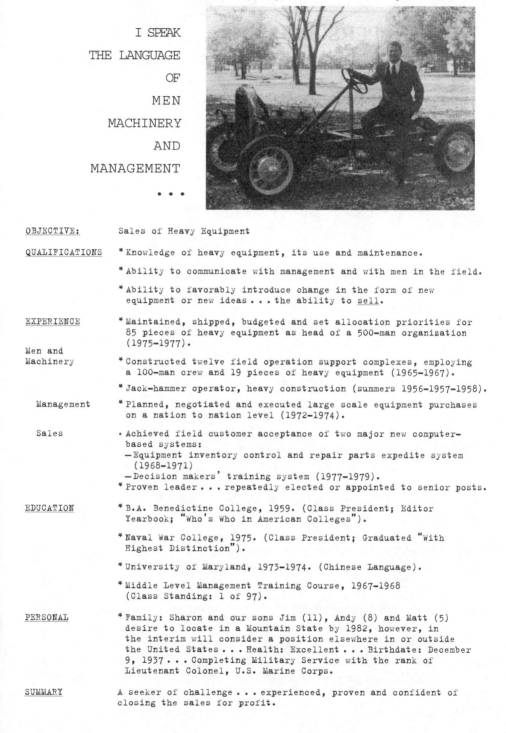

OBJECTIVE: Sales of Heavy Equipment

QUALIFICATIONS * Knowledge of heavy equipment, its use and maintenance.

                * Ability to communicate with management and with men in the field.

                * Ability to favorably introduce change in the form of new
                  equipment or new ideas . . . the ability to sell.

EXPERIENCE   * Maintained, shipped, budgeted and set allocation priorities for
                  85 pieces of heavy equipment as head of a 500-man organization
Men and   (1975-1977).
Machinery
                * Constructed twelve field operation support complexes, employing
                  a 100-man crew and 19 pieces of heavy equipment (1965-1967).

                * Jack-hammer operator, heavy construction (summers 1956-1957-1958).

   Management   * Planned, negotiated and executed large scale equipment purchases
                  on a nation to nation level (1972-1974).

   Sales   · Achieved field customer acceptance of two major new computer-
                  based systems:
                  —Equipment inventory control and repair parts expedite system
                    (1968-1971)
                  —Decision makers' training system (1977-1979).
                * Proven leader . . . repeatedly elected or appointed to senior posts.

EDUCATION   * B.A. Benedictine College, 1959. (Class President; Editor
                  Yearbook; "Who's Who in American Colleges").

                * Naval War College, 1975. (Class President; Graduated "With
                  Highest Distinction").

                * University of Maryland, 1973-1974. (Chinese Language).

                * Middle Level Management Training Course, 1967-1968
                  (Class Standing: 1 of 97).

PERSONAL   * Family: Sharon and our sons Jim (11), Andy (8) and Matt (5)
                  desire to locate in a Mountain State by 1982, however, in
                  the interim will consider a position elsewhere in or outside
                  the United States . . . Health: Excellent . . . Birthdate: December
                  9, 1937 . . . Completing Military Service with the rank of
                  Lieutenant Colonel, U.S. Marine Corps.

SUMMARY   A seeker of challenge . . . experienced, proven and confident of
                closing the sales for profit.

Trouble is, you don't know which employer likes *what*. That's why many job-hunters, if they use resumes, pray as they mail their resume: *Please, dear God, let them be employers who like resumes in general, and may the form of my resume appeal to those employers I care the most about, in particular.*

Conclusion: Start with What You Want, Not with What the Job-Market Wants

How employers job-hunt *is of no concern to you* if you are planning on launching your own business, and being self-employed—which is the goal and intention of one out of every ten job-hunters. In which case, it is you who gets to set the rules of the game, and determine how customers or clients will find you. Plus, you can forget about preparing your own resume, mostly, or any other noxious aspects of job-hunting in America. You call the shots. You determine the path. It's all about your agenda, your wishes, your plans. You determine the rules of the game.

But if you're going to work for someone else, as nine out of every ten job-hunters intend, then you need to pay large attention to this chapter, and how employers go hunting. You need to use contacts and networking. And resumes. Because employers are the ones who, in this case, determine the rules of the game.

Yes, it's all a kind of game, no matter who determines the rules thereof. So, let's turn now and take a look at the Playing Field where the game is played, namely, the planet Earth.

I hold the world but as the world, Gratiano, a stage, where every man must play a part .

Antonio, in *The Merchant of Venice,* act 1 sc 1, by William Shakespeare (1564–1616)

The
Playing
Field

The picture on page 44 of the Earth and the Moon together, features images that were taken in 1992 by the spacecraft Galileo. Separate images of the Earth and the Moon were combined, to the same scale and relative color, to generate this picture. For those who care about such things, the image of the Earth is centered on the Pacific Ocean at about latitude 20 degrees south. The Moon shows the bright ray crater of the Tycho impact basin, at the bottom. The picture was produced by USGS Flagstaff.

CHAPTER SIX

The Playing Field

The Death of Distance[1]

On December 26, 2004, a monstrous 9.3 earthquake and tidal wave struck the Earth in Asia, and scientists said this caused the entire Earth to "ring like a bell."

In fact, every part of the Earth's surface moved, every seventeen minutes, by as much as half an inch, and for weeks on end thereafter. "No point on Earth remained undisturbed," wrote one scientist in awe, at the University of Colorado. The force was awesome. A thousand miles away from the epicenter of the earthquake, the ground moved up and down by almost four inches.

Of course, this powerful shaking of the Earth as though it were just one gigantic physical bell, brought with it terrible destruction and heartbreaking loss of life, with up to 232,000 people losing their lives; and the survivors facing a nightmare, in trying to put their lives back together, even months later. The response of human hearts elsewhere in the world to this tragedy

---

1. This phrase was coined by Frances Cairncross, senior editor for the *Economist*, in her 1997 book of the same name. Her thesis is that the growing ease and speed of communication is increasingly creating a world where the miles have little to do with our ability to work and interact together, whoever we are, whatever our skills.

was immediate. A kind of spiritual earthquake—an unprecedented, worldwide, benign tidal wave of compassion, aid, and humanitarian efforts, sped almost instantaneously around the whole globe. In sympathy, we were all one. And the World seemed a very small size: a bell ringing in space.

But looking back, if you were not an Earthquake, and it were not the twenty-first century, it can, could, and did, take you an awfully long time to travel around this bell called Earth. For much of human history, *distance* was a great barrier, for everyone involved in work or commerce. For example, it used to take ships three years to travel around the World. At least that was true for Ferdinand Magellan's ships, 1519–1522.[2]

Ever since 1522, things have sped up. If we skip to the year 1843, we notice it took just 5 months to travel by wagon train from Missouri to California in the U.S.

In 1846 it took just 4 months to travel from the East Coast to the West Coast (California) by sea.

In 1858 it took just 25 days to go from coast to coast by stagecoach.

In 1920 it took just 78 hours for U.S. Airmail Route #1 to go from coast to coast by a combination of air and rail.

In 1930 it took just 16 hours to fly from coast to coast.

On January 22, 1970, it took 6 and ½ hours for a Boeing 747 to fly from New York to London.

On February 7, 1996, it took a Concorde supersonic jet just two hours 52 minutes and 59 seconds to fly from New York to London. The Concorde flew at twice the speed of sound—around 1,350 miles per hour.

Now, Japanese and French engineers are working together on a jet engine that can theoretically fly more than five times the speed of sound.

In 2005, NASA spacecraft flew to a comet 83 million miles away, between January 12 and July 3 (factually, since it went roundabout, the spacecraft actually flew 280 million miles in those six months).

---

2. His *ships*, mind you; Ferdinand himself didn't make it beyond the Philippines.

Chapter Six

You can see where all this is leading: down through history every time a new *Thing*—*a* new method of transportation—has been invented, be it ship, pony express, stagecoach, wagon train, railroad train, airplane, jet, supersonic jet, or spacecraft, etc.—it has led to this one result: the increasing death of distance, the death of *distance as an obstacle*, anyway.

You can see this same phenomenon with information. Up until 1844, reliable communications—messages—could never be transmitted faster than people, pigeons, smoke, or mirrors could carry them. No information or data could move faster than people.

But with the invention of the telegraph, messages for the first time in history could move faster than people. And ever since 1844, every new method of communications invented— telegraph, telephone, radio, television, wireless, cellphone, the Internet, the World Wide Web—has led to this one result: the increasing death of distance. Again, *as obstacle*. To the spread of information.

> And there you have it:
> The death of distance for People.
> The death of distance for Information, or Data.
> The two main components of our daily work.

The Playing Field

There is a sense in which *work* is like a game or sport—in the same sense as, say, football. And even as any game, such as football, has a playing field, so too does *work*. The Earth—this big bell hanging and ringing in space—is *work's* playing field.

In any game, what happens to the playing field affects the game being played there. In football, for example, it matters where the field is built, how far apart the goal posts are, how much driving rain is falling on that playing field on a particular day, or where the sun is in the players' eyes, what the rules of the game are, who sets those rules, what is the fairness of the players and the officials, etc., etc. These all affect how football gets played.

So too, with work's playing field, the Earth. What's going on, out there, definitely affects our *work*. With the death of *distance-as-obstacle*, the first thing going on out there, is greater freedom. You can now live anywhere. You can communicate with any place. *(That's something of an oversimplification, but there is some substantial truth, and wonder, and awe, to it.)* It now takes only seven minutes for communication to travel over 83 million miles (as, to a spacecraft deliberately instructed to collide with a comet).

The Future Is Already Here: It's Just Unevenly Distributed[3]

Of course, *distance-as-obstacle* is only dying in certain countries and in certain economies and among certain peoples. By contrast, for example, distance still matters, and matters greatly, to the people in Darfur. One hundred miles is *forever*. So, too, in the mountains of Afghanistan. And among nomadic peoples. And in rural areas all around the globe. Distance is as much an obstacle in these places today, as it was in the 1500s.

But this is the twenty-first century, and not the sixteenth, for people in Western civilization, for workers in developed countries, for industries in developing countries now rising from economic sleep, such as China, and India.

---

3. Attributed, in various wordings, to the author William Gibson.

In those places, and in increasing numbers, you or I or anyone running a business can search the World for the clients or customers we need, for the help we need, the resources we need, etc.—and at the cheapest costs that we can find; and then work with those hires without ever having to move them to the U.S. We no longer have to restrict our search just to the country where we are living, or were born.

China Calling, or Even Timbuktu[4]

With the death of *distance-as-obstacle,* many job-hunters are rethinking and reinventing their jobs.

For example, look at *career counseling*—or *career-coaching*, as it more and more tends to be called. For many decades, it was taken for granted that it was a face-to-face business. Indeed, some career counselors and coaches still insist on that definition, often vehemently. *What? Do counseling without ever meeting my client? Are you nuts?*

But in this twenty-first century, as the miles have begun to matter less and less, an increasing number now do most of their counseling over the telephone.

One counselor I know from the San Francisco Bay Area has telephone clients, for example, in many places overseas, including France and China. Think what this turn of events—the death of distance—means to job-hunters living in some remote rural area in either France or China. Now they can access the very best counselors anywhere else in the world.

Conversely, if you are the career counselor in the San Francisco Bay Area, your search for clients is not restricted merely to job-hunters who happen to live nearby. You can go as far afield as France or China, or Timbuktu, to find clients.

Furthermore, you yourself can live anywhere a phone line or wireless can reach, such as a remote rural cabin in the Austrian Alps listening to *The Sound of Music.* Or listening to some Mozart, or Bono or Coldplay, while you work.

---

4. A metaphor for "the ends of the earth." It is an actual place, however—a region in northern Mali, West Africa, bordering Mauritania on the northwest, Algeria on the northeast, and the regions of Gao on the east, and Mopti and Ségou on the south. It is entirely within the Sahara desert, except for the extreme southern area along the Niger River.

You can be a hugely expensive executive coach, who charges client companies two hundred thousand dollars per executive client *(Yep! there are such coaches)*; or you can be a coach for the common man or woman, who charges only forty to eighty bucks an hour. I know both types, and they each say they have never laid eyes on over 90 percent of their clients. Wouldn't know what they looked like, if they tripped over them! Of course, telephone coaches can exchange pictures, so each knows what the other looks like. Down the road *(we can see it coming)* they will be tying in video cams with their phoning, so neither counselor nor job-hunter will be working blind. *(Although some telephone counselors like things the way they are; they prefer not to be visually distracted, and while operating essentially as blind people, they have developed their listening to the nth degree, by way of what psychologists call* compensation.*)*

Anyway, this is but one example of how, with the death of *distance-as-obstacle*, many job-hunters are rethinking and reinventing their jobs, these days. It's a constant, endless, evolving *process*, as the kinks gradually get worked out.

The Coming of the Bogeyman[5]

Every decade creates its own "bogeyman" to scare job-hunters, and make them fear for their jobs. One decade it may be *illegal immigrants.*[6] In another, *"Made in Japan."* In another decade it turns out to be *the taking over of manufacturing by robots.* And in yet another decade it turns out to be China. Each and every one of them—so the fear goes—is going to rob us of our jobs.

In this decade, our bogeyman is *outsourcing* in general, and China in particular.

---

5. As any fan of horror movies knows, this is a monstrous imaginary figure used in frightening children out of their wits—or moviegoers out of their wallets.

6. As of March 2004, an estimated 10.3 million unauthorized migrants were in the U.S. and 6.3 million of them had found employment. (*Pew Hispanic Center report, 6/14/05*). As of May 2005, "unauthorized workers" made up approximately 4.3 percent of our labor force in the U.S. Some 57 percent of them are from Mexico, according to the Pew Report. (*The Population Reference Bureau*)

If you haven't been living in a cave the last five years, you probably know what *outsourcing* is, or—more particularly— offshore outsourcing. With the death of *distance-as-obstacle*, employers can increasingly send jobs overseas, jobs which once would have been *ours*, and give those jobs to cheaper labor elsewhere in the world, including not only China, but also India, Mexico, and Eastern European countries.[7] The average computer programmer in India, for example, only demands around $10 an hour, compared to the more than $60 per hour that the average American computer programmer can command.

What kinds of jobs do employers try to outsource? Well, currently almost any kind of job you can think of. (Or, with a bow to Winston Churchill, *every job of which you can think.*) As long as it doesn't involve touch.

Massage therapists seem safe. So do doctors and nurses. And local delivery trucks. And waiters or waitresses. And garbage disposal jobs.

When jobs do move overseas, it's all about salaries.

---

7. In Europe, future outsourcing centers are predicted to include the Czech Republic, Poland, and Hungary.

Scared and Depressed

In a recent online poll 49 percent of all the respondents said that offshoring had had "a somewhat negative" impact on employee morale, while an additional 37 percent said the impact was "extremely negative." The reason these developments on *the playing field* called Earth matter so greatly to job-hunting and job-hunters in this twenty-first century, is precisely this issue of "morale." Outsourcing or the threat of it, is the biggest kick-in-the-head to job-hunters' morale in a long time.

However, the U.S. is not alone in these fears. Job-hunters in other countries are also afraid of outsourcing, or any variation on that theme. In Europe, they are afraid of their jobs being taken away when less expensive workers from other nations, come to their shores. French voters, for example, overwhelmingly turned down ratification of the European Union constitution on May 30, 2005, in part because of their fears about some mythical "Polish plumber"—symbol of the workers from eastern EU countries who are increasingly free to move west, as to France, and are willing to work for lower pay than French workers.

As in France, so in the rest of Europe. Researchers report that "outsourcing continues to accelerate in Europe, with the level of deal activity rivaling that in the US. The UK still stands out as Europe's dominant market, but outsourcing has gained ground in Germany, Spain, and France."[8] Yes, job-hunters are afraid. The $64 million question: just how realistic are these fears?

Good question! One U.S. report cautions:

> "Despite numerous efforts, both public and private sector agencies have yet to determine a clear accurate measure of how many U.S. jobs are being lost to outsourcing, or how many might be lost in the future."[9]

---

8. Forrester's Report: Trends 2005: Outsourcing in Europe, by Richard Peynot, issued on November 9, 2004. www.forrester.com/Research/Document/Excerpt/0,7211,35706,00.html.

9. "Outsourcing Statistics in Perspective," from the Center for American Progress.

In the absence of concrete data, *fear* has given birth to fantastical estimates of how many U.S. jobs could potentially be lost to outsourcing in the future. Such estimates run as high as 14.1 million U.S. jobs.

The reality? Actual U.S. outsourcing-job-losses to date, appear to total a mere 500,000 jobs, out of the 140,000,000 jobs that are in the U.S. workforce currently.

And experts' predictions of the actual number of U.S. jobs that *will* be lost annually in the future, hover around 220,000[10]— which works out to mean: only two-hundredths of one percent of the U.S. workforce stand to lose their jobs to outsourcing.

Bogeyman, indeed!

Jobs Are Mortal, by Their Very Nature

Let's face it. If you wanted to find something to worry about, there are a million things you can choose between—besides outsourcing—that cause jobs to be lost in the U.S. There is a constant turnover in the job-market, which experts call "churning." Churning is created by factors, developments, inventions, and current events—that wipe out old kinds of jobs, and maybe—

"Let's put it this way — if you can find a village without an idiot, you've got yourself a job."

10. Ibid.

maybe—get replaced by new kinds of jobs. Each year in the U.S. thirty million jobs come to an end, and have to be refilled.[11] Plus 2,400,000 *new* jobs get born in the U.S., in a typical year, when the economy is healthy.

It is useful, then, to think of jobs as mortal—and mortal for a hundred reasons. So if your job gets ground up in the future, or has already gotten ground up, in all of this churning, *puhlease* don't take it personally! Just repeat to yourself our simple truth: *jobs are mortal*, by their very nature. Jobs get born. That is what jobs do. Jobs live for a time. Sometimes a long time. That is what jobs do. But then, inevitably, jobs die. (And sometimes, long before they die, they are moribund and on "life-support.") Again, they die because that is what jobs do.

A Philosophy of Work

The most useful thing you can do is to adopt, ahead of time, what we might call *a philosophy of work.* That philosophy should have, at a minimum, five points:

1. The typical job these days is best viewed **as a temp job**. That is, *of uncertain length.* If you work for someone else, as 90 percent of the U.S. workforce does, then how long your job lasts is up to the people you work for, and not just you. Your job can end at any time and without warning. Therefore, you must always be mentally prepared to go out job-hunting again, at the drop of a hat.

---

11. On March 30, 2004, the brilliant Ben S. Bernanke—at that time a Regional Governor of the Federal Research Board, now the successor to Alan Greenspan—gave a speech at Duke University in Durham, North Carolina, in the course of which he revealed that "about 30 million jobs are lost each year in the United States." Fifteen million of them, he said, are short-term, temporary contracts that run their course and then end, as they are supposed to. But, the other 15 million become vacancies that in the job-hunting game of musical chairs have to be filled—in the course of a year. That works out to 1,250,000 each month. And this has been the case, for at least the past ten years. That 1,250,000 has to be added, each month, to the net figure that the Monthly Unemployment Report declares, the first Friday of each month, as new jobs. If that Report says "only 146,000 *new* jobs were added to the economy this past month" (as it did, at the end of June 2005), that isn't the number of vacancies. The actual number of vacancies for that month was 146,000 plus 1,250,000—all of which had to get filled, during the course of that month.

2. The typical job these days is best viewed as **a seminar**. Almost every job these days is moving and changing so fast in its content or form, that there is a lot you will have to learn on the job, not only when you begin but throughout the whole time you are there. You would be wise not to think of your job just in terms of what you can accomplish. You must look at it in terms of what you can learn, or did learn, while you are there. If you want to be a prized employee, you must not only be *ready* to learn, but *eager* to learn. And, if it is true, you must emphasize to every would-be employer how much you love to learn new stuff, new tasks and procedures, and how fast you pick up new stuff.

3. The typical job these days is best viewed as **an adventure**. If you end up working for an organization that is of any size, it is very likely that the dramas which will be played out there, daily, weekly, and monthly, will rival any soap opera on television. Power plays! Ambition! Double-dealing! Cheating! Strange alliances! Rumors! Betrayal! Revolution! Overthrow! Sudden plot twists, that no one could have predicted! Sometimes you'll love it. Sometimes you'll hate it.

4. The typical job these days is best viewed as **one where the satisfaction lies in the work itself,** and not in some hoped-for future reward. In the old days, most of us hoped we would not only find work we enjoyed, but also work where we were appreciated, saluted, singled-out, and praised to the skies. In other words, we looked for love, where we worked. And a raise. And a promotion. Unfortunately, despite your best research and hopes during your job-hunt, you may end up in a job where your bosses fail to recognize or acknowledge the fine contribution that you are making to the organization, leaving you feeling unloved and unappreciated, until—finally—even after many months or years, you may be suddenly let go, and without warning, as they cite a business turndown, merger, bankruptcy, the need they have for *new blood*, reduced costs, or the full moon.

5. You need to approach any job with the philosophy that **it can be transformed**. No job is set in stone, just as it is. Your power

lies in your conviction that you can, you may, you must, transform that job by the attitude you bring with you. And by the grace of God.

Who Are My Brothers and Sisters?

The best way to think about this new playing field called Earth is through a parable. Imagine that you have been reborn into a family of twelve children, everyone of whom is of a different nationality, race, religion, values held, degree of education, and so forth. Moreover, you are all blind. You cannot see what the other eleven of your brothers and sisters look like. Nor can they see what you look like, either. But you have to all learn to work together, helping each other, even so. That is the new world.

And now to the good news: you are more gifted and talented, because of this. As I said, in this parable you are blind. It is well-known that those who are blind often become extremely gifted. They often develop their other senses to a really keen degree, to make up for their lack of sight. As we saw earlier, it's called *compensation.* And developing our other senses to a really keen degree, is necessary for those of us who live, work, and play on this new playing field, where distance is swallowed up.

The Earth Moves; You Can Too

We need to keep reminding ourselves that this *death of distance* thing is not just about employers.

For us job-hunters too, the world has changed. When you go job-hunting, you job-hunt on a vastly different playing field than, say, ten years ago. You have more opportunities.

And if you choose to be self-employed, you now have a much larger market at your disposal where you can sell your skills, knowledge, services, and products.

If you need to find a partner with certain skills, to complement your own, you have the whole World to pick from.

If you need to sublet some of your work, products, or services, you can choose among people all over the World.

If you need to have something printed or produced, as inexpensively as possible, you have the whole World to search for an inexpensive printer, vendor, or manufacturer.

If you need a larger market for your product or services, you can now draw on the whole World.

Increasingly, the miles are no obstacle to your ability to work and interact with other people, no matter what you do, no matter what your goals, no matter what your skills. Distance is becoming more and more irrelevant to your now and future work, because it is more and more irrelevant to the World. At least in some places.

Hence, as a job-hunter today, you've got more freedom. The world is *your* oyster.

It's not simply that your job can move; you can too.

You can decide to go and work in other parts of the world. Or other parts of the country. Or other parts of the state. Or other parts of the city or county, where you currently live. Maybe you won't be able to achieve your dream; but you'll never know, unless you first define what your dream is.

So, when you start out job-hunting or trying to change careers, the question you want to address first of all, is this: *where* would you most like to live, on this Bell hanging and ringing in space?

Two roads diverged in a yellow wood,
And sorry I could not travel both
And be one traveler, long I stood
And looked down one as far as I could
To where it bent in the undergrowth;

Then took the other, as just as fair,
And having perhaps the better claim,
Because it was grassy and wanted wear;
Though as for that the passing there
Had worn them really about the same,

And both that morning equally lay
In leaves no step had trodden black.
Oh, I kept the first for another day!
Yet knowing how way leads on to way,
I doubted if I should ever come back.

I shall be telling this with a sigh
Somewhere ages and ages hence:
Two roads diverged in a wood, and I—
I took the one less traveled by,
And that has made all the difference.

—Robert Frost (1874–1963)[1]

---

1. The title of this poem is "The Road Not Taken," from *The Poetry of Robert Frost* edited by Edward Connery Lathem. Copyright 1916, © 1969 by Holt, Rinehart & Winston. Copyright 1944 by Robert Frost. Henry Holt and Company, Publisher. Used with permission. Incidentally, the late M. Scott Peck's classic, *The Road Less Traveled*, took its title from this poem. (*The Road Less Traveled, 25th Anniversary Edition: A New Psychology of Love, Traditional Values and Spiritual Growth*—by M. Scott Peck, M.D.; Paperback. 2003.)

Where on Earth Do You Want to Live?

A s we have just seen, the dominant theme on the playing field called Earth is *energy* and *motion*.

The Earth moves.

Information moves.

You move.

We've talked, already, about the Earth, and information. Now let's talk about You.

We Are a Nomadic People, Sort Of . . .

Oh, a lot of us stay put, to be sure. Some of us have lived in the same city, the same house, for forty-one years, or more.

But many of us *could* move, if we wanted to; and a lot of us *do* move. Some *fourteen million* of us move, lock, stock, and barrel each year, in the U.S. That's a lot of people!

And yet, according to an analysis of Census Bureau data from the year 2003, which was published in the February 2005 issue of *The Gerontologist*, it was discovered that only 14 percent of the population moved that year, which is the lowest rate since the Census Bureau began collecting these data in 1948.

On the other hand, experts agree that young adults of today are an exception to the general trend of decreasing mobility.

Young adults feel less and less bound to any particular place on earth. They are much more ready than previous generations to pull up stakes, and move to a new place—often a huge distance away—in order to secure the right job. "Have resume, will travel," might be *the* bumper-sticker of the twenty-first century.

So, when we move, why *do* we move, in this country, or anywhere else in the world? The reasons are various and manifold; I count fourteen, just for starters.

1. Catastrophies that are of Biblical proportions. Currently, twenty-five million people have at least temporarily lost their homes, worldwide, according to the United Nations. This is due to mammoth *natural* or *man-made* disasters, such as the uprooting of millions of people in Sudan in the early twenty-first century *(and before)*, or the aforementioned 9.3 earthquake and tsunami in the Pacific region of the world on December 26, 2004, or the monstrous assault by the Category 4 hurricane called Katrina, upon the city of New Orleans and one hundred miles of Gulf Coast line on Monday, August 29, 2005, where up to a million and a half people in the U.S. lost their homes, and became dispossessed.

2. A Safe Haven. People will move, sometimes even to another country, to escape harsh—often intolerable—circumstances: when they find themselves facing long-standing, hurtful, domestic abuse, or sexual molestation, and no one will play their champion, or deliver them from such meanness, in the place or country where they are—not the law, not family, not social agencies, *not no one*. In which case, experts advise: Move!! Please! Not much guidance on the web, but for a place to start, try: www .domesticviolence.org/who.html.

3. New life, new place. Release from the military, finishing college, death of a loved one, release from prison, divorce, a new marriage, etc.—you are starting a new chapter in your life, and you decide you want to start it in a new place, away from the memories of the past.

4. Medical attention. Maybe you need more medical expertise than is offered in the place where you are; you need to go to the kind of country, place, or hospital, where you or your family can get the medical attention that you need. Don't know where

to start? Type *best hospitals best doctors* into your favorite search engine on the Internet.

5. Education. Maybe you live where there is only a two-year college, and you want four years of college. Or where there's only four years, and you want a place where you can get a graduate degree. Or maybe there's a far better school in some other country, that has exactly the professors you'd most like to study with, for your field. Type *best universities best professors* into your favorite search engine, to find the best in the U.S., Europe, Asia, Australia, etc.

6. Geography as Career Guidance. I once met a waitress who moved from one city to another, never staying more than five months in any one place; she was a keen observer of the local scene, wherever she was, and was hoping to get from her observations some new ideas of what else she could do with her life, besides waitressing. I was quite taken with her approach. I thought to myself, "Ah, geography as a career search tool. Never thought of that!" But someone did. I later found out that someone has turned this into a business. His name is Brian Kurth. His business is called Vocations Vacations.[2] Very popular! So, geography is not a bad way to explore future kinds of

---

2. www.vocationvacations.com. A bit superficial, perhaps (one to three days). A bit pricey, perhaps ($500–$1000). But, who knows? You just might find out what you want to do, next, with your life.

jobs. Plus, careers aside, maybe you'll meet Prince Charming in your travels. Or a female rock star. Or the new Donald Trump. *"One never know, do one?" (Fats Waller)*

7. Jobs. Of course, *of course*. Just within the good ol' U.S. of A., for example, there are varying job opportunities, as you move from city to city, and from state to state. Your local federal/state employment office can usually give you the current unemployment statistics about all fifty states. The figures are also on the Internet.[3] You want to look, of course, for the states with the lowest overall unemployment rate, where finding jobs is the easiest.

As of the latest figures, released June 17, 2005, the five states with the lowest jobless rates (those rates stated as a percentage of that state's work force), where it's therefore easiest to find a job (in theory) were:

1. Hawaii (2.7 percent unemployment rate)
2. Vermont (3.1 percent unemployment rate)
3. North Dakota (3.5 percent unemployment rate)
4. New Hampshire (3.6 percent unemployment rate)
5. Virginia (3.6 percent unemployment rate)

On the other hand, the five states with the highest jobless rates (stated as a percentage of that state's work force) where it's therefore hardest to find a job (in theory) were:

1. District of Columbia (7.9 percent unemployment rate)
2. Mississippi (7.1 percent unemployment rate)
3. Michigan (7.1 percent unemployment rate)
4. Oregon (6.5 percent unemployment rate)
5. Alaska (6.4 percent unemployment rate)

If you want to move, in order to pursue the jobs, pick one of the first five states, say the one that appeals to you the most, get your hands on a map of that state, pick one or more areas in that state—metropolitan or rural—and write to their chamber of commerce. You can ask *Information* for their phone number, or if you

---

3. For the states see: www.bls.gov/web/laumstrk.htm For metropolitan areas in the U.S. see: www.bls.gov/web/laummtrk.htm

prefer you can of course look it up online, at: `www.chamberof` `commerce.com/forms/search_state_chambers.htm`. Then you ask those chambers for all the information they have in writing, about businesses that deal with your trade or specialty, assuming you know your trade or specialty.

8. Money. Minimum hourly wages in some civilized places around the world run $1.75 or less. Sometimes much, much less. *(Try: fifty cents a day.)* Some people, when their families can manage it financially, will be sent to places that pay better for the work they do best and most enjoy doing; and they then send the money back home. Alternatively, you may move back in with your family for a while if you have no wages, and just can't find a job to save your life.

9. "Going Rural." Maybe you're looking for a simpler life, away from urban centers, out where the buffalo roam, and the deer and the antelope play, where seldom is heard a discouraging word, and the skies are not cloudy all day, etc. Good for you! Further details about this, in the body of this chapter.

10. "Going Urban." You may want more choices in life, than are available to you where you are. So you move from a remote place to a more crowded one.

11. Wanderlust. You just want to be moving around. Period. You've got itchy feet. You're bored, and it feels better to be in motion, than it does to be stuck still in the same old same old. You're like a gifted dancer, looking for a new ballroom.

12. Curiosity and Love of Adventure. There's some place, city, country, continent you've heard about, and you always wanted to see it with your own eyes, just out of curiosity, or for the love of adventure, or maybe even to find out if you want to live there—*maybe*. One woman I know, newly single, has made a list of twelve countries she wants to visit and work in, before she retires or dies. If you're starting fresh, and need some ideas, there's a great book to help you; it's called *1000 Places to See Before You Die*.[4]

---

4. By Patricia Schultz, Workman Publishing Company, May 22, 2003. Very popular book, as I write. (*NY Times* best-seller list; also among the top 150 best-selling titles on Amazon.com, etc.)

13. Love of beauty. You want to visit or move to a more beautiful place, which fills your soul with serenity and takes your breath away. It can be the gardens of England, the music of Aspen, Colorado, Yosemite National Park in California, the mountains of Switzerland, some South Sea Island, Hawaii, Guilin in China, Ha Long Bay in Vietnam, the Tetons in Wyoming, etc. Need ideas? If you have access to the Internet, enter at the same time the words *photos* and *most beautiful places on earth* into your favorite search engine (say, www.google.com or www.a9.com). Or enter your favorite kind of scenery or environment: *music,*

art, museums, mountains, lakes, gardens, ocean, universities, tropical, buildings, etc., together with the word *photos*, into that search engine. See what you find. Try also the Discovery Channel on your TV.

14. Compassion for Family or for Mankind. As families age, become injured, or fall ill, you may move home or at least *closer* to home, in order to be their caregivers during their dying or other life crisis. Or, if we define *family* more broadly, you may want to fight AIDS/HIV, or malaria, or poverty, or bird flu, or any other of the scourges of mankind, in some near or far-off place.

Katrina

So much for the geographical possibilities. Summing up: in some cases you *want* to move; in other cases, as with Katrina and similar catastrophies, where 80 percent of your city (*e.g., New Orleans*) lies underwater, you *have* to move. Immediately. With only a garbage bag of your lifelong possessions, under your arm. You *have* to move, for now. Even if, maybe—*maybe*—some day you'll be back.

The question for now is: how do you go about choosing a new place, when you haven't got even a clue where to go.

The *diaspora* or dispersion, that occurred in Katrina's wake, found hundreds of thousands of people fleeing New Orleans, and other low-lying Gulf Coast cities, searching—most immediately—for a safe place, above all else. A higher ground, where the floodwaters could not reach them, and a place where lawlessness did not reign. They found what they were looking for, temporarily, in a nearby *parish*, or in a city or state far away.[5]

In all of our lives, there may come such a time when without any warning *Survival* will be our issue and our first consideration in defining *a new place*.

---

5. Events move swiftly, but for months if not years to come, help will be desperately needed for this largest displacement of people in the U.S. since the Civil War in the 1860s. If your heart is moved to help them (*"There, but for the grace of God, go I."*) there is a central website you can turn to, to donate online to any of a tremendously wide variety of helpers. It is called Network for Good, located at: www.networkforgood.org/topics/animal_environ/hurricanes/.

Most Immediately, Choose Any Place Where You Feel Safe

I have argued elsewhere[6] that each time we find ourselves in a new situation, there are four issues we must solve, in turn—and in this order: 1. **What's Happening?** What exactly is the situation I am facing? 2. **Survival.** What do I have to do, to survive, physically, economically, mentally, and spiritually, in the midst of all that's happening? 3. **Meaning or Mission.** How can I then find some meaning to all of this, and some meaning or mission for my future life and work? 4. **Effectiveness.** And, how can I measure how well I am achieving my goals?

The point? The point is that when *Survival* is your issue, you usually have to solve *that* first, before you can go on to deal with any other issues you may face. Hence, you must find, first of all, a place where you feel safe.

Next, Choose a Place Where You Formerly Lived, and Have, Still, Family or Friends There

That place, whatever its name, has the virtue of familiarity. We've been there before. We know, basically, how to make our way around. When we feel lost and bewildered, *familiar surroundings* count for a lot.

---

6. In my book, *The Three Boxes of Life, and How to Get Out of Them: An Introduction to Life Work Planning* (Bolles, 1981. Ten Speed Press, Berkeley, CA).

That place has also the virtue of support. If our family is there, they offer a haven, a place of refuge and recovery, when we have nowhere else to turn. If there once was love for us there, love waits there for us still. Family will take care of us, for a time, when no one else will. Ditto for friends—*true* friends as defined by Jesus' standard: *"I was hungry and you gave me something to eat, I was thirsty and you gave me something to drink, I was a stranger and you invited me in, I needed clothes, and you clothed me, I was sick and you looked after me . . ."*[7]

To such friends, or to a loving family, we instinctively turn when we are broke and out of money, and have no job to mention. That's true of the thousands if not millions of victims of Katrina. That's true even in lesser circumstances, as when you are an unemployed college graduate, who has to move temporarily back in with your parents, when you just can't find a job. A chance for you to exercise the good old-fashioned virtue of gratitude. Think it. Say it. Out loud. Thank you.

---

7. In, *The Gospel* according to Matthew, chapter 25, verses 34–40.

Beyond Survival:
Picture a Place
Where You'd Most Like to Live

If *survival* is not your issue, but rather your issue is that of *meaning and mission,* i.e., choosing a more appropriate place where your work and your spirit can flourish, then where do you begin?

Well, begin simply. Ask yourself, *if I could live anywhere in the country (or the world), what place would it be?*

Got a name? Good!

Got some doubts? Well yes, of course, you do. That proves you're human. You've got doubts that you will ever be able to figure out a way to get there, and live there.

Well, let's be honest. It *could* all stay a daydream. But ah! maybe it won't. You'll never know 'til you try. And try hard. So, don't set yourself up for failure, with your thinking. Picture your dream coming true. Picture yourself in that place. Keep that vision strongly in your head.

Places are like jobs.
The stronger a picture
you can see in your mind
of what you want,
the more enthusiasm you will feel,
and the more time you will put in,
toward achieving that dream.

Chapter Seven

My own motto for many many years now, is: *Pray as though everything depended on God; then work, as though everything depended on you.*

Here's how you begin, as though everything depended on you:

1. You start by interviewing all your friends and acquaintances, to ask them what places *they* have loved the most, in the U.S. or in whatever country you live. And *why*. This task can be a lot of fun, and a great conversation-starter with all your friends. But be sure and write their suggestions down—don't just nod thoughtfully! And when you have a lengthy list, choose the two or three places that intrigue you the most, and do further investigation.

2. Too shy to interview your friends and family? Well, then, you can turn to books or to the Internet. Books used to be the way to go. In the U.S., there were quite a number of them that rated various cities and towns according to *factors* that might be important to you, such as *weather, crime, educational system, recreational opportunities*, etc.

The best of these, by a long shot, was David Savageau's and Ralph B. D'Agostino's *Places Rated Almanac (Special Millennium Edition)*. Problem with books: they sometimes go years without being revised or updated in any but the most superficial way. *Places Rated*, for example, hasn't been updated in over five years, as I write.

I grant you, cities don't necessarily change *that* much over the years. In New York City, the Metropolitan Museum of Art is still standing right where it's always been. But on the other hand, the World Trade Center isn't.

Currently, the most recent book offering you geographical guidance is *Cities Ranked and Rated: More than 400 Metropolitan Areas Evaluated in the U.S. and Canada*, 1st Edition, by Bert Sperling and Peter Sander, published March 30, 2004. Bert is the creator of *Money* magazine's original "Best Places to Live" list. He's been at this, for seventeen years or more. On the Internet, he is at Bert Sperling's BestPlaces Site: www.bestplaces.net/.

Web sites for exploring Places where you might love to live, are: FindYourSpot, at www.FindYourSpot.com/. It has an interesting article called *The Best Place to Live—and Other Fairy Tales*. And, then there is also CNN/Money's site: money.cnn.com/best/bplive/.

When You Want to "Go Rural"

Outdoors. Away from civilization. Wilderness. Do these words strike a chord with you? It may be, as you think about moving someday, that your idea of *paradise* turns out to be "going rural"—and moving, at last, to *the country*.

Sometimes the root of this lies in the desire for a simpler life; sometimes, the root lies in the desire for a less expensive way of living. Whatever the reasons, if this is your vision, take that vision seriously. Remember: you only have one life to live, on this earth at least.

Begin by interviewing anyone you know who has moved from urban to the rural life, and ask them what they liked the most about that move, and what they missed the most about their former locale. Then weigh what you learn.

Next, if you have a particular place in mind, investigate that place *thoroughly*. "Look before you leap" is always a splendid caution, and it means—in this particular case—that if there's a place that sounds *just great* to you, do your best to go visit it before you up and move there. This applies not only to rural places, but to urban, suburban, and every other kind of place, as well.

I repeat, if you can scrape together the necessary funds, *go there*, and talk to *everyone*. Through some persistent questioning on your part, search for both the good side and the bad. The dream you save may be your own.

When You Want to Just Wander

So much for finding a *place*. If you don't want to settle down, but you are thinking of leasing/buying an RV (recreational vehicle) in which to roam the U.S., you will doubtless be interested in getting your hands on, and reading, *Workamper News* (for "work camper"): www.workamper.com/WorkamperNews/WNIndex.cfm—a tabloid which, since 1987, has helped more than 70,000 people find jobs while roaming the West.

Incidentally, the champion work camper in the U.S. is a man named Chuck Woodbury who started his quarterly tabloid *Out West* as a hobby back in 1987. His story is an inspiring one for anyone considering a career change. His idea was to roam the West in a motor home rigged up as a newsroom, and to write about what he found along the way. He said, "I figured if I earned enough in subscriptions to cover my gasoline I'd be happy." But the media soon got wind of his unusual "on-the-road" newspaper, and the number of subscriptions shot up to 10,000. Since then, in his ten years on the road, Woodbury has logged more than 200,000 miles, written a million or so words, and snapped about 15,000 pictures. His paper, *Out West*, complete with a picture of him, is on the Internet at: www.outwest newspaper.com/home.html.

Alternative scenario: You love being outdoors but you've got no RV. And you wouldn't mind putting down roots for a spell? Then you might be interested in *caretaking* jobs. These are house-sitting or ranch-sitting contracts. A man named Gary Dunn says that for those who are spiritually connected with the earth, but don't own land, *caretaking* is an ideal career. Opportunities are listed in Gary Dunn's *Caretaker Gazette*, which he emails to subscribers *(there are 12,000 of them)* bi-monthly *(that means once every two months—okay so you knew that, but I always forget)*. Cost? $29 a year. Details can be found on the Internet at www.care taker.org or you can order it directly from Gary, at *The Caretaker Gazette*, Gary C. Dunn, Publisher, PO Box 4005-M, Bergheim, TX 78004, or call him at (830) 336-3939, or email him at caretaker@caretaker.org. Approximately 150 caretaker/house-sitting opportunities in each issue. Over 1,000 new assignments are available each year, and these opportunities are worldwide!

When You Want to Work Overseas

Speaking of "worldwide," 3.2 million Americans currently live abroad (not including the military stationed in Iraq, Afghanistan, and elsewhere). If you've always wanted to live and work overseas, then that is a dream you should explore. I am talking about job-hunters in the U.S. who want to move to Europe, Africa, Asia, South America, or even next door, to Canada.[8]

There is a site on the Internet that should prove immensely helpful. It is: www.escapeartist.com/expatriate/resources.htm. But there are some cautions that need to be voiced about living overseas. These are from Will Cantrell, former editor of *International Employment Hotline,* now merged with *International Career Employment Weekly:*

First of all, be sure you're not going overseas in order to find Utopia. Utopia rarely lives up to expectations. Even if (big *if*) you do not find the same things that irritate you about the country where you presently live, I guarantee you that you will find some brand new things to irritate you.

Regarding the mechanics of going overseas: many people assume you find an overseas job by packing a bag, buying a ticket and passing out resumes once you reach your foreign destination. No, no, no. Work-permit requirements and high unemployment make finding jobs at foreign destinations often difficult, and sometimes impossible.

For example, if you were to study employment classifieds in, say, a newspaper from London, England, you would at first sight think you had found some grand opportunities for yourself. *Unfortunately,* these are in most cases job opportunities open only to British nationals or citizens of EU nations ("European Union"). What is true in England is true elsewhere. Your U.S. citizenship will actually preclude you from working in a foreign country—even Canada—unless your employer can prove that a local national is unavailable to take the job, and thus secure a work permit for *you.*

Your wisest approach to overseas employment is to conduct your job-hunt for an overseas job while you are still here in the U.S. How do you go about it?

Well, first of all, research the country or countries that interest you, as to living conditions, conditions of employment, et cetera.

---

8. However, there are readers of this book who live in those places and want to move to the U.S. Much of what I have to say here will apply, as general principles, to them.

Talk to everyone you possibly can who has in fact been overseas, most especially to those country or countries. A nearby large university will probably have such faculty or students *(ask)*. Companies in your city which have overseas branches *(your library should be able to tell you which they are)* should be able to lead you to people also—possibly to the names and addresses of personnel who are still "over there" to whom you can write for the information you are seeking.

Alternatively, try asking every single person you meet for the next week (at the supermarket checkout, at your work, at home, at church or synagogue, etc.) if they know someone who used to live overseas and now lives here in your city or town. You may be amazed at how many normal looking people are actually world travelers. By doing research with such people, you will learn a great deal. Find out what they liked and didn't like, about the country which interests you. Find out what they know about the conditions for working over there.

Next, you need to research what kinds of job possibilities exist in that country. Every *successful* overseas search starts with *some* sources of information on "who's hiring now." *Which* sources you access, and how you make use of them, will greatly affect your chances of landing an overseas assignment.

What do I mean? Well, for openers, beware of such sources as employment agencies that promise to find you an overseas job for an advance fee. Ninety-eight percent of their clients *do not* find an overseas job. This fleecing industry has flourished for years, with a few individuals often running scores of companies under an assortment of names. Such companies regularly go out of business or file for bankruptcy *once they've fleeced enough suckers.* On the Internet, see the Rip-Off Report at http://bad businessbureau.com/default.asp.

Beware also of directories advertised on the Internet, or in newspapers, etc. as listing *overseas employers.* Many, though not all, of these job listings are out of date and tend to report on "who *was* hiring" rather than "who is hiring *now.*"

You can still make effective use of any such directory by taking care that *if* you contact an organization listed therein, you include a cover letter which requests that your resume be kept on file "for further consideration *if there are no current openings.*" As

I have emphasized elsewhere in this book, pure dumb luck—which means, having your name in the "right place at the right time"—plays a crucial role in finding most jobs. Since you can't get *over there*, at the moment, you will have to rely more heavily on resumes here than I would normally advise, to keep your name in the right place. In the case of overseas employment, the more employers who have your resume, the better.

Also, in your job-search do not forget that the U.S. Government is a heavy overseas employer.

If you run into an absolute stonewall in your search for an overseas job, there are two backup strategies for you to consider. The first is to seek an international internship. Web resources giving lists, etc. can be found at: www.umich.edu/~icenter/overseas/study/studyabroad1.html.

The second strategy begins with the fact that many companies operating in this country, both domestic and foreign-owned, *have branches overseas*. Thus, *sometimes* your ticket to getting overseas may be to start working here in the U.S. for such a company, hoping they will eventually send you overseas. It *does* happen. And if it happens, they will likely take care of the visa and work permit red tape, pick up your travel bill, and provide other helpful benefits. Unfortunately, however, you can't *count* on their ever sending you overseas. In other words, it's a big fat gamble. *You* have to decide whether you're willing to take it, or not.

If you decide to do either of the above strategies, you'll find the names of organizations by going to your local library and asking the reference librarian to help you find such directories as these: *Principal International Businesses*, published by Dun's Marketing Service; *International Directory of Corporate Affiliations*, published by Corporate Affiliations Information Services, of the National Register Publishing Company; and *International Organizations, revised annually*, published by Gale Research, Inc.

Last, contact every friend you have who already lives overseas—even if it's not in the country that is your target. Ask for their counsel, advice, help, and prayers. They went before you; hopefully they can now be your guide, and door-opener.

No such friends? Then try a book. If you're not easily scared, there is a fascinating book called, *The World's Most Dangerous*

Places, by Robert Young Pelton. The fifth edition was published in 2003, and you can get it from bookstores or online.

One final word about hunting for an overseas job: above all, be patient. The search for an overseas job takes *more* time than looking for a job in this country. Don't expect to be in an exotic foreign capital within ninety days. Perseverance is the key.

How to Research Your New Town or City

And now, whether your choice is overseas or here in your own country, whether your choice is urban or rural, there is the $64,000 question: how do you go about finding out about *jobs* in your chosen target city or town?

If your finances are tight, it may not be possible for you to go to visit your new chosen destination, at least in the immediate future. In which case, you want to research the place, as best you can, from a distance:

How do you do this, while still remaining in your present location. More specifically, how do you find out about *jobs*, at a distance?

There are *ways*.

- If your chosen city or town has a local newspaper, *subscribe*, even while you are still living *here*. Read the whole paper, when it comes, however long delayed. Look particularly for: news of companies that are *expanding*, news of *promotions* or *transfers* (that creates vacancies *down below* in "the company store"), and the like.

Where on Earth Do You Want to Live?

• You first want to discover some organizations that, at a distance, look interesting to you.

• Then you want to research them, at a distance, as much as you can.

• It will help if you can regard the city or town where you presently are, as a kind of *parallel city* to the town or city you are interested in. In which case, some of your research can be done where you are, and then its *learnings* transferred. For example, suppose you wanted to use your interests in psychiatry, plants, and carpentry, in your future career. In the city where you presently are, you would try to learn how to combine these three. You might learn, right where you are, that there is a branch of psychiatry which uses plants in the treatment of deeply withdrawn patients, and these plants have to be put, of course, in wooden planters. Now, having learned *that* where you presently are, you would then explore your chosen city or town to see what psychiatric facilities they have there, and which ones—if any—use plants in their healing program. Thus you can conduct your research where you are, and then transfer its *learnings* to the place where you want to be.

• In doing your research of organizations that interest you, it is perfectly permissible for you to write to the library in your target city, asking for information that may be only there. If the librarian is too busy to answer, then use one of your contacts there to find out. "Bill (or Billie), I need some information that I'm afraid only the library in your town has. Specifically, I need to know about company x." Or whatever.

• Develop contacts, even at a distance, as much as you can.

• Ask your friends where you currently live, if they know of anyone who lives in that city or town. The best contacts are those who know your target employer really well.[9]

---

9. Unless—the job-hunter's nightmare—your mutual "friend"/contact has *misrepresented* how close he or she is to your target employer, and as a matter of fact said employer can't stand the sight of this "mutual friend." *It has happened.* It is to die. Asking a question beforehand, of the "mutual friend," like "How *well* do you know him—or her?" may help avoid this.

- If you went to college, find out if any graduates of that college live in this chosen city or town of yours. (Contact the alumni office of your college, and ask.)

- Also any church, synagogue, or national organization you belong to, that has a presence in that city or town, may yield true helpfulness to you, *if you know what it is you want to know.* Write or phone them, and tell them that you're one of their own and you need some information. *"I need to know who can tell me what nonprofit organizations there are in that city, that deal with x."* "I need to know how I can find out what corporations in town have departments of mental hygiene." *Or, whatever.*

- If you decide to approach the places which interest you, first of all by mail, you will want to research each organization so that you know *who* to address the letter to, *by name.* Get the name spelled absolutely accurately, and double-check. Nothing turns off a prospective employer like your misspelling her or his name.

- Your letter will carry a lot more weight if you can mention, in it, the name of any contacts you may know there.

- As for whether or not you should enclose a resume with your initial contact letter, experts' opinions vary widely. *Everything* depends on the nature of the resume, and the nature of the person you are sending it to. With some employers I know, the sight of a resume is *death* to any future rapport between you and this person. It will *ensure* that your letter is carelessly tossed aside. Other employers *like* to see resumes. It's a big fat gamble, unless you know someone who knows them, and their preferences.

- Personally, I think a well-composed letter summarizing all you would say in a resume, may be your best bet; with a closing paragraph indicating that your resume is available, should they wish it.

- Once you've turned up some promising job prospects you will need to set up interviews; and this means you will have to go there, to that town or city, in almost all cases.

- If you have trouble setting up interviews with a particular person at a particular place, see if that town or city has any church, synagogue, or national organization that you belong to here. If so, write and tell them of your local affiliation, and ask for their help in finding the person you're trying to connect with.

- When to go? Well if you are dirt-poor you might not be able to get there right away; you might have to wait until there's a professional convention, or business meeting nearby there, that your present boss could send you to. Or you might want to reschedule your next summer's vacation so that it is *there*.

- If this is your first-ever visit to the place, try to go there a week or so ahead of whatever interviews you have set up, so you can look the whole place over, and decide: *Do I really want to move here?* It's a little late to do on-site explorations, experts will tell you; but, hey, better late than never!

- *Needless to say*, if you have a spouse or partner, who is going to be moving there with you, they should be doing this same kind of research of that place, and setting up the same kinds of interviews, as you are planning.

How Hard Should I Work at This?

We kept score with one man's job-hunt. While still at a distance he turned up—by means of diligent research—107 places that seemed interesting to him. Over a period of some time, he sent a total of 297 letters to them. He also made a total of 126 phone calls to that city. When he was finally able to go there in person, he had narrowed the original 107 that looked interesting, down to just 45. He visited all 45, while there. Having done his homework on himself thoroughly and well—and having obviously conducted *this* part of his search in an extremely professional manner, he received 35 job offers. When he had finished his survey, he went back to the one job he most wanted—and accepted it.

No one can argue that you should be dealing with numbers of this magnitude. But this may at least give you some idea of *how hard you may need to work* at this. Certainly, we're not just talking about five letters and two phone calls. We're talking about rolling up your sleeves, and being *very thorough*.

Conclusion

There is a great joy in moving to a new place, particularly if it is to a place that you love. One job-hunter described this joy to me, in words which many other job-hunters could echo:

"[Not long ago,] my wife and I took a trip out to the Southwest from our home in Annapolis, Maryland, to see the Grand Canyon and sights like that. We both fell in love with the Southwest, and said, 'Wouldn't it be great if I could get a job out here as a highway engineer, and maybe we could work with the Native Americans.' Back in Annapolis, I purchased Parachute *and read it with extreme interest. So I started some network planning, and scheduled another upcoming trip to Arizona in February of the following year, planning to visit various engineering offices and check out living conditions.*

"Meanwhile, I visited the U.S.G.S. Headquarters in Reston, Virginia. On the way out, I noticed an ad on the bulletin board for 'Highway Engineer—Bureau of Indian Affairs, Gallup, New Mexico.' Naturally, I applied for the job but received notice that the position had been cancelled. Disappointed, my wife and I decided to each spend a

Chapter Seven

day in prayer. On the following day I received a call from that office in Gallup informing me there was another position for Highway Planner now open; was I still interested? Still interested?!

"Using your advice [to go after the person-who-has-the-power-to-hire-me] I called the Bureau in Gallup and got the names of the bosses of the various divisions or sections that would impinge upon my application. I sent in the application to the person by name who was the chief decision-maker. In February of the following year we carried out the trip I had been planning, now including a visit to Gallup. We visited headquarters there, though they weren't yet ready to formally interview, since not all applicants had yet been screened. However, it was a useful visit, and on returning, I wrote Thank You notes to all the people I had met, and hoped for the best.

"In March I received another phone call, asking for further information; I used this to invite myself out for an actual interview, at my expense. My offer was accepted, I was out there in two days, the interview went well, and I received official notice to report for work in May. We were ecstatic! And we found a house in Gallup, through a friend in Annapolis who had a friend in Gallup, who knew of a co-worker who was moving out.

"In short, ours is a wonderful story. Who would think a sixty-six-year-old man could leave one job and move into another full-time job, at a salary almost equal to his present one, in a place 2,600 miles away, that he and his wife truly love! What a blessing! And what you said has stuck with me all this time: I've remembered to write my Thank You notes."

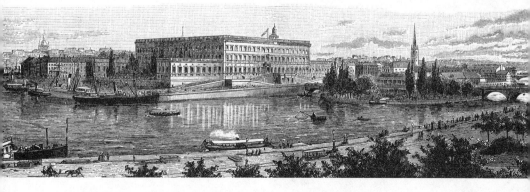

Choosing
or Changing
Careers

You've Got a Lot of Choices, Believe Me

As the map on pages 84 and 85 shows clearly, when it comes time for you to choose a career, choose a major, choose what you're going to do with your life, or change careers, you've got a lot of choices.

You want, of course, not just to keep busy. You want to find work that is best *for you.*

The best work—the best career—for you is going to be one which uses: *your* favorite transferable skills, in *your* favorite subjects or fields of fascination; it's going to be one that offers you *your* preferred people environments, *your* preferred working conditions, and *your* preferred salary, and one which works toward *your* preferred goals and values. And your vision of what you always dreamed of doing with your life.

Pictures, not Words

To begin with, think not in terms of words but in terms of pictures. Try to picture yourself in various kinds of jobs. As much

The Brain as a Treasure Chest of Alternative Strategies

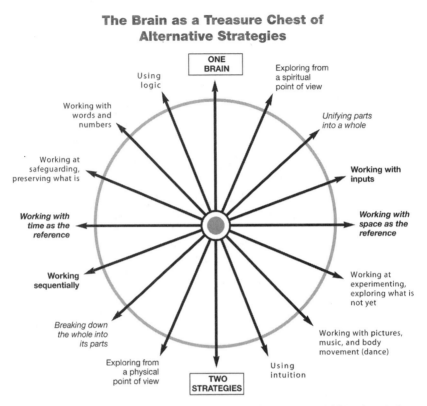

as you can, and for as long as you can, keep yourself in the right side of your brain, rather than in the left side. Don't look for job titles. Look for your vision or picture of your life.

The Power of the Beckoning Vision

No matter what other people tell you, you won't increase your likelihood of finding your dream job by just polishing up your resume, or taking a few more tests, or memorizing a few more techniques, or reading a few better answers to an employer's interview questions.

Okay, then what is the key? It's found in the words of one reader who said that the sentence in *Parachute* which changed her life was:

"The clearer your vision of what you seek, the closer you are to finding it."

It is the vision, the picture of *the life you really want*, that you need to be concentrating on. It has the power to bring about the very change you desire. And the more detailed the picture, the more it is *fleshed out*, the more power it has. You make it more detailed by asking yourself such questions as: What is it that I most want to be doing with my life? What are my unfulfilled dreams? What hunches, what yearnings, do I have about why I was put here, on earth? What have I always put off for the future, that I ought to actually go after, now?

"The clearer your vision of what you seek, the closer you are to finding it." Here are four exercises to help you refine your vision:

Exercise #1:
Draw a Picture of Your Ideal Life

Take a large piece of white paper, with some colored pencils or pens, and draw a picture of your ideal life: where you live, who's with you, what you do, what your dwelling looks like, what your ideal vacation looks like, etc. Don't let *reality* get in the way. Pretend a magic wand has been waved over your life, and it gives you everything you think your ideal life would be.

Now, *of course* you can't draw. Okay, then make symbols for things, or create little "doodads" or symbols, with labels— anything so that you can *see* all together on one page, your vision of your ideal life—however haltingly expressed.

The power of this exercise is sometimes amazing. Reason? By avoiding words and using pictures or symbols as much as possible, it bypasses the left side of the brain ("the safekeeping self," as George Prince calls it) and speaks directly to the right side of your brain ("the experimental self"), whose job it is to engineer change.

Exercise #2:
Pick Your Ideal Job from Some List

Well, sure, *words* tend to arouse your "safekeeping self." But not always. Sometimes words can be useful, as when they are put in the form of *lists*.

Don't think of them as *lists*, however. Think of them as a menu of options at some Vocational Restaurant.

Matching Yourself with the World of Work: 2004[1]

Symbols in the "Matching" table

The table on the following pages provides information about personal skills and job characteristics for many occupations. Below is a guide to interpreting the symbols found there.

Key for personal skills:
● — essential or high-skill level
◉ — somewhat essential or moderate-skill level
○ — basic-level skill
— nonessential skill

Key for job characteristics:
● — highly probable
◉ — somewhat probable
○ — no more or less probable than improbable
— improbable

---

1. This list is from the Occupational Outlook Quarterly, Fall 2004; last updated March 29, 2005. Authored by Henry T. Kasper, an economist in the Office of Occupational Statistics and Employment Projections. In the public domain. Source: the Bureau of Labor Statistics; Page URL: www.bls.gov/opub/ooq/2004/fall/contents.htm.

Chapter Eight

	Personal Skills							Job Characteristics				
	Artistic	Communication	Interpersonal	Managerial	Mathematics	Mechanical	Science	Economically sensitive	Geographically concentrated	Hazardous conditions	Outdoor work	Physically demanding
Management, business, and financial operations occupations												
Management occupations												
Administrative services managers	○	●	●	●	◉			○				
Advertising, marketing, promotions, public relations, and sales managers	●	●	●	●	●	◉						
Computer and information systems managers		●	●	●	●	●	●	●				
Construction managers	○	●	●	●	●	●	◉			◉	●	○
Education administrators		●	●	●	◉		○					
Engineering and natural sciences managers		●	●	●	●	●	●	◉				
Farmers, ranchers, and agricultural managers		●	●	●	◉	●	◉	○	●	◉	●	◉
Financial managers		●	●	●	●	○		◉				
Food service managers	◉	●	●	●	◉	◉	○	◉				○
Funeral directors	○	●	●	◉	◉	○	○					○
Human resources, training, and labor relations managers and specialists		●	●	●	○			○				
Industrial production managers		●	●	●	●	○	◉	○				○
Lodging managers	○	●	●	●	◉	○		○				
Medical and health services managers		●	●	●	◉	◉	◉					
Property, real estate, and community association managers	○	●	●	●	○	○		○			○	
Purchasing managers, buyers, and purchasing agents		●	●	●	◉		○	○				
Top executives	○	●	●	●	●			◉	○			
Business and financial operations occupations												
Accountants and auditors		○	○	◉	●			○				
Budget analysts		○	○	○	●							
Claims adjusters, appraisers, examiners, and investigators		◉	○	◉	◉	◉	○				◉	
Cost estimators		○	○	○	●	○		◉			◉	
Financial analysts and personal financial advisors		●	●	○	●		○	●				

Choosing or Changing Careers

91

		Personal Skills							Job Characteristics				
	Artistic	Communication	Interpersonal	Managerial	Mathematics	Mechanical	Science	Economically sensitive	Geographically concentrated	Hazardous conditions	Outdoor work	Physically demanding
Insurance underwriters		○	○	○	●							
Loan counselors and officers		◉	●	○	◉			◉				
Management analysts		●	◉	○	●			○				
Tax examiners, collectors, and revenue agents		○	○	○	●							
Professional and related occupations												
Computer and mathematical occupations												
Actuaries		○	○	○	●		◉					
Computer programmers		◉	○	○	●	◉	●	○				
Computer software engineers		◉	◉	◉	●	●	●	○				
Computer support specialists and systems administrators		◉	◉	○	◉	●	◉	○				
Computer systems analysts, database administrators, and computer scientists		◉	○	○	●		●	○				
Mathematicians		○	○	○	●		◉					
Operations research analysts		○	○	○	●		◉	○				
Statisticians		○	○	○	●		◉					
Architects, surveyors, and cartographers												
Architects, except landscape and naval	●	◉	◉	◉	●	●	◉	◉			◉	○
Landscape architects	●	◉	◉	◉	◉	●	◉	◉			●	○
Surveyors, cartographers, photogrammetrists, and surveying technicians	◉	◉	◉	○	◉	◉	◉	◉			◉	◉
Engineers												
Aerospace engineers	○	◉	○	◉	●	●	●	◉	◉			
Agricultural engineers	○	◉	○	◉	●	●	●	○	◉			
Biomedical engineers	○	◉	○	◉	●	●	●	○				
Chemical engineers	○	◉	○	◉	●	●	●	○		○		
Civil engineers	◉	◉	○	◉	●	●	●	○			◉	
Computer hardware engineers	○	◉	○	◉	●	●	●	◉				
Electrical and electronics engineers, except computer	○	◉	○	◉	●	●	●	○				
Environmental engineers	○	◉	○	◉	●	●	●				○	

	Personal Skills							Job Characteristics				
	Artistic	Communication	Interpersonal	Managerial	Mathematics	Mechanical	Science	Economically sensitive	Geographically concentrated	Hazardous conditions	Outdoor work	Physically demanding
Industrial engineers, including health and safety	◉	◉	○	◉	●	●	●	○			○	
Materials engineers	○	◉	○	◉	●	●	●	○				
Mechanical engineers	◉	◉	○	◉	●	●	●	○		○		
Mining and geological engineers, including mining safety engineers	○	◉	○	◉	●	●	●	◉	●	◉	●	○
Nuclear engineers	○	◉	○	◉	●	●	●	○	◉	○		
Petroleum engineers	○	◉	○	◉	●	●	●	○	●	○	●	
Drafters and engineering technicians												
Drafters	●	◉	○		◉	●	○	◉				
Engineering technicians	○	◉	○		●	●	●	○		○	○	○
Life scientists												
Agricultural and food scientists		◉	○	◉	●	●	●			○	◉	○
Biological scientists		◉	○	◉	●	●	●	○		○	◉	○
Medical scientists		◉	○	◉	●	●	●	○		○		
Conservation scientists and foresters		◉	○	◉	●	●	●	○	●	○	●	◉
Physical scientists												
Atmospheric scientists		◉	○	◉	●	●	●	○			◉	
Chemists and materials scientists	○	◉	○	◉	●	●	●	◉		○		
Environmental scientists and geoscientists	○	◉	○	◉	●	●	●	○			●	○
Physicists and astronomers	○	◉	○	○	●	●	●	○	○		○	
Social scientists and related occupations												
Economists		◉	○	◉	●							
Market and survey researchers		●	●	○	●			◉				
Psychologists		●	●	○	◉		◉					
Urban and regional planners	◉	◉	◉	◉	●	○	○	○			○	
Social scientists, other		◉	◉	○	◉	○	○					
Science technicians	○	◉	○		●	●	●	◉		○	○	○

	Personal Skills							Job Characteristics				
	Artistic	Communication	Interpersonal	Managerial	Mathematics	Mechanical	Science	Economically sensitive	Geographically concentrated	Hazardous conditions	Outdoor work	Physically demanding
Community and social service occupations												
Clergy	○	●	●	●	○							○
Counselors		●	●	○	○		○					
Probation officers and correctional treatment specialists		◉	◉	○	○	○	○			●		
Social and human service assistants		◉	●				○					
Social workers		●	●	○	○		○					
Legal occupations												
Court reporters		◉	○			●						○
Judges, magistrates, and other judicial workers		●	○	○	○		○					
Lawyers		●	●	●	○		○	◉				
Paralegals and legal assistants		●	●	○	○		○	◉				
Education, training, library, and museum occupations												
Archivists, curators, and museum technicians	●	◉	○	○	◉	●	●		◉			○
Instructional coordinators	○	●	●	◉	◉	◉	◉					
Librarians	○	●	◉	●	○	◉	○					
Library technicians	○	◉	○	○	○	◉	○					○
Teacher assistants	◉	●	●	◉	○		◉					
Teachers—adult literacy and remedial and self-enrichment education	◉	●	●	●	◉		◉					
Teachers—postsecondary	◉	●	●	●	●		◉					
Teachers—preschool, kindergarten, elementary, middle, and secondary	◉	●	●	●	◉	○	◉					
Teachers—special education	◉	●	●	●	◉	○	◉					
Art and design occupations												
Artist and related workers	●	○	○	○	○	◉	○	◉			○	○
Designers	●	◉	◉	●	○	●	○	◉				
Entertainers and performers, sports and related occupations												
Actors, producers and directors	●	●	●	◉		◉	○	○	●		○	●
Athletes, coaches, umpires, and related workers	◉	◉	◉	●		○	○				○	●

	Personal Skills							Job Characteristics				
	Artistic	Communication	Interpersonal	Managerial	Mathematics	Mechanical	Science	Economically sensitive	Geographically concentrated	Hazardous conditions	Outdoor work	Physically demanding
Dancers and choreographers	●	◉	◉	◉			○	○	●			●
Musicians, singers, and related workers	●	◉	◉	○		○	○		○			○
Media and communication-related occupations												
Announcers	◉	●	●		○	○			○		○	
Broadcast and sound engineering technicians and radio operators		○	◉		◉	●	◉		○		○	
Interpreters and translators	●	●	○									
News analysts, reporters, and correspondents	◉	●	●	○	○	○	◉				◉	
Photographers	●	○	○	○	○	●	○	◉			◉	◉
Public relations specialists	◉	●	●	○	○				◉			
Television, video, and motion picture camera operators and editors	●	○	○	○	○	●	○			●	◉	◉
Writers and editors	●	●	●	○	○		○					
Health diagnosing and treating practitioners												
Audiologists		●	◉	●	◉	○	●					
Chiropractors		●	◉	●	◉	○	●					○
Dentists	○	●	●	●	◉	●	●			◉		○
Dieticians and nutritionists		●	●	○	◉	○	●					
Occupational therapists		●	●	◉	◉	◉	◉			◉		○
Optometrists	○	●	◉	●	◉	◉	●			◉		
Pharmacists		●	◉	◉	●	○	●					○
Physical therapists		●	●	○	◉	○	●			◉		●
Physician assistants		●	●	○	●	◉	●			◉		◉
Physicians and surgeons	◉	●	●	●	◉	●	●			◉		◉
Podiatrists	○	●	●	●	◉	◉	●					
Recreational therapists	●	●	●	○	○	○	○				●	◉
Registered nurses		●	●	◉	●	●	●			◉		◉
Respiratory therapists		●	●	○	●	●	●			◉		○
Speech-language pathologists	○	●	●	○	●	○	●					
Veterinarians	○	●	●	●	●	●	●			●	○	●

	Personal Skills							Job Characteristics				
	Artistic	Communication	Interpersonal	Managerial	Mathematics	Mechanical	Science	Economically sensitive	Geographically concentrated	Hazardous conditions	Outdoor work	Physically demanding
Health technologists and technicians												
Cardiovascular technologists and technicians		◉	○	○	●	●	●					○
Clinical laboratory technologists and technicians		◉	○	○	●	●	●			○		○
Dental hygienists		◉	◉	○	◉	●	◉			◉		○
Diagnostic medical sonographers		◉	○	○	●	●	●					
Emergency medical technicians and paramedics		●	●	●	○	●	●			●	●	●
Licensed practical and licensed vocational nurses		◉	●	○	○	●	●			◉		◉
Medical records and health information technicians		◉	○	○	◉		◉					
Nuclear medicine technologists		◉	○	○	●	●	●			◉		
Occupational health and safety specialists and technicians		◉	○	◉	◉	◉	◉			◉	○	◉
Opticians, dispensing	◉	◉	◉	○	◉	◉	○	○				○
Pharmacy technicians		◉	◉	○	◉	◉	◉					○
Radiologic technologists and technicians		◉	◉	○	●	●	◉			◉		◉
Surgical technologists		◉	◉	○	●	●	●			◉		◉
Veterinary technologists and technicians		◉	◉	◉	◉	●	◉	○		●	○	●
Service occupations												
Healthcare support occupations												
Dental assistants		◉	◉	○	○	●	◉			◉		◉
Medical assistants		◉	◉	○	◉	●	●			◉		◉
Medical transcriptionists		●	○	○	○	○	●					
Nursing, psychiatric, and home health aides		◉	◉	○	○	◉	○			●		●
Occupational therapist assistants and aides		◉	●	○	○	●	◉			◉		◉
Pharmacy aides		◉	◉	○	○		○					○
Physical therapist assistants and aides		◉	◉	○	○	◉	◉			◉		●
Protective service occupations												
Correctional officers		◉	○	○	○	○				●		◉
Fire fighting occupations		●	○	○	○	●	○			●	●	●

	Personal Skills							Job Characteristics				
	Artistic	Communication	Interpersonal	Managerial	Mathematics	Mechanical	Science	Economically sensitive	Geographically concentrated	Hazardous conditions	Outdoor work	Physically demanding
Police and detectives		●	○	◉	○	●	○			●	●	●
Private detectives and investigators		●	○	◉	○	●	○			○	◉	○
Security guards and gaming surveillance officers		○	○	○		○		○		●	◉	○
Food preparation and serving related occupations												
Chefs, cooks, and food preparation workers	●	◉	◉	●	○	◉	○	●		○		◉
Food and beverage serving and related workers	○	◉	●		○			●			○	●
Building and grounds cleaning and maintenance occupations												
Building cleaning workers	○	○			○	●		○		○		●
Grounds maintenance workers	◉	○			○	●	○	○		◉	●	●
Pest control workers		○			○	●	○		◉	●	○	●
Personal care and service occupations												
Animal care and service workers		○	○		○	◉	○	◉		●	◉	●
Barbers, cosmetologists, and other personal appearance workers	●	◉	○		○	◉	○	◉			○	○
Child care workers	○	◉	●	○	○	○					○	◉
Flight attendants		●	●	○	○	○		●	◉	○		●
Gaming services occupations	○	◉	●	●	○	○		◉	●			●
Personal and home care aides		◉	●	○	○		○				◉	●
Recreation and fitness workers	○	●	●	○	○	○	○	◉			◉	●
Sales and related occupations												
Advertising sales agents	◉	●	●		○			●				
Cashiers		○	◉		◉			◉				●
Counter and rental clerks		○	◉		◉			◉				◉
Demonstrators, product promoters, and models	●	●	●		○	○		◉				◉
Insurance sales agents		●	●		◉			◉				
Real estate brokers and sales agents	○	●	●	◉	◉			◉			○	
Retail salespersons	○	◉	●		○			◉				
Sales engineers	○	●	●		◉	○	◉	●				
Sales representatives, wholesale and manufacturing	○	●	●		◉		○	●				

	Personal Skills							Job Characteristics				
	Artistic	Communication	Interpersonal	Managerial	Mathematics	Mechanical	Science	Economically sensitive	Geographically concentrated	Hazardous conditions	Outdoor work	Physically demanding
Sales worker supervisors	○	●	●	●	◉	○	○	◉				
Securities, commodities, and financial services sales agents		●	●	●	●			●	●			
Travel agents		◉	●		○			●				

Office and administrative support occupations

	Artistic	Communication	Interpersonal	Managerial	Mathematics	Mechanical	Science	Economically sensitive	Geographically concentrated	Hazardous conditions	Outdoor work	Physically demanding
Communications equipment operators		◉	◉		◉	◉	○	◉				
Computer operators		○			○	◉	○	◉				
Customer service representatives		●	●		◉		○	○				
Data entry and information processing workers		○	○		○	◉		●				
Desktop publishers	●	○	○		○	◉	○	○				
Financial clerks		○	○		●			○				
Bill and account collectors		○	●		●			◉				
Billing and posting clerks and machine operators		○	○		○	○		○				
Bookkeeping, accounting, and auditing clerks		○	○		●			○				
Gaming cage workers		○	○		◉			◉	●			
Payroll and timekeeping clerks		○	○		◉			○				
Procurement clerks		○	○		◉			○				
Tellers		◉	●		●			○				
Information and record clerks		◉	○		◉			○				
Brokerage clerks		○	○		◉			○	●			
Credit authorizers, checkers, and clerks		◉	○	○	◉			◉				
File clerks		○	○		○							
Hotel, motel, and resort desk clerks	○	◉	●	○	○			●				◉
Human resources assistants, except payroll and timekeeping		○	○		◉			○				
Interviewers		●	◉	◉	○		○	○				
Library assistants, clerical		○	○		○	◉	○					
Order clerks		○	○		◉			◉				
Receptionists and information clerks		●	●		◉	◉		○				

	Personal Skills							Job Characteristics				
	Artistic	Communication	Interpersonal	Managerial	Mathematics	Mechanical	Science	Economically sensitive	Geographically concentrated	Hazardous conditions	Outdoor work	Physically demanding
Construction laborers	○	○	○		○	●	○	●		●	◉	●
Drywall installers, ceiling tile installers, and tapers	○	○	○		○	●	○	●		○	○	●
Electricians		○	○		◉	●	◉	●		●	○	◉
Elevator installers and repairers		○	○		○	●	○	●		●	○	●
Glaziers	◉	○	○		○	●	○	●		○	●	●
Hazardous materials removal workers		○	○		○	●	●			●	●	●
Insulation workers		○	○		○	●	○	●		○	○	●
Painters and paperhangers	◉	○	○		○	●	○	●		○	●	●
Pipelayers, plumbers, pipefitters, and steamfitters		○	○		○	●	◉	●		○	○	●
Plasterers and stucco masons	○	○	○		○	●	○	●		○	●	●
Roofers	○	○	○		○	●	○	○		●	●	●
Sheet metal workers	○	○	○		○	●	○	●		●		●
Structural and reinforcing iron and metal workers	○	○	○		○	●	○	●		●	●	●
Installation, maintenance, and repair occupations												
Electrical and electronic equipment mechanics, installers, and repairers												
Computer automated teller, and office machine repairers		○	○		○	●	○				○	○
Electrical and electronics installers and repairers		○	○		◉	●	○			◉		○
Electronic home entertainment equipment installers and repairers	◉	○	○		◉	●	○	●				◉
Radio and telecommunications equipment installers and repairers		○	○		◉	●	◉	○	◉		●	◉
Vehicle and mobile equpment mechanics, installers, and repairers												
Aircraft and avionics equipment mechanics and service technicians		○	○		◉	●	◉	◉	◉	○	●	◉
Automotive body and related repairers	○	○	○		○	●	○	○		○	○	◉
Automotive service technicians and mechanics		○	○		○	●	○	◉		○	○	◉
Diesel service technicians and mechanics		○	○		○	●	◉	◉		○	○	◉

	Personal Skills							Job Characteristics				
	Artistic	Communication	Interpersonal	Managerial	Mathematics	Mechanical	Science	Economically sensitive	Geographically concentrated	Hazardous conditions	Outdoor work	Physically demanding
Heavy vehicle and mobile equipment service technicians and mechanics		○	○		○	●	◉	●		○	○	◉
Small engine mechanics		○	○		○	●	◉	◉		○	○	◉
Other installation, maintenance, and repair occupations												
Coin, vending, and amusement machine servicers and repairers		○			○	●				○	○	◉
Heating, air conditioning, and refrigeration mechanics and installers		○	○		○	●	○	◉		○	○	◉
Home appliance repairers		○	○		○	●	○				○	◉
Industrial machinery installation, repair, and maintenance workers, except millwrights		○			○	●	○	○	○	◉		◉
Line installers and repairers		○			◉	●	○	○		◉	●	◉
Maintenance and repair workers, general		○	○		○	●	○			◉	◉	◉
Millwrights		○	○		◉	●	○	●	◉	◉	○	◉
Precision instrument and equipment repairers	○	○			◉	●	○					◉
Production occupations												
Assemblers and fabricators	○	○			○	●	○				◉	
Food processing occupations		○			○	●			●		●	
Metal workers and plastics workers												
Computer control programmers and operators		○			◉	◉	○	○				
Machinists	◉	○			●	●	◉	○		◉		◉
Machine setters, operators, and tenders—metal and plastic		○			●	●	◉	○		◉		◉
Tool and die makers	○	○			●	●	◉	○		◉		◉
Welding, soldering, and brazing workers	○	○			○	●	○	○		●	◉	●
Printing occupations												
Bookbinders and bindery workers	○	○			○	●	○	○				◉
Prepress technicians and workers	◉	◉	○		◉	◉	○	○				○
Printing machine operators		○			○	●	○	○		◉		●
Textile, apparel, and furnishings occupations	◉	○			○	●		◉	◉	○		●
Woodworkers	◉	○			◉	●	○	◉		◉		○

| | Personal Skills | | | | | | | Job Characteristics | | | | |
	Artistic	Communication	Interpersonal	Managerial	Mathematics	Mechanical	Science	Economically sensitive	Geographically concentrated	Hazardous conditions	Outdoor work	Physically demanding
Reservation and transportation ticket agents and travel clerks		○	●		◉			●				
Material recording, scheduling, dispatching, and distributing occupations		○	○		○	○		○				
Cargo and freight agents		○	○	○	◉		○	○	◉		◉	○
Couriers and messengers		○	○		○	○		●		◉	◉	○
Dispatchers		◉	○	◉	○							
Meter readers, utilities		○			◉	○					◉	○
Production, planning, and expediting clerks		◉	○	○	◉		○	○				
Shipping, receiving, and traffic clerks		○	○		○	◉		○				
Stock clerks and order fillers		○	○		○	○		○				
Weighers, measurers, checkers, and samplers, recordkeeping		○	○		◉	◉	◉	○				○
Office and administrative support worker supervisors and managers		●	●	●	◉	○		○				
Office clerks, general		○	◉		○			◉				
Postal service workers		○	○	○	○	○					●	●
Secretaries and administrative assistants	○	●	●		○	○		○				
Farming, fishing, and forestry occupations												
Agricultural workers		○	○	○	○	●	○		●	◉	●	●
Fishers and fishing vessel operators		◉	○	○	○	●	○		●	●	●	●
Forest, conservation, and logging workers		○	○	○	○	●	○	○	●	●	●	●
Construction trades and related workers												
Boilermakers	○	○	○		○	●	○	●	◉	●		●
Brickmasons, blockmasons, and stonemasons	◉	○	○		○	●	○	●		○	◉	●
Carpenters	◉	○	○		◉	●	○	●		●	◉	
Carpet, floor, and tile installers and finishers	◉	○	○		○	●	○	●		○	◉	●
Cement masons, concrete finishers, segmental pavers, and terrazzo workers	◉	○	○		○	●	○	●		○	◉	●
Construction and building inspectors		○	○	○	○	●	◉	○		○	◉	○
Construction equipment operators		○	○		○	●	○	●		●	●	●

	Personal Skills							Job Characteristics				
	Artistic	Communication	Interpersonal	Managerial	Mathematics	Mechanical	Science	Economically sensitive	Geographically concentrated	Hazardous conditions	Outdoor work	Physically demanding
Plant and system operators												
Power plant operators, distributors, and dispatchers		○	◉	○	●	○	●			◉		
Stationary engineers and boiler operators		○	○	○	○	●	○			◉		
Water and liquid waste treatment plant and system operators		○	○	○	◉	●	◉			●	◉	◉
Other production occupations												
Dental laboratory technicians	◉	○			○	●	◉					○
Inspectors, testers, sorters, samplers, and weighers	○	◉	○		◉	●	◉					○
Jewelers and precious stone and metal workers	●	○	○		○	●	◉	●				○
Ophthalmic laboratory technicians	○	○	◉		○	●	◉					○
Painting and coating workers, except construction and maintenance	○	○			○	●		○		◉		◉
Photographic process workers and processing machine operators	○	○			○	●	○	○		◉		○
Semiconductor processors		○			●	◉	●	◉	●			○
Transportation and material moving occupations												
Air transportation occupations												
Aircraft pilots and flight engineers	●	●	●	●	◉	●	●	●	○	●	○	◉
Air traffic controllers	●	◉	◉	◉		◉		○				○
Material moving occupations	○				●			●		●	●	●
Motor vehicle operators												
Bus drivers		○	○		○					●	○	◉
Taxi drivers and chauffeurs		○	○		○				◉	●	○	◉
Truck drivers and driver / sales workers		○			○			●		●	○	●
Rail transportation occupations		◉	○	○	●	○		◉	◉	◉	◉	◉
Water transportation occupations		◉	○	●	◉	●	◉	●	●	●	◉	◉

Chapter Eight

How useful is it to look over a list like this? Well, if there is some kind of job that has always intrigued you, you can catch a glimpse, here, of what basic skills may be required (e.g., mathematical skills, or communication skills, etc.) and what the challenges of the job are.

On the other hand, if you don't know the labor market very well, say you're just out of high school or whatever, this gives you a good overview of the possibilities. Job titles or careers that maybe you never heard of.

You may, of course, find the list too short, or too long. Too short? Well, take comfort: there are at least 12,741 different careers or occupations *out there*, with 8,000 alternative titles; and a description of them all can be found in a volume known as the *U.S. Dictionary of Occupational Titles* (4th ed.). It is online, and searchable, at www.occupationalinfo.org. A more current edition, the fifth, bound together with its successor system, O*Net, is available, but only in book form. And it is expensive. Try your local library. O*Net itself, a database of only 950 occupations, is online, and searchable by skills (nice list!), occupations, or occupational codes at http://online.onetcenter.org.

Too long a list on the previous pages? Experts are continually trying to boil the list down to just the top ten hottest jobs or the top ten hottest careers.

Type the phrase "hot jobs" or "hottest careers" into your favorite Internet search engine, such as the wildly popular Google (www.google.com) or Yahoo (www.yahoo.com) or Metacrawler (http://metacrawler.com) and see what you get.

(Metacrawler, incidentally, summarizes the best results from both Google and Yahoo! searches, as well as many other of the world's leading search engines: MSN Search, Ask Jeeves, About, MIVA, LookSmart and more, all with one single click.)

The *hottest* jobs or careers are often listed *offline*. *Fortune* magazine, for example, had an article called "20 Hot Careers for the Next Ten Years" in its March 21, 2005 issue.

Variations on "the ten hottest jobs," such as "the employers offering the most entry-level jobs to college grads" can be found on the Net, at: www.collegegrad.com/topemployers.

On the Web, try these sites:

Top Jobs Matching Your Interests and Needs: Top Ten Jobs for People Who . . .

    www.princetonreview.com/cte/articles/
    plan/tenjobs.asp

Ten Hottest Careers for College Grads

    www.collegeboard.com/article/
    0,3868,4-24-0-236,00.html

CareerPlanner's Top Jobs for the Future

    www.careerplanner.com/Career-Articles/
    Top_Jobs.htm

Ten Hottest Careers in Australia

    www.jobsearchexpress.com/jobsearchexpress/
    articles/careers/ten-hottest-careers.html

The fact that a career is "hot" doesn't mean a thing, unless it turns you on. *Hot* only refers to how much demand there is for a particular job or career, and how easy therefore it is to get into such a career. But that's not very relevant, if you are seeking a job that you love. For example, if some *hot* new career involves always working with computers, but you much prefer working with people, then that career is going to make you miserable, no matter how easy it may be to find that kind of job.

Hence, it doesn't matter that a career is *hot* or *easy* to get into. What matters is that you and the career should be happy with each other. Better yet, that you and your career should be in love with each other. Work that you can't wait to get up in the morning and go do. Work that you love so much, you can't believe you are being paid to do it—since you'd be willing to do it for nothing. There are few greater joys in life, than to find such a career.

So, in the end, each individual must form his or her *own* list of "ten best careers." No one else can do it for you; therefore no one else's list should be taken seriously by you for even one minute—unless you see something on that list that causes you to go, *Aha!*

As a *primer of the pump*, such a list may be useful. As *a recipe* for where you should go next, it can be a disaster.

Exercise #3:
The Mirror Method of Identifying
Your Dream Job

In this method you use other people as though they were mirrors to yourself. You look at everyone you know, everyone you've ever seen on TV, or read about, and you think to yourself, "Well, whose job would I most like to have, in all the world?" Make a second and third choice. On three separate sheets of paper, write what each of these three people does. Underneath that, then, break down their job into its parts: what is it about the job that attracts you? List as many things as possible. Then look at all three sheets of paper, choose which job is actually of greatest interest to you, and figure out how you could go talk to someone actually doing such a job.[2]

One woman who changed careers this way decided that the job she most admired was that of a woman she saw on national TV, who hosted a children's program. So, she prepared a careful outline of what she thought a good children's TV program should look like, then went to her local TV station (which had no such program) and told them her ideas. They liked her proposal, hired her to host just such a program, and she became a big success. Later, she triumphantly wrote me, "I am in my ideal career . . . without ever having done any of the exercises in your book!" *Bravo*, say I.

Exercise #4:
Letting a Test Tell You What to Do

When you're puzzled about what to do next with your life, the idea of taking some kind of career test may strike you as a really great idea. There are a lot of such tests out there. They are not really "tests"—you can't flunk them. Experts call them "questionnaires" or "assessment instruments." But most people still call them "tests."

---

2. This assumes, of course, that you can move from one career into another without spending much time "re-tooling."

They come in many forms and flavors—skills tests, interests tests, values tests, psychological tests, etc.—and their names form a veritable alphabet soup: SDS, MBTI, SII, CISS, and the like.

In the past, if you wanted to take them, you had to get dressed and get yourself down to a community college counseling center, or career counselor's office, or state unemployment office, or one-stop career center, or a Johnson O'Connor Human Engineering Laboratory—where the tests and the test administrators can be found. You can still do that. Ask around, in your community, to see where such tests can be found.

But in this Internet Age, a new wrinkle has developed. If you have Internet access, career tests can now be plucked off the Internet, and taken by you in the privacy of your own home. *Our eyes light up! Now you're talking!*

Here's the best of what's available in your home, by title (most sites explain what their particular test or instrument is trying to measure). I have tried to indicate which are free, and which charge for the privilege of taking them.

Measuring Interests

▶ **The Princeton Review Career Quiz**
www.princetonreview.com/cte/quiz/default.
   asp?menuID=0&careers=6
Free. A brief twenty-four-part questionnaire, related to the Birkman Method, with intriguing career suggestions.

▶ **Analyze My Career**
www.analyzemycareer.com
Tests for sale: Aptitude tests, personality tests, occupation interests, entrepreneurial index ($69.95 for *everything*).

(More tests can be found at
   http://directory.google.com/Top/
      Science/Social_Sciences/Psychology/
      Tests_and_Testing)

▶ **John Holland's Self-Directed Search**
www.self-directed-search.com
The queen of career tests (in my opinion), it has been taken by more than twenty-four million people. The SDS online takes fif-

teen minutes and costs only $9.95. Your eight- to sixteen-page personalized report will appear on your screen. This printable assessment report provides a list of the occupations and fields of study that most closely match your interests.

▶ **CareerPlanner.com's "Career Planning Test"**

`www.careerplanner.com`

As the website says, this proprietary on-line career assessment test is based on the well-established RIASEC system developed by Dr. John Holland. It will cost you at least $19.95 to take this test, however (more if you want your results back faster), so you must decide if it is worth twice the cost (or more) of John L. Holland's original (above). It does show more contemporary careers that did not exist a few years ago, including Java Programmer, Web Master, Marketing Communications Specialist, Software Alliance Manager, Network Specialist, and more. The test report is approximately eight to eleven pages long and includes listings for thirty to more than 100 unique careers, related to your "Holland Code."

▶ **The Career Interests Game**

`www.career.missouri.edu/modules.php`
`    ?name=News&file=article&sid=146`

Free. Many years ago, I invented a visual short-cut to the RIASEC system called "The Party Exercise" (page 215), and here is a beautiful presentation of it (here called *The Career Interests Game*), supplemented by pages of skills, suggested careers, and favorite traits. First rate.

▶ **The Career Key**

`www.careerkey.org/english/you`

Free. Related to Holland.

Now, before you reach for your modem, there are six rules to keep in mind when approaching career tests in general, on- or offline.

The Six Rules About Taking Career Tests

Okay, here are six rules to keep in mind, when you're going to take a test on the Internet *(or anywhere else).*

1. *No test can measure YOU. It can only describe the family to whom you belong.* Tests tend to divide the world into what we might call *groups,* or *tribes,* or *families*—namely, all those people who answered the test the same way you did. They come out as: *You are an ISFJ.* Or *You are an SAE.* Or *You are a Blue.* The results are an accurate description of "those people," that tribe, that family, in general; but they may or may not be true in every respect of YOU. So, when you see your test results, keep in mind that these are the test results for the *family* who answered the questions the same way you did. You may be totally like that family, or you may be different in important ways. It's your call. You're free to say "I am like this *family* in these eighteen respects, but not in these other four"—or, whatever. Do remember: you are unique, and you are like nobody else on earth.

2. *Don't predetermine how you want the test to come out. Stay loose and open to new ideas.* It's easy to have an emotional investment that the test should come out a certain way. I remember one time I was administering a test about geographical preferences, where job-hunters had to prioritize a whole bunch of factors, and then decide what state that pointed to. One woman was long-delayed in arriving at an answer, so I asked her if she was running into any problems. She said, "No, I'm just prioritizing it. And . . . I'm gonna keep on prioritizing it, until it comes out **Texas**!"

3. *You're looking for clues, hunches, or suggestions, rather than for a definitive picture that tells you exactly what you should do with your life.* "A light bulb going off, over my head" is how some people describe what they got out of taking a test—at the most. If your goal in taking a test (or tests) is that you're just looking for light bulbs, you will enjoy tests much much more.

4. *Take several tests and not just one.* One may send you horribly down the wrong path. Three can offer a more balanced picture or a more balanced set of clues.

5. *An online test isn't likely to be as insightful as one administered by a qualified psychologist or counselor.* Counselors may see things that you don't. But who they are, is more important than all the degrees they may have on their walls. If you hit it off with them, and they seem loving, wise, and professional, then trust them. But if you basically don't like them, quietly take your leave—with thanks—and go elsewhere. They may be good, but they're not good for you. Rapport is everything.

6. *Finally, don't try to force your favorite online tests on your friends.* (This caution applies to job-hunters, career-changers, and counselors.) You may take a particular test, think it's the best thing since the invention of the wheel, and try to "sell" it to everyone you meet. Don't. Just because it worked well for you, doesn't necessarily mean it will work well for them. If you ignore this caution, your friends will start running when they see you coming.

Try on the Suit First

In all of the four exercises, above, don't believe what lists, tests, experts, or well-meaning friends try to claim is an ideal job *for you.* Just as you would when buying a suit, test it, try it on, make up your own mind. *Puh-leeze.*

Go talk to at least three people who are actually *doing* this career that you find so appealing, and ask them these questions:

How did you get into this field?

What do you like best about it?

What do you like least about it?

How do I get into this career, and how much of a demand is there for people who can do this work?

Is it easy to find a job in this career, or is it hard?

Who else would you recommend or suggest I go talk to, to learn more about this career?

You *want* to know all this! Believe me, you *want* to know! Especially if, in order to prepare for this career that interests you, it's going to take some time for you to go get some schooling, or perhaps a degree.

If you fail to ask such questions *ahead of time* you may be bitterly disappointed after you get all that training, or that degree.

Getting a Job by Degrees

And do yourself a big favor: don't go get a degree because you think that will guarantee you a job! No, mon ami, it will not.

I wish you could see my mail, filled with bitter letters from people who believed such tests as you have just seen, went and got a degree in that field, thought it would be a snap to find a job, but are still unemployed after two years. You would weep! They are bitter (often), angry (always), and disappointed in a society which they feel lied to them.

They found there was no job that went with that degree. They feel lied to, by our society and by the experts, about the value of going back to school, and getting a degree in this or that "hot" field.

Now that they have that costly worthless degree, and still can't find a job, they find a certain irony in the phrase, "*Our country believes in getting a job by degrees.*"

If you already made this costly mistake, you know what I mean.

Chapter Eight

How to Find Information, Using the Internet

Besides doing *informational interviewing*, face-to-face, in the fashion I just described, there are other ways to find out helpful information, especially if you have access to the Internet. Here are tutorials *on the Internet*, about how to find information on the Internet, beginning with the tutorial that I like the best:

▶ Search the Internet
A guide to finding information on the Internet; very informative
```
www.lib.berkeley.edu/TeachingLib/
    Guides/Internet/FindInfo.html
```

▶ Searching the Internet
Good article on Internet searches; also very informative and up-to-date page on search engines
```
www.sldirectory.com/search.html
www.sldirectory.com/searchf/engines.html#
```

▶ University at Albany Libraries
A Primer In Boolean Logic: Boolean Searching on the Internet
```
http://library.albany.edu/internet/
    boolean.html
```

▶ Bright Planet Tutorial
Guide to Effective Searching of the Internet
The Complete Source for Search Engines and Databases Tutorial
```
www.brightplanet.com/deepcontent/
    tutorials/search/index.asp
```

▶ Kids Research Tools (Wordsmythe, Britannica.com, etc.)
Like faith, the Internet is best-approached with the eyes of a child.
```
www.rcls.org/ksearch.htm
```

 ▶ Rules for Conducting Informational Interviews in Order to Find Out About Fields and Jobs, Before You Ever Commit Yourself
```
http://danenet.wicip.org/jets/
    jet-9407-p.html
```

▶ Guidelines for Informational Interviews
```
www.quintcareers.com/informational_
    interviewing.html
```

How to Find Career Information, Using Site/Books

Some of the very best online job-hunting experts have put up sites, that are immensely useful, and are—in each case—accompanied by a companion book. In other words, these are site/books. The sites are listed below. The books can be procured from Barnes and Noble, Amazon.com, Borders, or your local independent bookstore.

The Riley Guide is the best of these, by far. If you can only go to one gateway job-site on the web, or book off-site, this should be it. Margaret Dikel is the mother of all that is intelligent about job-hunting on the Internet. *(And her on-site listings are always completely up to date.)*

 ▶ The Riley Guide: Employment Opportunities and Job Resources on the Internet
Compiled by Margaret F. Dikel
www.rileyguide.com
The companion book to this site is entitled *The Guide to Internet Job Searching, 2004–2005 Edition,* by Margaret F. Dikel and Frances E. Roehm.

 ▶ *Job-Hunting on the Internet* (4th ed.), by Richard Nelson Bolles and Mark Emery Bolles, 2005, Ten Speed Press. This is a companion to *What Color Is Your Parachute?* teaching readers, in detail, how to use the Internet in their job-hunt. Originally, it was just a part of this book you are holding in your hands, but it soon outgrew its space. The companion free website is my own www.jobhunters bible.com.

"We who lived in concentration camps can remember the men who walked through the huts comforting others, giving away their last piece of bread. They may have been few in number, but they offer sufficient proof that everything can be taken from a man but one thing: the last of the human freedoms—to choose one's attitude in any given set of circumstances . . ."

Victor Frankl

▶ *WEDDLE's*
Approaching Fields, etc. through their Associations
  www.weddles.com/associations/index.htm
The companion book to this site is entitled, *WEDDLE's Job-Seeker's Guide to Employment Web Sites (revised annually)*. Amacom, N.Y., N.Y. Pete Weddle is one of the true experts in the field of employment sites, recruiters, etc. on the Internet.

▶ CareerXRoads
This is a site which promotes the authors' book and online database.
  www.careerxroads.com
The companion book to this site is entitled, *CareerXRoads 2005: The Directory to Job, Resume and Career Management Sites on the Web,* by Gerry Crispin and Mark Mehler. Be aware that the title is something of a misnomer as they do not review any career management sites unless they have a job or resume database. They offer helpful information about those sites that are among the five hundred they reviewed, however.

How to Find Career Information, Using Just Books

▶ Quintessential Careers: A Career and Job-Hunting Resources Guide
One of the best *book* lists available. Forget the irony that you have to first print it from the web (if you don't have web access yourself, get a computer-friendly colleague to print this out for you).
  www.quintcareers.com/career_books.html
Maintained by Randall S. Hansen, who has great taste!

How to Find Career Information, through Individals on the Internet

Back in the spring of 2001, Google acquired the Usenet newsgroup directory and archive formerly maintained by the legendary *Deja.com*—in this archive more than 650 million messages had been posted since 1995. A great venue for online networking.
  http://groups.google.com

Conclusion:
When a Dream Job Isn't Enough:
The Search for Serenity

The search for a "dream job" is, on its surface, a search for happiness. We want to be happier in our work, and life, than we have been, up to now.

More specifically, we want that brand of happiness to which I give a special name, namely, *serenity*. And the pathway to serenity is found through *attitude*.

Your attitude is the first (and last) thing everyone notices about you. It is the creator of the texture of your life. As someone has said, "What you have, is God's gift to you. How you use it, is your gift to God." Also it is your gift to all of those around you.

How to Start Your Own Business

The Art of Self-Employment or Working for Yourself

"All I Do the Whole Day Through Is Dream of You . . . "

Sure, you've thought about it, a million times. Hasn't everyone? Everytime you're tied up in traffic going to or from work. You've toyed with the idea of not having to go to an office or other place of business, but of running your own business, maybe even out of your own home, making your own product or selling your own services, being your own boss, and keeping all the profits for yourself. It's called *self-employment*, or being *an independent contractor*, or *freelancing* or *contracting out your services*. Great idea! *But*, nothing's ever come of all this daydreaming. Until now. Now, you're out of work, or maybe you're still working but you're really fed up with your job, and—dusting off those old dreams—you're thinking to yourself: *Maybe it's now, or never. Maybe I ought to just* do *it.*

Home Business in General

Three hundred years ago, of course, nearly everybody did it. They worked at home or on their farm. But then the industrial revolution came, and the idea of working *away from* home became normal. In recent times, however, the idea of working at home has been finding new life, due to congestion on the highways, and the development of new technologies. If you can afford them, a telephone,[1] a fax machine, a computer with a modem, a Palm Pilot, e-mail, online services, mail-order houses, and the like, all make working for yourself feasible, as never before.

The Three Major Problems of Home Businesses

1. The first major problem of home businesses, according to experts, is that on average home-based workers *(in the U.S. at least)* only earn 70 percent of what their full-time office-based equals do. So, you must think carefully whether you could make enough money to survive—*or prosper.*

2. The second major problem of home businesses is that it's often difficult to maintain the balance between business and family time. Sometimes the *family* time gets shortchanged, while in other cases the demands of family (particularly with small children) may become so interruptive, that the *business* gets shortchanged. So, do investigate thoroughly, ahead of time, *how* you would go about doing this *well.*

3. Last, a home business puts you into a perpetual job-hunt.

Some of us who are unemployed *hate* job-hunting, and are attracted to the idea of a home business because this seems like an ideal way to cut short our job-hunt. The irony is, that a home business makes you in a very real sense a *perpetual* job-hunter—because you have to be *always* seeking new clients or customers—

---

1. This *telephone family* includes cell phones, camera cell phones, video phones, and the new ROKR combination phone from Apple and Motorola; "call-forwarding"—the technology where people call your one fixed telephone number, and then get automatically forwarded to wherever you have told the phone company you currently are—and voice/electronic mail.

which is to say, new *employers*. (Well, yes, they are *employers*, because they *pay* you for the work you are doing. The only difference between this and a full-time job is that here *the contract is limited*. But if you are running your own business, you will have to *continually* beat the bushes for new clients or customers—who are in fact *short-term employers*.)

Of course, the dream of most home business people is to become so well known, and so in demand, that clients or customers will be literally beating down your doors, and you will be able to stop this endless job-hunt. But that only happens to a relative minority, and your realistic self must know that.

The greater likelihood is that you will *always* have to beat the bushes for employers/clients. It may get easier as you get better at it, or it may get harder, if economic conditions take a severe downturn. In any event, it will probably be the one aspect of

"YES, THE BUSINESS HAS BECOME BIGGER, BUT FRED STILL LIKES TO WORK AT HOME."

How to Start Your Own Business **119**

your work that you will *always* cordially dislike. If you're going to go this route, you must learn to make your peace with it—however grudgingly.

If you can't manage that, if you avoid that task like the plague until there's literally no bread on the table, you're probably going to find *a home business* is just a glamorous synonym for *"starving."* I know *many* home business people to whom this has happened, and it happened precisely because they couldn't stomach going out to beat the bushes for clients or customers. If that's true for you, you should plan to start out by *hiring*, *co-opting*, or *volunteering* somebody part-time, who is willing to do this for you—one who, in fact, "eats it up"—or abandon the idea of having your own business.

When You Don't Know What Kind of Home Business to Start

Okay, so basically the *idea* of working at home intrigues the life out of you, but you can't figure out what kind of business to start. *Minor little detail!*

There are fortunately seven steps you can take, to nail this down.

First, read. There are oodles of books out there that are *filled* with ideas for home businesses. The best of them is: *Working from Home: Everything You Need to Know About Living and Working Under the Same Roof* by Paul Edwards and Sarah Edwards

Chapter Nine

(paperback, June 1999), called "the Bible on working from home." For other titles, browse Amazon's categories, or your local library, or the business shelves in your local bookstore.

Second, dream. In evaluating any ideas that you pick up, the first thing you ought to look at are your dreams. What have you always dreamed about doing? Since childhood? Since last week? Now is the time to dust off those dreams.

And please don't pay any attention, for now, to whether those dreams represent *a step up* for you in life, or not. Who cares? Your dreams are yours. You may have been dreaming of earning *more* money. But then again, you may have been dreaming of doing work that you really love, even if it means a lesser salary or income than you have been accustomed to. Don't *judge* your dreams, and don't let anyone else judge them either.

Third, look around your own community, and ask yourself what services or products people seem to need the most. Or what service or product already offered in the community could stand a lot of *improving?* There may be something there that *grabs* you.

The underlying theme to 90 percent of the businesses that are *out there* these days is *things that save time.* It's what single parents, families where both parents work, and singles who have overcrowded lives, most want.

You might consider: Offering home deliveries of local restaurants' dinners, or home delivery of grocery orders from any downtown supermarket. (Pay no attention to the fact that delivery services such as *Webvan* went "belly-up" on the Internet. Local delivery services may still be wanted.) There is also: Evening delivery services of laundry, etc. Daytime or evening office cleaning services and/or home cleaning services. Home repairs, especially in the evening or on weekends, of TVs, radios, audio systems, laundries, dishwashers, etc. Lawn care. Care for the elderly in their own homes. Childcare in their own homes. Pickup and delivery of things (even personal stuff, like cleaning) at the office. Automobile care or repair services, with pickup and delivery. Offering short-term business consultancy in various fields. Other successful businesses these days deal with such arenas as leisure activities.

Fourth, consider mail order. If you find no needs within your own community, you may want to broaden your search, to ask what is needed in this country—or the world. After all, mail-order businesses can be started *small* at home, and catalogs can be sent *anywhere*. If this interests you, read up on the subject. Also, for heaven's sake, go talk to other mail-order people (for names, just look at the catalogs you're already likely receiving). There are books "out there" about mail-order businesses, but they are of very unequal value.

Fifth, consider telecommuting. Telecommuting is "working at home for others." The people who do this are called *"telecommuters"*— a term coined by Jack Nilles in 1973. To learn more about telecommuting, a good place to start is at PortaJobs, whose website is: www.portajobs.com.

One way to go about easing yourself into telecommuting, if you already have a job, is to talk your boss into letting you do at least *some* of your work at home. You can find plans for how you "sell" your employer on the idea, at such sites as:

www.workoptions.com/telecom.htm.

Your boss, of course, may take the initiative here, before it has even occurred to you, and they may *ask* you to work at home, connected to the office by computer-network telephone lines.

If you are thinking about becoming a telecommuter, I advise you to investigate the idea thoroughly. In this case, the Internet is your best friend. For example, you can find more telecommuting information, including a database of work-at-home jobs, at:

www.careersfromhome.com.

And another, similar, site with job listings is at www.tjobs .com and you can find **an association for telecommuters,** ITAC (International Telework Association and Council) with conventions and everything, at: www.telecommute.org.

Sixth, consider a franchise. Franchises are for people who want their own business, but don't care if it's not *in the home.* (Though some franchises can be done from your home, the majority require an outside site.)

Franchises exist because some people want to have their own business, but don't want to go through the agony of starting it up. They want to *buy in* on an already established business, and they have the money in their savings with which to do that (or

WELL, I FINALLY DID IT.

I GOT SICK OF THE DAILY RAT RACE, SO I STARTED MY OWN COMPANY! I'M SELF-EMPLOYED! I'M MY OWN BOSS!

AND SO YOU DISCOVERED ...

THAT I'M WORKING FOR AN IDIOT.

they know where they can get a bank loan). Fortunately for them, there are a lot of such franchises. In the U.S., the overall failure rate for franchises is less than 4 percent. You want to keep in mind that some *types* of franchises have a failure rate *far* greater than that. The ten *riskiest* small businesses, according to experts, are local laundries and dry cleaners, used car dealerships, gas stations, local trucking firms, restaurants, infant clothing stores, bakeries, machine shops, grocery or meat stores, and car washes—though I'm sure there will be some new nominees for this list, by the time you read this. *Risky* doesn't mean you can't make them succeed. It only means the odds are greater than they would be with other small businesses.

You want to keep in mind also that some individual franchises are *terrible*—and that includes well-known names. They charge too much for you to *get on board*, and often they don't do the advertising or other commitments that they promised they would.

There isn't a franchising book that doesn't warn you eighteen times to go talk to people who have *already* bought that same franchise, before you ever decide to go with them. And I mean *several* people, not just one. Most experts also warn you to go talk to *other* franchises in the same field, not just the kind you're thinking about signing up with. Maybe there's something better, that such research will uncover.

If you are drawn to the idea of a franchise, because you are in a hurry, and you don't want to do any homework first, *'cause it's just too much trouble,* you will deserve what you get, believe me. That way lies madness.

Seventh, if you've invented something, weigh doing something with it. If you are inclined toward invention or tinkering, you might want to start by improving on an idea that's already *out there.* Start with something you like, such as bicycles. You might experiment with making—let us say—a folding bicycle.

Or, if you like to go to the beach, and your skills run to sewing, you might think about making and selling beach towels with weights sewn in the corners, against windy days.

If you've already invented something, and it's been sitting in your drawer, or the garage, but you've never attempted to duplicate or manufacture it before, now might be a good time to try. Think out very carefully just how you are going to get it manufactured, advertised, and marketed, etc.

There are also promoters out there (on and off the Internet) who claim to specialize in promoting inventions *such as yours*, if *you* will pay *them* a fee. However, according to the Federal Trade Commission, in a study of 30,000 people who paid such promoters, *not a single inventor* ever made a profit after giving their invention to such promoters or firms. If you want to gamble some of your hard-earned money on such firms, consider whether you might better drop it at the tables in Las Vegas. I think the odds are *better* there.

You're much better off, *of course*, if on your own, on or off the Internet, you locate other inventors, and ask if they were successful in marketing their own invention. When you find those who were, pick their brains for everything they're worth. (Of course one of the first things they're going to tell you is to go get your invention copyrighted or trademarked or patented.)

When You Know What Kind of Home Business to Start

The above seven steps are, of course, if you don't know what kind of business you'd like to start. But, it may be that you already know exactly *what* business you want to start, because you've been thinking about it for *years*, and may even have been *doing* it for years—only, in the employ of someone else.

But now, the turning point: you're about to set out on your own. You're thinking about doing this kind of work yourself, and for yourself, whether it be business services, or consultancy, or repair work, or some kind of craft, or the making of some kind of product, or teaching, or offering of home services, such as childcare or delivery by night.

Some sorts of jobs are just made for working out of one's home, as when you are already some kind of writer, artist, performer, business expert, lawyer, consultant, craftsperson, or the like. Be prepared for the fact that your present home may not be big enough for the kind of thing you're dreaming of. For example, your dream may be: *I want a horse ranch, where I can raise and sell horses.* Or *I want to run a bed-and-breakfast place.* Stuff like that.

Well, the nice thing about deciding to work out of your home is that you get to define what *home* is. Given today's technology, you could *literally* work wherever your preferred environment in the whole world is—whether that be out in nature, or at your favorite vacation spot, or skiing chalet, or in some other country altogether.

The only rule is, if it involves a possible move, be sure to go talk to other people who have already done that. Pick their brains for everything they're worth. No need for you to step on the same *land mines* that they did.

You Want to Succeed!

And that brings us to the most important part of this chapter. The key to successfully starting your own business turns out to be this one *crucial* rule: *Find out what's involved, before you hurl yourself into this new world.*

This **research** has two steps to it:

1. Finding out what skills it takes to make this kind of enterprise work. *This involves figuring out what is "A – B = C."*

2. Finding out just exactly what is involved in setting up any home-based business. *This involves going on the Internet, or reading some books.*

Step #1:
Figure Out What Is
"A – B = C"

Over the past thirty years I have found it *mindboggling* to discover how many people start their own business, at home or elsewhere, without *ever* first going to talk to anybody who started the same kind of business earlier.

One job-hunter told me she started a home-based soap business, without ever talking to anyone who had started a similar endeavor before her. Not surprisingly, her business went belly-up within a year and a half. She concluded: no one should go into such a business. Ah, but there *are* successful home-based soap businesses—Paula Gibbons's "Paula's Soap" of Seattle, Washington, for one. *Someone is already doing the work you are dreaming of. The key to your success, is that you go talk to them.*

This involves a simple series of methodical steps:

1. You first write out *in as much detail as you can* just exactly what kind of business you are thinking about starting. Do you want to be a freelance writer, or a craftsperson, or a consultant, independent screenwriter, copy writer, digital artist, songwriter, photographer, illustrator, interior designer, video person, film person, counselor, therapist, plumber, electrician, agent, filmmaker, soap maker, bicycle repairer, public speaker, or *what?*

2. You identify towns or cities that are at least fifty to seventy-five miles away, and you try to get their phone books, so you can look up addresses of their chambers of commerce, etc. In some cases, the Internet will also help. An index to such help can be found at my website, www.JobHuntersBible.com.

3. By using the Internet or the yellow pages or the chamber of commerce, you try to identify three businesses in those towns, that are identical or similar to the business you are thinking of starting. You journey to that town or city, and talk to the founder or owner of each such business.

4. When you talk to them, you explain that you're exploring the possibility of starting your own business, similar to theirs, but seventy-five miles away. You ask them if they would mind sharing what pitfalls or obstacles they ran into when they started their own business. You ask them what skills or knowledge do they think are necessary to running that kind of business successfully. Will they give you such information? Yes, most likely. Most people love to help others get started in their same business, *if* they love it, although—let's face it—occasionally you may run into owners who are of an ungenerous nature. In such a case, thank them politely for their time, and go on to the next name on your list. When you've found three people willing to help you by reminiscing about their own history, you interview each of them in turn, and make a list of the necessary skills and knowledge they all agreed were necessary. Give this list a name. Let's call it "**A**."

5. Back home you sit down and inventory your own skills and knowledge, with the information you will draw from the exercises in chapter 10, or in the Flower Exercise. Give this list a name, also. Let's call it "**B**."

6. Having done this, you then subtract "**B**" from "**A**." This gives you another new list, which you should name. Let's

PEANUTS reprinted by permission of United Features Syndicate, Inc.

How to Start Your Own Business

call it "C." "C" is by definition a list of the skills or knowledge that you *don't* have, but must find—either by taking courses yourself, or by hiring someone with those skills, or by getting a friend or family member (who has those skills) to volunteer.

Why fifty to seventy-five miles away? Well, actually, that's a minimum. You want to interview businesses which, *if they were in the same geographical area as you,* would be your rivals. And if they were in the same geographical area as you, wouldn't likely tell you how to get started. After all, they're not going to train you just so you can then take business away from them.

But, when a guy, a gal, or a business is fifty to seventy-five miles away—you're not as likely to be perceived as a rival, and therefore they're much more likely to tell you what you want to know about their own experience, and how *they* got started, and where the land mines are hidden.

A − B = C

Skills and Knowledge Needed to Run This Kind of Business Successfully	Skills and Knowledge Which I Have	Skills and Knowledge Needed, Which I Have to Learn or Get Someone to Volunteer, or I Will Have to Go Out and Hire
Precision-working with tools and instruments	Precision-working with tools and instruments	
Planning and directing an entire project	Planning and directing an entire project	
Programming computers, inventing programs that solve physical problems		Programming computers, inventing programs that solve physical problems
Problem solving: evaluating why a particular design or process isn't working	Problem solving: evaluating why a particular design or process isn't working	
Being self-motivated, resourceful, patient, and persevering, accurate, methodical, and thorough	Being self-motivated, resourceful, patient, and persevering, accurate, methodical, and thorough	
Thorough knowledge of: Principles of electronics	*Thorough knowledge of:*	*Thorough knowledge of:* Principles of electronics
Physics of strings	Physics of strings	
Principles of vibration	Principles of vibration	
Properties of woods	Properties of woods	
Accounting		Accounting

Doubtless at this point you would like an example of this whole process. Okay. Our job-hunter is a woman who has been making harps for some employer, but now is thinking about going into business for herself, not only *making* harps at home, but also *designing* harps, with the aid of a computer. After interviewing several home-based harp makers and harp designers, and finishing her own self-assessment, her chart of $A - B = C$ came out looking like the previous page.

If she decides to try her hand at becoming an independent harp maker and harp designer, she now knows what she needs but lacks: *computer programming, knowledge of the principles of electronics, and accounting.* In other words, List C. These she must either go to school to acquire for herself, OR enlist from some friends of hers in those fields, on a volunteer basis, OR go out and hire, part-time. These are the essential steps for any new enterprise that you are considering: $A - B = C$.

You may also want to talk to people who have juggled two (or more) careers, at the same time. If you want to start up more than one venture, you need to interview people *in each line of work* to find out $A - B = C$ for both jobs.

How Can You Do A – B = C, When No One Has Done What You Want to Do?

No matter how inventive you are, you're probably *not* going to invent a job that *no one* has ever heard of, before. You're only going to invent a job that *most* people have never heard of, before. But the likelihood is *great* that someone, somewhere, in this world of endless creativity, has already put together the kind of job you're dreaming about. Your task: to find them and interview them thoroughly. And then . . . well, you know the drill: $A - B = C$.

If there isn't someone doing *exactly* what you are dreaming of doing, there is at least someone who is *close*. This is how you find them.

1. Break down your projected business or new career into its parts.

2. If there are more than two parts, take any two of these parts to begin with. See what kind of job or person they describe.

3. Find out the names of such persons. You want three names, or more.

4. Go see, phone, or e-mail them. You can learn a great deal from them, and even if they are not in the same business as you are dreaming of, you will learn a great deal that is relevant to your dream.

5. They in turn may be able to give you a lead to someone whose business is even closer to what you are dreaming of. Ask for names. Go interview them.

Let's see how this works out, in practice. For our example, let's suppose your dream is—here we take a ridiculous case—to use computers to monitor the growth of plants at the South Pole. And suppose you can't find anybody who's ever done such a thing. The way to tackle this seemingly insurmountable problem, is to break the proposed business down into its parts, which—in this case—are: *computers, plants,* and *the Antarctic.*

Then you try combining any two parts, together, to define the person or persons you need to talk to. In this case, that would mean finding someone who's *used computers with plants here in the States,* or someone who's *used computers at the Antarctic,* or someone who has *worked with plants at the Antarctic,* etc. You go talk to them, and along the way you may discover there *is* someone who has used computers to monitor the growth of plants at the South Pole. Then again, you may not. In any event, you will learn most of the pitfalls that wait for you, by hearing the experience of those who are in *parallel* businesses or careers.

Thus, it is *always* possible—with a little blood, sweat, and imagination—to find out what $A - B = C$ is, for the business you're dreaming of doing.

Step #2:

Going on the Internet

or

Reading Some Books

The Internet offers five kinds of help to the job-hunter or career-changer:

1. **Job-posting** on the part of employers (*used to be called "classified ads," and still is, when it's not on the Internet but in newspapers*).
2. **Resume-posting** on the part of job-hunters.
3. **Testing and career advice.**
4. **Research** on careers, fields, companies, and salaries.
5. **Contacts** with other job-hunters or resource people.

While the first two kinds of help do not work nearly as well as all the *hype* suggests, the last three kinds of help (above) work superbly. Here the Internet comes into its own, and is truly a Godsend.

So, it's **career advice and research** that we're talking about here, in the arena of self-employment and/or working at home. There are some tremendously useful sites that you should visit before ever launching your own enterprise, and a list of them starts on the following page.

Websites Dealing with Home-Based Business

I and my Web consultants have combed through the various home-based business *sites*, testing them (this is all very subjective, believe me) for sensible advice, ease of use, and trustworthiness *in our judgment*.

There are probably a lot of good home-business sites that we didn't find; but among those we looked at, here is a Sampler of the ones we liked the best:

▶ **CCH Inc.**
SOHO Guidebook
`www.toolkit.cch.com/text/P04_0750.asp`
Many articles and much information on home businesses:
`www.toolkit.cch.com/BOToC.asp`

▶ **FreeAgent.com**
Home & Work, FreeAgent 101
`www.freeagent.com/resource/index.asp#`

▶ **AHBBO—Elena Fawkner**
Look Before You Leap: Is a Home-Based Business REALLY For You?
`www.ahbbo.com/lookb4uleap.html`
`www.ahbbo.com/articles.html`

▶ **U.S. Small Business Administration**
How to Get Started as a Small Business
`www.sba.gov/starting_business/index.html`

▶ **IdeaCafe**
IdeaCafe's Work at Home
`www.businessownersideacafe.com/workathome/`

▶ **Nolo Press**
Independent Contractors Legal Encyclopedia
`www.nolo.com/lawcenter/index.cfm/catID/EC0EEB1C`
`-16EA-4F81-833ED5890B19383A?t`
`=0030LFNAV03202000`

▶ **Jobs & Moms**
Work-at-Home for the Working Mother
`www.jobsandmoms.com/work_at_home.html`

▶ **Working at Home—Work-at-Home Schemes**
Avoiding work-at-home scams and cyberschemes
`www.geocities.com/freehomebasedbusiness/`
`bbb2.htm`

▶ **Better Business Bureau**

Tips on work-at-home schemes *(separating scams from real opportunities)*

    www.bbb.org/alerts/article.asp?ID=205

▶ **Y & E: The Magazine for Teen Entrepeneurs**

The Kauffman Center for Entrepreneurial Leaders

    http://ye.entreworld.org/librarE_search.cfm

▶ **Working Solo**

Working Solo: FAQs for Solo Entrepreneurs

    www.workingsolo.com/faqstarting.html

▶ **Resources for the Small Office/Home Office (SOHO) Worker**

    www.workingsolo.com/
        resources/resources.html

▶ **Inc.com**

Articles about setting up your own business, even outside the home.

    www.inc.com/home

Fall-Back Strategies When You Just Can't Get a Business Going, at First

When I first started out in this field, more than thirty-five years ago, I read every book there was, on job-hunting and career-change. One thing that frustrated me was that they would offer some recommended strategies, and then act as though, *Well, of course, now you've got that job you've always wanted.*

I always wondered, as I read, *"But what if they don't?"* What if all the strategies here recommended *don't work?* So, naturally I'm concerned for my own readers who try *everything* in this chapter, and you're still out of work, and your finances are getting to the crisis stage. The advice that follows applies not only to starting your own business, but to any kind of job target.

You know about welfare, of course. It varies from country to country, but it is a safety net that most countries have constructed.

But what if you don't want to go on welfare. Then what do you do? Well, you have several choices:

- A stop-gap job
- Temp work
- Holding down two different part-time jobs
- Job-sharing

A Stop-Gap Job

The first life-preserver is: *a stop-gap job.* This phrase, used by many experts, refers to the situation where your money is about gone, and you have exhausted all job-hunting strategies. At this point, the advice of every expert is to take *any kind of work you can get.* That fills, or stops-up, the gap between the balance in your bank account and what you need to live on—hence, it is called a *stop-gap job.*

The mark of a stop-gap job is simple: it's a short-term job that you would *hate* if it was anything but short-term. It isn't supposed to be anything you really *like* to do. Its only requirement is that it be honest work, and that it bring in some money. It will probably be less money than you are used to making, per hour. It will probably also be hard work—or boring work. *But,* who cares? Its sole purpose is to put some honest money on the table, so you can eat. And pay the rent. And that's *it.*

The way you go about finding a stop-gap job is simple. You get your local newspaper, you look at the help-wanted ads, and you circle *any* and *every* job that you could see yourself doing *for a short time*, simply for the money. Then you go and apply for those jobs.

You also go to employment agencies, and say, "I'll do *any-thing*; what have you got?"

Unhappily, this spirit—"I'll do anything" is rarer than it ought to be. Many job-hunters refuse to even consider a stop-gap job; they'd rather go on welfare, first. One reason for this financially suicidal feeling is the conviction that "such jobs are *beneath* me." You know: *"I wouldn't be caught* dead *washing dishes."*

I need to state the obvious here: namely, that **any honest hard work neither demeans you, nor makes you less important as a person.** The "you" who is doing that work, remains the same. Except that it is a "you" who *needs this money.* I should also add, while I'm at it, that there are many salutary lessons for the soul, to be learned from temporarily taking a stop-gap job. And this is especially true if that job is at a different level and in a different world than you have been accustomed to.[4]

Many of us delay in seeking a stop-gap job for a somewhat higher reason: namely, the conviction that we must have full-time to devote to our job-hunt. Well, that's important, of course; but so is eating. You may want to consider a part-time stop-gap job, in order to address both concerns, fairly. (Also you might want to keep a *time-log* for two weeks, to see just how much time you actually *are* spending on your job-hunt. The easiest person in the world to deceive is *ourselves.*)

---

4. At one point in my life, I myself took a stop-gap job which involved cutting grass, helping lay cement sidewalks, and building retaining walls. It was one of the most educational experiences of my life. It also brought in exactly the money that I so badly needed.

Chapter Nine

A final reason many refuse to seek a stop-gap job is that they are receiving unemployment benefits, which of course would be cut off, if they took a job of any kind. But, needless to say, unemployment benefits do run out, and should they run out before you have found a job, then it is a very different story. Run, do not walk, to find a job, any job, apply for it and take it, once offered—as a stop-gap measure . . . only. Keep working on chapters 9 to 13. And *keep looking*.

For, as the birds say (*I overheard them just the other day*): "A stop-gap job is like a frail branch of a tree: a lovely place to stop and catch your breath, but a lousy place to build a permanent nest."

Temp Work

After stop-gap jobs, your next life-preserver is *temp work*. In these difficult times, many many employers are cutting their staff to the bone. Trouble is, as time goes on, some extra work may then come their way, work which their reduced staff can't keep up with.

At that point, employers won't usually hire back the staff they cut, but they will turn to what are called "Temporary Help" agencies, for either full- or part-time work. If you are having trouble finding a long-term full-time job, you certainly want to go register at one or more of these agencies.

In the old days, temporary agencies were solely for clerical workers and secretarial help. But the field has seen an explosion of services in recent years.

Now there are temporary agencies (*at least in the larger cities*) for many different occupations. In your city you may find temporary agencies for: accountants, industrial workers, assemblers, drivers, mechanics, construction people, engineering people, management/executives, nannies (for young and old), health care/dental/medical people, legal specialists, insurance specialists, sales/marketing people, underwriting professionals, financial services, and the like, as well as for the more obvious specialties: data processing, secretarial, and office services.

You will find the agencies listed in the yellow pages of your local phone book, under *Employment-Temporary*. Their listing or their ads will usually indicate what their specialities are.

They may find for you: a full-time job that lasts for a number of days or weeks or even months.

Or they may find for you: a part-time job that lasts for a number of days or weeks or even months.

Or they may not find anything for you. It is the case, as with all employment agencies, that there are often many more job-hunters who list themselves with such agencies, than there are employers who come there looking for help.

So, this cannot be your only strategy for finding work.

But it is certainly worth a try. You can increase the likelihood of the agency linking you up with a job, if you help them a little. For example, if you are in environmental engineering, and you know your field well, you can increase your chances of getting employment through a particular agency by compiling *for them* a list of the companies in your field, together with (if you know it) the name of the contact person there.[5] The temporary agency will do what it always does, initiate calls to those companies, soliciting their business; and if they uncover a vacancy, the odds are very great that it will be your name which is put forth for that job there.

Holding Down Two Different Part-Time Jobs

If the temporary agencies never call, and you still can't find any full-time job, your next strategy for finding work is to look for part-time work. While there are many *involuntary* part-time workers these days[6] there are also many *voluntary* part-time workers. They don't *want* to work full-time. Period. End of story. And you of course may be among them.

But suppose you do want full-time work. Often you can put a couple of part-time jobs together, so as to make the equivalent of full-time work.

In some cases, you may even prefer this to one full-time job. Perhaps you feel yourself to be multi-talented and/or perhaps you have a couple of very different interests. You can sometimes

---

5. I am indebted to one of our readers, Tathyana Pshevlozky, for this idea.

6. Involuntary part-time workers are those who want a full-time job, can't find one, so take a part-time job until a full-time job comes along.

find a part-time job in one of your fields of interest and a second part-time job in another one of your fields of interest, thus allowing you to use *all* your favorite skills and interests—in a way that no one full-time job might be able to do.

You can put together two part-time jobs in a variety of ways. One can be a job where you work for someone else, the other can be your own business or consultancy.

One can be a job advertised in a newspaper (or agency) or *online*, and the other can be a job that you create for yourself by approaching someone you'd really like to work with (or for), and asking what kind of help they need.

One can be a job with someone you never met before, and the other can be a job with your father, mother, brother, sister, aunt, uncle, or your best friend.

One can be a job during the daytime, on weekdays, and the other can be a job you do on weekends, or on certain evenings.

How you find such jobs, will depend on the nature of the job. If it's with a family member or friend, you ask them. If one of the jobs involves starting your own business, you start it. Newspaper ads also are a way of finding part-time jobs. If they want part-time workers, they will say so. Experience usually dictates that these jobs will either be at places you like, for much less money than you want, or they will be at places you hate, for a lot more money (e.g., toll-booth collectors, check-out people at supermarkets, etc.). The general rule is: the more boring the job, the higher the pay. You decide.

Job-Sharing

You're looking for part-time work. But one day, while you're looking through the ads or talking to some friends, you discover a full-time job that you are really interested in, and it's at just the kind of place where you would like to work. But they want someone full-time, and you only want to work part-time. There is a *possible* solution.

You can sometimes sell the organization on the idea of letting *two* of you fill that one job *(one of you from 8–12 noon, say, and the other from 1–5 p.m.).* Of course in order to do this, you have to find someone else—a relative, friend, or acquaintance—who is also looking for part-time work, *and* is very competent, *and* would be willing to share that job with you. And you have to find them *first*, and talk them into it, before you approach the boss at that place that interests you. This arrangement is called *job-sharing*, and there are a number of books and places you can write to, if you need some further guidance about how to do it, and how to sell the employer on the idea.

Incidentally, don't omit larger employers, from this particular search just because they would seem to you to be too bound by their own bureaucratic rules—*some* of them are very open to the idea of job-sharing. *On the other hand, of course, a lot of them aren't.* But it never hurts to ask.

Conclusion:
New Ways to Work

It takes a lot of guts to try ANYTHING new *(to you)* in today's economy. It's easier, however, if you keep three rules in mind:

1. There is always some risk, in trying something new. Your job is not to avoid risk—there is no way to do that—but to make sure ahead of time that the risks are *manageable*.
2. You find this out before you start, by first talking to others who have already done what you are thinking of doing; then you evaluate whether or not you still want to go ahead and try it.
3. Have a Plan B, already laid out, *before you start*, as to what you will do if it doesn't work out; i.e., know where you are going to go, next. Don't wait, *puh-leaze!* Write it out, now. *This is what I'm going to do, if this doesn't work out:*_____

_____

These rules always apply, no matter where you are in your life: just starting out, already employed, unemployed, in midlife, recovering after a crisis or accident, facing retirement, or whatever. Do take them very seriously.

If you're sharing your life with someone, sit down with that partner or spouse and ask what the implications are *for them* if you try this new thing. Will it require all your joint savings? Will they have to give up things? If so, what? Are they willing to make those sacrifices? And so on.

If you aren't out of work, you will need to debate the wisdom of quitting your job before you start up the new company, or business. And what do the experts say, here? In a word, they say, if you have a job, *don't* quit it. Better by far to move *gradually* into self-employment, doing it as a moonlighting activity first of all, while you are still holding down that regular job somewhere else. That way, you can test out your new enterprise, as you would test a floorboard in an old run-down house, stepping on it cautiously without at first putting your full weight on it, to see whether or not it will support you.

If your investigation revealed that it takes good accounting practices in order to turn a profit, and you don't know a thing about accounting, you go out and hire a part-time accountant *immediately*—or, if you absolutely have no money, you talk an accountant friend of yours into giving you some volunteer time, for a while.

It is up to you to do your research thoroughly, weigh the risks, count the cost, get counsel from those intimately involved with you, and then if you decide you want to do **it** (whatever **it** is), go ahead and try—no matter what your well-meaning but pessimistic acquaintances may say.

You only have one life here on this earth, and that life is *yours* (under God) to say how it will be spent, or not spent. Parents, well-meaning friends, etc. get no vote. Just you, and God.

How to Start Your Own Business

Where

What

How

YOUR DREAM JOB
A Visit to
The Isle of You

The Creative Approach
to Finding Meaning
for Your Life:

What,
Where,
and How

144

The Secret to Finding Your Dream Job

For the past thirty-five years I have heard from thousands and thousands of readers who write each year to tell me that my book changed their life. I am always curious to know exactly *what* in my book changed their life. So, I often ask.

I remember one reader wrote back to say, "It was that sentence where you said, *'You can do anything you want to.'* "

Another reader wrote that it was the sentence where I said, *"The clearer your vision of what you seek, the closer you are to finding it."*

And yet another reader, more mystically inclined, said it was the sentence, *"What you are seeking is seeking you."*

What has always fascinated me is how often, in a book of many many pages, it is just one particular sentence (*varying from reader to reader*) that does it. It is as if our whole being is trembling on the brink of new life, sometimes, and needs only the slightest encouragement—often a simple sentence will do—to launch itself into a new and more satisfying orbit.

What Did You Come into the World to Do?

It may be that as you read this, *your* whole being has wanted for some time, a new, better, more satisfying, more fulfilling life.

And now—due to your being laid off or made redundant, or due to some internal time clock ticking *within*, or some life-changing event occurring *without* (such as a death or divorce)—you find yourself at a crossroads; and the moment to actually seek that new life and new work has arrived.

There is a name for this moment in your life; in fact, there are several names.

We call it "at last going after your dreams."
We call it "finding more purpose and meaning for your life."
We call it "making a career-change."
We call it "deciding to try something new."
We call it "setting out in a different direction in your life."
We call it "getting out of the rat race."

We call it "going after your dream job."

We call it "finding your mission in life, at last."

But what you call it doesn't really matter. It is instantly recognizable as that moment when you decide that *this time* you're not going to do just a traditional job-hunt; you're going to do a life-changing job-hunt or career-change: one that begins with you and what it is that *you* want out of life.

This time it's all about: *Your* agenda. *Your* wishes. *Your* dreams. *Your* mission in life, given you by the Great God, our Creator.

This is a life-changing moment, and we should celebrate its arrival, in any life.

Why Now? And, Why You?

Let's face it, dear reader, neither one of us is getting any younger. If you don't go after your dreams *now*, when will you?

Now is the time to fulfill your dreams and the vision that you once had of what your life could be. Even if it can't be done in a night and a day. Even if it takes patience. Even if it means hard work. Even if it means changing careers. Even if it means going out into the unknown, and taking risks. *(Manageable risks, please!)*

You may think that this is a selfish activity—because this deals with You, you, you. But it is not. It is related to what *the world* most needs from you. That world currently is *filled* with workers whose weeklong question is, *When is the weekend going to be here?* And, then, *Thank God It's Friday!* Their work puts bread on the table *but* . . . they are bored out of their minds. Some of them are bored because even though they know what they'd rather be doing, they can't get out of their dead-end jobs, for one reason or another. But too many others, unfortunately, are bored simply because they have *never* given this sufficient priority in their life. They've kept busy with work and their social life, and partying, and vacation; and never taken the time to *think*—to think out what they uniquely can do, and what they uniquely have to offer to the world. They've flopped from one job to another, letting *accident, circumstance, coincidence,* and *whim* carry them wheresoever it would.

What the world most needs *from you* is not to add to their number, but to figure out, and then contribute to the world, what you came into this world to do.

The Road to a Dream Job
Is a Road that Passes
First of All Through You

> Most job-hunters who fail to master the job-hunt or find
> their dream job, fail not because they lack information
> about the job-market, but because they lack information
> about themselves.

The secret of finding your dream job is to first of all find You.
And to find out everything about You that you possibly can.

Of course, being human, our first instinct is to protest that we
already know loads of information about ourselves. After all,
we've lived with ourselves all these years. We *surely* know who
we are, by now.

Well, let's test that premise.

1. Take ten sheets of blank paper. Write, at the top of each one,
the words: **Who Am I?**

2. Then write, on each sheet in turn, one answer to that question. And only one.

3. When you're done, go back over all ten sheets and expand
now upon what you have written on each sheet. Looking at each
answer, write below it, *why* you said that, and *what turns you on*
about that answer.

4. When finished with all ten sheets, go back over them and
arrange them in order of priority. That is, which identity is the
most important to you? That page goes on top. Then, which is
next? That goes immediately underneath the top one. Continue
arranging the rest of the sheets in order, until the least important
identity is at the bottom of the pile.

5. Finally, go back over the ten sheets, in order, and look particularly at your answer, on each sheet, to *What Turns Me On
About This?* See if there are any common denominators, or
themes, among the ten answers you gave. If so, jot them down
on a separate piece of paper. Voila! You have begun to put your

finger on some things that your dream job or career, vocation, mission, or whatever, needs to give you, if you are to feel truly excited, fulfilled, used, effective, and operating at the height of your powers.

Here, incidentally, is an example, of how one man did this exercise:

Who am I?

1. A man
2. An urban dweller (and lover)
3. A loving person
4. A creator
5. A writer
6. A lover of good movies and music
7. A skilled counselor and teacher
8. An independent
9. An executive
10. An enabler

What turns me on about this?

1. Taking initiative, having inner strength; being open, growing, playful
2. Excitement, variety of choices available, crowds, faces
3. Feelings, empathizing, playfulness, sex, adoration given, happiness
4. Transforming things, making old things new, familiar wonderous
5. Beauty of words, variety of images, new perspectives, new relationships of ideas, words, understandings
6. Watching people up close, merging of color, photography, music
7. Using intuition, helping, seeing totalities of people, problem solving, long-term close helpful relationships
8. Making own decisions, carrying out own plans
9. Taking responsibility, wise risks, using mind, seeing totalities of problems overall
10. Helping people to become freed-up, to be what they want to be.

Any common denominators? Variety, totalities, rearranging of constellations, dealing with a number of different things and showing relationships between them all in a new way, helping others.

What must my career use (and include) for me to be truly happy, used and effective? A variety of different things that have to be dealt with, with people, where seeing totalities, rearranging their relationships, and interpreting them to people in a new way is at the heart of the career.

Well you were right. You do indeed know something about yourself. *But* we must go deeper. In order to survive in this increasingly more complex technological world, where we all have witnessed the death of distance *as an obstacle*, it is urgent for you to know more about who you are, individually and uniquely.

That knowledge is your secret weapon, to keep from being overwhelmed and overcome.

This is true if you're just having trouble with the common, everyday, garden-variety job-hunt.

But it is especially true if you are not just job-hunting, but are in the process of either choosing or changing careers, as you search for your dream job.

The Secret
to Finding Your Dream Job

The late Barbara B. Brown who was the first to bring *biofeedback* to the public's awareness back in 1974, with her groundbreaking book, *New Mind, New Body*, sometime later gave a public lecture on what *brain scientists* had discovered—on the way to biofeedback—about **how best to gather information about yourself, so that you can make better decisions about your life.**

Her findings were of great interest because of our own finding that the road to your dream job is a road that passes first of all *through You*. Want to see your dream job more clearly? Want to see the road to that job more clearly? Then first of all see yourself more clearly.

Barbara Brown said *brain scientists* had discovered there were three things you can do, that greatly facilitate such decision making.

Their first finding was: **Put everything you know about yourself, on one piece of paper.** Jot down anything and everything that occurs to you about yourself. This doesn't mean you can only *ever* use just one piece of paper. *That* would require you to learn how to write the Declaration of Independence on the head of a pin. No, the "one piece of paper" is merely the final destination of your collecting information about your Self. Let's call it something obvious, like: "That One Piece of Paper."

On your way to that final destination, you can of course use as many different pieces of paper as you want to—give them whatever name you will. I call those other pieces of paper simply "Scribble sheets."

Brain scientists' second finding, according to Barbara, was: **Use some kind of graphic** on that piece of paper, in order to organize the information *about yourself.* A graphic—any graphic—keeps "That One Piece of Paper" interesting, and not just a mess of words and space.

Their third, and last, finding was: **Prioritize** all this information, when you have finished gathering it. Put it in its order of importance, to you. On "That One Piece of Paper." That way, when you finally go looking for a dream job or career that matches *you,* if it is not a *perfect* overlap, at least you will know what you should make sure *is* included in the overlap.

I have followed this prescription for the past twenty-five years, as I have taught millions of job-hunters and career-changers how to find their dream job. With great results.

We have called "That One Piece of Paper" by various names over the years: *The Beginning Job-Hunting Map, The Quick Job-Hunting Map, The What Color is Your Parachute Workbook, The Flower Exercise*, etc.

And, over the years, we have tried out various graphics on "That One Piece of Paper": a Parachutist and his/her parachute, a Grecian temple, a clown holding a bunch of round balloons, a tree with several branches, etc., etc. The common denominator has been that each graphic has had seven or eight parts, inasmuch as any dream job has seven or eight parts. Ultimately we settled on a diagram of a Flower, with seven or eight petals[1] because readers preferred it above all other graphics. Something about it being a living entity, and being beautiful, I guess, and therefore a reflection of them at their best.

Here's what it came out looking like:

---

1. Seven vs. eight depends on whether you put Goals and Values on one petal, or two.

The Flower

"That One Piece of Paper"

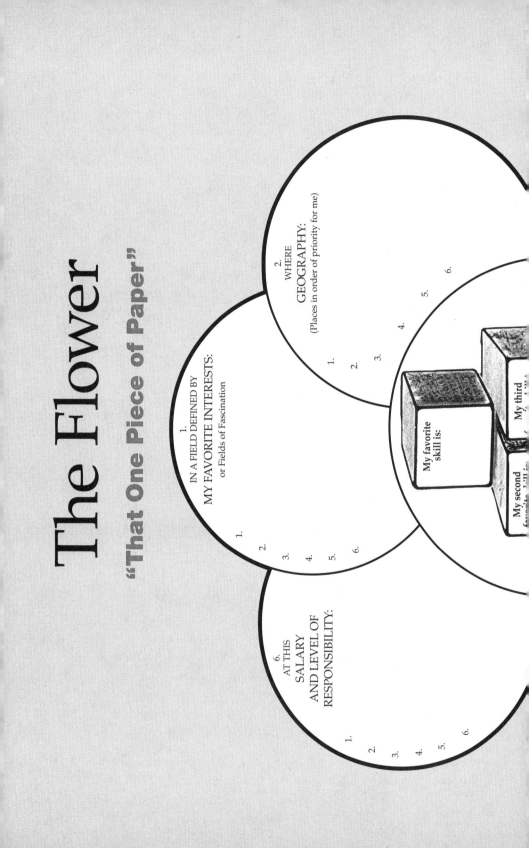

1.
IN A FIELD DEFINED BY
MY FAVORITE INTERESTS:
or Fields of Fascination

1.
2.
3.
4.
5.
6.

2.
WHERE
GEOGRAPHY:
(Places in order of priority for me)

1.
2.
3.
4.
5.
6.

6.
AT THIS
SALARY
AND LEVEL OF
RESPONSIBILITY:

1.
2.
3.
4.
5.
6.

My favorite
skill is:

My second

My third

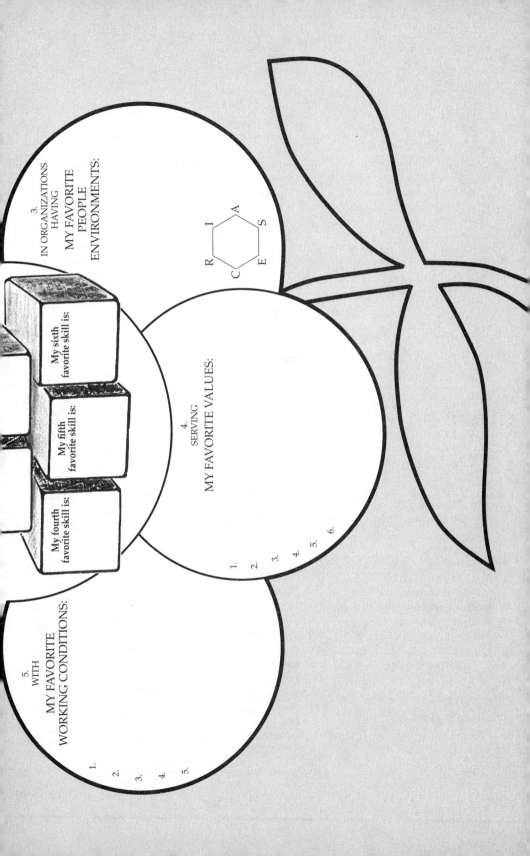

3.
IN ORGANIZATIONS
HAVING
MY FAVORITE
PEOPLE
ENVIRONMENTS:

R   I   A
C   E   S

My sixth
favorite skill is:

My fifth
favorite skill is:

My fourth
favorite skill is:

4.
SERVING

MY FAVORITE VALUES:

1.
2.
3.
4.
5.
6.

5.
WITH
MY FAVORITE
WORKING CONDITIONS:

1.
2.
3.
4.
5.

Example
(Rich Feller's Flower)

Favorite Interests

1. Large conference planning
2. Regional geography & culture
3. Traveling on $20/day 4. Career planning seminars 5. Counseling techniques / theories 6. American Policies 7. Fundamentals of sports 8. Fighting Sexism 9. NASCAR Auto Racing
10. Interior design

Salary and Level of Responsibility

1. Can determine 9/12 month contract 2. Can determine own projects 3. Considerable clout in organization's direction without administrative responsibilities 4. Able to select colleagues 5. 3 to 5 assistants 6. $35K to $50K 7. Serve on various important boards 8. Can defer clerical and budget decisions and tasks 9. Speak before large groups 10. Can run for elected office

Geography

1. Close to major city
2. Mild winters / low humidity
3. Change in seasons 4. Clean and green 5. 100,000 people 6. Nice shopping malls. 7. Wide range of athletic options 8. Diverse economic base 9. Ample local culture
10. Sense of community (pride)

Favorite Skills

1. Observational / learning skills • continually expose self to new experiences • perceptive in identifying and assessing potential of others 2. Leadership Skills • continually searches for more resonsibility • sees a problem / acts to solve it 3. Instructing / interpreting / guiding • committed to learning as a lifelong process • create atmosphere of acceptance 4. Serving / helping / human relations skills • shapes atmosphere of particular place • relates well in dealing with public 5. Detail / follow-through skills • handle great variety of tasks • resource broker 6. Influencing / persuading skills • recruiting talent / leadership • inspiring trust 7. Performing skills • getting up in front of a group (if I'm in control) • Addressing small and large groups 8. Intuitional / Innovative skills • continually develop / generate new ideas 9. Develop / Plan / Organize / Execute • designing projects • utilizing skills of others 10. Language / Read / Write • communicate effectively • Can think quickly on my feet

Favorite People Environment

1. Strong social, perceptual skills
2. Emotionally and physically healthy
3. Enthusiastically include others 4. Heterogeneous in interests and skills 5. Social changers, innovators 6. Politically, economically astute 7. Confident enough to confront / cry and be foolish 8. Sensitive to nontraditional issues
9. I and R, (see page 216)
10. Nonmaterialistic

Favorite Working Conditions

1. Receive clinical supervision 2. Mentor relationship 3. Excellent Secretary 4. Part of larger, highly respected organization with clear direction 5. Near gourmet and health food specialty shops 6. Heterogeneous colleagues (race, sex, age) 7. Flexible dress code 8. Merit system 9. Can bike / bus / walk to work 10. Private office with window

Favorite Values

1. Improve the human condition
2. Promote interdependence and futuristic principles 3. Maximize productive use of human / material resources 4. Teach people to be self-directed / self-responsible 5. Free people from self-defeating controls (thoughts, rules, barriers) 6. Promote capitalistic principles 7. Reduce exploitation 8. Promote political participation 9. Acknowledge those who give to the community 10. Give away ideas

People like to see just what "That One Piece of Paper" looks like, when it is all filled out, and done. Rich W. Feller, once a student of mine back in 1982, now a world-famous professor and expert in this field, filled out his paper as you see, on the facing page. He said "That One Piece of Paper" has been his life-long companion ever since 1982, and his guiding star, as it has turned out to be more and more a description of where he has gone, and is going, with his life. I hear such testimony, again and again.

What Do You Put on "That One Piece of Paper"?

Anything. We have discovered that anything you know about yourself, that you *have the impulse* to put there, should go there. You be the judge. No censorship. Because any- and everything you know about yourself, and jot down in full view, ultimately makes you a better job-hunter, a better resume writer, a better interviewer or inter-viewee, a better career-changer, and ultimately, a better worker.

Anything.

Even if it's something ridiculous, like: *"I would die to be able to be an airline pilot, but I cannot be an airline pilot."* Don't prejudge where that can lead.

For example, a seventeen-year-old high school student in France did indeed want to be an airline pilot, but he had a physical handicap that prevented him from pursuing that dream seriously. The way he wrote it down on his *one piece of paper*, during a session with a career counselor, was: "My dream is to be a pilot, but I can never achieve my dream."

Seemed like a downer, if not a completely useless bit of information. But his counselor gave him a pen and a pad of paper, one day, and said, "I want you to spend a day out at the airport *(it was a big airport)* and jot down every job you run into or hear about there— from the shoe-shine man to the pilot himself. Talk to any worker there who will give you even a minute of their time, to find out what other jobs each of them knows about, there in the airport or in the airline industry. Make a list of every job you hear about."

The seventeen-year-old did as he was told, and met with his counselor the following day. The counselor asked him how it had gone. The young man's eyes glistened with delight: "I found a job I really would love to do." "And what was that?" the counselor asked. "Well," he replied, "The airline seats—the ones the passengers sit in? I would love to make those seats!" And so, he began to set his sights on that job, and what kind of preparation or training it would take to do it.

The Secret to Finding Your Dream Job   **155**

Finding the Twenty Dollar Bills

Okay then, if our first rule is: **Put everything you know about yourself, on one piece of paper,** then we really do mean *everything*. Or *anything*. You can make it simple, or complex. I recommend *simple*.

Are some pieces of information more valuable than others? Oh, yes. And thank God, or you'd be jotting down stuff, forever. (Maybe what you know about yourself would fill an encyclopedia, a wikipedia,[2] a blog,[3] an all-day podcast,[4] a tape-recording *(of an interview with yourself)*, or whatever.)

But here's the deal. Let us say you are a U.S. job-hunter, and you have in your purse or wallet some $5 bills, $1 bills, and some $20 bills. You wouldn't throw any of those bills away, would you? They are all *money*, and they are all valuable. But some of those bills are more valuable than others. A $20 bill, for example, is twenty times as valuable as a $1 bill.

So it is, with information about yourself. It's all valuable; *by analogy*, it's all money. But some of the information about yourself is comparable to $20 bills, and some of it is comparable to $1 bills, and some of it is in between.

Now, let's cut to the chase. What is the $20 information about yourself?

Well, it turns out to be:

1. Any information you have about your most favorite **transferable skills**, *and specific examples of when and how you used those skills, in the past.*

2. Any information you have about those **fields** that most fascinate you, *and specific examples of when and how you had experience with those fields in the past.*

These two, together, are called *competencies*. They are your $20 information about yourself. They are valuable in a million ways, and offer the basis for Behavioral Interviews—should you run into them.

There are some $10 bits of information about yourself, of course. These are: your favorite **people-environments**, your favorite **values and goals**, your favorite **working conditions**, and your desired **salary** and **level of responsibility**.

These $20 and $10 pieces of information are all included in the Flower Diagram, as you may have already noticed.

---

2. http://en.wikipedia.org/

3. www.technorati.com/

4. www.thepodcastingebook.com/

The rest of the stuff you jot down about yourself on "That One Piece of Paper," in the margins, will likely turn out to be $1 bits of information, but you never know. Since you are jotting down *anything* and *everything*, there may be some $10 or $20 information about you, that hits you, right out of the blue. Scrutinize it all, carefully.

It is time now to begin. Here are the basic steps you must go through, in order to choose a career, or figure out what you want to do next, with your life, or change careers, or (best of all) identify your dream job.

HOW DO YOU IDENTIFY YOUR DREAM JOB, Step by Step?

1. **Favorite Transferable Skills.** You do a systematic inventory of the *transferable skills* which you already possess.

2. **Fields of Fascination.** You do a systematic inventory of the fields or *bodies of knowledge* that fascinate you the most.

3. **The Flower.** From these two inventories, you fashion a description—a picture, if you will—of what your new career *looks like*.

4. **Names of Jobs that Fit.** Then you interview people, sharing this picture, to find out *what its name is* (or names).

5. **Informational Interviewing.** Once you know your skills, and know what kind of work you want to do, you go talk to people who are doing it. Find out how they like the work, how they found their job.

6. **Research of Organizations.** Do some research, in your chosen geographical area, on organizations which interest you, to find what they do and what kinds of problems they or their industry are wrestling with.

7. **Network.** Then identify and seek out the person who actually has the power to hire you there, for the job you want.

8. **Contacts.** Use your contacts to get in to see him or her. Show this person with the power to hire you how you can help them with their problems, and how you would stand out as "one employee in a hundred."

9. **Closure.** In all of this, cut no corners, take no shortcuts.

This creative approach to career-choice, or career-change, has three main parts to it. These parts are in the form of the questions:

What, Where, and **How**

• WHAT ?

The full question here is *what are the skills you most enjoy using?* To answer this question, you need to identify or inventory what **skills/gifts/talents** you have; and then you need to prioritize them, in their order of importance and enjoyment for you. Experts call these transferable skills, because they are transferable to any field/career that you choose, regardless of where you first picked them up, or how long you've had them.

• WHERE ?

The full question here is *where do you most want to use those skills?*

This has to do *primarily* with the **fields of fascination** *you have already acquired*, which you most enjoy using. But *where* also has to do with your preferred working conditions, what kinds of data or people or things you enjoy working with, etc.

• HOW ?

The full question here is *how do you find such jobs, that use your favorite skills and your favorite fields of knowledge?*

To answer this question, you need to do some **interviewing of various people in order to find the information you are looking for.** You begin this interviewing with the awareness that *skills* point toward job-titles; and *Fields of Fascination* point toward a career *field*, where you would use those skills. You want also to find out the names of *organizations* in your preferred geographical area which have such jobs to offer. *And,* the names of the people or person there who actually has the *power* to hire you, as well as the challenges they face. You then secure an interview with them, by using your contacts, and show them how your skills can help them with their challenges.

A Systematic Approach to
the Job-Hunt and Career-Change:

PART I

What

Skills Do You
Most Enjoy Using?

Steven M. Johnson

"WHAT?" Is a Matter of Skills

You are looking here for what you may think of as the basic building-blocks of your work. So, if you're going to identify your dream job, and/or attempt a thorough career-change, you should begin by first of all identifying your functional, transferable skills. And while you may think you know what your best and favorite skills are, in most cases your self-knowledge could probably use a little work.

A weekend should do it! In a weekend, you can inventory your *past* sufficiently so that you have a good picture of the *kind* of work you would love to be doing *in the future. (You can, of course, stretch the inventory over a number of weeks, maybe doing an hour or two one night a week, if you prefer. It's up to you as to just how you do it.)*

The Secret to Finding Your Dream Job **159**

A Crash Course on "Transferable Skills"

Many people just "freeze" when they hear the word "skills."

It begins with high school job-hunters: "I haven't really got any skills," they say.

It continues with college students: "I've spent four years in college. I haven't had time to pick up any skills."

And it lasts through the middle years, especially when a person is thinking of changing his or her career: "I'll have to go back to college, and get retrained, because otherwise I won't have any skills in my new field." Or: "Well, if I claim any skills, I'll start at a very entry kind of level."

All of this fright about the word "skills" is very common, and stems from a total misunderstanding of what the word means. A misunderstanding that is shared, we might add, by altogether too many employers, or human resources departments, and other so-called "vocational experts."

By understanding the word, you will automatically put yourself way ahead of most job-hunters. And, especially if you are weighing a change of career, you can save yourself much waste of time on the folly called "I must go back to school." I've said it before, and I'll say it again: *maybe* you need some further schooling, but very often it is possible to make a dramatic career-change without any retraining. It all depends. And you won't really *know* whether or not you need further schooling, until you have finished all the exercises in this section of the book.

Chapter Ten

All right, then, if transferable skills are the heart of your vision and your destiny, let's see just exactly what transferable skills *are*.

Here are the most important truths you need to keep in mind about transferable, functional, skills:

1 Your transferable *(functional)* skills are the most basic unit—the atoms—of whatever career you may choose. You can see this from this diagram:

Skills as the Basic Unit of Work

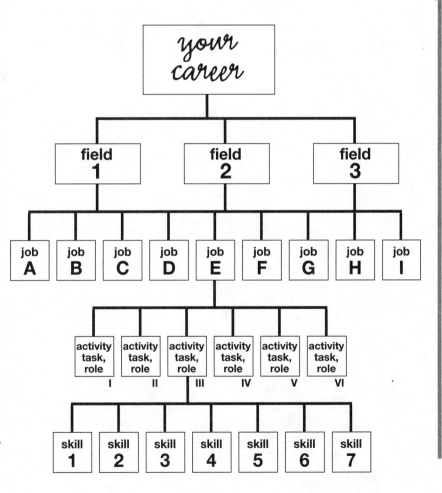

The skills you need to inventory, for yourself, are called functional or transferable skills. Here is a famous diagram of them:

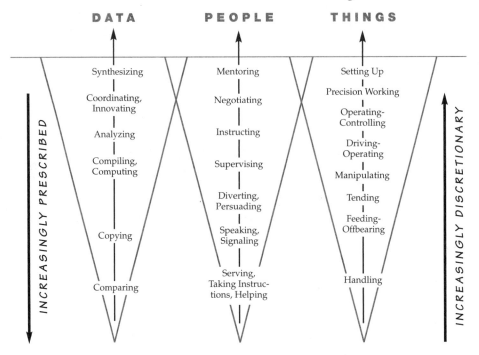

2 You should always claim the *highest* skills you legitimately can, on the basis of your past performance.

As we see in the functional/transferable skills diagram above, your skills break down into three *families*, according to whether you use them with **Data/Information,** or **People** or **Things.** And again, as this diagram makes clear, within each family there are *simple* skills, and there are higher, or *more complex* skills, so that these can be listed as inverted pyramids, with the simpler skills at the bottom, and the more complex ones in order above it, as in the diagram.

Incidentally, as a general rule—to which there are exceptions—each *higher* skill requires you to be able also to do all those skills listed below it, on the diagram. So of course you can usually claim *those,* as well. But you want to particularly claim the highest skill you legitimately can, on each transferable skills pyramid, based on what you have already proven you can do in the past.

3 The higher your transferable skills, the more freedom you will have on the job.

Simpler skills can be, and usually are, heavily *prescribed* (by the employer), so if you claim *only* the simpler skills, you will have to *"fit in"*—following the instructions of your supervisor, and doing exactly what you are told to do. The *higher* the skills you can legitimately claim, the more you will be given discretion to carve out the job the way you want to—so that it truly fits *you*.

4 The higher your transferable skills, the less competition you will face for whatever job you are seeking, because jobs which use such skills will rarely be advertised through normal channels.

Not for you the way of classified ads, resumes, and agencies, that we spoke of in earlier chapters. No, if you can legitimately claim higher skills, then to find such jobs you *must* follow what I have called "the life-changing job-hunting method" described in this and the next two chapters.

The essence of this approach to job-hunting or career-change is that once you have identified your favorite transferable skills, and your favorite Fields of Fascination, you may then approach *any organization that interests you, whether or not they have a known vacancy.* Naturally, whatever place you visit—and particularly those which have not advertised any vacancy—you will find far fewer job-hunters that you have to compete with.

In fact, if the employers you visit happen to like you well enough, they may be willing to create for you a job that does not presently exist. *In which case, you will be competing with no one, since you will be the sole applicant for that newly created job.* While this doesn't happen all the time, it is astounding to me how many times it *does* happen. *The reason* it does is that the employers often have been *thinking* about creating a new job within their organization, for quite some time—but with this and that, they just have never gotten around to *doing* it. Until they saw you.

Then they decide they didn't want to let you get away, since *good employees are as hard to find as are good employers.* And they suddenly remember that job they have been thinking about creating for many weeks or months, now. So they dust off their *intention*, create the job on the spot, and offer it to you! And if that new job is not only what *they* need, but is exactly what *you* were looking for, then you have a dream job. Match-match. Win-win.

From our country's perspective, it is also interesting to note this: by this job-hunting initiative of yours, you have helped accelerate the creation of more jobs in your country, which is so much on everybody's mind here in the new millennium. How nice to help your country, as well as yourself!

5 Don't confuse transferable skills with traits.
Functional/transferable skills are often confused with **traits, temperaments**, or **type.** People think transferable skills are such things as: *has lots of energy, gives attention to details, gets along well with people, shows determination, works well under pressure, is sympathetic, intuitive, persistent, dynamic, dependable,* etc. Despite popular misconceptions, these are not functional/transferable skills, but traits, or the *style* with which you do your transferable skills. For example, let's take *"gives attention to details."* If one of your *transferable skills* is *"conducting research"* then *"gives attention to details"* describes the manner or style with which you do

---

5. The Myers-Briggs Type Indicator, or "MBTI®," measures what is called *psychological type.* For further reading about this, see:

Paul D. Tieger & Barbara Barron-Tieger, *Do What You Are: Discover the Perfect Career for You Through the Secrets of Personality Type.* Third Edition. 2001. Little, Brown & Company, Inc., division of Time Warner Inc., 34 Beacon St., Boston MA 02108. For those who cannot obtain the MBTI®, this book includes a method for readers to identify their personality types. This is one of the most popular career books in the world. It's easy to see why. Many have found great help from the concept of Personality Type, and the Tiegers are masters in explaining this approach to career-choice. Highly recommended.

Donna Dunning, *What's Your Type of Career? Unlock the Secrets of Your Personality to Find Your Perfect Career Path.* 2001. Davies-Black Publishing, an imprint of Consulting Psychologists Press, Inc., 3803 East Bayshore Road, Palo Alto, CA 94303, 1-800-624-1765. This is a dynamite book on personality type. I found it to be the best written, most insightful, and most helpful book I have ever read about using "Type" in the workplace. Donna Dunning's knowledge of "Type" is encyclopedic!

David Keirsey and Marilyn Bates, *Please Understand Me: Character & Temperament Types.* 1978. Includes the Keirsey Temperament Sorter—again, for those who cannot obtain the MBTI® (Myers-Briggs Type Indicator)—registered trademark of Consulting Psychologists Press.

that transferable skill called *conducting research.* If you want to know what your traits are, popular tests such as the *Myers-Briggs Type Indicator,* measure that sort of thing.[5]

If you have access to the Internet, there are tests—and articles about tests—to be found there, that will give you some clues, at least, about your traits or "type":

▶ Working Out Your Myers-Briggs Type
    `www.teamtechnology.co.uk/tt/t-articl/`
        `mb-simpl.htm`
An informative article about the Myers-Briggs

▶ What Is Your Myers-Briggs Personality Type?
    `www.personalitypathways.com/type_inventory.html`
    `www.personalitypathways.com`
Another article about personality types; also, there's a Myers-Briggs Applications page, with links to test resources

▶ Myers-Briggs Foundation home page
    `www.myersbriggs.org`
The official website of the Foundation; testing resources

▶ Human Metrics Test (Jung Typology)
    `www.humanmetrics.com/cgi-win/JTypes2.asp`
Free test, loosely based on the Myers-Briggs

▶ Myers-Briggs Type Indicator Online
    `www.discoveryourpersonality.com/MBTI`
Official Myers-Briggs test, $60

▶ The Keirsey Temperament Sorter
    `www.keirsey.com`
Free test, similar to the Myers-Briggs

"I Wouldn't Recognize My Skills If They Came Up and Shook Hands with Me"

Well, now that you know what transferable skills technically *are,* the problem that awaits you now, is figuring out your own. If you are one of the few lucky people who already know what your transferable skills are, blessed are you. Write them down, and put them in the order of preference, for you, on "That One Piece of Paper," page 152 and 153.

The Secret to Finding Your Dream Job   **165**

If, however, you don't know what your skills are (and 95 percent of all workers *don't*), then you will need some help. Fortunately there is an exercise to help. A great exercise!

It involves the following steps:

1. Write a Story

Here is a specific example of such a story, so you can see how it is done:

"A number of years ago, I wanted to be able to take a summer trip with my wife and four children. I had a very limited budget, and could not afford to put my family up, in motels. I decided to rig our station wagon as a camper.

"First I went to the library to get some books on campers. I read those books. Next I designed a plan of what I had to build, so that I could outfit the inside of the station wagon, as well as topside. Then I went and purchased the necessary wood. On weekends, over a period of six weeks, I first constructed, in my driveway, the shell for the "second story" on my station wagon. Then I cut doors, windows, and placed a six-drawer bureau within that shell. I mounted it on top of the wagon, and pinioned it in place by driving two-by-fours under the station

wagon's rack on top. I then outfitted the inside of the station wagon, back in the wheel-well, with a table and a bench on either side, that I made.

"The result was a complete homemade camper, which I put together when we were about to start our trip, and then disassembled after we got back home. When we went on our summer trip, we were able to be on the road for four weeks, yet stayed within our budget, since we didn't have to stay at motels.

"I estimate I saved $1,900 on motel bills, during that summer's vacation."

Ideally, each story you write should have the following parts, as illustrated above:

I. **Your goal: what you wanted to accomplish:** *"I wanted to be able to take a summer trip with my wife and four children."*

II. **Some kind of hurdle, obstacle, or constraint that you faced** (self-imposed or otherwise): *"I had a very limited budget, and could not afford to put my family up, in motels."*

III. **A description of what you did, step by step** (how you set about to ultimately achieve your goal, above, in spite of this hurdle or constraint): *"I decided to rig our station wagon as a camper. First I went to the library to get some books on campers. I read those books. Next I designed a plan of what I had to build, so that I could outfit the inside of the station wagon, as well as topside. Then I went and purchased the necessary wood. On weekends, over a period of six weeks, I . . ." etc., etc.*

IV. **A description of the outcome or result:** *"When we went on our summer trip, we were able to be on the road for four weeks, yet stayed within our budget, since we didn't have to stay at motels."*

V. **Any measurable/quantifiable statement of that outcome,** that you can think of: *"I estimate I saved $1,900 on motel bills, during that summer's vacation."*

Now write *your* story, using the next page as a guide.

Don't pick a story where you achieved something *big*. At least to begin with, write a story about a time when you had fun!

MY LIFE STORIES

Column 1	Column 2	Column 3	Column 4	Column 5
Your Goal: What You Want to Accomplish	Some Kind of Obstacle (or limit, hurdle, or restraint you had to overcome before it could be accomplished)	What You Did Step-by-Step (It may help if you pretend you are telling this story to a whining 4-year-old child, who keeps asking, after each of your sentences, "An' then whadja do? An' then whadja do?")	Description of the Result (What you accomplished)	Any Measure or Quantities to Prove Your Achievement

Note: Reproduce this page as much as you need to.

2. Analyze the Story for Transferable Skills

Once you have written Story #1 (and before you write the other six), you will want to analyze it for the transferable skills you *used*. (You can decide later if you loved those skills or not. For now, just do an inventory.)

To do this inventory, go to the list of Skills Keys found on pages 170 to 175, which resemble a series of keyboard keys. Transferable skills divide into:

1. Physical Skills: the transferable skills you enjoy, using primarily *your hands or body*—with things, or nature;

2. Mental Skills: the transferable skills you enjoy, using primarily *your mind*—with data/information, ideas, or subjects;

3. Interpersonal Skills: the transferable skills you enjoy, involving primarily *personal relationships*—as you serve or help people or animals, and their needs or problems.[6]

Therefore you will find three sets of Skills Keys, labeled accordingly.

As you look at each key in the three sets, the question you need to ask yourself, is: "Did I use this transferable skill *in this Story* (#1)?"

That is the *only* question you ask yourself (at the moment). Then you go to the little box named #1 (under each Skill Key), and this is what you do:

If the answer is "Yes," fill in the little box, as shown (right):

Ignore the other little boxes there, for the time being; they belong to your other stories (all the little boxes named #2 belong to Story #2, all the little boxes named #3 belong to Story #3, etc.).

Taking
Instructions,
Serving,
or Helping

Did I Use This Skill in Story

Yes

---

6. For the curious, "animals" are placed in this category with "people," because the skills required to deal with animals are more like those used with people, than like those used with "things."

My Physical Skills

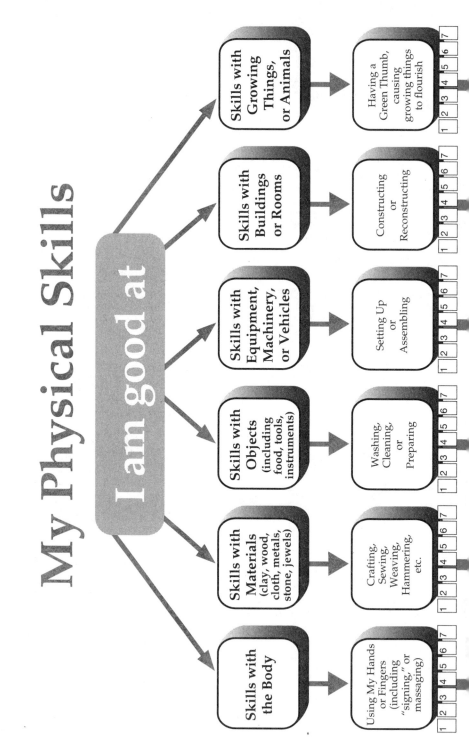

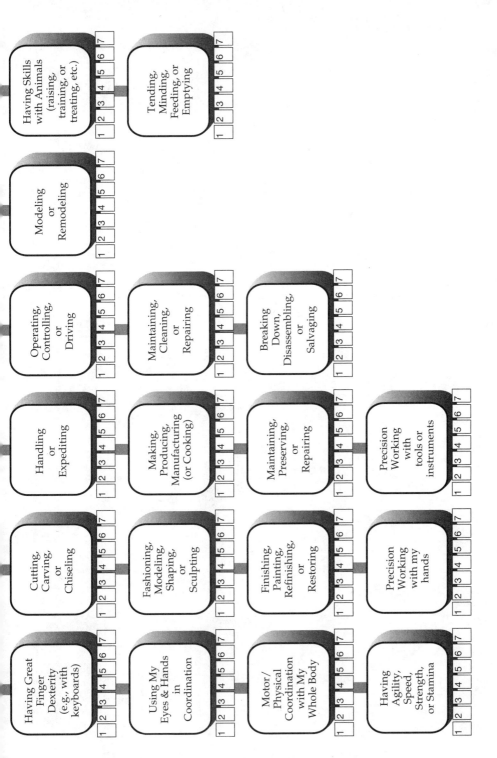

171

My Mental Skills

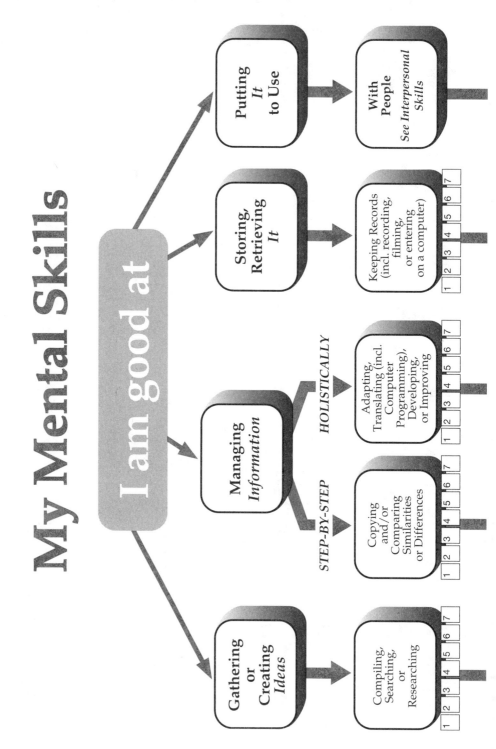

I am good at

Gathering or Creating Ideas

Compiling, Searching, or Researching

1 2 3 4 5 6 7

Managing Information

STEP-BY-STEP

Copying and/or Comparing Similarities or Differences

1 2 3 4 5 6 7

HOLISTICALLY

Adapting, Translating (incl. Computer Programming), Developing, or Improving

1 2 3 4 5 6 7

Storing, Retrieving *It*

Keeping Records (incl. recording, filming, or entering on a computer)

1 2 3 4 5 6 7

Putting *It* **to Use**

With People *See Interpersonal Skills*

With
Things
*See Physical
Skills*

Storing or Filing
(in file cabinets,
microfiche,
video, audio,
or computer)
1 2 3 4 5 6 7

Retrieving
Information,
Ideas,
Data
1 2 3 4 5 6 7

Enabling
Other People
to Find or
Retrieve
Information
1 2 3 4 5 6 7

Having a
Superior
Memory,
Keeping Track
of Details
1 2 3 4 5 6 7

Visualizing,
Drawing,
Painting,
Dramatizing,
Creating Videos
or Software
1 2 3 4 5 6 7

Synthesizing,
Combining
Parts into
a Whole
1 2 3 4 5 6 7

Problem
Solving
or Seeing
Patterns Among
a Mass of Data
1 2 3 4 5 6 7

Deciding,
Evaluating,
Appraising,
or Making
Recommendations
1 2 3 4 5 6 7

Computing,
Working with
Numbers,
Doing
Accounting
1 2 3 4 5 6 7

Analyzing,
Breaking
Down
into Its
Parts
1 2 3 4 5 6 7

Organizing,
Classifying,
Systematizing,
and/or
Prioritizing
1 2 3 4 5 6 7

Planning,
Laying Out
a Step-by-Step
Process for
Achieving a Goal
1 2 3 4 5 6 7

Gathering
Information by
Interviewing
or Observing
People
1 2 3 4 5 6 7

Gathering
Information by
Studying
or Observing
Things
1 2 3 4 5 6 7

Having an Acute
Sense of
Hearing,
Smell, Taste,
or Sight
1 2 3 4 5 6 7

Imagining,
Inventing,
Creating, or
Designing
New Ideas
1 2 3 4 5 6 7

173

My Interpersonal Skills

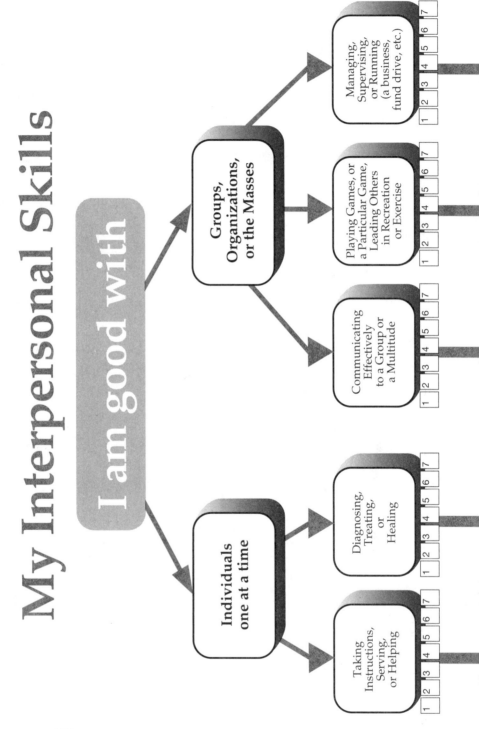

I am good with

Individuals one at a time

- Diagnosing, Treating, or Healing
  1 2 3 4 5 6 7

- Taking Instructions, Serving, or Helping
  1 2 3 4 5 6 7

Groups, Organizations, or the Masses

- Communicating Effectively to a Group or a Multitude
  1 2 3 4 5 6 7

- Playing Games, or a Particular Game, Leading Others in Recreation or Exercise
  1 2 3 4 5 6 7

- Managing, Supervising, or Running (a business, fund drive, etc.)
  1 2 3 4 5 6 7

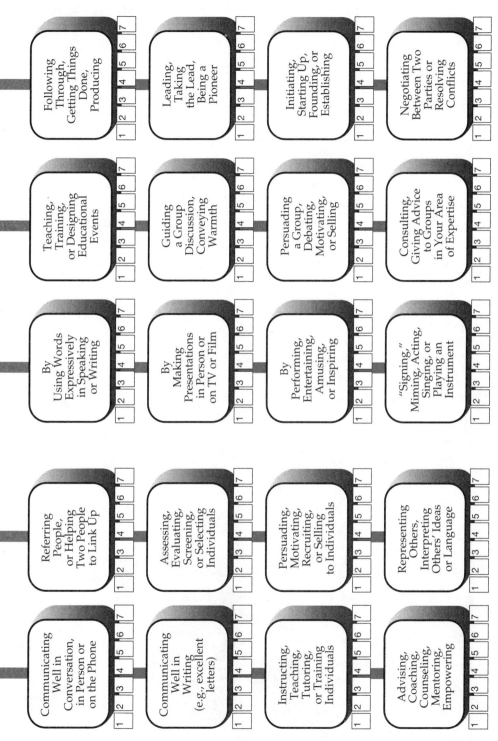

Following Through, Getting Things Done, Producing
1 2 3 4 5 6 7

Leading, Taking the Lead, Being a Pioneer
1 2 3 4 5 6 7

Initiating, Starting Up, Founding, or Establishing
1 2 3 4 5 6 7

Negotiating Between Two Parties or Resolving Conflicts
1 2 3 4 5 6 7

Teaching, Training, or Designing Educational Events
1 2 3 4 5 6 7

Guiding a Group Discussion, Conveying Warmth
1 2 3 4 5 6 7

Persuading a Group, Debating, Motivating, or Selling
1 2 3 4 5 6 7

Consulting, Giving Advice to Groups in Your Area of Expertise
1 2 3 4 5 6 7

By Using Words Expressively in Speaking or Writing
1 2 3 4 5 6 7

By Making Presentations in Person or on TV or Film
1 2 3 4 5 6 7

By Performing, Entertaining, Amusing, or Inspiring
1 2 3 4 5 6 7

"Signing," Miming, Acting, Singing, or Playing an Instrument
1 2 3 4 5 6 7

Referring People, or Helping Two People to Link Up
1 2 3 4 5 6 7

Assessing, Evaluating, Screening, or Selecting Individuals
1 2 3 4 5 6 7

Persuading, Motivating, Recruiting, or Selling to Individuals
1 2 3 4 5 6 7

Representing Others, Interpreting Others' Ideas or Language
1 2 3 4 5 6 7

Communicating Well in Conversation, in Person or on the Phone
1 2 3 4 5 6 7

Communicating Well in Writing (e.g., excellent letters)
1 2 3 4 5 6 7

Instructing, Teaching, Tutoring, or Training Individuals
1 2 3 4 5 6 7

Advising, Coaching, Counseling, Mentoring, Empowering
1 2 3 4 5 6 7

175

3. Write Six Other Stories, and Analyze Them for Transferable Skills

Voila! You are done with Story #1. However, "one swallow doth not a summer make," so the fact that you used certain skills in this first Story doesn't tell you much. What you are looking for is **patterns**—transferable skills that keep reappearing in story after story. They keep reappearing because they are your favorites (assuming you chose stories where you were *really* enjoying yourself).

So, now, write Story #2, from any period in your life, analyze it using the keys, etc., etc. And keep this process up, until you have written, and analyzed, seven stories.

4. Decide Which Skills Are Your Favorites, and Prioritize Them

When you're done writing and analyzing all Seven Stories, you should now go back and look over the six pages of "Skills Keys" to see which skills got used the most often. Make a list.

Cross out any that you don't enjoy using.

Prioritize the remainder, using one of the Prioritizing Grids on the following pages.

The Prioritizing Grid

How to Prioritize Your
Lists of Anything

Here is a method for taking (say) ten items, and figuring out which one is most important to you, which is next most important, etc.

- Insert the items to be prioritized, in any order, in Section A. Then compare two items at a time, circling the one you prefer—between the two—in Section B. Which one is more important to you? State the question any way you want to: In the case of geographical factors, you might ask. "If I were being offered two jobs, one in an area that had factor #1, but not factor #2; the other in an area that had factor #2, but not factor #1, all other things being equal, which job would I take?" Circle it. Then go on to the next pair, etc.

- When you are all done, count up the number of times each number got circled, all told. Enter these totals on the TIMES line in Section C. Then notice the number of times each item was circled ("Times" = "Times Circled"). This determines the item's ranking. Most circled = #1, next most circled = #2, etc. Enter this ranking on the RANK line in Section C. If two items are circled the same number of times, look back in Section B to see—when those two were compared there—which one you preferred. Give that one an extra half point. List the items, now in their proper rank, in Section D.

The question to ask yourself, on the Grid, as you confront each "pair" is: "If I were offered two jobs, and in one job I could use the first skill, but not the second; while in the other job, I could use the second skill, but not the first, which job would I choose?" When you've got your ten favorite transferable skills, in order, copy the top six onto the Flower Diagram.

Since you will be using this Prioritizing Grid more than once in these exercises you will want to go down to Kinko's or your local copy shop and make a number of copies of this form before you begin filling it in, for the first time. Show the staff there, this, for authorization.

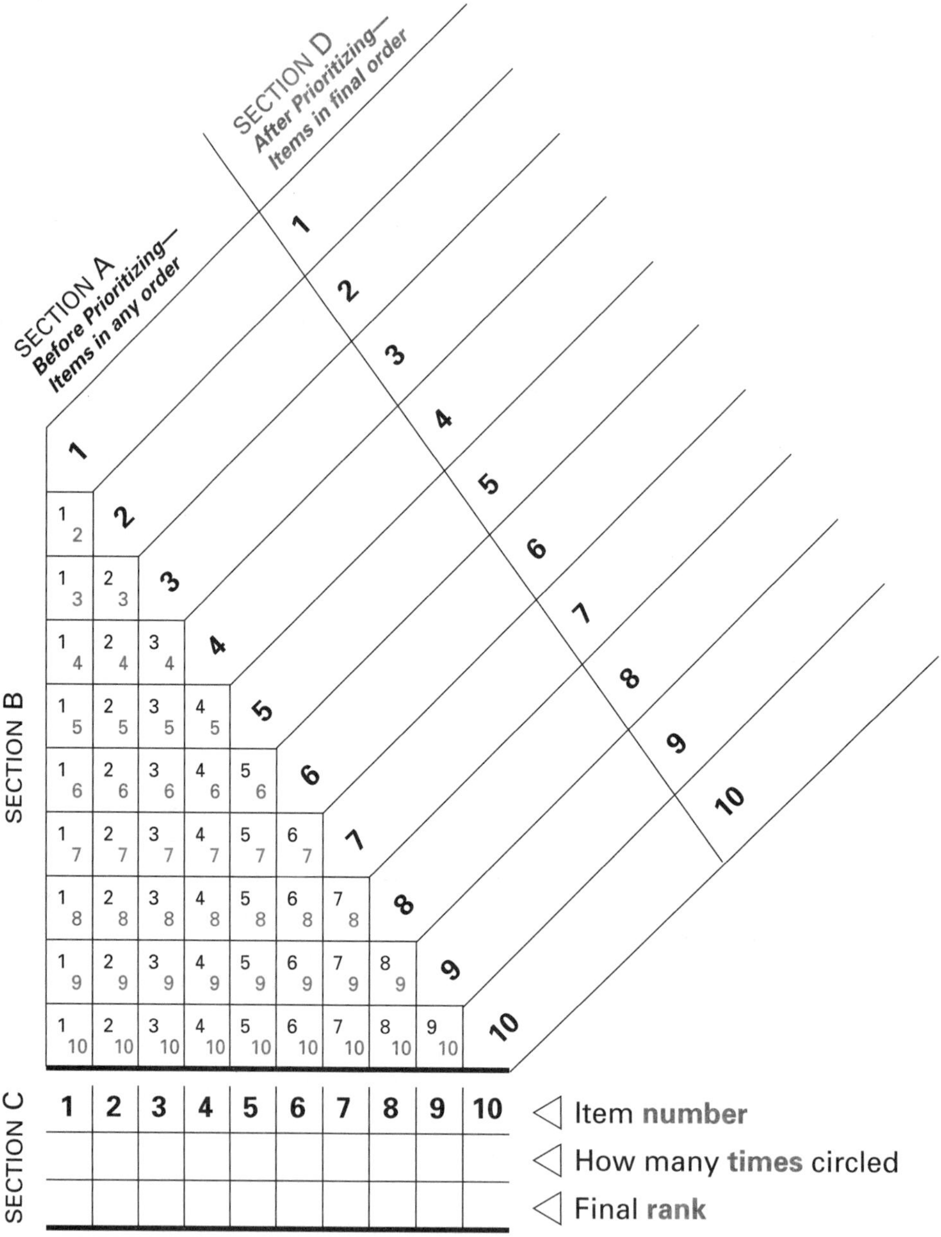

SECTION D
After Prioritizing—
Items in final order
SECTION A
Before Prioritizing—
Items in any order
SECTION B
SECTION C
1 2 3 4 5 6 7 8 9 10
Item number
How many times circled
Final rank

Prioritizing Grid for 10 Items

```
1  1  1  1  1  1  1  1  1  1  1  1  1  1  1  1  1  1  1  1  1  1  1
  2  3  4  5  6  7  8  9  10 11 12 13 14 15 16 17 18 19 20 21 22 23 24

2  2  2  2  2  2  2  2  2  2  2  2  2  2  2  2  2  2  2  2  2  2
  3  4  5  6  7  8  9  10 11 12 13 14 15 16 17 18 19 20 21 22 23 24

3  3  3  3  3  3  3  3  3  3  3  3  3  3  3  3  3  3  3  3  3
  4  5  6  7  8  9  10 11 12 13 14 15 16 17 18 19 20 21 22 23 24

4  4  4  4  4  4  4  4  4  4  4  4  4  4  4  4  4  4  4  4
  5  6  7  8  9  10 11 12 13 14 15 16 17 18 19 20 21 22 23 24

5  5  5  5  5  5  5  5  5  5  5  5  5  5  5  5  5  5  5
  6  7  8  9  10 11 12 13 14 15 16 17 18 19 20 21 22 23 24

6  6  6  6  6  6  6  6  6  6  6  6  6  6  6  6  6  6
  7  8  9  10 11 12 13 14 15 16 17 18 19 20 21 22 23 24

7  7  7  7  7  7  7  7  7  7  7  7  7  7  7  7  7
  8  9  10 11 12 13 14 15 16 17 18 19 20 21 22 23 24

8  8  8  8  8  8  8  8  8  8  8  8  8  8  8  8
  9  10 11 12 13 14 15 16 17 18 19 20 21 22 23 24

9  9  9  9  9  9  9  9  9  9  9  9  9  9  9
  10 11 12 13 14 15 16 17 18 19 20 21 22 23 24

10 10 10 10 10 10 10 10 10 10 10 10 10 10
  11 12 13 14 15 16 17 18 19 20 21 22 23 24

11 11 11 11 11 11 11 11 11 11 11 11 11
  12 13 14 15 16 17 18 19 20 21 22 23 24

12 12 12 12 12 12 12 12 12 12 12 12
  13 14 15 16 17 18 19 20 21 22 23 24

13 13 13 13 13 13 13 13 13 13 13
  14 15 16 17 18 19 20 21 22 23 24

14 14 14 14 14 14 14 14 14 14
  15 16 17 18 19 20 21 22 23 24

15 15 15 15 15 15 15 15 15
  16 17 18 19 20 21 22 23 24

16 16 16 16 16 16 16 16
  17 18 19 20 21 22 23 24

17 17 17 17 17 17 17
  18 19 20 21 22 23 24

18 18 18 18 18 18
  19 20 21 22 23 24

19 19 19 19 19
  20 21 22 23 24

20 20 20 20
  21 22 23 24

21 21 21
  22 23 24

22 22
  23 24

23
  24
```

Total times each number got circled.

1	2	3	4	5	6
7	8	9	10	11	12
13	14	15	16	17	18
19	20	21	22	23	24

Prioritizing Grid
for 24 Items

Once you've checked off your favorites, prioritize them (using another copy of the Prioritizing Grid if necessary), and then integrate your favorites into the building blocks of transferable skills below, then on The Flower.

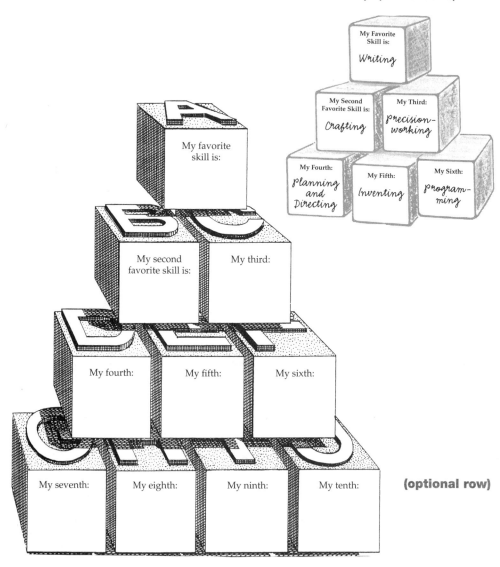

Example (Six Favorite Skills)

My Favorite Skill is: *Writing*

My Second Favorite Skill is: *Crafting*

My Third: *precision-working*

My Fourth: *planning and Directing*

My Fifth: *Inventing*

My Sixth: *programming*

My favorite skill is:

My second favorite skill is:

My third:

My fourth:

My fifth:

My sixth:

My seventh:

My eighth:

My ninth:

My tenth:

(optional row)

Chapter Ten

A Picture Is Worth a Thousand Words

When you have your top favorite skills in order, and *fleshed out*, it is time to put them on the central petal of the Flower Diagram.

The Flower
"That One Piece of Paper"

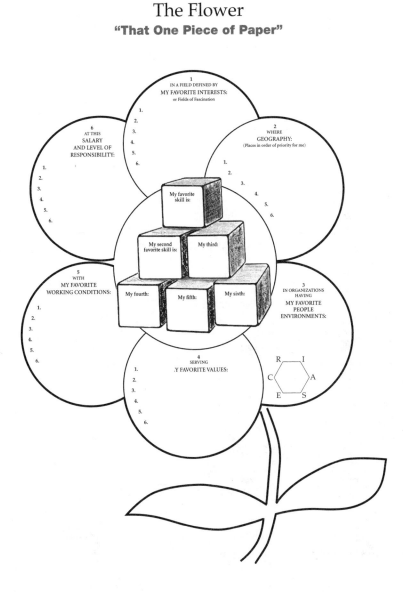

5. "Flesh Out" Your Favorite Transferable Skills with Your Traits

In general, traits describe:
How you deal with time, and promptness.
How you deal with people and emotions.
How you deal with authority, and being told what to do at your job.
How you deal with supervision, and being told how to do your job.
How you deal with impulse vs. self-discipline, within yourself.
How you deal with initiative vs. response, within yourself.
How you deal with crises or problems.

A CHECKLIST OF MY STRONGEST TRAITS
I am very . . .

- ❏ Accurate
- ❏ Achievement-oriented
- ❏ Adaptable
- ❏ Adept
- ❏ Adept at having fun
- ❏ Adventuresome
- ❏ Alert
- ❏ Appreciative
- ❏ Assertive
- ❏ Astute
- ❏ Authoritative
- ❏ Calm
- ❏ Cautious
- ❏ Charismatic
- ❏ Competent
- ❏ Consistent
- ❏ Contagious in my enthusiasm
- ❏ Cooperative
- ❏ Courageous
- ❏ Creative
- ❏ Decisive
- ❏ Deliberate
- ❏ Dependable/have dependability
- ❏ Diligent
- ❏ Diplomatic

- ❏ Discreet
- ❏ Driving
- ❏ Dynamic
- ❏ Extremely economical
- ❏ Effective
- ❏ Energetic
- ❏ Enthusiastic
- ❏ Exceptional
- ❏ Exhaustive
- ❏ Experienced
- ❏ Expert
- ❏ Firm
- ❏ Flexible
- ❏ Humanly oriented
- ❏ Impulsive
- ❏ Independent
- ❏ Innovative
- ❏ Knowledgeable
- ❏ Loyal
- ❏ Methodical
- ❏ Objective
- ❏ Open-minded
- ❏ Outgoing
- ❏ Outstanding
- ❏ Patient
- ❏ Penetrating
- ❏ Perceptive

- ❏ Persevering
- ❏ Persistent
- ❏ Pioneering
- ❏ Practical
- ❏ Professional
- ❏ Protective
- ❏ Punctual
- ❏ Quick/work quickly
- ❏ Rational
- ❏ Realistic
- ❏ Reliable
- ❏ Resourceful
- ❏ Responsible
- ❏ Responsive
- ❏ Safeguarding
- ❏ Self-motivated
- ❏ Self-reliant
- ❏ Sensitive
- ❏ Sophisticated, very sophisticated
- ❏ Strong
- ❏ Supportive
- ❏ Tactful
- ❏ Thorough
- ❏ Unique
- ❏ Unusual
- ❏ Versatile
- ❏ Vigorous

You need to *flesh out* your skill-description for each of those ten, so that you are able to describe each of your talents or skills with more than just a one-word verb or gerund, like *organizing*.

Let's take *organizing* as our example. You tell us proudly: "I'm good at *organizing*." That's a fine start at defining your skills, but unfortunately it doesn't yet tell us much. Organizing WHAT? *People*, as at a party? *Nuts and bolts*, as on a workbench? Or *lots of information*, as on a computer? These are three entirely different skills. The one word *organizing* doesn't tell us which one is *yours*.

So, please *flesh out* each of your favorite transferable skills with an object—some kind of *Data/Information*, or some kind of *People*, or some kind of *Thing*, and then add an adverb or adjective, too.

Why adjectives? Well, "I'm good at organizing information *painstakingly and logically*" and "I'm good at organizing information *in a flash, by intuition,*" are two *entirely different* skills. The difference between them is spelled out not in the verb, nor in the object, but in the adjectival or adverbial phrase there at the end. So, expand each definition of your ten favorite skills, in the fashion I have just described.

> When you are face-to-face with a person-who-has-the-power-to-hire-you, you want to be able to explain what makes you different from nineteen other people who can basically do the same thing that you can do. It is often the adjective or adverb that will save your life, during that explanation.

In trying to identify your skills, it will not be surprising if you run into some problems. Let us look at the five most common ones that have arisen for job-hunters in the past:

1. "When I write my skill stories, I don't know exactly what is an achievement."

When you're looking for a story/achievement to illustrate one of your skills, you're *not* looking for something that only you have done, in the history of the world. What you're looking for is a lot simpler than that. You're looking for *any* time in your life when you did something that was, at that time of your life, a source of pride and accomplishment *for you*. It might have been learning to ride a bike. It might be achieving your first quota, at work. It might be a particularly significant project that you designed, in mid-life. It doesn't matter whether or not it pleased anybody else; it only matters that it pleased you.

I like Bernard Haldane's definition of an achievement. He says it is: something you yourself feel you have done well, that you also enjoyed doing and felt proud of. In other words you are looking for an accomplishment which gave you two pleasures: enjoyment while doing it, and satisfaction from the outcome. That doesn't mean you may not have sweated as you did it, or hated *some parts* of the process, but it does mean that basically you enjoyed *most of* the process. The pleasure was not simply in the outcome, but along the way as well.

2. "I don't see why I should look for skills I enjoy; it seems to me that employers will only want to know what skills I do well. They will not care whether I enjoy using the skill or not."

Well, sure, it is important for you to find the skills you do well, above all else. But, generally speaking, that is hard for you to evaluate about yourself. *Do I do this well, or not? Compared to whom?* Even aptitude tests can't resolve this dilemma for you. So it's better to take the following circular equation, which experience has shown to be true:

If it is a skill you do well, you will generally enjoy it.

If it is a skill you enjoy, it is generally because you do it well.

With these equations in hand, you will see that—since they are equal anyway—it is much more useful to ask yourself, "Do I enjoy doing it?" instead of hunting for the elusive "Do I do it well?" I repeat: listing the skills you most *enjoy* is—in most cases—just another way of listing the skills you do *best*.

The reason why this idea—of making *enjoyment* the key—causes such feelings of uncomfortableness in so many of us is that we have an old historical tradition in this country which insinuates you shouldn't really enjoy yourself in life. To suffer is virtuous.

Sample: Two girls do babysitting. One hates it. One enjoys it thoroughly. Which is more virtuous in God's sight? According to that old tradition, the one who hates it is more virtuous. Some of us feel this instinctively, even if more logical thought says, Whoa!

We have this subconscious fear that if we are caught enjoying life, punishment looms. Thus, the story of two Scotsmen who met on the street one day: "Isn't this a beautiful day?" said one. "Aye," said the other, "but we'll pay for it."

We feel it is okay to talk about our failures, but not about our successes. To talk about our successes appears to be boasting, and that is manifestly a sin. Or so we think. We shouldn't be enjoying so much about ourselves.

But look at the birds of the air, or watch your pets at play. You will notice one distinctive fact about that part of God's creation: when a bird or a pet does what it is meant to do, by God and nature, it manifests true joy.

Joy is so clearly a part of God's plan for us. God wants us to eat; therefore He made eating enjoyable. God wants us to sleep; therefore He made sleeping enjoyable. God wants us to procreate, love, and make love; therefore He made sex enjoyable, and love even more so.

Likewise, God gives to each of us unique combinations of skills and talents which He wants us to contribute to His general plan—to the symphony of the world, and the music of the spheres. Therefore, **when we use the talents He most wants each of us to use, He attends it with a feeling of great joy.** Everywhere in God's plan for His creation, joy rewards right action.

Bad employers will not care whether you enjoy a particular task, or not. But good employers will care greatly. They know that unless a would-be employee has **enthusiasm** for his or her work, the quality of that work will always suffer.

3. *"I have no difficulty finding stories to write up, from my life, that I consider to be enjoyable achievements; but once these are written, I have great difficulty in seeing what the skills are—even if I stare at the skills keys in the Exercises for hours. I need somebody else's insight."*

You may want to consider getting two friends or two other members of your family to sit down with you, and do skill identification through the practice of "Trioing," which I invented some twenty years ago to help with this very problem. This practice is fully described in my book, *Where Do I Go From Here With My Life?* But to save you the trouble of reading it, here is—in general—how it goes:

a. Each of the three of you quietly writes up some story of an accomplishment in their life that was enjoyable.

b. Each of the three of you quietly analyzes just your own story to see what skills you see there; you jot these down.

c. One of you then volunteers to go first. You read your story aloud. The other two jot down on a piece of paper whatever skills they hear you using. They ask you to pause if they're having trouble keeping up. You finish your story. You read aloud the skills *you* picked out in that story.

d. Then the second person tells you what's on their list: what skills *they* heard you use in your story. You copy them down, below your own list, even if you don't agree with every one of them.

e. Then the third person tells you what's on their list; what skills *they* heard you use in your story. You copy them down, below your own list, even if you don't agree with every one of them.

f. When they're both done, you ask them any questions for further elaboration that you may have. *"What did you mean by this skill? Where did you think you heard me using it?"*

g. Now it is the next person's turn, and you repeat steps "c" through "f" with them. Then it is the third person's turn, and you repeat steps "c" through "f" with them.

h. Now it is time to move on to a second story for each of you, so you begin with steps "a" through "g" all over again, except that each of you writes a new story. And so on, through seven stories.

4. ***"I don't like the skill words you offer in the Exercises. Can't I use my own words, the ones I'm familiar with from my past profession?"***

It's okay to invent your own words for your skills, but it is not useful to state your transferable skills in the jargon of your old profession, such as (in the case of ex-clergy), *"I am good at preaching."* If you are going to choose a new career, out there in what people call the secular world, you must not use language that locks you into the past—or suggests that you were good in one profession but in one profession only. Therefore, it is important to take jargon words such as *preaching* and ask yourself what is its larger form? *"Teaching?"* Perhaps. *"Motivating people?"* Perhaps. *"Inspiring people to the depths of their being?"* Perhaps. Only you can say what is true, for you. But in one way or another be sure to get your skills out of any jargon that locks you into your past career.

5. ***"Once I've listed my favorite transferable skills, I see immediately a job-title that they point to. Is that okay?"***

Nope. Once you've finished your skill-identification, steer clear of prematurely putting a job-title on the skills you see. Skills can point to *many* different jobs, which have a multitude of titles. Therefore, don't lock yourself in, prematurely. *"I'm looking for a job where I can **use** the following skills,"* is fine. But, *"I'm looking for a job where I can **be** a (job-title)"* is a no-no, at this point in your job-hunt. Always define WHAT you want to do with your life and WHAT you have, to offer to the world, in terms of your favorite talents/gifts/skills—not in terms of a job-title. That way, you can stay mobile in the midst of this constantly changing economy, where you never know what's going to happen next.

Conclusions: Shortcuts

I know, I know, you look at this whole process and it just feels like too much work. You want something shorter, briefer, either on or off the Internet, that you can turn to.

Okay, here's a shortcut toward identifying your favorite transferable skills. Following is a List. It is, in fact, a *sampler* of skill-verbs, to help you quickly identify your favorite.

The way in which this list is typically used by job-hunters or career-changers is to put a check mark in front of each skill that:

a) you believe you possess.

And a separate check mark in front of each skill that:

b) you also enjoy doing.

And a separate check mark in front of each skill that:

c) you also believe you do well.

Thus a skill could end up with three check marks—and these, in fact, are the skills you want to look the hardest at, to see what kind of job they suggest:

Internet Shortcuts: Transferable Skills Tests

We saw in the last chapter that there are a number of *tests*, or *assessment instruments* that are available to help you figure out what you want to do with your life.

What we want to know now is: are there tests specifically focussed on Identifying Transferable Skills?

And the answer is, Oh yes, indeed there are. Here's a sampler:

▶ "Transferable Skills" and "Transferable Skills Checklist" from the State of Wisconsin's Department of Workforce Development

`www.dwd.state.wi.us/dwd/`
    `publications/223e_28a.htm`

Very thorough checklist, though it does not point to particular jobs.

▶ Internet Transferable Skills Analysis with
O*Net by VocRehab
`www.vocrehab.com/webtsa.htm`

This site has a very well-done analysis available for U.S. job-hunters *in particular,* which points you to particular jobs, using

The Secret to Finding Your Dream Job

A List of 246 Skills as Verbs

achieving	acting	adapting	addressing	administering
advising	analyzing	anticipating	arbitrating	arranging
ascertaining	assembling	assessing	attaining	auditing
budgeting	building	calculating	charting	checking
classifying	coaching	collecting	communicating	compiling
completing	composing	computing	conceptualizing	conducting
conserving	consolidating	constructing	controlling	coordinating
coping	counseling	creating	deciding	defining
delivering	designing	detailing	detecting	determining
developing	devising	diagnosing	digging	directing
discovering	dispensing	displaying	disproving	dissecting
distributing	diverting	dramatizing	drawing	driving
editing	eliminating	empathizing	enforcing	establishing
estimating	evaluating	examining	expanding	experimenting
explaining	expressing	extracting	filing	financing
fixing	following	formulating	founding	gathering
generating	getting	giving	guiding	handling
having responsibility	heading	helping	hypothesizing	identifying
illustrating	imagining	implementing	improving	improvising
increasing	influencing	informing	initiating	innovating
inspecting	inspiring	installing	instituting	instructing
integrating	interpreting	interviewing	intuiting	inventing
inventorying	investigating	judging	keeping	leading
learning	lecturing	lifting	listening	logging
maintaining	making	managing	manipulating	mediating
meeting	memorizing	mentoring	modeling	monitoring
motivating	navigating	negotiating	observing	obtaining
offering	operating	ordering	organizing	originating
overseeing	painting	perceiving	performing	persuading
photographing	piloting	planning	playing	predicting
preparing	prescribing	presenting	printing	problem solving
processing	producing	programming	projecting	promoting
proofreading	protecting	providing	publicizing	purchasing
questioning	raising	reading	realizing	reasoning
receiving	recommending	reconciling	recording	recruiting
reducing	referring	rehabilitating	relating	remembering
rendering	repairing	reporting	representing	researching
resolving	responding	restoring	retrieving	reviewing
risking	scheduling	selecting	selling	sensing
separating	serving	setting	setting-up	sewing
shaping	sharing	showing	singing	sketching
solving	sorting	speaking	studying	summarizing
supervising	supplying	symbolizing	synergizing	synthesizing
systematizing	taking instructions	talking	teaching	team-building
telling	tending	testing & proving	training	transcribing
translating	traveling	treating	trouble-shooting	tutoring
typing	umpiring	understanding	understudying	undertaking
unifying	uniting	upgrading	using	utilizing
verbalizing	washing	weighing	winning	working
writing				

the U.S. O*Net system. This site is geared toward vocational re-hab professionals and the like, and you must register to use their services; but they do offer the first transferable skills analy-sis test for free.

▶ **Transferable Skills Sets for Job-Hunters**
   `www.quintcareers.com/transferable_skills.html`
There are links to some good articles on transferable skills, in-cluding a very good skills list, here at Quintessential Careers.

▶ **Assessing Your Skills and Accomplishments**
   `www.uwrf.edu/ccs/assessskills.htm`
Another good article, with an even better skills list

▶ **Transferable Skills Survey**
   `www.d.umn.edu/student/loon/car/self/`
      `career_transfer_survey.html`
An online skills assessment; free

▶ **Career Tests at HotJobs**
   `http://hotjobs.careerid.com/articles.html`
Yahoo!Hotjobs has skills tests here. The tests are free, although you must register

And now, on to **WHERE?**

*A Systematic Approach to
the Job-Hunt and Career-Change:*

PART II

Where

Do You Want to
Use Your Skills?

Your heart has its own geography, where it prefers to be. It may be by a mountain stream. It may be in the Alps. It may be in the hustle and bustle of the streets of London or New York. It may be on an Oregon farm. It may be in a beach town. It may be in the quiet recollection of your own backyard. Your heart knows the places that it loves.

Likewise, your mind has its own geography, where it prefers to be. It may be among books on psychology. It may be among books of art. It may be among books of romances. It may be books of travel. It may be books on business trends. It may be on computers. Your mind knows the subjects that it loves.

Your body also has its own geography, where it prefers to be. It may be walking in the hills. It may be in a yoga class. It may be working out with weights. It may be in a marathon. It may be on a bicycle path. It may be in a physical therapy class. It may be in the local gym. It may be on a basketball court. It may be with massage. Your body knows the workout that it loves.

Your soul, too, has its own geography, where it prefers to be. It may be in a quiet place, it may be in a church, or synagogue or mosque. It may be among honest folk. It may be among those

190

Chapter Ten

who're fixed on a kind of social change. It may be almost any-where, where the values you prize—community, God, compassion, generosity, faith—are valued still by others. Your soul knows the values that it loves.

Therefore, my friend, what "a dream job" is all about (beyond skills) is identifying these favorite geographies, defining for yourself the *places* that your skills, your soul, and body, heart and mind, most often yearn to be.

If you would find your dream job, then, you must define these things.

There are two ways to approach this task—the *intuitional "leap-to-a-conclusion"* way, and the more labored, logical, step-by-step way. This *hurry-up* culture in which we live values most the method that is quick. Intuition is quick, and sometimes can provide just the clues you're looking for. So it is there that we begin.

Where you use your favorite skills, where you do your favorite tasks is largely a matter of what "field" you choose to use your skills in. Hence, these are the kinds of intuitions you should be searching your heart about:

Intuitions

Toward deciding WHERE, *in a dream job,*
your skills, your soul and body, heart and mind,
would most like to be.

1 What are your favorite interests *(Computers? Gardening? Span-
ish? Law? Physics? Department stores? Hospitals? etc., etc.)?* If
you just can't think of any favorite interest, ask yourself: "If
I could talk about *something* with someone all day long, day
after day, what would that subject or field of interest be? *Or,* if
I were stuck on a desert island with a person who only had the
capacity to speak on a few subjects, what would I pray those
subjects were?"

If you turn out to have more than one favorite interest, take
two of them at a time, and ask yourself: if you were in a conversation with someone covering two of your favorite subjects at
once, toward which of the two interests would you try to steer
the conversation. Repeat with another pair of favorite subjects,
and keep "sifting down."

2 What are your favorite subjects—the ones you're drawn to
in magazines, libraries, bookstores, trade expos, and so
forth? It doesn't have to be a subject you studied in school. It can
be a field that you just picked up along the way in life—say, *antiques,* or *cars,* or *interior decorating,* or *music* or *movies* or *psychology,* or *the kind of subjects that come up on television "game shows."*

The only important thing is that you *like* the subject a lot, and
that you picked up a working knowledge of it—who cares where
or how? As the late John Crystal used to say, it doesn't matter
whether you learned it in college, or sitting at the end of a log.

Let's take *antiques* as an example. Suppose it's one of your favorite subjects, yet you never studied it in school. You picked up
your knowledge of antiques by going around to antique stores,
and asking lots of questions. And you supplemented this by
reading a few books on the subject, and you subscribe to an antiques magazine. You've also bought a few antiques, yourself.
That's enough, for you to put *antiques,* on your list of fields/in-
terests/languages. Your degree of *mastery* of this whole field of

antiques is irrelevant—*unless you want to work at a level in the field that demands and requires* mastery.

3 What are your favorite words? Every field has its own peculiar language, vocabulary, or jargon. What words or jargon do you like to use, or listen to, the most?

To illustrate this, I'll *freeze* the job-title or skills, for a moment. I'll choose "secretary." By looking then at different kinds of *secretary*, we can see how favorite *words* can give you a helpful clue about where you might like to find your dream job.

For example, if you work as a legal secretary, you have to endure a lot of talk there, all day long, about *legal procedures*. Do you like that vocabulary and *language*? If so, consider law as the field you might work in—for your next job or career.

Again, if you work as a secretary at a gardening store, there's a lot of talk there, all day long, about gardens and such. Do you like that vocabulary and *language*? If so, consider gardening as the field you might work in—for your next job or career.

If you work as a secretary at an airline, there's a lot of talk there, all day long, about airlines procedures and such. Do you like that vocabulary and *language*? If so, consider the airlines as the field you might work in—for your next job or career.

If you work as a secretary at a church, there's a lot of talk there, all day long, about church procedures and matters of faith. Do you like that vocabulary and *language*? If so, consider religion as the field you might work in—for your next job or career.

And so it continues. If you work as a secretary in a photographic laboratory, there's a lot of talk there, all day long, about photographic procedures. Do you like that vocabulary and *language*? If so, choose photography as the field you might work in—for your next job or career.

Again, if you work as a secretary at a chemical plant, there's a lot of talk there, all day long, about chemicals manufacturing. Do you like that vocabulary and *language*? If so, consider the chemical industry as the field you might work in—for your next job or career.

If you work as a secretary for the federal government, there's a lot of talk there, all day long, about government procedures.

Do you like that vocabulary and *language*? If so, consider government work as the field you might work in—for your next job or career.

And so it goes. The point is not that you should be a secretary. I just *froze* the job-title and skills for a moment, so that you could see how many different fields you might use those skills in.

All of this proceeds from a simple intuition: the source of joy in your dream job derives, to a great extent, from the fact that you enjoy the *language* and vocabulary that you will be speaking or listening to all day long (provided, of course, that you also get to use your favorite skills there).

Whereas, if you don't enjoy the vocabulary or *language* that is spoken at work—you want to talk about *gardening* but you work at a place where *law* (which has a vocabulary you hate) is what you have to listen to, and work with, all day long—then you are not going to like that job or career.

4 Once you know what subjects, fields, interests, vocabulary, etc., fascinate you the most, look back at your answers to *What skills you most enjoy,* and see if you can put skills and subjects together, in terms of a particular job. For example, if you love to work with figures *(financial, that is),* and your favorite field is hospitals, you would want to think about working in the accounting department at a hospital.

5 Once you have some idea of what jobs interest you, go visit places where those jobs are, and talk to people doing those jobs, to see if this job or career *really* interests you, or not. This is called "informational interviewing." Fancy name for *informal research.*

6 If you have decided to try a new career or go into a new field (for you), and you are dismayed at how much preparation it looks as though it would take, go talk to people doing that work. And don't look for the rules or generalizations. Look for the exceptions to the rules. For example, everyone may tell you the rule is: *"In order to do this work you have to have a master's degree and ten years' experience at it."* So what? That's a statement about the majority of people in this field. You want to find out about the exceptions. *"Yes, but do you know of anyone in the field who*

hasn't gone and gotten all those credentials? And where might I find him or her? I need to find out how they did it."

7 If you have decided to try to stay with your old career *(which you lost through downsizing or whatever)* then you need to find "leads." You find them by asking yourself the question: *"Who might be interested in the skills and problem-solving that I learned at my last job?"*

For example, ask yourself who you served in your last job, or came in contact with, *who might be in a position to hire someone with your talents.*

Ask yourself who supplied training or staff development in your last company or field; *do you think any of them might be interested in hiring you?* (Ask them.)

Ask yourself what machines or technology you learned, mastered, improved on, at your last job; *and, who is interested in those machines or technology?*

Ask yourself what raw materials *(e.g., Kodak paper in a darkroom)*, equipment or support services you used at your last job; *would any of those suppliers know of other places where their equipment or support services are used?*

Ask yourself who were the subcontractors, outsourcing agencies, or temp agencies that were used at your last job; *would any of them be interested in hiring you?*

Ask yourself what community or service organizations were interested in your projects at your last job; *would any of them be interested in hiring you?*[7]

Step-by-Step
Ways of deciding WHERE, in a dream job,
your soul and body, heart and mind, would most like to be.

Well, that's about it, for the *intuitional approach* to finding your favorite fields of fascination. Now we turn to the other approach, where we go *step-by-step*, using "That One Piece of Paper" again, with its Flower graphic.

---

7. These suggestions courtesy of Chuck Young, former Administrator for the Oregon Commission on the Blind; and Martin Kimeldorf, career counselor and author.

Your Favorite Interests, or "Fields of Fascination"

We are talking here about the major element of "Where?" It follows on the heels of "What?" "What transferable skills, that you have, do you most enjoy using?"

"Where?" is a matter of "Where would you most like to use your favorite skills?" In other words, we are talking about Fields, and particularly, those Fields that fascinate you.

Now, there are three basic kinds of Fields or Interests that you may have:

1. Fields That Use Your Mental Skills (the "Subjects list")

2. Fields Dealing with People's Problems or Needs (the "People list")

3. Fields Dealing with Things, Tools, or Products (the "Things list")

Let us do some exercises, dealing with each of them in turn:

1. Fields That Use Your Mental Skills

Before you begin looking at Fields, you must fight against the natural tendency to think that a Field will automatically determine what job you will do. It does not.

Think of a Field of Knowledge as, literally, *a field*—a meadow, a *large* meadow. Lots of people are standing in that meadow, or Field, no matter what Field it is. And they have many different skills, do many different things, have many different job titles.

Let us take the Field called "Movies" as our example. Suppose you love Movies, and want to choose this Field for your next job or career. Your first instinct will be to think that this automatically means you have to be either *an actor or actress, or a screenwriter, or a director, or a movie critic.* Not so. There are many other people standing out in that Field, helping to produce Movies. Just look at the closing credits at the end of any movie, and you will see: *researchers (especially for movies set in another time), travel experts (to scout locations), interior designers (to design sets), carpenters (to build them), painters (for backdrops, etc.), artists, computer graphics designers (for special effects), costume designers, makeup artists, hair stylists, photographers (camera operators), lighting technicians, sound mixers and sound editors, composers (for soundtrack), conductors, musicians, singers, stunt people, animal trainers, caterers, drivers, first-aid people, personal assistants, secretaries, publicists, accountants, etc., etc.* My, there are a lot of people standing in that Field—some of whom are *outstanding* in their Field!

And so it is with any Field. No matter what your skills are, they *can* be used in *any* meadow or Field that you may choose as your favorite.

For some people, incidentally, Subjects yield *the least* helpful information about future Fields. Reason? Subjects often *don't* point to jobs. Example? Liberal Arts. But, might as well inventory everything we've learned so far, *just in case* (using the exercise called **The Subjects Chart**). *Then* you can go on to the exercise called **The People List**, and then the exercise called **The Things Phone Book**).

Everyone has mental skills.

Your mental skills are such things as: *the ability to gather information, to analyze information, to organize information, to present information,* and the like. The question here is: **what kinds of information, subjects, bodies of knowledge, ideas, or languages, do you like to use your mental skills with?**

In order for you to answer this question, it is helpful to fill out the following chart; *you may first copy it onto a larger piece of paper, if you wish, in order to have more room to write.*

Please note that this chart is asking you what subjects you know *anything* about, whether you *like* the subject or not. (*Later*, you will ask yourself which of these you like or even *love*.) For now, the task facing you is merely *inventory*. That is a task similar to inventorying what clothes you've got in your closet, before you decide which ones to give away. Only, here, *the closet is your head*, and you're inventorying all the stuff that's in *there*. Don't try to evaluate your degree of mastery of a particular subject. Put down something you've only read a few articles about *(if it interests you)* side by side with a subject you studied for three semesters in school.

Throwaway comes later *(though, obviously, if there's a subject you hate so much you can barely stand to write it down, then . . . don't . . . write . . . it . . . down).*

When filling this chart out, do not forget to list those things you've learned—no matter how—about *Organizations (including volunteer organizations),* and what it takes to make them work.

It is not necessary that you should have ever taken a course in management or business. As the late John Crystal used to say, "Who cares *how* you learned it, whether in school or by sitting on the end of a log?" Examples of things you may know something about (and should list here) are: *accounting or bookkeeping; administration; applications; credit collection of overdue bills; customer relations and service; data analysis; distribution; fiscal analysis, controls, reductions; government contracts; group dynamics or work with groups in general; hiring, human resources; or manpower; international business; management; marketing, sales; merchandising; packaging; performance specifications; planning; policy development; problem solving or other types of troubleshooting with operations or management systems; production; public speaking/addressing people; R & D program management; recruiting; show or conference planning, organization and management; systems analysis; travel or travel planning, especially international travel; etc.*

The Subjects Chart

Which column you decide to put a subject in, below, doesn't matter at all. The columns are only a series of pegs, to hang your memories on. Which peg is of no concern. Jot down a subject anywhere you like.

Column 1	Column 2	Column 3	Column 4	Column 5
Studied in High School or College or Graduate School	Learned on the Job	Learned from Conferences, Workshops, Training, Seminars	Learned at Home: Reading, TV, Tape Programs, Study Courses	Learned in My Leisure Time: Volunteer Work, Hobbies, etc.
Examples: Spanish, Typing, Accounting, Computer Literacy, Psychology, Geography	*Examples: Publishing, Computer graphics, How an organization works, How to operate various machines*	*Examples: Welfare rules, Job-hunting, Painting, How to use the Internet*	*Examples: Art Appreciation, History, Speed Reading, A Language*	*Examples: Landscaping, How to sew, Antiques, Camping, Stamps*

The Secret to Finding Your Dream Job

199

Prioritizing
"The Subjects Chart"

When you're done, you may want to let this Chart just sit on your refrigerator door for a few days, while you see if there's anything you want to add.

But when you're sure you've listed all you want to, on the chart, it is crucial then to sort and then prioritize all these subjects. See the Prioritizing Grids on pages 178 and 179.

When you've got your ten prioritized Subjects, then go on to the next item, here.

✳ 2. Fields Dealing with
People's Problems or Needs

Now, on to the Fields category.

The question here is: **if you like to help people, what problems or needs do you like to help them with?** Each of these is a field.

In order to answer this question, it is helpful to fill out either of two kinds of exercises: *A checklist,* or *"fill in the blank."* Better yet, the two together, *like this:*

---

1. Check off any kind of need you think you *might* like to help people with, and then
2. Add *which part of it,* or *what aspect of it,* you find particularly interesting or *appealing.*

The People List

I'd like to help people with their need for:

❑ **Clothing** (people's need to find and choose appropriate and affordable clothing); *and in my case what interests me particularly is*_____.

❑ **Food** (people's need to be fed, to be saved from starvation or poor nutrition) *and in my case what interests me particularly is*_____.

❑ **Housing and real estate** (people's need to find appropriate and affordable housing, apartment, office, or land); *and in my case what interests me particularly is*_____.

❑ **Languages** (people's need for literacy, to be able to read, or to learn a new language); *and in my case what interests me particularly is*_____.

❑ **Personal services or service occupations** (people's need to have someone do tasks they can't do, or haven't time to do, or don't want to do, for themselves—ranging from childcare to helping run a farm); *and in my case what interests me particularly is*_____.

❑ **Family and consumer economics** (people's need to have help with budgeting, taxes, financial planning, money management, etc.); *and in my case what interests me particularly is*_____.

❑ **Retail sales** (people's need for help in buying something); *and in my case what interests me particularly is*_____.

❑ **Automobile sales** (people's need for transportation); *and in my case what interests me particularly is*_____.

❑ **Legal services** (people's need for expert counseling concerning the legal implications of things they are doing, or things that have been done to them); *and in my case what interests me particularly is*_____.

❑ **Child development** (people's need for help with various problems as their children are moving from infancy through childhood, including behavioral disabilities); *and in my case what interests me particularly is*_____.

❑ **Physical fitness** (people's need to get their body in tune through physical or occupational therapy, body-work, exercise, or diet); *and in my case what interests me particularly is*_____.

❑ **Health services** (people's need to have preventative medicine or help with ailments, allergies, and disease); *and in my case what interests me particularly is*_____.

❑ **Healing including alternative medicine and holistic health** (people's need to have various injuries, ailments, maladies, or diseases healed); *and in my case what interests me particularly is*_____.

❑ **Medicine** (people's need to have help with diagnosing, treating various diseases, or removing diseased or badly injured parts of their body, etc.); *and in my case what interests me particularly is*_____.

☑ **Mental health** (people's need for help with stress, depression, insomnia, or other forms of emotional or mental disturbance); *and in my case what interests me particularly is*_____.

☑ **Psychology or psychiatry** (people's need for help with mental illness); *and in my case what interests me particularly is*_____.

☑ **Personal counseling and guidance** (people's need for help with family relations, with dysfunctions, or with various crises in their life, including a lack of balance in their use of time); *and in my case what interests me particularly is*_____.

☑ **Career counseling, career-change, or life/work planning** (people's need for help in choosing a career or planning a holistic life); *and in my case what interests me particularly is*_____.

❑ **Job-hunting, job-placement, or vocational rehabilitation** (people's need to have help in finding the work they have chosen, particularly when handicapped, or unemployed, or enrolling for welfare under the new regulations); *and in my case what interests me particularly is*_____.

☑ **Training or learning** (people's need to learn more about something, at work or outside of work); *and in my case what interests me particularly is*_____.

❑ **Entertainment** (people's need to be entertained, by laughter, wit, intelligence, or beauty); *and in my case what interests me particularly is*_____.

☑ **Spirituality or religion** (people's need to learn as much as they can about God, character, and their own soul, including their values and principles); *and in my case what interests me particularly is_____*.

❑ **I'm interested in working with animals or plants** (their need for nurturing, growth, health, and other life cycles that require the kinds of sensitivities often referred to as interpersonal skills); *and in my case what interests me particularly is_____*.

❑ **Other fields** (or people's needs) not listed above, or a new field I just invented
(I think): _____.

In each question where it says *". . . and in my case what interests me particularly is . . ."* think whether or not there are *particular age groups* you prefer to work with, *a particular gender* you prefer to work with (*or sexual orientation*), and whether you prefer to work with *individuals or groups, people of a particular background or set of beliefs, or people in a particular place (the Armed Forces, government, prison, mental institutions, etc.).* If so, write it in.

Prioritizing "The People List"

When you're done, you may want to let this List just sit on your refrigerator door for a few days, while you see if there's anything you want to add.

But when you're sure you've listed all you want to, on the List, it is crucial then to sort and then prioritize these Fields. See the Prioritizing Grids on pages 178 and 179.

3. Fields Dealing with Things, Tools, or Products

When you're done with the People list, go on to this third Fields list.

The question here is: **what things or products interest you the most?** (A product may be "a service," incidentally.)

Sampler: do you love to deal with, handle, construct, operate, market, or repair: *airplanes, antiques, bicycles, blueprints, books, bridges, clothing, computers, crops, diagrams, electricity, electronics, drugs, farms, farm machinery, fish, flowers, gardens, groceries, guidebooks, houses, kitchen appliances, lawns, machines, magazines, makeup, manuals, medicines, minerals, money, music, musical instruments, newspapers, office machines, paints, paper, plants, radios, rivers, rooms, sailboats, security systems, sewing machines, skiing equipment, soil, telephones, toiletries, tools, toys, trains, trees, valuable objects, videotapes, wine, wood*—or what?

What things or products do you *love* to deal with? In order to answer this question, you need to compile *a list*. And it is important that it is complete—that is, it's important that it list *all* the things or products that you love to deal with, in any way, shape, or form.

So, the brief *Sampler* above will not do. You need a longer list, and one that identifies what Fields those *things or products* are in. Fortunately, there is such a directory—at your very fingertips. It's called: *the yellow pages*, from your local telephone company. It has it all: things, products, fields, *and*—what you'll need later—the *location* of relevant organizations in your chosen geographical area.

If you don't plan to stay in your current community for this next job-hunt or career-change, then you will want to write to the phone company in the geographical area you are planning to move to, and secure *its* phone book. In the meantime, you can use the local phone directory for this exercise (just ignore locations).

The Secret to Finding Your Dream Job　　　　　　　　**205**

The instructions for this exercise are simple. Go through the *table of contents* or *the index* of *the yellow pages* (in a phone book you don't mind marking up), and highlight any and every category or field where you think you *might* like to deal with, or handle, or construct, or operate, or market, or repair *that thing, product, or service*. It is best to work your way backward, from Z to A. Then, go back, and looking only at the items you highlighted, circle in *red* the ones that you care the most about. Jot down their names on the next page.

Prioritizing
"The *Things* Phone Book"

When you're done, you may want to let this Phone Book exercise just sit on your refrigerator door for a few days, while you see if there's anything you want to add.

But when you're sure you've listed all you want to, on the Phone Book exercise, it is crucial then to sort and then prioritize all these "Things" Fields. Use the Prioritizing Grids on pages 178 and 179.

Putting All Your
Favorite Fields Together

And now that you are done with all three Fields lists, it is time to put all three lists together, and make one unified list of Your Favorite Fields.

And then, choose your top five Favorite Fields, and copy them on the Favorite Interests/Fields of Fascination petal on page 152.

Chapter Ten

The *Things* Phone Book

_____   _____   _____   _____

_____   _____   _____   _____

_____   _____   _____   _____

_____   _____   _____   _____

_____   _____   _____   _____

_____   _____   _____   _____

_____   _____   _____   _____

_____   _____   _____   _____

_____   _____   _____   _____

_____   _____   _____   _____

_____   _____   _____   _____

_____   _____   _____   _____

_____   _____   _____   _____

_____   _____   _____   _____

_____   _____   _____   _____

_____   _____   _____   _____

_____   _____   _____   _____

_____   _____   _____   _____

_____   _____   _____   _____

Your Favorite Places To Live
(Geography)

The Point of this Petal: To answer this question: *to the degree you have a choice—now or down the line—where would you most like to live?*

Why This is Important for You to Know: Human beings are like flowers. Our soul flourishes in some environs, but withers and dies—or at least becomes extremely unhappy—in others.

What You Want to Beware of: Thinking that where you live is not important. Or thinking, if you have a partner, and you each want to live in different places, that one of you can get their way, but the other is going to have to give up *their* dream. Nonsense! If this were part of a course about Thinking, what would the Lesson be? The subject of the Lesson would be: how can two partners, who initially disagree, learn to agree on a place where both get what they want.

Now, of course, *Chapter 7, Where on Earth Do You Want to Live?* may have already solved this question for you. But in case it didn't, and you still haven't got a clue, there is an interesting exercise you can do. It begins with your past *(the places where you used to live)*, and extracts from it some information that is tremendously useful in plotting your future.

It is particularly useful when you have a partner, and the two of you can't seem to agree on where you want to live.

1. Copy the chart that is on pages 212 and 213, onto a larger *(e.g., 24" x 36")* piece of paper or cardboard, which you can obtain from any Wal-Mart, Target, Office Depot/Office Max, or arts and crafts store, in your town or city. If you are doing this exercise with a partner, make a copy for them too, so that each of you is working on a clean copy of your own, and can follow these instructions independently.

2. In *Column 1,* list all the places where you have ever lived.

3. In *Column 2,* list all the factors you disliked (and still dislike) about each place. The factors do not have to be put exactly opposite the name in *Column 1.* The names in *Column 1* exist simply to jog your memory. Once you have listed the negative factors each place reminds you of (e.g., "the sun never shone, there") you can cross out that place's name in *Column 1.*

   If, as you go, you remember some good things about that place, put *those* factors at the bottom of the next column, *Column 3.*

   If the same factors keep repeating, from place after place, just put a checkmark after the first listing of that factor, each time it repeats.

   Keep going until you have listed the factors you hated about each and every place you named in *Column 1.* Now, in effect, throw away *Column 1;* discard it from your thoughts. The negative factors were what you were after. *Column 1* has served its purpose.

4. In *Column 3,* you look at the negative factors you listed in *Column 2,* and try to list each one's opposite. For example, "the sun never shone, there" would, in *Column 3,* be turned into "mostly sunny, all year 'round." It will not always be *the exact opposite.* For example, the negative factor "rains all the time" does not necessarily translate into the positive: "sunny all the time." It might be something more like "sunny at least 200 days a year." It's your call. Keep going, until every negative factor in *Column 2* is turned into its opposite, a positive factor,

in *Column 3*. At the bottom, note the positive factors you already listed there, that you thought of, when you were working on *Column 2*.

5. In *Column 4*, now, list the positive factors in *Column 3*, in the order of most important (to you), down to least important (to you). For example, if you were looking at, and trying to name a new town, city, or place, where you could be happy, and flourish, what is the first thing you would look for? Would it be, say, good weather? or lack of crime? or good schools? or access to cultural opportunities, such as music, art, museums, or whatever? or would it be inexpensive housing? etc., etc. Rank all the factors in *Column 4*. Use the Priority Grids (pages 178 and 179) if you need to.

6. If you are doing this by yourself, list on a *scribble sheet* the top ten factors, in order of importance to you, and show it to everyone you meet for the next ten days, with the question: "Can you think of any places that have these ten factors, or at least the first five?" Jot down their suggestions on the back of the *scribble sheet*. When the ten days are up, look at the back of your sheet and circle the three places others suggested, that look the most interesting to you. If there is only a partial overlap between your dream factors and the places your friends and acquaintances suggested, be sure the overlap is in the factors that count the most. Now you have some names that you will want to find out more about, until you are sure which is your absolute favorite place to live, and then your second, and third, as backups.

   Put the names of the three places, and/or your top five factors, on **That One Piece of Paper** with the Flower Graphic, on the Geography petal.

7. If you are doing this with a partner, skip *Column 5*. Instead, when you have finished your *Column 4*, look at your partner's *Column 4*, and copy it into *Column 6*. The numbering of *your* list in *Column 4* was 1, 2, 3, 4, etc. Number your partner's list, as you copy it into *Column 6*, as a., b., c., d., etc.

8. Now, in *Column 7*, combine your *Column 4* with *Column 6* (your partner's old *Column 4*, renumbered). Both of you can work now from just one person's chart. Combine the two lists as illustrated on the chart. First your partner's top favorite geographical factor ("a."), then *your* top favorite geographical factor ("1."), then your partner's second most important favorite geographical factor ("b."), then *yours* ("2."), etc., until you have ten or fifteen favorite geographical factors *(yours and your partner's)* listed, in order, in *Column 7*.

9. List on a *scribble sheet* the top ten factors, and both of you show it to everyone you meet, for the next ten days, with the same question as above: "Can you think of any places that have these ten factors, or at least the first five?" Jot down their suggestions on the back of the *scribble sheet*. When the ten days are up, you and your partner should look at the back of your sheet and circle the three places others suggested, that look the most interesting to the two of you. If there is only a partial overlap between your dream factors and the places your friends and acquaintances suggested, be sure the overlap is in the factors that count the most to the two of you, i.e., the ones that are at the top of your list in *Column 7*. Now you have some names of places that would make you both happy, that you will want to find out more about, until you are sure which is the absolute favorite place to live for both of you, and then your second, and third, as backups.

Put the names of the top three places, and/or your top six factors, on **That One Piece of Paper** with the Flower Graphic, on number two, the Geography petal.

Conclusion: Was all of this too much work? Then do what one family did: they put a map of the U.S. up on a corkboard, and then they each threw a dart at the map from a few feet away, and when they were done they saw where the most darts landed. It turned out to be around "Denver." So, *Denver* it was!

The Secret to Finding Your Dream Job

My Geographical Preferences
Decision Making for Just You

Column 1 Names of Places I Have Lived	*Column 2* From the Past: Negatives	*Column 3* Translating the Negatives into Positives	*Column 4* Ranking of My Positives
	Factors I Disliked and Still Dislike About That Place		1. 2. 3. 4. 5. 6. 7. 8. 9. 10. 11. 12. 13. 14. 15.
	Factors I Liked and Still Like About That Place		

Column 5 Places That Fit These Criteria	Column 6 Ranking of His/Her Preferences	Column 7 Combining Our Two Lists (Columns 4 & 6)	Column 8 Places That Fit These Criteria

Our Geographical Preferences
Decision Making for You and a Partner

Column 5 Places That Fit These Criteria	Column 6 Ranking of His/Her Preferences	Column 7 Combining Our Two Lists (Columns 4 & 6)	Column 8 Places That Fit These Criteria
	a.	a. 1.	
	b.	b. 2.	
	c.	c. 3.	
	d.	d. 4.	
	e.	e. 5.	
	f.	f. 6.	
	g.	g. 7.	
	h.	h. 8.	
	i.	i. 9.	
	j.	j. 10.	
	k.	k. 11.	
	l.	l. 12.	
	m.	m. 13.	
	n.	n. 14.	
	o.	o. 15.	

Your Favorite People

With the great emphasis upon the importance of the environment, in recent years, it has become increasingly realized that jobs are environments too. The most important environmental factor always turns out to be people, since every job, except possibly that of a full-fledged hermit, surrounds us with people to one degree or another.

Indeed, many a good job has been ruined by the people one is surrounded by. Many a mundane job has been made delightful, by the people one is surrounded by. Therefore, it is important to think out what kinds of people you want to be surrounded by.

Dr. John L. Holland offers the best description of people-environments. He says there are six principal ones:

1. The **Realistic** People-Environment: filled with people who prefer activities involving "the explicit, ordered, or systematic manipulation of objects, tools, machines, and animals." "Realistic," incidentally, refers to Plato's conception of "the real" as that which one can apprehend through the senses.

I summarize this as: **R** = people who like nature, or athletics, or tools and machinery.

2. The **Investigative** People-Environment: filled with people who prefer activities involving "the observation and symbolic, systematic, creative investigation of physical, biological, or cultural phenomena."

I summarize this as: **I** = people who are very curious, liking to investigate or analyze things or people.

3. The **Artistic** People-Environment: filled with people who prefer activities involving "ambiguous, free, unsystematized activities and competencies to create art forms or products."

I summarize this as: **A** = people who are very artistic, imaginative, and innovative.

4. The **Social** People-Environment: filled with people who prefer activities involving "the manipulation of others to inform, train, develop, cure, or enlighten."

I summarize this as: **S** = people who are bent on trying to help, teach, or serve people.

5. The **Enterprising** People-Environment: filled with people who prefer activities involving "the manipulation of others to attain organizational or self-interest goals."

I summarize this as: E = people who like to start up projects or organizations, and/or influence or persuade people.

6. The **Conventional** People-Environment: filled with people who prefer activities involving "the explicit, ordered, systematic manipulation of data, such as keeping records, filing materials, reproducing materials, organizing written and numerical data according to a prescribed plan, operating business and data processing machines." "Conventional," incidentally, refers to the "values" which people in this environment usually hold— representing the broad mainstream of the culture.

I summarize this as: C = people who like detailed work, and like to complete tasks or projects.

According to John's theory and findings, everyone has three preferred people-environments, from among these six. The letters for your three preferred people-environments gives you what is called your "Holland Code."

There is, incidentally, a relationship between the people you like to be surrounded by *and* your skills *and* your values. See John Holland's book, *Making Vocational Choices* (3rd. ed., 1997). You can procure it by writing to Psychological Assessment Resources, Inc., Box 998, Odessa, FL 33556. Phone: 1-800-331-8378. *The book is $29.95 at this writing.* PAR also has John Holland's instrument, called *The Self-Directed Search* (or SDS, for short) for discovering what your Holland Code is. PAR says you can take the test online for a small fee ($9.95) at www.self-directed-search.com.

For those who don't have Internet access (or are in a hurry), I invented (many years ago) a quick and easy way to get an *approximation* of your "Holland Code," as it's called. I call it "The Party Exercise." Here is how the exercise goes (do it!):

On the next page is an aerial view of a room in which a two-day (!) party is taking place. At this party, people with the same or similar interests have (for some reason) all gathered in the same corner of the room.

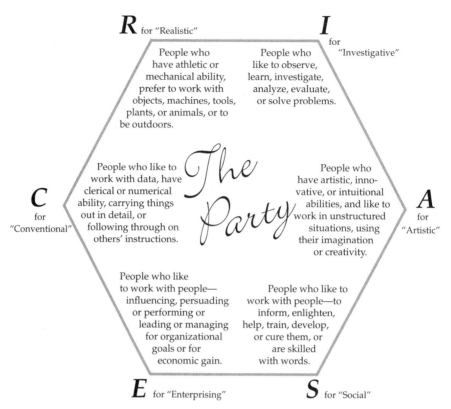

R for "Realistic"

People who have athletic or mechanical ability, prefer to work with objects, machines, tools, plants, or animals, or to be outdoors.

I for "Investigative"

People who like to observe, learn, investigate, analyze, evaluate, or solve problems.

C for "Conventional"

People who like to work with data, have clerical or numerical ability, carrying things out in detail, or following through on others' instructions.

The Party

People who have artistic, innovative, or intuitional abilities, and like to work in unstructured situations, using their imagination or creativity.

A for "Artistic"

People who like to work with people—influencing, persuading or performing or leading or managing for organizational goals or for economic gain.

People who like to work with people—to inform, enlighten, help, train, develop, or cure them, or are skilled with words.

E for "Enterprising"

S for "Social"

1) Which corner of the room would you instinctively be drawn to, as the group of people you would most enjoy being with for the longest time? (Leave aside any question of shyness, or whether you would have to talk to them.) Write the letter for that corner here: R

2) After fifteen minutes, everyone in the corner you have chosen leaves for another party crosstown, except you. Of the groups that still remain now, which corner or group would you be drawn to the most, as the people you would most enjoy being with for the longest time? Write the letter for that corner here: A

3) After fifteen minutes, this group too leaves for another party, except you. Of the corners, and groups, which remain now, which one would you most enjoy being with for the longest time? Write the letter for that corner here: S

Chapter Ten

The three letters you just chose, in the three steps, are called your "Holland Code." Here is what you should now do:

1. Circle them on the People petal, on your Flower Diagram.

Put three circles around your favorite corner; two circles around your next favorite; and one circle around your third favorite.

2. Once the corners are circled, you may wish to write up (for yourself and your eyes only) a temporary statement about your future job or career, using the descriptors above.

If your "Code" turned out to be IAS, for example, you might write: *"I would like a job or career best if I was surrounded by people who are very curious, and like to investigate or analyze things (I); who are also very innovative (A); and who are bent on trying to help or serve people (S)."*

3. Finally, here, look over the skills you have just described *in others*, and see how much of this is also true of *you*.

What I call "The Mirror Theory" holds that we often see *ourselves* best by looking into the faces of others. Hence, once we have described the people we would most like to be surrounded by, in many cases we have also described ourselves. ("Birds of a feather flock together.") So, look over the circled items on your People petal. Are these, perchance, *your* favorite proclivities, skills, tasks, etc.? Or not?

PETAL #4

Your Favorite Values

Values are a matter of what guides you through every day, every task, every encounter with another human being. Yet, we are often unaware of what our values are.

One way to bring values to your consciousness is to imagine that shortly before the end of your life you are invited to dinner—and to your great surprise people have secretly come in from all over the country and all over the world, to attend a surprise testimonial dinner for You.

At the dinner, to your great embarrassment, there is one testimonial after another about the good things you did, or the good person that you were, in your lifetime. No mention of any parts of your life that you don't want to have remembered. Just the good stuff.

So, this brings us to some questions. If you get the life you really want between now and then, what would you hope you would hear at that dinner, as they looked back on your life?

If you do achieve what you want with your life, what about you would you like to have remembered, after you are gone from this earth? Here is a checklist to help you:[8]

It would be a good life, if at its end here, people remembered me as one who (check as many items as are important to you):

☑ Served or helped those who were in need.

☑ Impressed people with my going the second mile, in meeting their needs.

☑ Was always a great listener.

---

8. I am indebted to Arthur Miller, of People Management, Inc., for many of these ideas.

- ❏ Was always good at carrying out orders, or bringing projects to a successful conclusion.
- ☑ Mastered some technique, or field.
- ❏ Did something that everyone said couldn't be done.
- ❏ Did something that no one had ever done before.
- ❏ Excelled and was the best at whatever it is I did.
- ❏ Pioneered or explored some new technology.
- ☑ Fixed something that was broken.
- ☑ Made something work, when everyone else had failed or given up.
- ☑ Improved something, made it better, or perfected it.
- ☑ Combatted some bad idea/philosophy/force/influence/ pervasive trend—and I persevered and/or prevailed.
- ☑ Influenced people and gained a tremendous response from them.
- ☑ Had an impact, and caused change.
- ☑ Did work which brought more information/truth into the world.
- ☑ Did work which brought more beauty into the world, through gardens, or painting, or decorating, or designing, or whatever.
- ☑ Did work which brought more justice, truth, and ethical behavior into the world.
- ❏ Brought people closer to God.
- ❏ Growing in wisdom and compassion was my great goal all my life.
- ☑ Had a vision of what something could be, and helped that vision to come true.
- ❏ Developed or built something, where there was nothing.
- ❏ Began a new business, or did some project from start to finish.
- ❏ Exploited, shaped, and influenced some situation, market, before others saw the potential.
- ❏ Put together a great team, which made a huge difference in its field, industry, or community.

☑ Was a good decision-maker.

☐ Was acknowledged by everyone as a leader, and was in charge of whatever it was that I was doing.

☑ Had status in my field, industry, or community.

☐ Was in the spotlight, gained recognition, and was well-known.

☑ Made it into a higher echelon than I originally was in, in terms of reputation, and/or prestige, and/or membership, and/or salary.

☐ Was able to acquire possessions, things, or money.

☐ Other goals which occur to me:_____

_____

When you're done checking off all the values that are important to you, go back, and pick out the ten that you care the most about, and then prioritize them in exact order of importance to you. As always, if you just can't prioritize them by guess and by gosh, then use the Prioritizing Grids on pages 178 and 179.

The question to ask yourself, there, as you confront each "pair" on the Grid is: "If I could only have this true about me, at the end of my life, but not the other, which would I prefer?" *Try not to pay attention to what others might or might not think of you, if they knew this was your heart's desire. This is just between you and God.*

Put your top six values on the Values petal, in the Flower Diagram.

Chapter Ten

Your Favorite
Working Conditions

Plants that grow beautifully at sea level, often perish if they're taken ten thousand feet up the mountain. Likewise, we do our best work under certain conditions, but not under others. Thus, the question: What are your favorite "working conditions"? actually is a question about "Under what circumstances do you do your most effective work?"

The best way to approach this is by starting with the things you *disliked* about all your previous jobs, using the following chart to list these. The chart, as you can see, has three columns, and you fill them out in the same order, and manner, that you filled out the geography chart earlier. Here too, you may copy this chart onto a larger piece of paper if you wish, before you begin filling it out. *Column A may begin with such factors as: "too noisy," "too much supervision," "no windows in my workplace," "having to be at work by 6 A.M.," etc.*

Of course, when you get to Column B, you must rank these factors that are in Column A, in their exact order of importance, to you.

As always, if you are baffled as to how to prioritize these factors in exact order, use the Prioritizing Grid.

The question to ask yourself, there, as you confront each "pair" is: "If I were offered two jobs, and in the first job I would be rid of this first distasteful working condition, but not the second; while in the second job, I would be rid of the second distasteful working condition, but not the first, which distasteful working condition would I choose to get rid of?"

Note that when you later come to Column C, the factors will be already prioritized. Your only job, there, is to think of the "positive" form of that factor that you hated so much (in Column B). (It is not always "the exact opposite." For example, *too*

The Secret to Finding Your Dream Job   **221**

much supervision, listed in Column B, does not always mean *no supervision,* in Column C. It *might* mean: *a moderate amount of supervision, once or twice a day.*)

Once you've finished Column C, enter the top five factors from there on the Working Conditions petal of the Flower Diagram.

DISTASTEFUL WORKING CONDITIONS

	Column A — Distasteful Working Conditions	*Column B* — Distasteful Working Conditions Ranked	*Column C* ✚ The Keys to My Effectiveness at Work
Places I Have Worked Thus Far in My Life	*I Have Learned from the Past That My Effectiveness at Work is Decreased When I Have to Work Under These Conditions:*	*Among the Factors or Qualities Listed in Column A, These Are the Ones I Dislike Absolutely the Most (in Order of Decreasing Dislike):*	*The Opposite of These Qualities, in Order:* *I Believe My Effectiveness Would Be at an Absolute Maximum, If I Could Work Under These Conditions:*

PETAL #6
Level & Salary

Salary is something you must think out ahead of
you're contemplating your ideal job or career. Level
in-hand with salary, of course.

**1. The first question here is at what level would you like to
work, in your ideal job?**

Level is a matter of how much responsibility you want, in an
organization:

❑ Boss or CEO (this may mean you'll have to form your own
  business)
❑ Manager or someone under the boss who carries out orders
❑ The head of a team
❑ A member of a team of equals
❑ One who works in tandem with one other partner
❑ One who works alone, either as an employee or as a consult-
  ant to an organization, or as a one-person business.

Enter a two- or three-word summary of your answer, on the
Salary and Level petal of your Flower Diagram.

**2. The second question here is what salary would you like to
be aiming at?**

Here you have to think in terms of minimum or maximum.
Minimum is what you would need to make, if you were just
barely "getting by." And you need to know this *before* you go
in for a job interview with anyone *(or before you form your own
business, and need to know how much profit you must make, just to
survive).*

Maximum could be any astronomical figure you can think of,
but it is more useful here to put down the salary you realistically
think you could make, with your present competency and experience, were you working for a real, *but generous*, boss. (If this
maximum figure is still depressingly low, then put down the
salary you would like to be making five years from now.)

Make out a detailed outline of your estimated expenses *now*,
listing what you need *monthly* in the following categories:[9]

The Secret to Finding Your Dream Job   **223**

...ing

Rent or mortgage payments . . . . $ _____

Electricity/gas . . . . $ _____

Water . . . . $ _____

Telephone . . . . $ _____

Garbage removal . . . . $ _____

Cleaning, maintenance, repairs[10] . . . . $ _____

Food

What you spend at the supermarket
and/or meat market, etc. . . . . $ _____

Eating out . . . . $ _____

Clothing

Purchase of new or used clothing . . . . $ _____

Cleaning, dry cleaning, laundry . . . . $ _____

Automobile/transportation[11]

Car payments . . . . $ _____

Gas . . . . $ _____

Repairs . . . . $ _____

Public transportation (bus, train, plane) . . . . . . $ _____

Insurance

Car . . . . $ _____

Medical or health-care . . . . $ _____

House and personal possessions . . . . $ _____

Life . . . . $ _____

Medical expenses

Doctors' visits . . . . $ _____

Prescriptions . . . . $ _____

Fitness costs . . . . $ _____

Support for other family members

Child-care costs (if you have children) . . . . $ _____

Child-support (if you're paying that) . . . . $ _____

Support for your parents (if you're helping out) . . $ _____

Charity giving/tithe (to help others). . . . . $ _____

School/learning

Children's costs (if you have children in school) . . $ _____

Your learning costs (adult education,
job-hunting classes, etc.) . . . . $ _____

Pet care (if you have pets) . . . . $ _____

Bills and debts (usual monthly payments)

Credit cards . . . . $ _____

Local stores. $ _____

Other obligations you pay off monthly . . . . . . $ _____

Taxes

    Federal[12] *(next April's due, divided by*
    months remaining until then). . . . . $ _____

    State *(likewise)* . . . . $ _____

    Local/property *(next amount due, divided by*
    months remaining until then). . . . . $ _____

    Tax-help *(if you ever use an accountant,*
    pay a friend to help you with taxes, etc.) . . . . $ _____

Savings . . . . $ _____

Retirement (Keogh, IRA, Sep, etc.) . . . . $ _____

Amusement/discretionary spending

    Movies, video rentals, etc. . . . . $ _____

    Other kinds of entertainment . . . . $ _____

    Reading, newspapers, magazines, books . . . . . $ _____

    Gifts *(birthday, Christmas, etc.)* . . . . $ _____

    Vacations . . . . $ _____

Total Amount You Need Each Month . . . . $ _____

---

9. If this kind of financial figuring is not your cup of tea, find a buddy, friend, relative, family member, or anyone, who can help you do this. If you don't know anyone who could do this, go to your local church, synagogue, religious center, social club, gym, or wherever you hang out, and ask the leader or manager there, to help you find someone. If there's a bulletin board, put up a notice on the bulletin board.

10. If you have extra household expenses, such as a security system, be sure to include the quarterly (or whatever) expenses here, divided by three.

11. Your checkbook stubs will tell you a lot of this stuff. But you may be vague about your cash or credit card expenditures. For example, you may not know how much you spend at the supermarket, or how much you spend on gas, etc. But there is a simple way to find out. Just carry a little notepad and pen around with you for two weeks or more, and jot down *everything* you pay cash (or use credit cards) for—on the spot, right after you pay it. At the end of those two weeks, you'll be able to take that notepad and make a realistic guess of what should be put down in these categories that now puzzle you. *(Multiply the two-week figure by two, and you'll have the monthly figure.)*

12. Incidentally, for U.S. citizens, looking ahead to next April 15, be sure to check with your local IRS office or a reputable accountant to find out if you can deduct the expenses of your job-hunt on your federal (and state) income tax returns. At this writing, some job-hunters can, if—big IF—this is not your first job that you're looking for, if you haven't been unemployed too long, and if you aren't making a career-change. Do go find out what the latest "ifs" are. If the IRS says you are eligible, keep careful receipts of everything related to your job-hunt, as you go along: telephone calls, stationery, printing, postage, travel, etc.

Multiply the total amount you need each month by 12, to get the yearly figure. Divide the yearly figure by 2,000, and you will be reasonably near the *minimum* hourly wage that you need. Thus, if you need $3,333 per month, multiplied by 12 that's $40,000 a year, and then divided by 2,000, that's $20 an hour.

Parenthetically, you may want to prepare two different versions of the above budget: one with the expenses you'd ideally *like* to make, and the other a minimum budget, which will give you what you are looking for, here: the floor, below which you simply cannot afford to go.

Enter the maximum, and minimum, on your Salary and Level petal on the Flower Diagram.

Chapter Ten

Optional Exercise: You may wish to put down other rewards, besides money, that you would hope for, from your next job or career. These might be:

❑ Adventure

❑ Challenge

❑ Respect

❑ Influence

❑ Popularity

❑ Fame

❑ Power

❑ Intellectual stimulation from the other workers there

❑ A chance to exercise leadership

❑ A chance to be creative

❑ A chance to make decisions

❑ A chance to use my expertise

❑ A chance to help others

❑ A chance to bring others closer to God

❑ Other:

If you do check off things on this list, arrange your answers in order of importance to you, and then add them to the Salary and Level petal.

Done!

Voila! Your Flower Diagram should now be complete. Reward yourself! Sleep for a week. Run up a mountain, or spend a week in your partner's arms.

PART III

How

Do You Find the Person
Who Has the Power to Hire You
for the Job You Want?

Well, you begin by seeing what "That One Piece of Paper"
tells you now that it's all completed. Compare it to Rich
Feller's flower.

Example
(Rich Feller's Flower)
Again

**Favorite
Interests**

1. Large conference planning
2. Regional geography & culture
3. Traveling on $20/day 4. Career planning seminars 5. Counseling techniques / theories 6. American Policies 7. Fundamentals of sports 8. Fighting Sexism 9. NASCAR Auto Racing
10. Interior design

**Salary
and Level of
Responsibility**

1. Can determine 9/12 month contract 2. Can determine own projects
3. Considerable clout in organization's direction without administrative responsibilities 4. Able to select colleagues 5. 3 to 5 assistants 6. $35K to $50K 7. Serve on various important boards 8. Can defer clerical and budget decisions and tasks 9. Speak before large groups 10. Can run for elected office

Geography

1. Close to major city
2. Mild winters / low humidity
3. Change in seasons 4. Clean and green 5. 100,000 people 6. Nice shopping malls. 7. Wide range of athletic options 8. Diverse economic base 9. Ample local culture
10. Sense of community
(pride)

Favorite Skills

1. Observational / learning skills • continually expose self to new experiences • perceptive in identifying and assessing potential of others 2. Leadership Skills • continually searches for more resonsibility • sees a problem / acts to solve it 3. Instructing / interpreting / guiding • committed to learning as a lifelong process • create atmosphere of acceptance 4. Serving / helping / human relations skills • shapes atmosphere of particular place • relates well in dealing with public 5. Detail / follow-through skills • handle great variety of tasks • resource broker 6. Influencing / persuading skills • recruiting talent / leadership • inspiring trust 7. Performing skills • getting up in front of a group (if I'm in control) • Addressing small and large groups 8. Intuitional / Innovative skills • continually develop / generate new ideas 9. Develop / Plan / Organize / Execute • designing projects • utilizing skills of others 10. Language / Read / Write • communicate effectively •
Can think quickly on my feet

**Favorite
People
Environment**

1. Strong social, perceptual skills
2. Emotionally and physically healthy
3. Enthusiastically include others 4. Heterogeneous in interests and skills 5. Social changers, innovators 6. Politically, economically astute 7. Confident enough to confront / cry and be foolish
8. Sensitive to nontraditional issues
9. I and R, (see page 216)
10. Nonmaterialistic

**Favorite
Working
Conditions**

1. Receive clinical supervision 2. Mentor relationship 3. Excellent Secretary 4. Part of larger, highly respected organization with clear direction 5. Near gourmet and health food specialty shops
6. Heterogeneous colleagues (race, sex, age) 7. Flexible dress code 8. Merit system 9. Can bike / bus / walk to work 10. Private office with window

Favorite Values

1. Improve the human condition
2. Promote interdependence and futuristic principles 3. Maximize productive use of human / material resources 4. Teach people to be self-directed / self-responsible 5. Free people from self-defeating controls (thoughts, rules, barriers)
6. Promote capitalistic principles 7. Reduce exploitation 8. Promote political participation
9. Acknowledge those who give to the community 10. Give away ideas

Then put your sheet on a wall, or on the door of your refrigerator. And there you have it: a simple picture (as it were) of You.

A Light Bulb Goes On

But, it's not *just* a picture of You. Just as importantly, it's a picture of Your Dream Job as well. It's both of these things at once, because you're looking for a dream job or career *that matches you.* You match it. It matches you. Bingo! Mirror images.

And now that you're looking at "That One Piece of Paper," what should happen? Well, for some of you there will be a big *Aha!* as you look at your Flower Diagram. A light bulb will go off, over your head, and you will say, "My goodness, I see *exactly* what sort of career this points me to." This happens particularly with intuitive people.

If you are one of those intuitive people, I say, "Good for you!" Just two gentle warnings, if I may:

Don't prematurely close out *other* possibilities.

THE VIRTUE OF "PASSION" OR ENTHUSIASM

Whether in stages or directly, it is amazing how often people do get their dream job or career. The more you don't *cut* the dream down, because of what you *think* you know about *the real world*, the more likely you are to find what you are looking for.

Hold on to *all* of your dream. Most people don't find their heart's desire, because they decide to pursue just half their dream—and consequently they hunt for it with only *half a heart*.

If you decide to pursue your whole dream, your best dream, the one you would die to do, I guarantee you that you will hunt for it *with all your heart*. It is this *passion* which often is the difference between successful career-changers, and unsuccessful ones.

And *don't* say to yourself: "Well, I see what it is that I would die to be able to do, but I *know* there is no job in the world like that, that *I* would be able to get." Dear friend, you don't know any such thing. You haven't done your research yet. Of course, it is always possible that when you've completed all that research, and conducted your search, you still may not be able to find *all* that you want—down to the last detail. But you'd be surprised at how much of your dream you may be able to find.

Sometimes it will be found in *stages*. One retired man I know, who had been a senior executive with a publishing company, found himself bored to death in retirement, after he turned sixty-five. He contacted a business acquaintance, who said apologetically, "We just don't have anything open that matches or requires your abilities; right now all we need is someone in our mail room." The sixty-five-year-old executive said, "I'll take that job!" He did, and over the ensuing years steadily advanced once again, to just the job he wanted: as a senior executive in that organization, where he utilized all his prized skills, for some time. He retired as senior executive for the second time, at the age of eighty-five. Like him, you may choose to go by stages.

Other times, it may be that you will be able to find your dream directly without having to go through stages.

Other Possibility,
You Look at Your Flower Diagram and . . .
a Light Bulb *Doesn't* Go On

In contrast to what I just said, many of you will look at your completed Flower Diagram, and you won't have *a clue* as to what job or career it points to. Soooo, we need a "fall-back" strategy. Of course it involves more "step-by-step-by-step" stuff.

Here's how it goes. Take a pad of paper, with pen or pencil, or go to your computer, with keyboard in hand, and make some notes.

1. First, look at your Flower Diagram, and from the center petal choose your three most *favorite* skills.
2. Then, look at your Flower Diagram and write down, from petal #2, your three *top* interests, or Fields of Fascination.
3. Now, take these notes, and show them to at least five friends, family, or professionals whom you know.

Chapter Ten

As you will recall, skills usually point toward a **job-title** or job-level, while interests or fields of fascination usually point toward a **career field**. So, you want to ask them, in the case of your skills, *What job-title or jobs do these skills suggest to you?*

Then ask them, in the case of your favorite Fields of Fascination, *What career fields do these suggest to you?*

4. Jot down *everything* these five people suggest or recommend to you.
5. After you have finished talking to them, you want to go home and look at all these notes. Anything helpful or valuable here? If not, if none of it looks valuable, then set it aside, and go talk to five more of your friends, acquaintances, or people you know in the business world and nonprofit sector. Repeat, as necessary.
6. When you finally have some worthwhile suggestions, sit down, look over their combined suggestions, and ask yourself some questions.

The Secret to Finding Your Dream Job

JOB FAMILIES

1. Executive, Administrative, and Managerial Occupations
2. Engineers, Surveyors, and Architects
3. Natural Scientists and Mathematicians
4. Social Scientists, Social Workers, Religious Workers, and Lawyers
5. Teachers, Counselors, Librarians, and Archivists
6. Health Diagnosing and Treating Practitioners
7. Registered Nurses, Pharmacists, Dieticians, Therapists, and Physician Assistants
8. Health Technologists and Technicians
9. Technologists and Technicians in Other Fields: Computer Specialists, Programmers, Information Technicians, Information Specialists, etc.
10. Writers, Artists, Digital Artists, and Entertainers
11. Marketing and Sales Occupations
12. Administrative Support Occupations, including Clerical
13. Service Occupations
14. Agricultural, Forestry, and Fishing Occupations
15. Mechanics and Repairers
16. Construction and Extractive Occupations
17. Production Occupations
18. Transportation and Material-Moving Occupations
19. Handlers, Equipment Cleaners, Helpers, and Laborers

- First, you want to look at what these friends suggested about your skills: *what job or jobs came to their mind?* It will help you to know that most jobs can be classified under nineteen headings or families. Which of these nineteen do your friends' suggestions predominantly point to? Which of these nineteen grabs you?

- Next, you want to look at what your friends suggested about your interests or *fields of fascination*: *what fields or careers came to their minds?* It will help you to know that most of the career fields above can be classified under four broad headings: *Agriculture, Manufacturing, Information Industries,* and *Service*

Industries. Which of these four do your friends' suggestions predominantly *point to*? Which of these four grabs you?

- The next question you want to ask yourself is: both job-titles and career-fields can be broken down further, according to whether you like to work primarily with *people* **or** primarily with *information/data* **or** primarily with *things.*

Let's take agriculture as an example. Within agriculture, you could be driving tractors and other farm machinery—and thus working primarily with *things;* or you could be gathering statistics about crop growth for some state agency—and thus working primarily with *information/data;* or you could be teaching agriculture in a college classroom, and thus working primarily with *people* and *ideas*. Almost all fields as well as career families offer you these three kinds of choices, though *of course* many jobs combine two or more of the three in some intricate way.

Still, you do want to tell yourself what your *preference* is, and what you *primarily* want to be working with. Otherwise your job-hunt or career-change is going to leave you very frustrated, at the end. In this matter, it is often your favorite skill that will give you the clue. If it *doesn't*, then go back and look at your skills *petal*, on your Flower Diagram. What do you think? Are your favorite skills weighted more toward working with *people*, or toward working with *information/data*, or toward working with *things*?

And, no matter what that *petal* suggests, which do you absolutely prefer?

Giving the Flower a Name

Once you have these *clues* from your friends, you need to go name your Flower. To do this, you need to answer four questions for yourself, in the order indicated below:

• QUESTION #1

What are the **names of jobs or careers** that would give me a chance to use my most enjoyable skills, in a field that is based on my favorite subjects?

Just be sure that you get the names of at least *two* careers, or jobs, that you think you could be happy doing. Never, ever, put all your eggs in one basket. The secret of surviving out there in the jungle is *having alternatives*.

Be careful. Be thorough. Be persistent. This is your life you're working on, and your future. Make it glorious. Whatever it takes, find out the name of your ideal career, your ideal occupation, your ideal job—*or jobs*.

• QUESTION #2

What **kinds of organizations** would and/or do employ people in these careers?

Before you think of individual places where you might like to work, it is necessary to step back a little, as it were, and think of all the *kinds* of places where one might get hired.

Let's take an example. Suppose in your new career you want to be a teacher. You must then ask yourself: *what kinds of places hire teachers?* You might answer, *"just schools,"*—and finding that schools in your geographical area have no openings, you might say, *"Well, there are no jobs for people in this career."*

But that is not true. There are countless other *kinds* of organizations and agencies out there, besides schools, which employ *teachers*. For example, corporate training and educational departments, workshop sponsors, foundations, private research firms, educational consultants, teachers' associations, professional and trade societies, military bases, state and local councils on higher education, fire and police training academies, and so on and so forth.

"Kinds of places" also means places with different *hiring modes*, besides full-time hiring, such as:

- places that would employ you part-time (maybe you'll end up deciding to hold down two or even three part-time jobs, which altogether would add up to one full-time job, in order to give yourself more variety);
- places that take temporary workers, on assignment for one project at a time;
- places that take consultants, one project at a time;
- places that operate with volunteers, etc.
- places that are nonprofit;
- places that are for profit;
- and, don't forget, places which you yourself would start up, should you decide to be your own boss. *(See chapter 9.)*

5,708,000 POSSIBLE TARGETS (EMPLOYERS)

57,000 POSSIBLE TARGETS

5,700 POSSIBLE TARGETS

1,000 POSSIBLE TARGETS

500 POSSIBLE TARGETS

300 POSSIBLE TARGETS

60 POSSIBLE TARGETS

10 POSSIBLE TARGETS

YOUR SPIRITUAL VALUES

YOUR PREFERRED LEVEL AND SALARY

YOUR PREFERRED WORKING CONDITIONS

THINGS, KINDS OF PEOPLE, AND INFORMATION YOU PREFER

YOUR PREFERRED TASKS OR SKILLS

YOUR PREFERRED FIELD (OF KNOWLEDGE) OR CAREER FIELD

YOUR PREFERRED GEOGRAPHICAL LOCATION

Don't forget that as you talk to workers about their jobs or careers (in the previous section), they will accidentally volunteer information about the *kinds* of organizations. Listen keenly, and keep notes.

• **QUESTION #3**

Among the kinds of organizations uncovered in the previous question, what are the names of **particular places** that I especially like?

As you interview workers about their jobs or careers, they will along the way volunteer actual names of organizations that have such jobs—including what's good or bad about the place where *they* work or used to work. This is important information for you. Jot it all down. Keep notes *as though it were part of your religion.*

Now when this name-gathering is all done, what do you have? Well, either you'll have *too few name*s of places to work, or you'll end up with *too much information*—too many names of places which hire people in the career that interests you. There are ways of dealing with either of these eventualities. We'll take this last scenario, first.

Cutting Down the Territory

If you end up with the names of too many places, you will want to **cut the territory down,** so that you are left with *a manageable number* of "targets" for your job-hunt.[13]

Let's take an example. Suppose you discovered that the career which interests you the most is *welding*. You want to be a welder. Well, that's a beginning. You've cut the 16 million U.S. job-markets down to:

- I want to work in a place
  that hires welders.

But the territory is still too large. There might be thousands of places in the country, that use welders. You can't go visit them all. So, you've got to cut the territory down, further. Suppose that on your geography *petal* you said that you really want to live and work in the San Jose area of California. That's helpful: that cuts the territory down further. Now your goal is:

- I want to work in a place
  that hires welders,
  within the San Jose area.

But, the territory is still too large. There could be 100, 200, 300 organizations which fit that description. So you look at your Flower Diagram for further help, and you notice that under *preferred working conditions* you said you wanted to work for an organization with fifty or fewer employees. Good, now your goal is:

---

13. If you resist this idea of *cutting the territory down*—if you feel you could be happy anywhere just as long as you were using your favorite skills—then almost no organization in the country can be ruled out. So if you aren't willing to take some steps to cut the territory down, then you'll have to go visit them all. Good luck! We'll see you in about forty-three years.

- I want to work in a place that hires welders,
  within the San Jose area,
  and has fifty or fewer employees.

This territory may still be too large. So you look again at your Flower Diagram for further guidance, and you see that on the Things *petal* you said you wanted to work for an organization which works with, or produces, *wheels*. So now your statement of what you're looking for, becomes:

- I want to work in a place that hires welders,
  within the San Jose area,
  has fifty or fewer employees,
  and makes wheels.

Using your Flower Diagram, you can thus keep cutting the territory down, until the *"targets"* of your job-hunt are no more than ten places. That's a manageable number of places for you to *start with*. You can always expand the list later, if none of these ten turn out to be very promising or interesting.

Expanding the Territory

Sometimes your problem will be just the opposite. We come here to the second scenario: if your Informational Interviewing doesn't turn up enough names of places where you could get hired in your new career, then you're going to have to expand your list. You're going to have to consult some directories.

Your salvation is going to be the yellow pages of your local phone book. Look under every heading that is of any interest to you. Also, see if the local chamber of commerce publishes a business directory; often it will list not only small companies but also local divisions of larger companies, with names of department heads; and sometimes will even include the NAICS industry codes, should you care. If you are diligent here, you won't lack for names, believe me—unless it's a very small town you live in, in which case you'll need to cast your net a little wider, to include other towns or villages that are within commuting distance.

Once you have about *ten names* of organizations or businesses that might hire you for the kind of work you are dying to do, you proceed to our fourth and last question involved in naming your Flower:

• QUESTION #4

Among the places that I particularly like, **what needs do they have** or what outcomes are they trying to produce, that my skills and knowledge could help with?

Talk to people, that's the key! And if shyness is a problem for you, as it is for me (believe me!!) I have some helpful things to suggest about how to deal with that, at the end of this chapter.

But I reiterate: to gather the information you will need, you must go talk to people.

Well and good, you may say, but how do you decide *which people*? Well, that's not as hard as it may seem. Let me give you an actual example of how it's done. (We'll take an actual career-changer's story, here.)

After our job-hunter did his Flower Diagram, it turned out that his top/favorite skill was: diagnosing, treating, or healing.

His three top/favorite *languages* or fields of fascination were: psychiatry, plants, and carpentry.

After showing five friends this information, and mulling over what they said, he concluded:

Among the nineteen *Job Families*, he was most attracted to (6) Health diagnosing and treating practitioners.

Among the four *broad divisions of career-fields*, he was most attracted to Service industries.

Among the *three kinds of skills*, he most wanted to use his skills with people.

So far, so good. Now, where does he go from there?

He's going to have to go talk to people. But, how does he choose who to talk to? Easy. He takes his favorite *languages* or fields of fascination, above—psychiatry, plants, and carpentry— and mentally translates them into *people* with those occupations: namely, a psychiatrist, a gardener, and a carpenter.

"Same career, change of career, same career . . . change of . . ."

Then he has to go find at least one of each. That's relatively easy: the yellow pages of the telephone directory will do, or he may know some of these among the friends or acquaintances he already has. What he wants to do, now, is go visit them and ask them: *how do you combine these three fields into one occupation?* He knows it may be a career that already exists, *or* it may be he will have to create this career for himself.

And, how does he decide which of these three to go interview *first*? He asks himself which of these persons is most likely to have the *largest overview. (This is often, but not always, the same as asking: who took the longest to get their training?)* The particular answer here: the psychiatrist.

He would then go see two or three psychiatrists—say, the head of the psychiatry department at the nearest colleges or universities,[14] and ask them: *Do you have any idea how to put these three subjects—carpentry, plants, and psychiatry—together into one*

---

14. If there were no psychiatrists at any academic institution near him, then he would do all his research with psychiatrists in private practice—getting their names from the phone book—and asking them for, and paying for, a half session. This, if there is no other way.

Chapter Ten

job or career? *And if you don't know, who do you think might?* He would keep going until he found someone who had a bright idea about how you put this all together.

In this particular case *(as I said, this is an actual career-changer's experience)*, he was eventually told: "Yes, it can all be put together. There is a branch of psychiatry that uses plants to help heal people. That takes care of your interest in plants and psychiatry. As for your carpentry interests, I suppose you could use that to build the planters for your plants."

Informational Interviewing

There is a name for this process I have just described. It is called *Informational Interviewing*—a term I invented many many years ago. But it is sometimes, incorrectly, called *by other names*. Some even call this gathering of information *Networking*, which it is not.

To avoid this confusion, I have summarized in the chart on pages 244 and 245 just exactly what *Informational Interviewing* is, and how it differs from the other ways in which *people* can help and support you, during your job-hunt or career-change— namely, *Networking, Support Groups,* and *Contacts.* I have also thrown in, at no extra charge, a *first* column in that chart, dealing with an aspect of the job-hunt that *never* gets talked about: namely, the importance before your job-hunt ever begins, of *nurturing the friendships you have let slip*—by calling them or visiting them early on in your job-hunt—just re-establishing relationships *before* you ever need anything from them, as you most certainly may, later on in your job-hunt. The first column in the chart explains this further.

Talking to Workers, "Trying on" Jobs

When you go talk to people, you are hoping they will give you ideas, as we saw, about *what careers* will use your skills and *languages* or Fields of Fascination and interest.

That's the first step.

The second step is that you want also to get some idea of *what that work feels like, from the inside.*

The Process ▼	1. Valuing Your *Community* Before the Job-Hunt	2. Networking
What Is Its Purpose?	To make sure that people whom you may someday need to do you a favor, or lend you a hand, know long beforehand that you value and prize them *for themselves*.	To gather a list of contacts now who might be able to help you with your career, or with your job-hunting, at some future date. And to go out of your way to regularly add to that list. *Networking is a term often reserved only for the business of adding to your list; but, obviously, this presupposes you first listed everyone you already know.*
Who Is It Done With?	Those who live with you, plus your family, relatives, friends, and acquaintances, however near (geographically) or far.	People in your present field, or in a field of future interest that you yourself meet; also, people whose names are given to you by others.
When You're Doing This Right How Do You Go About It? (Typical Activities)	You make time for them in your busy schedule, long before you find yourself job-hunting. You do this by: 1. Spending "quality time" with those you live with, letting them know you really appreciate who they are, and what kind of person they are. 2. Maintaining contact (phone, lunch, a thank-you note) with those who live nearby. 3. Writing friendly notes, regularly, to those who live at a distance— *thus letting them all know that you appreciate them* for themselves.	You deliberately attend, for this purpose, meetings or conventions in your present field, or the field/career you are thinking of switching to, someday. You talk to people at meetings and at "socials," exchanging calling cards after a brief conversation. Occasionally, someone may suggest a name to you as you are about to set off for some distant city or place, recommending that while you are there, you contact them. A phone call may be your best bet, with a follow-up letter after you return home, unless *they* invite *you* to lunch during the phone call. Asking *them* to lunch sometimes "bombs." (See below.)
When You've Really Botched This Up, What Are the Signs?	You're out of work, and you find yourself having to contact people that you haven't written or phoned in ages, suddenly asking them out of the blue for their help with your job-hunt. *The message inevitably read from this is that you don't really care about them at all, except when you can use them. Further, you get perceived as one who sees others only in terms of what they can do for you, rather than in a relationship that is "a two-way street."*	It's usually when you have approached a very busy individual and asked them to have lunch with you. If it is an aimless lunch, with no particular agenda—they ask during lunch what you need to talk about. and you lamely say, "Well, uh, I don't know, So-and-So just thought we should get to know each other" —you will not be practicing *Networking.* You will be practicing *antagonizing.* Try to restrict your *Networking* to the telephone.

Guide to Relationships with Others

3. Developing a Support Group	4. Informational Interviewing	5. Using Contacts
To enlist some of your family or close friends specifically to help you with your emotional, social, and spiritual needs, when you are going through a difficult transition period, such as a job-hunt or career-change—so that you do not have to face this time all by yourself.	To screen careers *before* you change to them. To screen jobs *before* you take them, rather than afterward. To screen places *before* you decide you want to seek employment there. To find answers to *very specific questions* that occur to you during your job-hunt.	It takes, let us say, 77 pairs of eyes and ears to find a new job or career. Here you recruit those 76 other people (don't take me literally— it can be any number you choose) to be your eyes and ears—once you know what kind of work, what kind of place, what kind of job you are looking for, *and not before.*
You try to enlist people with one or more of the following qualifications: you feel comfortable talking to them; they will take initiative in calling you, on a regular basis; they are wiser than you are; and they can be a hard taskmaster, when you need one.	Workers, workers, workers. You *only* do informational interviewing with people actually doing the work that interests you as a potential new job or career for yourself.	Anyone and everyone who is on your "networking list." (See column 2.) It includes family, friends, relatives, high school alumni, college alumni, former co-workers, church/synagogue members, places where you shop, etc.
There should be three of them, at least. They may meet with you regularly, once a week, as a group, for an hour or two, to check on how you are doing. One or more of them should also be available to you on an "as needed" basis: the Listener, when you are feeling "down," and need to talk; the Initiator, when you are tempted to hide; the Wise One, when you are puzzled as to what to do next; and the Taskmaster, when your discipline is falling apart, and you need someone to encourage you to "get at it." It helps if there is also a Cheerleader among them, whom you can tell your victories to.	You get names of workers from your co-workers, from departments at local community colleges, or career offices. Once you have names, you call them and ask for a chance to talk to them *for twenty minutes.* You make a list, ahead of time, of all the questions you want answers to. If nothing occurs to you, try these: 1. How did you get into this line of work? Into this particular job? 2. What kinds of things do you like the most about this job? 3. What kinds of things do you like the least about this job? 4. Who else, doing this same kind of work, would you recommend I go talk to?	Anytime you're stuck, you ask your contacts for help *with specific information.* For example: When you can't find workers who are doing the work that interests you. When you can't find the names of places which do that kind of work. When you have a place in mind, but can't figure out the name of "the-person-who-has-the-power-to-hire-you." When you know that name, but can't get in to see that person. At such times, you call every contact you have on your Networking list, if necessary, until someone can tell you the specific answer you need.
You've "botched it" when you have no support group, no one to turn to, no one to talk to, and you feel that you are in this, all alone. You've "botched it" when you are waiting for your friends and family to notice how miserable you are, and to prove they love you by taking the initiative in coming after you; rather than, as is necessary with a support group, *your* choosing and recruiting them—asking them for their help and aid.	You're trying to use this with people-who-have-the-power-to-hire-you, rather than with *workers.* You're claiming you want information when really you have some other hidden agenda, with this person. *(P.S. They usually can smell the hidden agenda, a mile away.)* You've botched it, whenever you're telling a lie to someone. The whole point of informational interviewing is that it is a search for Truth.	Approaching your "contacts" too early in your job-hunt, and asking them for help only in the most general and vague terms: "John, I'm out of work. If you hear of anything, please let me know." *Any what thing?* You must do all your own homework *before* you approach your contacts. They will not do your homework for you.

In the example above, you don't just want the job-title: *psychiatrist working with plants*. You want some feel for the substance that is underneath the title. In other words, you want to find out what the day-to-day work is like.

For this purpose you must leave your *interviewees*, above, and talk to actual people doing the work you think you'd love to do: in the particular example we have been discussing, you would have to go talk to *psychiatrists who actually use plants, in their healing work*.

Why do you want to ask them what the work feels like, from the inside? Well, in effect, you are mentally *trying on jobs* to see if they fit you.

It is exactly analogous to your going to a clothing store and trying on different suits (or dresses) that you see in their window or on their racks. Why do you try them on? Well, the suits or dresses that look *terrific* in the window don't always look so hotsy-totsy when you see them on *you*. Lots of pins were used, on the backside of the figurine in the window. On you, without the pins, the clothes don't hang quite right, etc., etc.

Likewise, the careers that *sound* terrific in books or in your imagination don't always look so great when you see them up close and personal, in all their living glory.

You need to know that. What you're ultimately trying to find is a career that looks terrific inside and out—in the window, *and* also on you. Essentially, you are asking what *this* job *feels* like. Here are some questions that will help *(you are talking, of course, with workers who are actually doing the career you think you might like to do)*:

- How did you get into this work?
- What do you like the most about it?
- What do you like the least about it?
- And, where else could I find people who do this kind of work? *(You should always ask them for more than one name, so that if you run into a dead end at any point, you can easily go back and visit the other names they suggested.)*

If it becomes apparent to you, during the course of any of these Informational Interviews, that this career, occupation, or job you were exploring definitely *doesn't* fit you, then the last question (above) gets turned into a different kind of inquiry:

- Do you have any ideas as to who else I could talk to, about my skills and Fields of Fascination or interests—so I can find out how they all might fit together, in one job or career?

Then go visit the people they suggest.

If they can't think of *anyone*, ask them if they know who *might* know. And so on. And so forth.

"They Say I Have to Go Back to School, but I Haven't the Time or the Money"

Next step: having found the names of jobs or careers that interest you, having mentally *tried them on* to see if they fit, you next want to find out *how much training, etc. it takes, to get into that field or career.* You ask the same people you have been talking to, previously.

More times than not, you will hear *bad news*. They will tell you something like: "In order to be hired for this job, you have to have a master's degree and ten years' experience at it."

If you're willing to do that, if you have the time, and the money, fine! But what if you don't? Then you search for *the exception:*

> *"Yes, but do you know of anyone in this field who got into it without that master's degree, and ten years' experience?*
> *And where might I find him or her?*
> *And if you don't know of any such person, who might know such information?"*

Throughout this Informational Interviewing, don't assume anything ("But I just assumed that . . ."). Question *all* assumptions, no matter how many people tell you that "this is the way things are."

Keep clearly in mind that there are people *out there* who will tell you something that absolutely *isn't* so, with every conviction in their being—because they *think* it's true. Sincerity they have, 100 percent. Accuracy is something else again. You will need to check and cross-check any information that people tell you or that you read in books (even this one).

No matter how many people tell you that such-and-so are the rules about getting into a particular occupation, and there are no exceptions—believe me there *are* exceptions, to almost *every* rule, except where a profession has rigid entrance examinations, as in, say, medicine or law.

Rules are rules. But what you are counting on is that somewhere in this vast country, somewhere in this vast world, *somebody* found a way to get into this career you dream of, without going through all the hoops that everyone else is telling you are *absolutely essential.*

You want to find out who these people are, and go talk to them, to find out *how they did it.*

Okay, but suppose you are determined to go into a career that takes *years* to prepare for; and you can't find *anyone* who took a shortcut? What then?

Even here, you can get *close* to the profession *without* such long preparation. Every professional speciality has one or more *shadow* professions, which require much less training. For example, instead of becoming a doctor, you can go into paramedical work; instead of becoming a lawyer, you can go into paralegal work, instead of becoming a licensed career counselor, you can become a career coach.

Have a "Plan B"

Sooner or later, as you interview one person after another, you'll begin to get some definite ideas about a career that is of interest to you. It uses your favorite skills. It employs your favorite Fields of Fascination or fields of interest. You've interviewed people *actually doing that work*, and it all sounds fine. This part of your Informational Interviewing is over.

Just be sure that you get the names of at least *two* careers, or jobs, that you think you could be happy doing. Never, ever, put all your eggs in one basket. The secret of surviving out there in the jungle is *having alternatives*.

Be careful. Be thorough. Be persistent. This is your life you're working on, and your future. Make it glorious. Whatever it takes, find out the name of your ideal career, your ideal occupation, your ideal job—*or jobs.*

Researching Places Before You Approach Them

Why should you research places, before you approach them for a hiring-interview? Well, first of all, you want to know something about the organization from the inside: what kind of work they do there. And what their needs or problems or challenges are. And what kind of goals are they trying to achieve, what obstacles are they running into, and how can your skills and knowledge help them? *(When you do at last go in for a hiring interview, you want above all else to be able to show them that you have something to offer, that they need.)*

Second, you want to find out if you would enjoy working there. You want to take the measure of that organization or organizations. Everybody takes the measure of an organization, but the problem with most job-hunters or career-changers is they take the measure of an organization *after* they are hired there.

In the U.S., for example, a survey of the federal/state employment service once found that 57 percent of those who found jobs through that service were not working at that job just thirty days later.

They were not working at that job just thirty days later, *because* they used the first ten or twenty days *on the job* to screen out that job.

By doing this research of a place ahead of time, you are choosing a better path, by far. Essentially, you are *screening out* careers, jobs, places *before* you commit to them. How sensible! How smart!

So, what you do is try to think of every way in the world that you could find out more about those organizations *(plural, not singular)* that interest you, *before you go to see if you can get hired there.* There are several ways you can do this research ahead of time:

- **Friends and Neighbors.** Ask *everybody* you know, if they know anyone who works at the place that interests you. And, if they do, ask them if they could arrange for you and that person to get together, for lunch, coffee, or tea. At that time, tell them why the place interests you, and indicate you'd like to know more about it. *(It helps if your mutual friend is sitting there with the two of you, so the purpose of this little chat won't be misconstrued.)* This is the vastly preferred way to find out about a place. However, obviously you need a couple of additional alternatives up your sleeve, in case you run into a dead end here:

- **What's in Print.** The organization itself may have stuff in print, or on its website, about its business, purpose, etc. The CEO or head of the organization may have given talks. The organization may have copies of those talks. In addition, there may be brochures, annual reports, etc., that the organization has put out, about itself. How do you get ahold of these? The person who answers the phone is the person to check with, in small organizations. In larger organizations, the publicity office, or human relations office, is the place to check. Also, if it's a decent-sized organization that you are interested in, public libraries may have files on the organization—newspaper clippings, articles, etc. You never know; and it never hurts to ask your friendly neighborhood research librarian.

- **People at the Organizations in Question, or at Similar Organizations.** You can also go directly to organizations and ask questions about the place, but here I must caution you about several *dangers.*

First, you must make sure you're not asking them questions that are in print somewhere, which you could easily have read for yourself instead of bothering *them.*

Second, you must make sure that you approach the people at that organization *whose business it is to give out information—*receptionists, public relations people, "the personnel office," etc.—*before* you ever approach other people higher up in that organization.

Third, you must make sure that you approach *subordinates* rather than the top person in the place, if the subordinates would know the answer to your questions. Bothering the boss there with some simple questions that someone else could have answered is committing *job-hunting suicide*.

Fourth, you must make sure you're not using this approach simply as a sneaky way to get in to see the boss, and make a pitch for them hiring you. This is supposed to be just information gathering. Keep it at that. Keep it honest.

- **Temporary Agencies.** Many job-hunters and career-changers have found that a useful way to explore organizations is to go and work at a temporary agency. Employers turn to these agencies in order to find: a) job-hunters who can work part-time for a limited number of days; and b) job-hunters who can work full-time for a limited number of days. The advantage to you of temporary work is that if there is an agency which loans out people with your particular skills and expertise, you get a chance to be sent to a number of different employers over a period of several weeks, and see each one from the inside. Maybe the temp agency won't send you to exactly the place you hoped for; but sometimes you can develop contacts in the place you love, even while you're temporarily working somewhere else—if both organizations are in the same field.

As I said earlier, some of you may balk at the idea of enrolling with a temporary agency, because you remember the old days when such agencies were solely for clerical workers and secretarial help. But the field has seen an explosion of services in the last decade, and there are temporary agencies these days *(at least in the larger cities)* for many different occupations. In your city you may find temporary agencies for: accountants, industrial workers, assemblers, drivers, mechanics, construction people, engineering people, software engineers, programmers, computer technicians, production workers, management/executives, nannies (for young and old), health care/dental/medical people, legal specialists, insurance specialists, sales/marketing people, underwriting professionals, financial services, and the like, as well as for the more obvious specialties: data processing, secretarial, and office services. See your local phone book, under "Temporary Agencies."

- **Volunteer Work.** Another useful way to research a place before you ever ask them to hire you there, is to volunteer your services at that place that interests you. Of course, some places will turn your offer down, cold. But others will be interested. If they are, it will be relatively easy for you to talk them into letting you work there for a while, because you offer your services *without pay,* and for a brief, limited period of time. In other words, from their point of view, if you turn out to be a *pain,* they won't have to endure you for long.

In this fashion, you get a chance to learn about organizations from the inside. Not so coincidentally, if you do decide you would really like to work there, and permanently, they've had a chance to see you in action, and when you are about to end your volunteer time there, *may* want to hire you permanently. I say *may.* Don't be mad if they simply say, "Thanks very much for helping us out. Goodbye. Farewell." (That's what *usually* happens.) Even so, you've learned a lot, and this will stand you in good stead, in the future—as you approach other organizations.

Send a Thank-You Note

After *anyone* has done you a favor, during this Informational Interviewing phase of your job-hunt, you must *be sure* to send them a thank-you note by the very next day, at the latest. Such a note goes to *everyone* who helps you, or who talks with you. That means friends, people at the organization in question, temporary agency people, secretaries, receptionists, librarians, workers, or whoever.

Ask them, at the time you are face-to-face with them, for their business card (if they have one), or ask them to write out their name and work address, on a piece of paper, for you. You *don't* want to misspell their name. It is difficult to figure out how to spell people's names, these days, simply from the sound of it. What sounds like "Laura" may actually be "Lara." What sounds like "Smith" may actually be "Smythe," and so on. Get that name and address, *but get it right,* please. And let me reiterate:

ALL RIGHT, WHO DID IT?
COME ON! CONFESS!

I WANNA KNOW!

WHO INVENTED
"THANK YOU" NOTES?!

write or e-mail the thank-you note that same night, or the very
next day at the latest. A thank-you note that arrives a week later,
completely misses the point.

Ideally it should be e-mailed immediately, followed by a
lovely printed copy, nicely formatted, and sent through the
mail. Most employers these days prefer a printed letter to a
handwritten one.

It can be just two or three sentences. Something like: "*I wanted
to thank you for talking with me yesterday. It was very helpful to me.
I much appreciated your taking the time out of your busy schedule, to
do this. Best wishes to you,*" and then your signature. *Do* sign it,
particularly if the thank-you note is printed. Printed letters sent
through the mail without any signature seem to be multiplying
like rabbits in the world of work, these days; the absence of a
signature on anything other than an e-mailed thank-you note
is usually perceived as making your letter *real* impersonal. You
don't want to leave that impression.

What If I Get Offered a Job Along the Way, While I'm Just Gathering Information?

You probably won't. Let me remind you that during this information gathering, you are *not* talking primarily to employers.
You're talking to workers.

Nonetheless, an occasional employer *may* stray across your
path during all this Informational Interviewing. And that employer *may* be so impressed with the carefulness you're showing, in going about your career-change and job-search, that they
want to hire you, on the spot. So, it's *possible* that you might get

The Secret to Finding Your Dream Job   **253**

offered a job while you're still doing your information gathering. Not *likely*, but *possible*. And if that happens, what should you say?

Well, if you're desperate, you will of course say *yes*. I remember one wintertime when I had just gone through the knee of my last pair of pants, we were burning old pieces of furniture in our fireplace to stay warm, the legs on our bed had just broken, and we were eating spaghetti until it was coming out our ears. In such a situation, *of course* you say yes.

But if you're not *desperate*, if you have a little time to be more careful, then you respond to the job-offer in a way that will buy you some time. You tell them what you're doing: that the average job-hunter tries to screen a job *after* they take it. But you are doing what you are *sure* this employer would do if they were in your shoes: you are examining careers, fields, industries, jobs, organizations *before* you decide where you can do your best and most effective work.

And you tell them that since your Informational Interviewing isn't finished yet, it would be premature for you to accept their job offer, until you're *sure* that this is the place where you could be most effective, and do your best work.

But, you add: "Of course, I'm tickled pink that you would want me to be working here. And when I've finished my personal survey, I'll be glad to get back to you about this, as my preliminary impression is that this is the kind of place I'd like to work in, and the kind of people I'd like to work for, and the kind of people I'd like to work with."

In other words, *if you're not desperate yet,* you don't walk immediately through any opened doors; but neither do you allow them to shut.

A CLOSING WORD TO THOSE WHO ARE SHY

The late John Crystal often had to counsel the shy. They were often *frightened* at the whole idea of going to talk to people for information, never mind for hiring. So John developed a system to help the shy. He suggested that before you even begin doing any Informational Interviewing, you first go out and talk to people about *anything* just to get good at *talking to people.* Thousands of job-hunters and career-changers have followed his advice, over the past thirty years, and found it really helps. Indeed, people who have followed John's advice in this regard have had a success rate of 86 percent in finding a job—and not just any job, but *the* job or new career that they were looking for.

Daniel Porot, Europe's premiere job-hunting expert, has taken John's system, and brought some organization to it. He observed that John was really recommending three types of interviews: this interview we are talking about, just for practice. Then Informational Interviewing. And finally, of course, the hiring-interview. Daniel decided to call these three the *"The PIE Method,"* which has helped thousands of job-hunters and career-changers in both the U.S. and in Europe.[15]

Why is it called *"PIE"*?

P is for the *warmup* phase. John Crystal named this warm-up "The Practice Field Survey."[16] Daniel Porot calls it **P** for *pleasure.*

I is for "Informational Interviewing."

E is for the employment interview with the-person-who-has-the-power-to-hire-you.

How do you use this **P** for *practice* to get comfortable about going out and talking to people *one-on-one?*

This is achieved by choosing a topic—*any* topic, however silly or trivial—that is a pleasure for you to talk about with your friends, or family. To avoid anxiety, it should not be connected to any present or future careers that you are considering. Rather, the kinds of topics that work best, for this exercise, are:

- **a hobby** you *love,* such as skiing, bridge playing, exercise, computers, etc.
- **any leisure-time enthusiasm** of yours, such as a movie you just saw, that you liked a lot

---

15. Daniel has summarized his system in a book published here in the U.S. in 1996: it is called *The Pie Method for Career Success: A Unique Way to Find Your Ideal Job,* 1996, and is available still from its publisher, JIST Works, Inc., 720 North Park Avenue, Indianapolis IN 46202-3431. Phone 317-264-3720. Fax 317-264-3709. It is a fantastic book, and I give it my highest recommendation.

16. If you want further instructions about this whole process, I refer you to "The Practice Field Survey," pp. 187–196 in *Where Do I Go From Here With My Life?* by John Crystal and friend. Ten Speed Press, Box 7123, Berkeley, CA 94707.

	Pleasure	Information	Employment
Initial:	**P**	**I**	**E**
Kind of Interview	Practice Field Survey	Informational Interviewing or Researching	Employment Interview or Hiring Interview
Purpose	To Get Used to Talking with People to Enjoy It; To "Penetrate" Networks	To Find Out If You'd Like a Job, Before You Go Trying to Get It	To Get Hired for the Work You Have Decided You Would Most Like to Do
How You Go to the Interview	You Can Take Somebody with You	By Yourself or You Can Take Somebody with You	By Yourself
Who You Talk To	Anyone Who Shares Your Enthusiasm About a (for You) Non-Job-Related Subject	A Worker Who Is Doing the Actual Work You Are Thinking About Doing	An Employer Who Has the Power to Hire You for the Job You Have Decided You Would Most Like to Do
How Long a Time You Ask for	10 Minutes (and DON'T run over—asking to see them at 11:50 may help keep you honest, since most employers have lunch appointments at noon)	Ditto	
What You Ask Them	Any Curiosity You Have About Your Shared Interest or Enthusiasm	Any Questions You Have About This Job or This Kind of Work	You Tell Them What It Is You Like About Their Organization and What Kind of Work You Are Looking For

	Pleasure	Information	Employment
Initial:	**P**	**I**	**E**
What You Ask Them *(continued)*	If Nothing Occurs to You, Ask: 1. How did you start, with this hobby, interest, etc.? 2. What excites or interests you the most about it? 3. What do you find is the thing you like the least about it? 4. Who else do you know of who shares this interest, hobby or enthusiasm, or could tell me more about my curiosity? a. Can I go and see them? b. May I mention that it was you who suggested I see them? c. May I say that you recommended them?	If Nothing Occurs to You, Ask: 1. How did you get interested in this work and how did you get hired? 2. What excites or interests you the most about it? 3. What do you find is the thing you like the least about it? 4. Who else do you know of who does this kind of work, or similar work but with this difference: _____? 5. What kinds of challenges or problems do you have to deal with in this job? 6. What skills do you need in order to meet those challenges or problems?	You tell them the kinds of challenges you like to deal with. What skills you have to deal with those challenges. What experience you have had in dealing with those challenges in the past.
	Get their name and address	*Get their name and address*	
AFTERWARD: That Same Night	SEND A THANK-YOU NOTE	SEND A THANK-YOU NOTE	SEND A THANK-YOU NOTE

PASSION OR ENTHUSIASM

Well, I said it before, but I'm going to say it again. Throughout the job-hunt and career-change, the key to informational "interviewing" for shy people is not found in memorizing a dozen questions about what you're supposed to say.

No, the key is just this one thing: now and always, be *sure* you are talking about something you feel *passionate about.*

Enthusiasm is the key—to *enjoying* "interviewing," and conducting *effective* interviews, at any level. What this exercise teaches us is that shyness always loses its power and its painful self-consciousness—*if* and *when* you are talking about something *you love.*

For example, if you love gardens you will forget all about your shyness when you're talking to someone else about gardens and flowers. *"You ever been to Butchart Gardens?"*

If you love movies, you'll forget all about your shyness when you're talking to someone else about movies. *"I just hated that scene where they. . . ."*

If you love computers, then you will forget all about your shyness when you're talking to someone else about computers. *"Do you work on a Mac or a PC?"*

That's why it is important that it be your enthusiasms that you are exploring and pursuing in these conversations with others.

- **a long-time curiosity,** such as how do they predict the weather, or what do policemen do
- **an aspect of the town or city you live in,** such as a new shopping mall that just opened
- **an issue** you feel strongly about, such as the homeless, AIDS sufferers, ecology, peace, health, etc.

There is only one condition about choosing a topic: it should be something you *love* to talk about with other people: a subject you know nothing about, but you feel a great deal of enthusiasm for it, is far preferable to something you know an awful lot about, but it puts you to sleep.

Having identified your enthusiasm, you then need to go talk to someone who is as enthusiastic about this thing, as you are. *For best results with your later job-hunt, this should be someone you don't already know.* Use the yellow pages, ask around among your friends and family, *who do you know that loves to talk about this?* It's relatively easy to find the kind of person you're looking for.

You love to talk about skiing? *Try a ski-clothes store, or a skiing instructor.* You love to talk about writing? *Try a professor on a nearby college campus, who teaches English.* You love to talk about physical exercise? *Try a trainer, or someone who teaches physical therapy.*

Once you've identified someone you think shares your enthusiasm, you then go talk with them. When you are face-to-face with your *fellow enthusiast*, the first thing you must do is relieve their understandable anxiety. *Everyone* has had someone visit them who has stayed too long, who has worn out their welcome. If your *fellow enthusiast* is worried about you staying too long, they'll be so preoccupied with this that they won't hear a word you are saying.

So, when you first meet them, ask for *ten minutes of their time, only.* Period. Stop. Exclamation point. And watch your wrist-watch *like a hawk,* to be sure you stay no longer. *Never* stay longer, unless they *beg* you to. And I mean, *beg, beg, beg.*[17]

Once they've agreed to give you ten minutes, you tell them why you're there—that you're trying to get comfortable about talking with people, for information—and you understand that you two share a mutual interest, which is . . .

Then what? Well, a topic may have its own unique set of questions. For example, I love movies, so if I met someone who shared this interest, my first question would be, "What movies have you seen lately?" And so on. If it's a topic you love, and often talk about, you'll *know* what kinds of questions you begin with. But, if no such questions come to mind, no matter how hard you try, the following ones have proved to be good conversation starters for thousands of job-hunters and career-changers before you, no matter what their topic or interest.

So, look these over, memorize them *(or copy them on a little card that fits in the palm of your hand),* and give them a try:

QUESTIONS SHY PEOPLE CAN PRACTICE WITH

Addressed to the person you're doing the Practice Interviewing with:

- How did you get involved with/become interested in this? (*"This"* is the hobby, curiosity, aspect, issue, or enthusiasm, that you are so interested in.)
- What do you like the most about it?
- What do you like the least about it?
- Who else would you suggest I go talk to who shares this interest?
- Can I use your name?
- May I tell them it was you who recommended that I talk with them?

---

17. A polite, "Oh do you have to go?" should be understood for what it is: politeness. Your response should be, "Yes, I promised to only take ten minutes of your time, and I want to keep to my word." This will almost always leave a *very* favorable impression behind you.

- *Then, choosing one person from the list of several names they may have given you, you say,* "Well, I think I will begin by going to talk to this person. Would you be willing to call ahead for me, so they will know who I am, when I go over there?"

Incidentally, during *this* Practice Interviewing, it's perfectly okay for you to take someone with you—preferably someone who is more outgoing than you feel you are. And on the first few interviews, let them take the lead in the conversation, while you watch to see how they do it.

Once it is *your turn* to conduct the interview, it will by that time usually be easy for you to figure out what to talk about.

Alone or with someone, keep at this Practice Interviewing until you feel very much at ease in talking with people and asking them questions about things you are curious about.

In all of this, *fun* is the key. If you're having fun, you're doing it right. If you're not having fun, you need to keep at it, until you are. It may take seeing four people. It may take ten. Or twenty. You'll know.

Summary of PIE

There is no limit to what you can find out about WHERE you'd like to work—careers, and places which hire for those careers—if you go out and talk to people. When you find places that interest you, it is irrelevant whether they happen to have a vacancy, or not. In this dance of life, called the job-hunt, you get to decide first of all whether or not *you* want *them*, through your research. Only after you have decided that, is it appropriate to ask, as in the next chapter, if they also want you.

262

Identifying Who Has the Power to Hire You

The First Crucial Question: How Large Is the Organization?

To begin with, most discussions of job-interviewing proceed from a false assumption. They *assume* you are going to be approaching a large organization—you know, the ones where you need a floor-plan of the building, and an alphabetical directory of the staff. There are admittedly *huge* problems in approaching such giants for a hiring-interview, not the least of which is that in troubled times, many do more downsizing than hiring.

But many job-hunters don't want to work for large corporations, anyway. They want to go after the so-called "small organizations"—those with fifty or fewer employees—which, in the U.S. for example, represent 80 percent of all private businesses, and one-fourth of all workers in the private sector.

The Virtues of Small Organizations

Experts have claimed for years that small organizations create up to two-thirds of all new jobs.[1] If that makes you prefer going after a small organization, I have good news: they are *much* easier to get into than large ones, believe me.

With a small organization, you don't need to wait until there's a *known* vacancy, because they rarely advertise vacancies even when there is one. You just go there and ask if they need someone.

With a small organization, there is no Personnel or Human Resources Department to screen you out.

With a small organization, there's no problem in identifying the person-who-has-the-power-to-hire-you. It's *the boss.* Everyone there knows who it is. They can point to his or her office door, easily.

With a small organization, you do not need to approach them through the mail; if you use your personal contacts, you can get in to see the boss. And if, by chance, he or she is well-protected from intruders, it is relatively easy to figure out how to get around *that.* Contacts are the answer, as I just indicated.

With a small organization, if it is growing, there is a greater likelihood that they will be willing to create a new position for you, *if you quietly convince them that you are too good to let slip out of their grasp.*

---

1. This statistic, first popularized by David Birch of M.I.T., and widely quoted for years, was challenged during the '90s by economists such as Nobel laureate Milton Friedman and Harvard economist James Medoff. The debate was fueled by a study conducted jointly by Steven J. Davis, a labor economist at the University of Chicago, John Haltiwanger at the University of Maryland, and Scott Schuh at the Federal Reserve. Their study, however, was of U.S. *manufacturing,* not of the economy as a whole. Anyway, what these researchers discovered at that time is that small *manufacturing* companies with fifty or fewer employees created only *one-fifth* of all new manufacturing jobs (*New York Times,* 3/25/94). Other researchers, notably Birch, claim that if you include all small companies, they create as many as two-thirds of all new jobs. Has this changed in the new millennium? Hard to tell. Certainly, the U.S. dot.com meltdown that began in April of 2000 made many people afraid to work for small companies—in the Internet field, at least, and in the so-called "New Economy" for sure.

Chapter Eleven

For all of these reasons and more, small organizations must be kept in mind, as much as, or more than, large organizations, when we begin talking about techniques or strategies for securing a hiring-interview. But let's take each separately, as they involve two different techniques:

Approaching Large Organizations for an Interview

In securing hiring-interviews, it's the large organizations that are the problem—the ones, as I mentioned above, where you need a floor-plan of the building, and an alphabetical directory of the staff.

But you can simplify your task, if you keep certain things in mind. To begin with, you don't want to just get into the building. You want to get in in order to see *a particular person* in that building, and only that person: namely, the person-who-has-the-power-to-hire-you for the job you are interested in.

Most job-hunters *don't* even *try* to find out *who* that person is, before approaching a large organization. Rather, they approach each large organization in what can only be described as a haphazard, scatter-shot fashion—sending them their resume or c.v.[2], with or without some covering letter, or posting their resume on that organization's website—hoping that their resume or covering letter will function as a kind of extended calling card, arousing employers' interest, who will then ask the job-hunter to come in and see them.

This blanket, depersonalized approach is many job-hunters' favorite way of approaching an organization, particularly a large organization, for a hiring-interview. It's their favorite because you don't have to *go* somewhere needlessly, you don't have to look into the employers' eyes when they reject you, and—let's admit it—sometimes it actually works: you do get invited in for a possible hiring-interview.

Also, to be truthful, *some* employers love this "mail approach," but for all the wrong reasons (from your point of view).

2. C.v. stands for *curriculum vitae,* a term for *resume* that is favored in academic circles in the U.S. and in other countries.

They love it, because it enables them to screen you out *in about eight seconds,* without ever "wasting their time" on your coming in for an interview.

It is not uncommon for job-hunters to approach eight hundred organizations or more in this fashion and not get *one* single invitation to come in for a hiring-interview.

But fortunately, there is a far far more effective way to approach employers—and that is to identify *who* at that organization has the power to hire you for the position you have in mind, and then to discover what mutual friend the two of you might have in common, who could help you get an appointment. The person-who-has-the-power-to-hire-you will see you because that mutual friend got the appointment for you.

How Do I Find Out Exactly Who Has the Power to Hire Me?

In a small organization with fifty or fewer employees, this is a relatively easy problem. Calling the place and asking for the name of the boss, should do it. It's what we call *The One-Minute Research Project.*

But if the place where you are dying to work is a much larger organization, then the answer is: "Through the *research* you already learned how to do in chapter 10; *and* by asking every *contact* you have."

Let's say that one of the places you are interested in is an organization which we will call *Mythical Corporation.*

You know the kind of job you'd like to get there, but first you know you need to find out the name of the person-who-has-the-power-to-hire-you there. What do you do?

If it's a large organization, you go on the Internet or you go to your local public library, and search the directories there. Hopefully that search will yield the name of the person you want.

But if it doesn't, which will particularly be the case with smaller organizations, *then you turn to your contacts.*

The Virtue of Contacts

So now, to our task. You want to approach, let us say, *Mythical Corporation* and you know that to get in there, you will need to use your contacts. So, what do you do? Well, you approach as many people from the above list as necessary and you ask each of them, "Do you know anyone who works, or used to work, at *Mythical Corporation*?"

WHO OR WHAT IS A "CONTACT"?

Since this subject of *contacts* is widely misunderstood by job-hunters and career-changers, let's be very specific, here.

Every person you know, is a contact.

Every member of your family.

Every friend of yours.

Every person in your address book.

Every person on your Christmas-card list.

Every person you met at any party you attended in the last year or two.

Every co-worker from your last five jobs.

Every person you know at your gym or athletic place.

Every person you know on any athletic team.

Every merchant or salesperson you ever deal with.

Every person who comes to your apartment or house to do any kind of repairs or maintenance work.

Every person you meet in line at the supermarket or bank.

Every check-out clerk you know.

Every gas station attendant you know.

Everyone who does personal work on you: your barber, hairdresser, manicurist, physical trainer, body worker, and the like.

The waiters, waitresses, and manager of your favorite restaurants.

All the people you meet on the Internet. All the people whose e-mail addresses you have.

Every leisure partner you have, as for walking, exercising, swimming, or whatever.

Every doctor, or medical professional you know.

Every professor, teacher, etc. you once knew or maybe still know how to get a hold of.

Identifying Who Has the Power to Hire You

Every person in your church, synagogue, mosque, or religious assembly.

Everyone you know in Rotary, Kiwanis, Lions, or other service organizations.

Every person you know at any group you belong to.

Every person you are newly introduced to.

Every person you meet, stumble across, or blunder into, during your job-hunt, whose name, address, and phone number you have the grace to ask for. (*Always have the grace to ask for it.*)

Got the picture?

You ask that question again and again of *everyone* you know, or meet, until you find someone who says, *"Yes, I do."*

Then you ask them:

"What is the name of the person you know who works, or used to work, at *Mythical Corporation*? Do you have their phone number and/or address?"

"Would you be willing to call ahead, to tell them who I am?"

You then either phone them yourself or make an appointment to go see them (*"I won't need more than twenty minutes of your time."*). Once you are talking to them, after the usual polite chit-chat, you ask them the question you are dying to know. Because they are *inside* the organization that interests you, they are usually able to give you the exact answer to the question that has been puzzling you: "Who would have the power to hire me at *Mythical Corporation*, for this kind of position *(which you then describe)*?" If they answer that they do not know, ask if they know *who* might know. If it turns out that they do know, then you ask them not only for that hiring person's name, address, phone, and e-mail address, but also what they can tell you about that person's job, that person's interests, and their style of interviewing.

Chapter Eleven

Then, you ask them if they could help you get an appointment with that person. You repeat once again the familiar refrain:

"Given my background, would you recommend I go see them?"

"Do you know them, personally? If not, could you give me the name of someone who does?"

"If you know them personally, may I tell them it was you who recommended that I talk with them?"

"If you know them personally, would you be willing to call ahead, to tell them who I am, and to help set up an appointment?"

Also, before leaving, you can ask them about the organization, in general.

Then you thank them, and leave; and you *never never* let the day end, without sitting down to write them a thank-you note. *Always* do it. *Never* forget to.

Getting In

If the contact you talked to, doesn't know the **person-who-has-the-power-to-hire-you** well enough to get you an interview, then you go back to your other contacts—now armed with the name of the person you are trying to get in to see—and pose a new question. Approaching as many of your contacts as necessary, you ask each of them, "Do you know Ms. or Mr. See, at *Mythical Corporation* or do you know someone who does?"

You ask that question again and again of *everyone* who is on your file cards, until you find someone who says, "*Yes, I do.*"

Then of course, over the phone or—better—in person, you ask them the same familiar questions, carefully, and in this exact order:

- "What can you tell me about him—or her?"
- "Given the kind of job I am looking for *(which you here describe)*, do you think it would be worth my while to go see them?"
- "Do you have their phone number and/or address?"

- "May I tell them it was you who recommended that I talk with them?"
- "Would you be willing to call ahead, to set up an appointment for me, and tell them who I am?"

May-Day, May-Day!

Whenever a job-hunter writes me and tells me they've run into a brick wall, and just can't find out the name of the person-who-has-the-power-to-hire-them, the problem *always* turns out to be: they aren't making *sufficient* use of their contacts. They're making a *pass* at using their contacts, but they aren't putting their whole heart and soul into it.

My favorite (true) story in this regard, concerns a job-hunter I know, in Virginia. He decided he wanted to work for a particular health-care organization in that state, and not knowing any better, he approached them by visiting their Human Resources Department. After dutifully filling out a job application, and talking to someone there in that department, he was told there were no jobs available. Stop. Period. End of story.

Approximately three months later he learned about this technique of approaching your favorite organization by using contacts. He explored his contacts *diligently*, and succeeded in getting an interview with the person-who-had-the-power-to-hire-him for the position he was interested in. The two of them hit it off, immediately. The appointment went swimmingly. "You're hired," said the person-who-had-the-power-to-hire-him. "I'll call Human Resources and tell them you're hired, and that you'll be down to fill out the necessary stuff."

Our job-hunter never once mentioned that he had previously approached that same organization through that same Human Resources Department, and been turned down cold.

Just remember: contacts are the key. It takes about eighty pairs of eyes, and ears, to help find the career, the workplace, the job that you are looking for.

Your contacts *are* those eyes and ears.

They are what will help you get the ideal job you are looking for, and they are key to finding out the name of the person-who-has-the-power-to-hire-you.

The more people you know, the more people you meet, the more people you talk to, the more people you enlist as part of your own personal job-hunting network, the better your job-finding success is likely to be. Therefore, you must try to grow your contacts wherever you go.

Here's how some people have gone about doing that. If they go to hear a speaker on some subject that interests them, they make it a point to join the crowd that gathers 'round the speaker at the end of the talk, and—with notepad poised—ask such questions as: "Is there anything special that people with my expertise can do?" And here they mention their *generalized* job-title: computer scientist, health professional, chemist, writer, or whatever. Very useful information has thus been turned up. You can also go up to the speaker afterwards, and ask if you can contact him or her for further information—"and at what address?"

Conventions, likewise, afford rich opportunities to make contacts. Says one college graduate: "I snuck into the Cable Advertisers Convention at the Waldorf in N.Y.C. That's how I got my job."

Identifying Who Has the Power to Hire You

Another way people have cultivated contacts, is to leave a message on their telephone answering machine which tells everyone who calls, what information they are looking for. One job-hunter used the following message: "This is the recently laid off John Smith. I'm not home right now because I'm out looking for a good job as a computer trouble-shooter in the telecommunications field; if you have any leads or just want to leave a message, please leave it after the tone."

You may also cultivate contacts by studying the *things* that you like to work with, and then writing to the manufacturer of that *thing* to ask them for a list of organizations in your geographical area which use that *thing*. For example, if you like to work on a particular machine, you would write to the manufacturer of that machine, and ask for names of organizations in your geographical area which use that machine. Or if you like to work in a particular environment, think of the supplies used in that environment. For example, let's say you love darkrooms. You think of what brand of equipment or supplies is usually used in darkrooms, and then you contact the sales manager of the company that makes those supplies, to ask where his (or her) customers are. Some sales managers will not be at all responsive to such an inquiry; but others graciously will, and thus you may gain some very helpful leads.

Because your memory is going to be overloaded during your job-hunt or career-change, it is useful to set up a filing system, where you put the name of each contact of yours on a 3 x 5 card, with addresses, phone numbers, and anything about where they work or who they know that may be of use at a later date. Those of you who are extremely computer literate can, if you prefer, use a database program to do the same thing. Go back over those cards (or their electronic equivalent) frequently.

That does add up to *a lot* of file cards, just because you've got *a lot* of contacts. But that's the whole point.

You may need *every one* of them, *when push comes to shove*.

Rescuing the Employer

As you can see, getting in to see someone, even for a hiring-interview, is not as difficult as people will tell you. It just takes some *know-how*, some *determination*, some *perseverance*, some *go-*

ing the extra mile. It works because everyone has friends, including this **person-who-has-the-power-to-hire-you.** You are simply approaching them through *their* friends. And you are doing this, not *wimpishly,* as one who is coming to ask a favor. You are doing it *helpfully,* as one who is asking to help rescue them.

Rescue? Yes, rescue! I cannot tell you the number of employers I have known over the years, who can't figure out how to find the right employee. It is absolutely mind-boggling, particularly in these hard times when job-hunters would seem to be gathered on every street corner.

You're having trouble finding the employer. The employer is having trouble finding you. *What a great country!*

So, if you now present yourself directly to the **person-who-has-the-power-to-hire-you,** you are not only answering your own prayers. You are hopefully answering the employer's, as well. You will be *just* what the employer is looking for, but didn't know how to find, if . . .

if you figured out what are your favorite and best skills, and

if you therefore figured out what are your favorite Fields of Fascination or *languages,* and

if you took the trouble to figure out what places *might* need such skills and such *languages,* and

if you researched these places with the intent of finding out what their tasks, challenges and problems are, and

if you took the trouble to figure out who there has the power to hire you.

Of course, you don't for sure *know* they need you; that remains for the hiring-interview to uncover. But at least by this thorough preparation you have *increased* the chances that you are at the right place—whether they have an announced vacancy or not. And, if you are, you are not imposing on this employer. You are coming not as "job-beggar," but as "resource person." You may well be absolutely rescuing him or her, believe me!

And yourself. *"The hiring-interview! I'm actually there."*

Yes, and so, it's time for the next section.

You're a bunch of jackasses. You work your rear ends off in a trivial course that no one will ever care about again. You're not willing to spend time researching a company that you're interested in working for. Why don't you decide who you want to work for and go after them?

Professor Albert Shapiro
The late William H. Davis Professor of the American Free Enterprise System at Ohio State University

274

Ten
Interviewing
Tips

HOW
Do You Land the Job?

The Most Important Things to Remember

1. The job-interview is not a test, where the employer decides whether you pass or fail. It is part of their data-collecting, and—more importantly—part of your data-collecting too, since you should be still trying to decide if this is a good place for you to work, or not. In other words, the interview resembles dating more than it resembles someone buying a used car (you).

2. You want to present yourself, not as a job-beggar, but as a resource-broker.

3. "Behavioral interviews" are very big with organizations that have 250 employees, or more. You may in fact run into them in much smaller organizations. In behavioral interviews, employers are looking for you to give them real-life examples from your past, that demonstrate your skills, performance, and achievement; not just vague claims on your part, like: "I'm good at . . ."

275

4. Employers are most impressed with examples that have the fourfold form of Goal, Obstacles, Solution, Numbers: "Here was the task we were trying to accomplish, these were the obstacles in our way, this is what I did to overcome those obstacles, and these were the results, expressed in numbers" (in whatever way you can put a figure or numbers, to the results).

5. Employers are particularly interested in your skills, as already demonstrated in the past; specifically, your transferable skills, your content skills, and your self-management skills, or traits.

6. At the end of the interview, if things look like they're going to just be left up in the air, **ask** for the job before you leave. "Can you offer me this job?" You'll be surprised how often this makes all the difference in the world. Ask for the job. Ask for the job.

Okay, now on to our ten tips.

First Interviewing Tip

To begin with, successful job-hunters have found it very useful to think of a job-interview as a picture, within a frame. The frame is how you mentally structure and prepare for the interview *ahead of time*. The picture inside is the content of what you say *during* the interview.

Interviewing books and articles often focus only on the *picture*—what you say once you're in the room with the interviewer. But, of equal importance is *the frame:* how you set up the whole interview, first of all in your mind, and second in the arrangements you make before going in.

Therefore, let us begin here with some tips about the *frame*.

Ask for Twenty Minutes, No More, When You First Set Up the Interview

---

If you are the one who asks for the job-interview, only ask for twenty minutes; and keep to this, religiously. Once you're into the interview, stay aware of the time and determine that you will not stay *one minute longer* than the twenty minutes you requested—unless the employer begs you to. And I mean *begs.*

Keep to your original agreement. ("I said I would only require twenty minutes of your time, and I like to honor agreements.") This will always impress an employer!

Research the Organization, Before You Go In

Wherever possible, you *must* research the organization ahead of time, before going in for an interview. This will put you ahead (in the employer's mind) of the other people they talk to.

Toward this end, when the appointment is first set up, ask them right then and there if they have anything *in writing* about their organization; if so, request they mail it to you, so you'll have time to read it before the interview. Or, if the interview is the next day, offer to come down that very day and pick it up, yourself.

Also go to their website *(if they have one)* and read everything they have there "About Us."

Also, go to your local library, and ask the librarian for help in locating any newspaper articles or other information about that organization.

Finally, ask all your friends if they know anyone who is working there, or used to work there; if they do, ask them to put you in contact with them, *please*. Tell them you have a job-interview there, and you'd like to know anything they can tell you about the place.

This is a matter of becoming familiar with their history, their purposes, and their goals. All organizations, be they large or small, profit or nonprofit, love to be loved. If you have gone to all this trouble, to learn so much about them—before you ever walk in their doors—they will be impressed, believe me, because most job-hunters never go to this trouble. *They* walk in knowing little or nothing about the organization. This drives employers *nuts.*

One time, the first question an IBM college recruiter asked a graduating senior was, "What do the initials IBM stand for?" The senior didn't know, and the interview was over.

Another time, an employer said to me, "I'm so tired of job-hunters who come in, and say, *'Uh, what do you do here?'* that the next time someone walks in who already knows something about us, I'm going to hire him or her, on the spot." And he did, within the week.

Thus, if *you* come in, and have done your homework on the organization, this immediately makes you stand out from other job-hunters, and dramatically speeds up your chances of being offered a job there.

During the Interview, Determine to Observe the 50-50 Rule

Studies have revealed that, in general, the people who get hired are those who mix speaking and listening fifty-fifty in the interview. That is, half the time they let the employer do the talking, half the time in the interview they do the talking. People who didn't follow that mix, were the ones who didn't get hired, according to the study.[1] My hunch as to the *reason* why this is so, is that if you talk too much about yourself, you come across as one who would ignore the needs of the organization; while if you talk too little, you come across as trying to hide something about your background.

In Answering the Employer's Questions, Observe the Twenty Second to Two-Minute Rule

---

Studies[2] have revealed that when it is your turn to speak or answer a question, you should plan ahead of time not to speak any longer than two minutes at a time, if you want to make the best impression. In fact, a good answer to an employer's question sometimes only takes twenty seconds to give. This is useful information for you to know, in conducting a successful interview—as you certainly want to do.

---

1. This one was done by a researcher at Massachusetts Institute of Technology, whose name has been lost in the mists of time.
2. This one was conducted by my friend and colleague, Daniel Porot, of Geneva, Switzerland.

Determine to Be Seen in the Interview as a Resource Person, Not a Job Beggar

Determine that during the interview you will stay focused on what you can do for the employer, rather than on what the employer can do for you. You want the employer to see you as a potential *Resource Person* for that organization, rather than as simply *A Job Beggar* (to quote Daniel Porot). You want to come across as *a problem solver*, rather than as *one who simply keeps busy*. You need to make it clear during the job-interview that you are there in order to make an oral proposal of what *you can do for them*, to help them with *their* problems. And determine that once the interview is over, you will follow this up with a carefully worded written proposal on the same theme. You will see immediately what a switch this is from the way most job-hunters approach an employer! (*"How much do you pay, and how much time off will I have?"*) Will he or she be glad to see you, with this different emphasis? In most cases, you bet they will. They *want* a resource person, and a problem-solver.

Determine to Be Seen as a Part of the Solution, Not as a Part of the Problem

Every organization has two main preoccupations for its day-by-day work: the problems they are facing, and what solutions to those problems people are coming up with, there. Therefore, the main thing the employer is going to be trying to figure out during the hiring-interview with you, is: will you be part of the *solution* there, or just another part of the *problem*.

In trying to answer this concern, figure out prior to the interview how a *bad* employee would "screw up," in the position you are asking for—such things as *come in late, take too much time off, follow his or her own agenda instead of the employer's, etc.* Then plan to emphasize to the employer during the interview how much you are the very opposite: your sole goal is to increase the organization's effectiveness and service and bottom line.

Be aware of the skills employers are looking for, these days, regardless of the position you are seeking. Overall, they are looking for employees: *who are punctual, arriving at work on time or early; who stay until quitting time, or even leave late; who are dependable; who have a good attitude; who have drive, energy, and enthusiasm; who want more than a paycheck; who are self-disciplined, well-organized, highly motivated, and good at managing their time; who can handle people well; who can use language effectively; who can work on a computer; who are committed to team work; who are flexible, and can respond to novel situations, or adapt when circumstances at work change; who are trainable, and love to learn; who are project-oriented, and goal-oriented; who have creativity and are good at problem solving; who have integrity; who are loyal to the organization; who are able to identify opportunities, markets, coming trends.* They also want to hire people who can bring in more money than they are paid. *Plan on claiming all of these that you* legitimately *can, during the hiring-interview.*

Realize That the Employer Thinks the Way You Are Doing Your Job-Hunt Is the Way You Will Do the Job

---

Plan on illustrating by the way you conduct your job-hunt whatever it is you claim will be true of you, once hired. For example, if you plan on claiming during the interview that you are very *thorough* in all your work, be sure to be thorough in the way

Chapter Twelve

you have researched the organization ahead of time. For, the manner in which you do your job-hunt and the manner in which you would do the job you are seeking, are not assumed by most employers to be two unrelated subjects, but one and the same. They can tell when you are doing a slipshod, halfhearted job-hunt (*"Uh, what do you guys do here?"*), and this is taken as a clear warning that you might do a slipshod, halfhearted job, were they foolish enough to ever hire you. Employers know this simple truth: Most people job-hunt the same way they live their lives, and the way they do their work.

Bring Evidence If You Can

Try to think of some way to bring evidence of your skills, to the hiring-interview. For example, if you are an artist, craftsperson, or anyone who produces a product, try to bring a sample of what you have made or produced—either in person, or through photos, or even videotapes.

Determine Ahead of Time Not to Bad-Mouth Your Previous Employer(s) During the Interview

During the hiring-interview, plan on never speaking badly of your previous employer(s). Employers often feel as though they are a fraternity or sorority. During the interview you want to come across as one who displays courtesy toward *all* members of that fraternity or sorority. Bad-mouthing a previous employer only makes this employer worry about what you would say about *them*, after they hire you.

I learned this in my own experience. I once spoke graciously about a previous employer, to my (then) present employer. Unbeknownst to me, my present employer already *knew* that my previous employer had badly mistreated me. He therefore thought very highly of me because I didn't drag it up. In fact, he never forgot this incident; talked about it for years afterward. Believe me, it always makes a *big* impression when you don't bad-mouth a previous employer.

Plan on saying something nice about your previous employer, or if you are afraid that the previous employer is going to give you a very bad recommendation, seize the bull by the horns. Say something simple like, "I usually get along with everybody; but for some reason, my past employer and I just didn't get along. Don't know why. It's never happened to me before. Hope it never happens again."

Determine That the Interview Will Be Part of Your Ongoing Research, and not Just a Sales Pitch

---

Your natural question, as you approach any job-interview, will tend to be, "How do I convince this employer to hire me?" Wrong question. It implies that you have already made up your mind that this would be a grand place to work at, and he or she a grand person to work for, so that all that remains is for you to sell yourself. But, in most cases, despite your best attempts to research the place thoroughly, you don't know enough about it yet, to say that. You have *got* to use the hiring-interview as a chance to gather further information about this organization, and this boss.

If you understand *this* about an interview, you will be ahead of 98 percent of all other job-hunters—who all too often go to the hiring-interview as a lamb goes to the slaughter, or as a criminal goes on trial before a judge.

You *are* on trial, of course, in the employer's eyes.

But, good news—so is that employer and that organization, in *your* eyes.

This is what makes the job-interview tolerable or even enjoyable: you are studying everything about this employer, at the same time that they are studying everything about you.

Two people, both sizing each other up. You know what that reminds you of, of course. *Dating.*

Well, the job-interview is every bit like the "dating game." Both of you have to like each other, before you can even discuss the question of *"going steady,"* i.e., a job. So, you're sitting there, sizing each other up.

The importance of your not just leaving the evaluation to the employer, but of doing your own weighing of this person, this organization, and this job, *during* the hiring-interview, cannot be overstated. The tradition in the U.S., and throughout the world for that matter, is to find a job, take it, and *then* after you're in it trying to figure out in the next three months whether it is a good job or not—and quitting if you decide it isn't.

You are going against this stupid custom, as any smartie should, by using the hiring-interview to screen the organization *before you decide to go to work there.* And if you decide you don't like what you're hearing during the job-interview, then you in effect, *quit before you're offered the job,* rather than *quitting after you've taken the job.* Believe me, if you show that kind of smartness, the employer will thank you, your Mother will thank you, your spouse or partner will thank you, and of course you will thank yourself.

Second Interviewing Tip

So much for the frame of the interview. Now for the picture within that frame, the actual content of what you say during the interview. We begin with this simple thought:

> **Many Employers Are as Scared as You Are During the Hiring Interview**

As you go in to the interview, keep in mind that **the person-who-has-the-power-to-hire-you** is sweating too. Why? Because, the hiring-interview is not a very reliable way to choose an employee. In a survey conducted some years ago among a dozen top United Kingdom employers,[3] it was discovered that the chances of an employer finding a good employee through the hiring-interview was only *3 percent better* than if they had picked a name out of a hat. In a further ironic finding, it was discovered that if the interview were conducted by someone

---

3. Reported in the *Financial Times Career Guide 1989* for the United Kingdom.

who would be working directly with the candidate, the success rate dropped to *2 percent below* that of picking a name out of a hat. And if the interview were conducted by a so-called personnel expert, the success rate dropped to *10 percent below* that of picking a name out of a hat.

No, I don't know how they came up with these figures. But they sure are a hoot! And, more important, they are totally consistent with what I have learned about the world of hiring during the past thirty years. I have watched so-called personnel or human resources experts make *wretchedly* bad choices about hiring *in their own office*, and when they would morosely confess this to me some months later, over lunch, I would playfully tease them with, "If you don't even know how to hire well for your own office, how do you keep a straight face when you're called in as a hiring consultant by another organization?" And they would ruefully reply, "We act *as though it were* a science." Well, let me tell you, dear reader, the hiring-interview is *not* a science. It is a very very hazy art, done badly by most of its employer-practitioners, in spite of their own past experience, their very best intentions, and their carloads of goodwill.

The hiring interview is not what it seems to be. It seems to be one individual *(you)* sitting there, scared to death while the other individual *(the employer)* is sitting there, blasé and confident.

But what it really is, is two individuals *(you and the employer)* sitting there scared to death. It's just that the employer has learned to *hide* his or her fears better than you have, because they've had more practice.

But this employer is, after all, a human being just like you. They were *never* hired to do *this*. It got thrown in with all their other duties. And they may *know* they're not very good at it. So, they're afraid.

> ## It Will Help If You Mentally Catalog, Ahead of Time, not Your Fears, but the Employer's

The employer's fears include *any or all* of the following:

A. That you won't be able to do the job: that you lack the necessary skills or experience, and the hiring-interview didn't uncover this.

B. That if hired, you won't put in a full working day, regularly.

C. That if hired, you'll be frequently "out sick," or otherwise absent whole days.

D. That if hired, you'll only stay around for a few weeks or at most a few months, and then quit without advance warning.

E. That it will take you too long to master the job, and thus it will be too long before you're profitable to that organization.

F. That you won't get along with the other workers there, or that you will develop a personality conflict with the boss himself (or herself).

G. That you will do only the minimum that you can get away with, rather than the maximum that they hired you for.

H. That you will always have to be told what to do next, rather than displaying initiative—always in a responding mode, rather than an initiating mode (and mood).

I. That you will have a work-disrupting character flaw, and turn out to be: dishonest, or totally irresponsible, a spreader of dissension at work, lazy, an embezzler, a gossip, a sexual harasser, a drug-user or substance abuser, a drunk, a liar, incompetent, or—in a word—*bad news.*

J. *If this is a large organization, and your would-be boss is not the top person:* that you will bring discredit upon them, and upon their department/section/division, etc., for ever hiring you in the first place—making them lose face, possibly also costing them a raise or a promotion.

K. That you will cost a lot of money, if they make a mistake by hiring you. Currently, in the U.S. the cost to an employer of a bad hire can far exceed $50,000 including relocation costs, lost pay for the period for work not done or aborted, and severance pay—if *they* are the ones who decide to let you go.

No wonder the employer is *sweating*.

In the old days, the employer had help in making this decision. They could get useful information by talking to your previous employers. No more. Employers have gotten badly burned since the 1980s by job-hunters filing lawsuits alleging "unlawful discharge," or "being deprived of an ability to make a living." Most employers have consequently adopted the policy of refusing to volunteer *any* information about past employees, except name, rank, and serial number—i.e., the person's job-title and dates of employment.

So now, during the hiring interview, the employer is completely on his or her own in trying to figure out whether or not to hire you. Their fears have moved to the front burner. The hiring-interview these days has become *everything*.

Fourth Interviewing Tip

> **You Don't Have to Spend Hours Memorizing a Lot of "Good Answers" to Potential Questions from the Employer; There Are Only Five Questions That Matter**

Of course, the employer is going to be asking you some questions, as a way of helping them to figure out whether or not they want to hire you. Books on *interviewing*, of which there are many, often publish lists of these questions—or at least some *typical* ones that employers often ask. They include such questions as:

- What do you know about this company?
- Tell me about yourself.
- Why are you applying for this job?
- How would you describe yourself?
- What are your major strengths?

- What is your greatest weakness?
- What type of work do you like to do best?
- What are your interests outside of work?
- What accomplishment gave you the greatest satisfaction?
- Why did you leave your last job?
- Why were you fired (if you were)?
- Where do you see yourself five years from now?
- What are your goals in life?
- How much did you make at your last job?

Well, the list goes on and on. In some books, you'll find eighty-nine questions, or more.

You are then told that you should prepare for the hiring-interview by writing out, practicing, and memorizing some devilishly clever answers to *all* these questions—answers which those books of course furnish you with.

All of this is well-intentioned, and has been *the state of the art* for decades. But, dear friend, Good News! We are in the new millennium, and things are getting simpler.

Beneath the dozens and dozens of possible questions that the employer could ask you, we now know that there are only *five basic questions,* that you really need to pay attention to.

Five. Just five. The people-who-have-the-power-to-hire-you usually want to know the answers to these five questions, which they may ask directly or try to find out obliquely:

1. **"Why are you here?"** *They mean by this, "Why are you knocking on my door, rather than someone else's door?"*
2. **"What can you do for us?"** *They mean by this, "If I were to hire you, would you be part of the problems I already have, or would you be a part of the solution to those problems? What are your skills, and how much do you know about some subject or field that is of interest to us?"*
3. **"What kind of person are you?"** *They mean by this, "Do you have the kind of personality that makes it easy for people to work with you, and do you share the values which we have at this place?"*
4. **"What distinguishes you from nineteen other people who can do the same tasks that you can?"** *They mean by this, "Do you have better work habits than the nineteen others, do*

you show up earlier, stay later, work more thoroughly, work faster, maintain higher standards, go the extra mile, or . . . what?"

5. **"Can I afford you?"** *They mean by this, "If we decide we want you here, how much will it take to get you, and are we willing and able to pay that amount—governed, as we are, by our budget, and by our inability to pay you as much as the person who would be above you, on the organizational chart?"*

These are the five principal questions that most employers are dying to know the answers to. *This is the case, even if the interview begins and ends with these five questions never once being mentioned overtly by the employer.* The questions are still *floating in the air* there, beneath the surface of the conversation, beneath all the other things that are being discussed. Anything you can do, during the interview, to help the employer find the answers to these five questions, will make the interview very satisfying to the employer.

Nothing for you to go memorize. If you just do the homework in this book, you will know the five answers. Period. End of story.

Fifth Interviewing Tip

> **You Need to Find Out the Answers**
> **to the Very Same Questions That the Employer**
> **Would Like to Ask You**

During the hiring-interview you have the right—nay, the duty—to find out the answers to the very same five questions *as the employer's*, only in a slightly different form. Your questions will come out looking like this:

1. **"What does this job involve?"** *You want to understand exactly what tasks will be asked of you, so that you can determine if these are the kinds of tasks you would really like to do.*
2. **"What are the skills a top employee in this job would have to have?"** *You want to know if your skills match those which the employer thinks a top employee in this job would have to have, in order to do this job well.*

Chapter Twelve

3. **"Are these the kinds of people I would like to work with, or not?"** *Do not ignore your intuition if it tells you that you would not be comfortable working with these people!! You want to know if they have the kind of personality that would make it easy for you to accomplish your work, and if they share the values which are important to you.*

4. **"If we like each other, and both want to work together, can I persuade them there is something unique about me, that makes me different from nineteen other people who can do the same tasks?"** *You need to think out, way ahead of time, what does make you different from nineteen other people who can do the same job. For example, if you are good at analyzing problems, how do you do that? Painstakingly? Intuitively, in a flash? By consulting with greater authorities in the field? You see the point. You are trying to put your finger on the "style" or "manner" in which you do your work, that is distinctive and hopefully appealing, to* this *employer.*

5. **"Can I persuade them to hire me at the salary I need or want?"** *This requires some knowledge on your part of how to conduct salary negotiation. See the next chapter.*

You will probably want to ask questions one and two out loud. You will *observe* quietly the answer to question three. You will be prepared to make the case for questions four and five, when the *appropriate* time in the interview arises (again, see the next chapter).

How do you get into these questions? You might begin by reporting to them just exactly how you've been conducting your job-hunt, and what impressed you so much about *their* organization during your research, that you decided to come in and talk to them about a job. Then you can fix your attention, during the remainder of the interview, on finding out the answers to the five questions above—in your own way.[4]

---

4. Additional questions you may want to ask, to elaborate upon these five:
   What significant changes has this company gone through in the
     last five years?
   What values are sacred to this company?
   What characterizes the most successful employees this company has?
   What future changes do you see in the work here?
   Who do you see as your allies, colleagues, or competitors in this business?

Yes, there are only *five* questions that really count in a job-interview; but how these five questions keep popping up! They pop up in a slightly different form (yet again), if you're there to talk *not* about a job that already exists but rather, one that you want them to *create* for you. In that kind of interview, or approach to an organization, these five questions get changed into five *statements*, that you make to this person-who-has-the-power-to-hire-you:

1. What you **like** about this organization.
2. What sorts of **needs** you find intriguing in this field and in this organization (unless you first hear the word *"problems"* coming out of their mouth, don't ever use the word *"problems,"* inasmuch as most employers prefer synonyms such as *"challenges"* or *"needs"*).
3. What **skills** seem to you to be needed in order to meet such needs.
4. **Evidence** from your past experience that demonstrates you have the very skills you claim. Employers are looking for *examples* from your past performance and achievement; not just vague statements like: "I'm good at . . ." They want concrete examples, specifically of your transferable skills, your content skills, and your self-management skills, i.e., traits.

If you read the previous chapters *(and didn't just leap to this section, because your interview is tomorrow),* you already know this. It's the underlying principle of what is called *Behavioral Interviewing,* or *competency-based interviewing.* This form of interviewing is extremely common these days in organizations with 250 employees or more; but you can run into it, even in smaller organizations. You just never know; so, you would be wise to be prepared.

You may be asked, or—if you're not—you can pose the same question yourself, near the top of the interview: "What are the three most important competencies, for this job?" (Competencies can mean your functional/transferable skills, and/or your content skills—what you need to know a lot about.) Then, of course, you need to show during the interview that you *have* those three—for the job that you are interested in.

5. What is **unique** about the way *you* perform those skills. As I said before: every prospective employer wants to know *what makes you different* from nineteen other people who can do the same kind of work as you do. You *have* to know what that is. And then not merely talk about it, but actually demonstrate it by the way you conduct your part of the hiring-interview. *For example, "I am very thorough in the way I would do the job for you"* translates into the imperative that you be thorough in the way you have researched the place before you go in for the hiring interview. That's *evidence* the employer can see with their own eyes.

A Special Note to *Those Who Consider Themselves Members of the Entitlement Generation:* Don't let "what is unique about you?" go to your head, please. If you're just out of college, and your idea of a job-interview is that you just waltz right in there and tell them how wonderful you are, how lucky they are to get you, and how you're expecting top dollar right out of college, equal to what they pay employees who've been there for twenty years, I recommend you do more reading on the subject of Conducting the Interview. Employers are searching for men and women of a humble spirit, who know their worth, but know other people's worth also. It's like the players in an orchestra.

Sixth Interviewing Tip

**Employers Don't Really Care About Your Past;
They Only Ask About It,
in Order to Try to Predict Your Future (Behavior)**

In the U.S. employers may only ask you questions that are related to the requirements and expectations of the job. They cannot ask about such things as your creed, religion, race, age, sex,

or marital status. Any other questions about your past are *fair game*. But don't be fooled by any employer's absorption with your past. You must realize that the only thing any employer can possibly care about is your future . . . with *them*. Since that future is impossible to uncover, they usually try to gauge what it would be by asking about your past (behavior).

Therefore, during the hiring-interview before you answer any question the employer asks you about your past, you should pause to think out what fear about the *future* lies underneath that question—and then address that fear, obliquely or directly.

In most cases, as I have been emphasizing, the person-who-has-the-power-to-hire-you is *scared*. If you think that is too strong a word, let's settle for *anxious*, or *afraid*, or *worried*. And this worry lies beneath all the questions they may ask.

Here are some *examples*:

Chapter Twelve

Employer's Question	The Fear Behind the Question	The Point You Try to Get Across	Phrases You Might Use to Get This Across
"Tell me about yourself"	The employer is afraid he/she isn't going to conduct a very good interview, by failing to ask the right questions. Or is afraid there is something wrong with you, and is hoping you will blurt it out.	You are a good employee, as you have proved in the past at your other jobs. (Give the briefest history of who you are, where born, raised, interests, hobbies, and kind of work you have enjoyed the most to date.) *Keep it to two minutes, max.*	In describing your work history, use any *honest* phrases you can about your work history, that are self-complimentary: "Hard worker." "Came in early, left late." "Always did more than was expected of me." Etc.
"What kind of work are you looking for?"	The employer is afraid that you are looking for a different job than that which the employer is trying to fill. E.g., he/she wants a secretary, but you want to be an office manager, etc.	You are looking for precisely the kind of work the employer is offering (but don't say that, if it isn't true). Repeat back to the employer, in your own words, what he/she has said about the job, and emphasize the skills you have to do *that.*	If the employer hasn't described the job at all, say, "I'd be happy to answer that, but first I need to understand exactly what kind of work this job involves." *Then* answer, as at left.
"Have you ever done this kind of work before?"	The employer is afraid you don't possess the necessary skills and experience to do this job.	You have skills that are transferable, from whatever you used to do; and you did it well.	"I pick up stuff very quickly." "I have quickly mastered any job I have ever done."

Employer's Question	The Fear Behind the Question	The Point You Try to Get Across	Phrases You Might Use to Get This Across
"Why did you leave your last job?" —or "How did you get along with your former boss and co-workers?"	The employer is afraid you don't get along well with people, especially bosses, and is just waiting for you to "bad-mouth" your previous boss or co-workers, as proof of that.	Say whatever positive things you possibly can about your former boss and co-workers *(without telling lies)*. Emphasize you usually get along very well with people— and then let your gracious attitude toward your previous boss(es) and co-workers prove it, right before this employer's very eyes (and ears).	If you left voluntarily: *"My boss and I both felt I would be happier and more effective in a job where [here describe your strong points, such as] I would have more room to use my initiative and creativity."* If you were fired: *"Usually, I get along well with everyone, but in this particular case the boss and I just didn't get along with each other. Difficult to say why." You don't need to say anything more than that.* If you were laid off and your job wasn't filled after you left: *"My job was terminated."*
"How is your health?" —or "How much were you absent from work during your last job?"	The employer is afraid you will be absent from work a lot, if they hire you.	You will not be absent. If you have a health problem, you want to emphasize that it is one which will not keep you from being at work, daily. Your productivity, compared to other workers', is excellent.	If you were *not* absent a lot at your last job: *"I believe it's an employee's job to show up every work day. Period."* If you *were* absent a lot, say why, and stress that it was due to a difficulty that is now *past*.

Employer's Question	The Fear Behind the Question	The Point You Try to Get Across	Phrases You Might Use to Get This Across
"Can you explain why you've been out of work so long?"—or "Can you tell me why there are these gaps in your work history?" *(Usually said after studying your resume.)*	The employer is afraid that you are the kind of person who quits a job the minute he/she doesn't like something at it; in other words, that you have no "stick-to-it-iveness."	You love to work, and you regard times when things aren't going well as challenges, which you enjoy learning how to conquer.	"During the gaps in my work record, I was studying/doing volunteer work/doing some hard thinking about my mission in life/finding redirection." (Choose one.)
"Wouldn't this job represent a step down for you?"—or "I think this job would be way beneath your talents and experience."—or "Don't you think you would be underemployed if you took this job?"	The employer is afraid you could command a bigger salary, somewhere else, and will therefore leave him/her as soon as something better turns up.	You will stick with this job as long as you and the employer agree this is where you should be.	"This job isn't a step down for me. It's a step up—from welfare." "We have mutual fears; every employer is afraid a good employee will leave too soon, and every employee is afraid the employer might fire him/her, for no good reason." "I like to work, and I give my best to every job I've ever had."
And, last "Tell me, what is your greatest weakness?"	The employer is afraid you have some character flaw, and hopes you will now rashly blurt it out, or confess it.	You have limitations just like anyone else, but you work constantly to improve yourself and be a more and more effective worker.	Mention a weakness and then stress its positive aspect, e.g., "I don't like to be oversupervised, because I have a great deal of initiative, and I like to anticipate problems before they even arise."

> ## As the Interview Proceeds, You Want to Quietly Notice the Time-Frame of the Questions the Employer Is Asking

When the interview is going favorably for you, the time-frame of the employer's questions will often move—*however slowly*—through the following stages.

1. Distant past: *e.g., "Where did you attend high school?"*
2. Immediate past: *e.g., "Tell me about your most recent job."*
3. Present: *e.g., "What kind of a job are you looking for?"*
4. Immediate future: *e.g., "Would you be able to come back for another interview next week?"*
5. Distant future: *e.g., "Where would you like to be five years from now?"*

The more the time-frame of the interviewer's questions moves from the past to the future, the more favorably you may assume the interview is going for you. On the other hand, if the interviewer's questions stay firmly in the past, the outlook is not so good. *Ah well, y' can't win them all!*

When the time-frame of the interviewer's questions moves firmly into the future, *then* is the time for you to get more specific about the job in question. Experts suggest you ask, at that point, these kinds of questions:

Chapter Twelve

What is the job, specifically, that I am being considered for?

If I were hired, what duties would I be performing?

What responsibilities would I have?

What would you be hiring me to accomplish?

Would I be working with a team, or group? To whom would I report?

Whose responsibility is it to see that I get the training I need, here, to get up to speed?

How would I be evaluated, how often, and by whom?

What were the strengths and weaknesses of previous people in this position?

Why did *you* yourself decide to work here?

What do you wish you had known about this company before you started here? What particular characteristics do you think have made you successful in your job here?

May I meet the persons I would be working with and for (if it isn't you)?

Remember, throughout this *weighing of each other*, we're not talking scientific measurement here. As Nathan Azrin has said for many years, *The hiring process is more like choosing a mate, than it is like deciding whether or not to buy a new house.* "Choosing a mate" here is a metaphor. To elaborate upon the metaphor a little bit, it means that *the mechanisms* by which human nature decides to hire someone, are *similar to* the mechanisms by which human nature decides whether or not to marry someone. Those mechanisms, of course, are impulsive, intuitional, non-rational, unfathomable, and often made on the spur of the moment.

> # Interviews Are Often Lost to Mosquitoes Rather Than to Dragons, and Lost within the First Two Minutes

Think about this: you can have all the skills in the world, have researched this organization to death, have practiced *interviewing* until you are a master at giving "right answers," be absolutely the perfect person for this job, and yet lose the hiring-interview because . . . *your breath smells terrible.* Or some other small personal reason. It's akin to your being ready to fight dragons, and then being killed by a mosquito.

It's the reason why interviews are most often lost, when they are lost, *during the first two minutes.* Believe it or not.

Let us look at *what* interview-mosquitoes *(as it were)* can fly in, during the first thirty seconds to two minutes of your interview so that *the person-who-has-the-power-to-hire-you* starts muttering to themselves, *"I sure hope we have some other candidates besides this person"*:

1. Your appearance and personal habits: interview after interview has revealed that if you are a male, *you are much more likely to get the job if:*

- you have obviously freshly bathed, have your face freshly shaved or your hair and beard freshly trimmed, have clean fingernails, and are using a deodorant; *and*

- you have on freshly laundered clothes, pants with a sharp crease, and shoes freshly polished; *and*

- you do not have bad breath, do not dispense gallons of garlic, onion, stale tobacco, or the odor of strong drink, into the enclosed office air, but have brushed and flossed your teeth; *and*

- you are not wafting tons of after-shave cologne fifteen feet ahead of you, as you enter the room.

Remember, since the hiring process is more like choosing a mate, than deciding whether or not to buy a new house, the employer is simply trying to determine if they like you. If you "bomb" in one of these areas just listed, *the person-who-has-the-power-to-hire-you may decide they really don't like you, in which case you're not going to get hired there*, no matter how qualified you otherwise may be. The same thing happens on dates, incidentally.

If you are a female, interview after interview has revealed that *you are much more likely to get the job if:*

- you have obviously freshly bathed; have not got tons of makeup on your face; have had your hair newly "permed" or "coiffed"; have clean or nicely manicured fingernails, that don't stick out ten inches from your fingers; and are using a deodorant; *and*

- you wear a bra, have on freshly cleaned clothes, a suit or sophisticated-looking dress, shoes not sandals, and are not wearing clothes so daring that they call *a lot* of attention to themselves. In these days of sexual harassment lawsuits, this tends to make many employers, male and female, *very* nervous. I grant you there are some employers who might like this kind of outfit, but—trust me—in most cases you don't want to work for *them* (as with all items here, I am only reporting what can affect your chances of getting hired—not whether or not I think this employer preoccupation with just outward appearance is asinine); *and*

- you do not have bad breath; do not dispense gallons of garlic, onion, stale tobacco, or the odor of strong drink, into the enclosed office air; but have brushed and flossed your teeth; *and*

- you are not wafting tons of perfume fifteen feet ahead of you, as you enter the room.

Remember, since the hiring process is more like choosing a mate, than deciding whether or not to buy a new house, the employer is simply trying to determine if they like you. If you "bomb" in one of these areas just listed, the person-who-has-the-power-to-hire-you may decide they really don't like you, in which case you're not going to get hired there, no matter how qualified you otherwise may be.

2. Nervous mannerisms: *it is a turnoff for employers if:*

- you continually avoid eye contact with the employer (that's a *big, big* no-no), *or*
- you give a limp handshake, *or*

- you slouch in your chair, or endlessly fidget with your hands, or crack your knuckles, *or* constantly play with your hair during the interview.

Remember, since the hiring process is more like choosing a mate, than deciding whether or not to buy a new house, the employer is simply trying to determine if they like you. If you "bomb" in one of these areas just listed, the person-who-has-the-power-to-hire-you may decide they really don't like you, in which case you're not going to get hired there, no matter how qualified you otherwise may be.

3. Lack of self-confidence: *it is a turnoff for employers if:*

- you are speaking so softly you cannot be heard, or so loudly you can be heard two rooms away, *or*
- you are giving answers in an extremely hesitant fashion, *or*
- you are giving one-word answers to all the employer's questions, *or*
- you are constantly interrupting the employer, *or*
- you are downplaying your achievements or abilities, or are continuously being self-critical in comments you make about yourself during the interview.

Remember, since the hiring process is more like choosing a mate, than deciding whether or not to buy a new house, the employer is simply trying to determine if they like you. If you "bomb" in one of these areas just listed, the person-who-has-the-power-to-hire-you may decide they really don't like you, in which case you're not going to get hired there, no matter how qualified you otherwise may be.

Chapter Twelve

4. The consideration you show to other people: *it is a turnoff for employers if:*

- you show a lack of courtesy to the receptionist, secretary, and (at lunch) to the waiter or waitress, *or*
- you display extreme criticalness toward your previous employers and places of work, *or*
- you drink strong stuff (Ordering a drink if and when the employer takes you to lunch is always an extremely bad idea, as it raises the question in the employer's mind, *Do they normally stop with one, or do they normally keep on going?* Don't . . . ever . . . do . . . it! Even if they do.), *or*
- you forget to thank the interviewer as you're leaving, or forget to send a thank-you note afterward. Says one human resources manager:

  "A prompt, brief, faxed business letter thanking me for my time along with a (brief!) synopsis of his/her unique qualities communicates to me that this person is an assertive, motivated, customer-service-oriented salesperson who utilizes technology and knows the rules of the 'game.' These are qualities I am looking for . . . At the moment I receive approximately one such letter . . . for every fifteen candidates interviewed."

Remember, since the hiring process is more like choosing a mate, than deciding whether or not to buy a new house, the employer is simply trying to determine if they like you. If you "bomb" in one of these areas just listed, the person-who-has-the-power-to-hire-you may decide they really don't like you, in which case you're not going to get hired there, no matter how qualified you otherwise may be.

- Incidentally, *many* an employer watches to see if you smoke, either in the office or at lunch. *In a race between two equally qualified people, the nonsmoker will win out over the smoker 94 percent of the time, according to a study done by a professor of business at Seattle University. If you hunt hard enough on the Internet or elsewhere you can find some experts giving detailed instructions on how to hide the fact that you smoke (if you do). Their advice runs along these lines: "If you are a smoker, do not think it will be easy to hide it. It will take a lot of work, on your part. The more that smoke has been hovering around you and your clothes, the more your clothes, hair, and breath will reek of smoke when you go in for the interview. You are so inured to it, that you will not be able to detect this; but the employer will know it, instantly, as you move forward to greet them. Breath mints and perfume/cologne will NOT cover it up; it will take much more formidable measures than that. Like what? Like this: don't smoke for at least four hours prior to the interview, bathe completely, including your hair, immediately before leaving for the interview, keep a set of smoke-free interview clothes, underwear, and shoes (at home) in a tight plastic bag in a room far-removed from anyplace you smoke in the house, and wear those smoke-free clothes to the interview." That's the advice of the You-Can-Hide-It school of thinking.*

Personally, I think none of this really works, in the end. So what if you do pull it off? It will come out that you smoke, after you are hired, and the employer who hates smoking can always manage to get you out of there after you are hired, on one pretext or another, without ever mentioning the word "smoke." So, my advice is: don't try to hide it.

On the other hand, it is legitimate, I think, to postpone *revealing it, if you can. But once a job-offer has been made, then I think it is important for you to tell the employer you smoke, and to offer an easy way out: "If this is a truly offensive habit to you, and one you don't want in any of your employees, I'd rather bow out gracefully now, than have it become an issue between us down the road."* Such consideration, thoughtfulness, and graciousness on your part may go a long way to soften the employer's resistance to the fact that you are a smoker. Many places, as you probably know, do allow their employees to go outside for a "smoke break" at stated intervals.

5. Your values: *it is a complete turnoff for most employers, if they see in you:*

- any sign of arrogance or excessive aggressiveness; any sign of tardiness or failure to keep appointments and commitments on time, including the hiring-interview; *or*
- any sign of laziness or lack of motivation; *or*
- any sign of constant complaining or blaming things on others; *or*
- any signs of dishonesty or lying—on your resume or in the interview; *or*
- any signs of irresponsibility or tendency to goof off; *or*

- any sign of not following instructions or obeying rules; *or*
- any sign of a lack of enthusiasm for this organization and what it is trying to do; *or*
- any sign of instability, inappropriate response, and the like; *or*
- the other ways in which you evidence your *values*, such as: what things impress you or don't impress you in the office; *or* what you are willing to sacrifice in order to get this job *and* what you are *not* willing to sacrifice in order to get this job; *or* your enthusiasm for work; *or* the carefulness with which you did or didn't research this company before you came in; and blah, blah, blah.

Remember, since the hiring process is more like choosing a mate, than deciding whether or not to buy a new house, the employer is simply trying to determine if they like you. If you "bomb" in one of these areas just listed, the person-who-has-the-power-to-hire-you may decide they really don't like you, in which case you're not going to get hired there, no matter how qualified you otherwise may be.

Well, dear reader, there you have it: the *mosquitoes* that can kill you, when you're only on the watch for dragons, during the hiring-interview.

One favor I ask of you: do not write me, telling me how picayune or asinine some of this is. Believe me, I already *know* that. I'm not reporting the world as it *should* be, and certainly not as I would like it to be. I'm only reporting what study after study has revealed about the hiring world as it *is*.

You may take all this to heart, or just ignore it. However, if you decide to ignore these points, and then—despite interview after interview—you never get hired, you might want to rethink your position on all of this. It may be *mosquitoes*, not dragons, that are killing you.

And, good news: you can *fix* all these mosquitoes. Yes, you control *every one* of these factors.

Read them all over again. There isn't a one of them that you don't have the power to determine, or the power to change. You can decide to bathe before going to the interview, you can decide to shine your shoes, you can decide not to smoke, etc., etc. All the little things which could torpedo your interview are within your control, and *you can fix* them, if they are keeping you from getting hired.

Ninth Interviewing Tip

There Are Some Questions You Must Ask Before You Let the Interview Close

Before you let the interview end, there are six questions you should *always* ask:

#1. *"Given my skills and experience, is there work here that you would consider me for?"* This is if you haven't come after a specific job, from the beginning.

#2. *"Can you offer me this job?"* **I know this seems stupid, but it is astonishing (at least to me) how many job-hunters have secured a job simply by being bold enough to ask for it, at the end of the interview, either with the words** *May I have this job,* **or something similar to it, in language they feel comfortable with.** I don't know *why* this is. I only know *that* it is. Maybe it has something to do with employers not liking to say "No," to someone who directly asks them for something. Anyway, if after hearing all about this job at this place, you decide you'd really like to have it, you must *ask for it.* The worst thing the employer can say is "No," or "We need some time to think about all the interviews we're conducting."

#3. *"Do you want me to come back for another interview, perhaps with some of the other decision-makers here?"* If you are a serious candidate in this employer's mind for this job, there usually *is* a second round of interviews. And, often, a third, and fourth. You, of course, want to make it to that second round. Indeed, many experts say the *only* purpose you should have in the first interview, at a particular place, is *to be invited back* for a second interview. If you've secured *that*, say they, it has been a successful first interview.

#4. *"When may I expect to hear from you?"* You *never* want to leave control of the ensuing steps in this process in the hands of the employer. You want it in your own hands. If the employer says, *"We need time to think about this,"* or *"We will be calling you for a second interview,"* you don't want to leave this as an undated good intention on the employer's part. You want to nail it down.

#5. *"Might I ask what would be* the latest *I can expect to hear from you?"* The employer has probably given you their *best* guess, in answer to your previous question. Now you want to know *what is the worst-case* scenario? Incidentally, one employer, when I asked him for the *worst-case* scenario, replied, *"Never!"* I thought he had a great sense of humor. Turned out he was dead serious. I never did hear from him, despite repeated attempts at contact, on my part.

#6. *"May I contact you after that date, if for any reason you haven't gotten back to me by that time?"* Some employers resent this question. You'll know that is the case if they snap at you, *"Don't you trust me?"* But most employers appreciate your offering them what is in essence a safety-net. They know they can get busy, become overwhelmed with other things, forget their promise to you. It's reassuring, in such a case, for you to offer to rescue them.

[Optional: #7. *"Can you think of anyone else who* might *be interested in hiring me?"* This question is invoked *only* if they replied *"No,"* to your first question, above.]

Jot down any answers they give you to the questions above, then stand up, thank them sincerely for their time, give a firm handshake, and leave. Write a thank-you note *that night*, to them, and mail it without fail the next morning.

Tenth Interviewing Tip

> **Always, Always Send a Thank-You Note the**
> **Same Night, at the Latest**

Every expert on interviewing will tell you two things: (1) Thank-you notes *must* be sent after *every* interview, by every job-hunter; and (2) Most job-hunters ignore this advice. Indeed, it is safe to say that it is the most overlooked step in the entire job-hunting process.

If you want to stand out from the others applying for the same job, send thank-you notes—to *everyone* you met there, that day. If you need any additional encouragement *(besides the fact that it may get you the job)*, here are six reasons for sending a thank-you note, most particularly to the employer who interviewed you:

First, you were presenting yourself as one who has good skills with people. Your actions with respect to the job-interview must back this claim up. Sending a thank-you note does that. The employer can see you *are* good with people; you remember to thank them.

Second, it helps the employer to remember you.

Third, if a committee is involved in the hiring process, the one man or woman who interviewed you has something to show the rest of the committee.

Fourth, if the interview went rather well, and the employer seemed to show an interest in further talks, the thank-you letter can reiterate *your* interest in further talks.

Fifth, the thank-you note gives you an opportunity to correct any wrong impression you left behind. You can add anything you forgot to tell them, that you want them to know. And from among all the things you two discussed, you can underline the main two or three points that you want to stand out in their minds.

Last, if the interview did not go well, and you lost all interest in working there, they may still hear of other openings, elsewhere, that might be of interest to you. In the thank-you note, you can mention this, and ask them to keep you in mind. Thus, from kindly interviewers, you may gain additional leads.

In the following days, rigorously keep to all that you said, and don't contact them except with that mandatory thank-you note, until after the *latest* deadline you two agreed upon, in answer to question #4, above. If you do have to contact them after that date, and if they tell you things are still up in the air, you must ask questions #3, #4, and #5, all over again. And so on, and so forth.

Incidentally, it is entirely appropriate for you to insert a thank-you note into the running stream, after *each* interview or telephone contact. Just keep it brief.

"I'll tell you why I want this job. I thrive on challenges.
I like being stretched to my full capacity. I like solving problems.
Also, my car is about to be repossessed."

Ten Interviewing Tips

When None of This Works, and You Never Get Invited Back

There is no magic in job-hunting. No techniques that always work, and work for everyone. Anyone who tells you there is magic, is delusional. I hear regularly from job-hunters who report that they paid attention to all the matters I have mentioned in this chapter and this book, and are quite successful at getting interviews—but they still don't get hired. And they want to know what they're doing wrong.

Well, unfortunately, the answer *sometimes* is: "Maybe nothing." I don't know *how often* this happens, but I know it does happen—because more than one employer has confessed it to me, and in fact at one point in my life it actually happened to *moi*: namely, *some* employers play wicked, despicable tricks on job-hunters, whereby they invite you in for an interview despite the fact that they have already hired someone for the position in question, and they know from the beginning that they have absolutely no intention of hiring you—not in a million years!

You are cheered, of course, by the ease with which you get these interviews. But unbeknownst to you, the manager who is interviewing you (we'll say it's a *he*) has a personal friend he already agreed to give the job to. Of course, one small problem remains: the state or the federal government gives funds to this organization, and has mandated that this position be opened to all. So this manager must comply. He therefore *pretends* to choose ten candidates, including his favorite, and pretends to interview them all *as though* the job opening were still available. But, he intended, from the beginning, to reject the first nine and choose his favorite, and since you were selected for the honor of being among those nine, you automatically get rejected—even if you are a much better candidate. This tenth person is, after all, his *friend*. But you have been very helpful, even without intending to be: you have helped the manager establish his claim that he followed the mandated hiring procedures to the letter.

You will of course be baffled as to *why* you got turned down. Trouble is, you will never know if it was because you met an employer who was playing this little trick, *or* not. All you know is: you're very depressed.

If you *never* get invited back for a second interview, there is always, of course, the chance that no games are being played. You are getting rejected, at place after place, because there is something really wrong with the way you are coming across, during these hiring-interviews.

Employers will rarely ever tell you this. You will never hear them say something like, "You come across as just too cocky and arrogant during the interview." You will almost always be left completely in the dark as to *what* it is you're doing wrong.

If you've been through a whole bunch of employers, one way around this deadly silence, is to ask for *generalized* feedback from whoever was the *friendliest* employer that you saw in your whole job-hunt. You can always try phoning the friendliest one, reminding them of who you are, and then asking the following question—deliberately kept generalized, vague, unrelated to just *that* place, and above all, *future-directed*: Something like: *"You know, I've been on several interviews at several different places*

now, where I've gotten turned down. From what you've seen, is there something about me in an interview, that you think might be causing me not to get hired at those places? If so, I'd really appreciate your giving me some pointers so I can do better in my future hiring-interviews."

Most of the time they'll *still* duck saying anything hurtful or helpful. First of all, they're afraid of lawsuits. Second, they don't know how you will use what they might have to say. (Said an old veteran to me once, "I used to think it was my duty to hit everyone with the truth. Now I only give it to those who can use it.")

But *occasionally* you will run into an employer who is willing to risk giving you the truth, because they think you will know how to use it wisely. If so, thank them from the bottom of your heart, no matter how painful their feedback is. Such advice, seriously heeded, can bring about just the changes in your interviewing strategy that you most need, in order to win the interview.

In the absence of any such help from employers who interviewed you, you might want to get a good business friend of yours to role-play a mock hiring-interview with you, in case they immediately see something glaringly wrong with how you're "coming across."

When all else fails, I would recommend you go to a career counselor that charges by the hour, and put yourself in their tender knowledgeable hands. Role-play an interview with them, and take their advice seriously (you've just paid for it, after all).

Conclusion

I have left out the subject of salary negotiation, in this chapter. It requires a chapter of its own (next!).

Hopefully, however, with that advice plus these ten tips for smarties, you will do well in your interviews. And if you do get hired, make one resolution to yourself right there on the spot. Plan to keep track of your accomplishments at this new job, on a weekly basis—jotting them down, every weekend, in your own private diary. Career experts, such as the late Bernard Haldane, recommend you do this without fail. You can then summarize these accomplishments annually on a one-page sheet, for your boss's eyes, when the question of a raise or promotion comes up.[5]

---

5. In any good-sized organization, you will often be amazed at how little attention your superiors pay to your noteworthy accomplishments, and how little they are aware at the end of the year that you really are entitled to a raise. Noteworthy your accomplishments may be, but no one is taking notes . . . unless you do. You may even need to be the one who brings up the subject of a raise or promotion. Waiting for the employer to bring this up may never happen.

The Six
Secrets
of Salary
Negotiation

HOW

Do You Negotiate for the Salary You Want?

I remember once talking to a breathless college graduate, who was elated at having just landed her first job. "How much are they going to pay you?" I asked. She looked startled. "I don't know," she said, "I never asked. I just assume they will pay me a fair wage." *Boy!* did she get a rude awakening when she received her first paycheck. It was so miserably *low*, she couldn't believe her eyes. And thus did she learn, painfully, what you must learn too: *Before accepting a job, always ask about salary.* Indeed, *ask and negotiate.*

It's the *negotiate* that throws fear into our hearts. We feel ill-prepared to do this. Well, it's not all that difficult. While whole books can be (and have been) written on this subject, there are basically just six secrets to keep in mind.

**The First Secret of Successful
Salary Negotiation:**

> ## *Never* Discuss Salary Until the End of the Interviewing Process, When They Have Definitely Said They Want You

"The end of the interviewing process" is difficult to define. It's the point at which the employer says, or thinks, "We've got to get this person!" That may be at the end of the first (and therefore the last) interview; or it may be at the end of a whole series of interviews, often with different people within the same company or organization. But assuming things are going favorably for you, whether after the first, or second, or third, or fourth interview, if *you* like them and *they* increasingly like you, a job offer *will* be made. Then, and only then, it is time to deal with the question that is inevitably on any employer's mind: *how much is this person going to cost me?* And the question that is on *your* mind: *how much does this job pay?*

If the employer raises the salary question earlier, in some form like "What kind of salary are you looking for?", you should have three responses at your fingertips.

Response #1: If the employer seems like a kindly man or woman, your best and most tactful reply might be: "Until you've decided you definitely want me, and I've decided I definitely could help you with your tasks here, I feel any discussion of salary is premature." That will work, in most cases.

Response #2: There are instances, however, where that doesn't work. You may be face-to-face with an employer who will not so easily be put off, and demands within the first two minutes that you're in the interview room to know what salary you are looking for. At this point, you use your second response: "I'll gladly come to that, but could you first help me to understand what this job involves?"

Response #3: That is a good response, *in most cases*. But what if it doesn't work? The employer with rising voice says, "Come, come, don't play games with me. I want to know what salary you're looking for." You have response #3 prepared for *this* very eventuality. It's an answer in terms of a *range*. For example, "I'm looking for a salary in the range of $35,000 to $45,000 a year."

If the employer still won't let it go until later, then consider what this means. Clearly, you are being interviewed by an employer who has no range in mind. Their beginning figure is their ending figure. No negotiation is possible.[1]

This happens, when it happens, because many employers are making salary their major criterion for deciding who to hire, and who not to hire, out of—say—nineteen possible candidates.

> *It's an old game, played with new determination by many employers these days, called* "among two equally qualified candidates, the one who is willing to work for the lower salary *wins.*"

---

1. One job-hunter said his interviews always began with the salary question, and no matter what he answered, that ended the interview. Turned out, this job-hunter was doing all the interviewing over the phone. That was the problem. Once he went face-to-face, salary was no longer the first thing discussed in the interview.

If you run into this situation, and you want that job badly enough, you will have no choice but to capitulate. Ask what salary they have in mind, and make your decision. (Of course you should always say, *"I need a little time, to think about this."*)

However, all the foregoing is merely the *worst-case scenario.* Usually, things don't go this way. Not by a long shot. In most interviews, these days, the employer will be willing to save salary negotiation until they've finally decided they want you (and you've decided you want them). And at that point, salary will be negotiable.

WHEN TO DISCUSS SALARY

Not until all of the following conditions have been fulfilled —

- *Not until they've gotten to know you, at your best, so they can see how you stand out above the other applicants.*

- *Not until you've gotten to know them, as completely as you can, so you can tell when they're being firm, or when they're flexible.*

- *Not until you've found out exactly what the job entails.*

- *Not until they've had a chance to find out how well you match the job-requirements.*

- *Not until you're in the final interview at that place, for that job.*

- *Not until you've decided, "I'd really like to work here."*

- *Not until they've said, "We want you."*

- *Not until they've said, "We've got to have you."*

    —should you get into salary discussion with this employer.

Chapter Thirteen

If you'd prefer this to be put in the form of a diagram, here it is:[2]

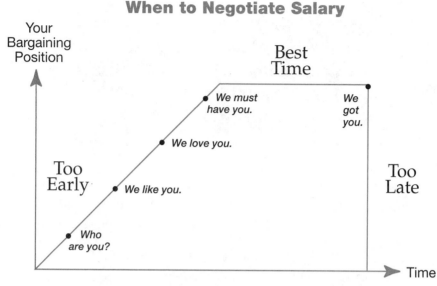

When to Negotiate Salary

Your Bargaining Position

Best Time

We must have you.

We got you.

We love you.

Too Early

We like you.

Too Late

Who are you?

Time

Why is it to your advantage to delay salary discussion? Because, if you really *shine* during the hiring-interview, they may—at the end—mention a higher salary than they originally had in mind, when the interview started—and this is particularly the case when the interview has gone so well, that they're *determined* to obtain your services.

2. Reprinted, by permission of the publisher, from *Ready, Aim, You're Hired*, by Paul Hellman, © 1986 Paul Hellman. Published by AMACOM, a division of American Management Association, New York. All rights reserved.

The Second Secret of Successful Salary Negotiation:

> # The Purpose of Salary Negotiation Is to Uncover the Most That an Employer Is Willing to Pay to Get You

Salary negotiation would never happen if *every* employer in *every* hiring-interview were to mention, right from the start, the top figure they are willing to pay for that position. *Some* employers do, as I was mentioning, above. And that's the end of any salary negotiation. But, of course, most employers don't. Hoping they'll be able to get you for less, they start *lower* than they're ultimately willing to go. This creates *a range*. And that range is what salary negotiation is all about.

For example, if the employer wants to hire somebody for no more than $12 an hour, they may start *the bidding* at $8 an hour. In which case, their *range* runs between $8 and $12 an hour. Or if they want to pay no more than $20 an hour, they may start the bidding at $16 an hour. In which case their range runs between $16 and $20 an hour.

So, why do you want to negotiate? Because, if a range *is* thus involved, you have every right to try to discover the highest salary that employer is willing to pay *within that range*.

The employer's goal, is to save money, if possible. Your goal is to bring home to your family, your partner, or your own household, the best salary that you can, for the work you will be doing. Nothing's wrong with the goals of either of you. But it does mean that, where the employer starts lower, salary negotiation is proper, and expected.

"WHILE YOU'RE WAITING FOR YOUR SHIP TO COME IN, WHY DON'T YOU DO SOME MAINTENANCE WORK ON THE PIER ?"

**The Third Secret of Successful
Salary Negotiation:**

During the Salary Discussion, Try Never to Be the First One to Mention a Salary Figure

Where salary negotiation has been kept *off stage* for much of the interview process, when it finally does come *on stage* you want the employer to be the first one to mention *a figure*, if you can.

Nobody knows why, but it has been observed over the years—where the goals are opposite, as in this case, you are trying to get the employer to pay the most that they can, and the employer is trying to pay the least that they can—in this back-and-forth negotiation, *whoever mentions a salary figure first, generally loses.* You can speculate from now until the cows come home, as to *why* this is; all we know is *that* it is.

Inexperienced employer/interviewers often don't know this quirky rule. But experienced ones are very aware of it; that's why they will *always* toss the ball to you, with some innocent-

sounding question, such as: "What kind of salary are you looking for?" *Well, how kind of them to ask me what I want*—you may
be thinking. No, no, no. Kindness has nothing to do with it.
They are hoping *you* will be the first to mention a figure, because
they know this odd experiential truth: that *whoever mentions a
salary figure first, generally loses salary negotiation, at the last.*

Accordingly, if they ask you to name a figure, the *counter-
move* on your part should be: "Well, you created this position, so
you must have some figure in mind, and I'd be interested in
knowing what that figure is."

Chapter Thirteen

The Fourth Secret of Successful Salary Negotiation:

Before You Go to the Interview, Do Some Careful Research on Typical Salaries for Your Field and/or that Organization

As I said earlier, salary negotiation is possible *anytime* the employer does not open their discussion of salary by naming the top figure they have in mind, but starts instead with a lower figure.

Okay, so here is our $64,000 question: how do you tell whether the figure the employer first offers you is only their *starting bid*, or is their *final final offer*? The answer is: by doing some research on the field *and* that organization, first.

Oh, come on! I can hear you say. *Isn't this all more trouble than it's worth?* No, not if you're determined.

If you're determined, this is one step you don't want to overlook. Trust me, salary research pays off *handsomely*.

Let's say it takes you from one to three days to run down this sort of information on the three or four organizations that interest you the most. And let us say that because you've done this research, when you finally go in for the hiring-interview you are able to ask for and obtain a salary that is $4,000 a year higher in range, than you would otherwise have gotten. In just the next three years, you will be earning $12,000 extra, because of your salary research. *Not bad pay, for one to three days' work!* And it can be even more. I know *many* job-hunters and career-changers to whom this has happened. Thus you can see that there is a financial penalty exacted from those who are too lazy, or in too much of a hurry, to go gather this information. In plainer language: *if you don't do this research, it'll cost ya!*

Okay then, how do you do this research? There are two ways to go: on the Internet, and off the Internet. Let's look at each, in turn:

SALARY RESEARCH ON THE INTERNET

If you have access to the Internet, and you want to research salaries for particular geographical regions, positions, occupations, or industries, here are some free sites that may give you just what you're looking for:

▶ The Bureau of Labor Statistics' survey of salaries in individual occupations, *The Occupational Outlook Handbook 2004–2005*.

www.bls.gov/oco

▶ The Bureau of Labor Statistics' survey of salaries in individual industries *(it's a companion piece to The Occupational Outlook Handbook 2004–2005)*.

http://stats.bls.gov/oco/cg/cgindex.htm

▶ "High Earning Workers Who Don't Have a Bachelor's Degree," by Matthew Mariani, appearing first in the Fall 1999 issue of the *Occupational Outlook Quarterly*. For those who want to know how to earn *a lot* without having to go to college first.

http://stats.bls.gov/opub/ooq/1999/
fall/art02.pdf

▶ The oldest of the salary-specific sites, and one of the largest and most complete lists of salary reviews on the Web; run by a genius (Mary Ellen Mort).

http://jobstar.org/tool/salary/index.cfm

▶ The most visited of all the salary-specific job-sites. Over two million visitors per month (as of 7/01), with fifty online partners that use their "Salary Wizard," such as AOL and Yahoo.

www.salary.com

▶ When you need a salary expert, it makes sense to go to the Salary Expert. Lots of stuff on the subject here, including a free "Salary Report" for hundreds of job titles, varying by area, skill level, and experience. Also has one of the salary calculators mentioned earlier.

www.salaryexpert.com

Incidentally, if these free sites don't give you what you want, you can always *pay* for the info, and hopefully get more-up-to-date surveys. Salary Source (`www.salarysource.com`) offers up-to-date salary information services starting at $19.95.

If you "strike out" on all the above sites, then you're going to have to get a little more clever, and work a little harder, and pound the pavements, as I describe below.

SALARY RESEARCH OFF THE INTERNET

Off the Internet, how do you go about doing salary research? Well, there's a simple rule: generally speaking, abandon books, and go talk to people. Use books and libraries only as a *second*, or *last*, resort. (Their information is often just way too outdated.)

You can get much more complete and up-to-date information from people who are in the same job *at another company or organization.* Or, people at the nearby university or college who *train* such people, whatever that department may be. Teachers and professors will usually know what their graduates are making.

Now, exactly how do you go about getting this information, by talking to people? Let's look at some concrete examples:

> *First Example:* Working at your first entry-level job, say at a fast-food place.

You may not need to do any salary research. They pay what they pay. You can walk in, ask for a job application, and interview with the manager. He or she will usually tell you the pay, outright. It's usually *inflexible.* But at least you'll find that it's easy to discover what the pay is. (Incidentally, filling out an application, or having an interview there, doesn't commit you to take the job—but you probably already know that. You can always decline an offer from *any place.* That's what makes this approach harmless.)

> *Second Example:* Working at a place where you can't discover what the pay is, say *at a construction company.*

The Six Secrets of Salary Negotiation

If that construction company where you would *hope* to get a job is difficult to research, go visit a *different* construction company in the same town—one that isn't of much interest to you—and ask what they make *there*. Or, if you don't know who to talk to there, fill out one of their applications, and talk to the hiring person about what kinds of jobs they have (or might have in the future), at which time prospective wages is a legitimate subject of discussion. Then, having done this research on a place you don't care about, go back to the place that *really* interests you, and apply. You still don't know *exactly* what they pay, but you do know what their competitor pays—which will usually be *close*.

> *Third Example:* Working in a one-person office, say *as a secretary*.

Here you can often find useful salary information by perusing the *Help Wanted* ads in the local paper for a week or two. Most of the ads probably won't mention a salary figure, but a few *may*. Among those that do, note what the lowest salary offering is, and what the highest is, and see if the ad reveals some reasons for the difference. It's interesting how much you can learn about salaries, with this approach. I know, because I was a secretary myself, once upon a time (dinosaurs were still roaming the earth).

Another way to do salary research is to find a *Temporary Work Agency* that places secretaries, and let yourself be farmed out to various offices: the more, the merrier. It's relatively easy to do salary research when you're *inside* the place. (Study what that place pays *the agency*, not what the agency then pays you.) If it's an office where the other workers *like* you, you'll be able to ask questions about a lot of things, including salary. It's like *summertime*, where the research is easy.

The Fifth Secret of Successful Salary Negotiation:

Define a Range That the Employer Has in Mind, and Then Define an Interrelated Range for Yourself

THE EMPLOYER'S RANGE

Before you finish your research, before you go into that organization for your final interview, you want more than just *one* figure. You want *a range*: what's the *least* the employer may be willing to offer you, and what's the *most* the employer may be willing to offer you. In any organization which has more than five employees, that range is relatively easy to figure out. It will be less than what the person *who would be above you* makes, and more than what the person *who would be below you* makes.

If the Person Who Would Be Below You Makes	And the Person Who Would Be Above You Makes	The Range for Your Job Would Be
$45,000	$55,000	$47,000–$53,000
$30,000	$35,500	$31,500–$33,500
$15,240	$18,000	$16,500–$17,200

The Six Secrets of Salary Negotiation

One teensy-tiny little problem: *how* do you find out the salary of those who would be above and below you? Well, first you have to find out their *names* or the names of their *positions*. If it is a small organization you are going after—one with twenty or fewer employees—finding this information out should be *duck soup*. Any employee who works there is likely to know the answer, and you can usually get in touch with one of those employees, or even an ex-employee, through your own personal contacts. Since up to two-thirds of all new jobs are created by companies that size, that's the size organization you are likely to be researching, anyway.

If you are going after a larger organization, then you fall back to our familiar life-preserver, namely, every contact you have (family, friend, relative, business, or church acquaintance) who might know the company, and therefore, the information you seek. In other words, you are looking for Someone Who Knows Someone who either is working, or has worked, at the particular place or places that interest you, and who therefore has or can get this information for you.

Chapter Thirteen

If you absolutely run into a blank wall on a particular organization (everyone who works there is pledged to secrecy, and they have shipped all their ex-employees to Siberia), then seek out information on their nearest *competitor* in the same geographic area. *For example,* let us say you were researching Bank X, and they were proving to be inscrutable about what they pay their managers. You would then try Bank Y as your research base, to see if the information were easier to come by, there. And if it were, you would then assume the two were similar in their pay scales, and that what you learned about Bank Y was applicable also to Bank X.

Also experts say that in researching salaries, you should take note of the fact that most governmental agencies have civil service positions matching those in private industry, and their job descriptions and pay ranges are available to the public. Go to the nearest city, county, regional, state, or federal civil service office, find the job description nearest what you are seeking in private industry, and then ask for the starting salary.

YOUR OWN RANGE

Once you've made a guess at what the employer's range might be, for the job you have in mind, you then define your own range *accordingly.* Let me give an example. Suppose you guess that the employer's range is one of those stated in the chart above, viz., $16,500 to $17,200. Accordingly, you now *invent* an "asking" range for yourself, where your *minimum* "hooks in" just below that employer's *maximum.*

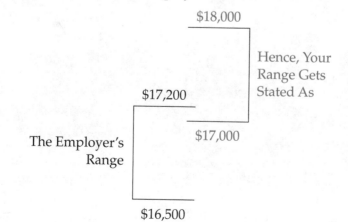

$18,000

Hence, Your
Range Gets
Stated As

$17,200

$17,000

The Employer's
Range

$16,500

And so, when the employer has stated a figure (probably around his or her *lowest*—i.e., $16,500), you will be ready to respond something like: "I understand of course the constraints under which all organizations are operating, considering the present economy, but I believe my productivity is such that it would *justify* a salary"—*and here you mention a range whose bottom hooks in just below the top of their range, and goes up from there, accordingly, as shown on the diagram above*—" in the range of $17,000 to $18,000."

It will help a lot if during this discussion, you are prepared to show in what ways you will *make money* or in what ways you will *save money* for that organization, such as will justify the higher salary you are seeking. Hopefully, this will succeed in getting you the salary you want.

Daniel Porot, the job-expert in Europe, suggests that if you and an employer really hit it off, and you're *dying* to work there, but they cannot afford the salary you need, consider offering them part of your time. If you need, and believe you deserve, say $25,000, but they can only afford $15,000, you might consider offering them three days a week of your time for that $15,000 (15/25 = 3/5). This leaves you free to take work elsewhere during those other two days. You will *of course* produce so much work during those three days per week, that they will be ecstatic that they got you for even those three days.

The Sixth Secret of Successful Salary Negotiation:

> ## Know How to Bring the Salary Negotiation to a Close; Don't Leave It "Just Hanging"

Your salary negotiation with this particular employer is not finished until you've addressed the issue of so-called fringe benefits. "Fringes" such as life insurance, health benefits or health plans, vacation or holiday plans, and retirement programs typically add anywhere from 15 to 28 percent to many workers' salaries. That is to say, if an employee receives $3000 salary per month, the fringe benefits are worth another $450 to $840 per month.

If your job is *at a high level*, benefits may include but not be limited to: health, life, dental, disability, malpractice insurance; insurance for dependents; sick leave; vacation; personal leave/personal days; educational leave; educational cost reimbursement for coursework related to the job; maternity and/or parental leave; health leave to care for dependents; bonus system or profit sharing; stock options; expense accounts for entertaining clients; dues to professional associations; travel reimbursement; fee sharing arrangements for clients that the employee generates; organizational memberships; parking; automobile allowance; relocation costs; sabbaticals; professional conference costs; time for community service; flextime work schedules; fitness center memberships.

You should therefore, before you walk into the interview, know what benefits are particularly important to you, then at the end of salary negotiation remember to ask what benefits are offered—and negotiate if necessary for the benefits you particularly care about. Thinking this out ahead of time, of course, makes your negotiating easier, by far.

You also want to achieve some understanding about what their policy is about future raises. You can prepare the ground at the end of salary negotiation, by saying: *"If I accomplish this job to your satisfaction, as I fully expect to—and more—when could I expect to be in line for a raise?"*

Finally, you want to get *all of this* summarized, in writing. Always request a letter of agreement—or employment contract— that they give to you. If you can't get it in writing, now's a good time to start wondering *why.* The Road to Hell is paved with oral promises that went unwritten, and—later—unfulfilled.

Many executives unfortunately "forget" what they told you during the hiring-interview, or even deny they ever said such a thing.

Also, many executives leave the company for another position and place, and their successor or the top boss may disown any *unwritten* promises: *"I don't know what caused them to say that to you, but they clearly exceeded their authority, and of course we can't be held to that."*

Conclusion:
The Greatest Secret

All of this, of course, presumes that your interview, and salary negotiation, goes well. There are times, however, when it looks like it's going well, and then all of a sudden and without warning it comes totally unraveled. You're hired, told to report next Monday, and then get a phone call on Friday telling you that all hiring has been put, mysteriously, "on hold." You're therefore back out "on the pavements." Having seen this happen so many times, over the years, I remind you of the truth at the beginning of this book: *successful* job-hunters and career-changers *always have alternatives.*

Alternative ideas of what they could do with their life.

Alternative ways of describing what they want to do right now.

Alternative ways of going about the job-hunt (not just the Internet, not just resumes, agencies, and ads).

Alternative job prospects.

Alternative "target" organizations that they go after.

Alternative ways of approaching employers.

And so on, and so forth.

What all this means for you, the seeker of secrets, is: be sure you are pursuing more than just one employer, right up until after you start your new job. That organization, that office, that group, that church, that factory, that government agency, that volunteer organization that you've targeted may be *the ideal place* where you would like to work. But no matter how appetizing this *first choice* looks to you, no matter how much it makes your mouth water at the thought of working there, *you are committing job-hunting suicide* if you don't have some alternative places in mind. Sure, maybe you'll get that dream-come-true. But—*big question*—what are your plans if you don't? You've *got* to have other plans **now**—not when that first target runs out of gas three months from now. You must go after more than one organization. I recommend five "targets," at least.

TARGET SMALL ORGANIZATIONS

Were I myself looking for a job tomorrow, this is what I would do. After I had figured out, as in the previous chapters, what my ideal job looked like, and after I had collected a list of those workplaces that have such jobs, in my chosen geographical area, I would then circle the names and addresses of those which are *small* organizations (personally I would restrict my *first draft* to those with twenty-five or fewer employees)—and then go after them, in the manner I have described in previous chapters. However, as the dot.com *downturn* of *April 2000 and following* taught us, small organizations can sometimes be fraught with danger *(a nova-like birth, a sudden black hole death)*, I would look particularly for small organizations that are *established* or *growing.* And if *"organizations with twenty-five or fewer employees"* eventually didn't turn up enough *leads* for me, then I would broaden my search to *"organizations with fifty or fewer employees,"* and finally—if that turned up nothing—to *"organizations with 100 or fewer employees."* But I would *start* small. Very small.

Remember, job-hunting always involves luck, to some degree. But with a little bit of luck, and a lot of hard work, plus determination, these instructions about how to get hired, should work for you, even as they have worked for so many hundreds of thousands before you.

Take heart from those who have gone before you, such as this determined job-hunter, who wrote me this heartfelt letter, with which I close:

"Before I read this book, I was depressed and lost in the futile job-hunt using Want Ads Only. I did not receive even one phone call from any ad I answered, over a total of four months. I felt that I was the most useless person on earth. I am female, with a two-and-a-half-year-old daughter, a former professor in China, with no working experience at all in the U.S. We came here seven months ago because my husband had a job offer here.

"Then, on June 11th of last year, I saw your book in a local bookstore. Subsequently, I spent three weeks, ten hours a day except Sunday, reading every single word of your book and doing all of the flower petals in the Flower Exercise. After getting to know myself much better, I felt I was ready to try the job-hunt again. I used Parachute throughout as my guide, from the very beginning to the very end, namely, salary negotiation.

"In just two weeks I secured (you guessed it) two job offers, one of which I am taking, as it is an excellent job, with very good pay. It is (you guessed it again) a small company, with twenty or so employees. It is also a career-change: I was a professor of English; now I am to be a controller!

"I am so glad I believed your advice: there are jobs out there, and there are two types of employers out there, and truly there are!

"I hope you will be happy to hear my story."

How to Find Your Mission in Life

GOD AND ONE'S VOCATION

FOREWORD

As I started writing this section, I toyed at first with the idea of following what might be described as an "all-paths approach" to religion. But, after much thought, I decided not to try that. This, because I have read many other writers who tried, and I felt the approach failed miserably. An "all-paths" approach to religion ends up being a "no-paths" approach, even as a woman or man who tries to please everyone ends up pleasing no one. It is the old story of the "universal" vs. the "particular."

Those of us who do career counseling could predict, ahead of time, that trying to stay universal is not likely to be helpful, in writing about religion. We know well from our own field that truly helpful career counseling depends upon defining the **particularity** or uniqueness of each person we try to help. No employer wants to know only what you have in common with everyone else. He or she wants to know what makes you unique and individual. As I have argued throughout this book, the identification and inventory of your uniqueness or *particularity* is crucial if you are ever to find meaningful work.

This particularity invades and carries over to *everything* a person does; it is not suddenly "jettisonable" when he or she turns to religion. Therefore, when I or anyone else writes about religion I believe we **must** write out of our own particularity—which *starts*, in my case, with the fact that I write, and think, and breathe as a Christian—as you might expect from the fact that I was an ordained Episcopalian minister for many years. Understandably, then, this article speaks from a Christian perspective. I want you to be aware of that, at the outset.

Balanced against this is the fact that I have always been acutely sensitive to the fact that this is a pluralistic society in which we live, and that I owe a great deal to my readers who may have religious convictions quite different from my own. It has turned out that the people who work or have worked here in my office with me, over the years, have been predominantly of other faiths, mainly Jewish. Furthermore, *Parachute*'s more than 8 million readers have not only included Christians of every variety and persuasion, Christian Scientists, Jews, members of the Baha'i faith, Hindus, Buddhists, adherents of Islam, but also believers in "new age" religions, secularists, humanists, agnostics, atheists, and many others. I have therefore tried to be very courteous toward the feelings of all my readers, *while at the same time* counting on them to translate my Christian thought forms into their own thought forms. This ability to thus translate is the indispensable *sine qua non* of anyone who wants to communicate helpfully with others, these days.

In the Judeo-Christian tradition from which I come, one of the indignant Biblical questions is, "Has God forgotten to be gracious?" The answer was a clear No. I think it is important *for all of us* also to seek the same goal. I have therefore labored to make this section gracious as well as helpful.

R.N.B

Turning Point

For many of us, the job-hunt offers a chance to make some fundamental changes in our whole life. It marks a turning point in how we live our life.

It gives us a chance to ponder and reflect, to extend our mental horizons, to go deeper into the sub-soil of our soul.

It gives us a chance to wrestle with the question, "Why am I here on Earth?" We don't want to feel that we are just another grain of sand lying on the beach called humanity, unnumbered and lost in the billions of other human beings.

We want to do more than plod through life, going to work, coming home from work. We want to find that special joy, "that no one can take from us," which comes from having a sense of Mission in our life.

We want to feel we were put here on Earth for some special purpose, to do some unique work that only we can accomplish.

We want to know what our Mission is.

The Meaning of the Word "Mission"

When used with respect to our life and work *Mission* has always been a religious concept, from beginning to end. It is defined by *Webster's* as "a continuing task or responsibility that one is destined or fitted to do or specially called upon to undertake," and historically has had two major synonyms: *Calling* and *Vocation*. These, of course, are the same word in two different languages, English and Latin. Both imply God. To be given a Vocation or Calling implies *Someone who* calls. To have a Destiny implies

Someone who determined the destination for us. Thus, the concept of Mission lands us inevitably in the lap of God, before we have hardly begun.

I emphasize this, because there is an increasing trend in our culture to try to speak about religious subjects without reference to God. This is true of "spirituality," "soul," and "Mission," in particular. More and more books talk about Mission as though it were simply "a purpose you choose for your own life, by identifying your enthusiasms."

This attempt to obliterate all reference to God from the originally religious concept of Mission, is particularly ironic because the proposed substitute word—enthusiasms—is derived from two Greek words, "en theos," and means "God in us."

In the midst of this "redefining culture" we find an oasis called the "job-hunting field." It is a field that was raised on a firm concept of "God." That's because most of its inventors, most of its leaders over the years—the late John Crystal, Arthur Miller, Ralph Mattson, Tom and Ellie Jackson, Bernard Haldane, Arthur and Marie Kirn, myself, and many others—have been people who believe firmly in God, and came into this field because we think about Him a lot, in connection with meaningful work.

Nor are we alone. Many many job-hunters also think about God a lot. In the U.S., 94 percent of us believe in God, 90 percent of us pray, 88 percent of us believe God loves us, and 33 percent of us report we have had a life-changing religious experience—and these figures have remained virtually unchanged for the past fifty years, according to opinion polls conducted by the Gallup Organization. (*The People's Religion: American Faith in the 90s*. Macmillan & Co. 1989.)

What is not so clear is whether we think about God in connection with our work. Often these two subjects—spiritual beliefs and Work—live in separate mental ghettos within the same person's head.

But unemployment offers us a chance to fix all that: to marry our work and our religious beliefs together, to talk about Calling, and Vocation, and Mission in life—to think out why we are here, and what plans God has for us.

That's why a period of unemployment can absolutely change our life.

The Secret of Finding Your Mission in Life: Taking It in Stages

> I will explain the steps toward finding your Mission in life that I have learned in my seventy-eight years on Earth. Just remember two things. First, I speak from a Christian perspective, and trust you to translate this into your own thought-forms.
>
> Second, I know that these steps are not the only Way—by any means. Many people have discovered their Mission by taking other paths. And you may, too. But hopefully what I have to say may shed some light upon whatever path you take.

I have learned that if you want to figure out what your Mission in life is, it will likely take some time. It is not a *problem* to be solved in a day and a night. It is a *learning process* which has steps to it, much like the process by which we all learned to eat. As a baby we did not tackle adult food right off. As we all recall, there were three stages: first there had to be the mother's milk or bottle, then strained baby foods, and finally—after teeth and time—the stuff that grown-ups chew. Three stages—and the two earlier stages were not to be disparaged. It was all Eating, just different forms of Eating—appropriate to our development at the time. But each stage had to be mastered, in turn, before the next could be approached.

There are usually three stages also to learning what your Mission in life is, and the two earlier stages are likewise not to be disparaged. It is all "Mission"—just different forms of Mission, appropriate to your development at the time. But each stage has to be mastered, in turn, before the next can be approached.

Of course, there is a sense in which you never master any of these stages, but are always growing in understanding and mastery of them, throughout your whole life here on Earth.

As it has been impressed on me by observing many people over the years (admittedly through *Christian spectacles*), it appears that the three parts to your Mission here on Earth can be defined generally as follows:

1. *Your first Mission here on Earth* is one which you share with the rest of the human race, but it is no less your individual Mission for the fact that it is shared: and it is, **to seek to stand hour by hour in the conscious presence of God, the One from whom your Mission is derived.** *The Missioner before the Mission*, is the rule. In religious language, your Mission here is: *to know God, and enjoy Him forever, and to see His hand in all His works.*

2. Second, once you have begun doing that in an earnest way, *your second Mission here on Earth* is also one which you share with the rest of the human race, but it is no less your individual mission for the fact that it is shared: and that is, **to do what you can, moment by moment, day by day, step by step, to make this world a better place, following the leading and guidance of God's Spirit within you and around you.**

3. Third, once you have begun doing that in a serious way, *your third Mission here on Earth* is one which is uniquely yours, and that is:

a) **to exercise that Talent which you particularly came to Earth to use—your greatest gift, which you most delight to use,**

b) **in the place(s) or setting(s) which God has caused to appeal to you the most,**

c) **and for those purposes which God most needs to have done in the world.**

Epilogue

When fleshed out, and spelled out, I think you will find that there you have the definition of your Mission in life. Or, to put it another way, these are the three Missions which you have in life.

The Two Rhythms of the Dance of Mission: Unlearning, Learning, Unlearning, Learning

The distinctive characteristic of these three stages is that in each we are forced to *let go* of some fundamental assumptions which the world has *falsely* taught us, about the nature of our Mission. In other words, throughout this quest and at each stage we find ourselves engaged not merely in a process of *Learning.* We are also engaged in a process of *Un*learning. Thus, we can restate the above three Learnings, in terms of what we also need to *un-learn* at each stage:

- We need in the first Stage to *un*learn the idea that our Mission is primarily to keep busy *doing* something (here on Earth), and learn instead that our Mission is first of all to keep busy *being* something (here on Earth). In Christian language (and others as well), we might say that we were sent here to learn how *to be* sons of God, and daughters of God, before anything else. "*Our Father, who art in heaven . . .*"

- In the second stage, "Being" issues into "Doing." At this stage, we need to *un*learn the idea that everything about our Mission must be *unique* to us, and learn instead that some parts of our Mission here on Earth are *shared* by all human beings: e.g., we were all sent here to bring more gratitude, more kindness, more forgiveness, and more love, into the world. We share this Mission because the task is too large to be accomplished by just one individual.

- We need in the third stage to *un*learn the idea that that part of our Mission which is truly unique, and most truly ours, is something Our Creator just *orders* us to do, without any agreement from our spirit, mind, and heart. (On the other hand, neither is it something that each of us chooses and then merely asks God to bless.) We need to learn that God so honors our free will, that He has ordained our unique Mission be something which we have some part in choosing.

- In this third stage we need also to *un*learn the idea that our unique Mission must consist of some achievement which all the world will see—and learn instead that as the stone does not always know what ripples it has caused in the pond whose surface it impacts, so neither we nor those who watch our life will always know *what we have achieved* by our life and by our Mission. *It may be* that by the grace of God we helped bring about a profound change for the better in the lives of other souls around us, but it also may be that this takes place beyond our sight, or after we have gone on. And we may never know what we have accomplished, until we see Him face-to-face after this life is past.

- Most finally, we need to *un*learn the idea that what we have accomplished is our doing, and ours alone. It is God's Spirit breathing in us and through us which helps us to do whatever we do, and so the singular first person pronoun is never appropriate, but only the plural. Not "*I* accomplished this" but "*We* accomplished this, God and I, working together . . ."

That should give you a general overview. But I would like to add some random comments on my part about each of these three Missions of ours here on Earth.

Some Random Comments About Your First Mission in Life

Your first Mission here on Earth is one which you share with the rest of the human race, but it is no less your individual Mission for the fact that it is shared: and that is, **to seek to stand hour by hour in the conscious presence of God, the One from whom your Mission is derived.** The Missioner before the Mission, is the rule. In religious language, your Mission is: to know God, and enjoy Him forever, and to see His hand in all His works.

Comment 1:
How We Might Think of God

Each of us has to go about this primary Mission according to the tenets of his or her own particular religion. But I will speak what I know out of the context of my own particular faith, and you may perhaps translate and apply it to yours. I will speak as a Christian, who believes (passionately) that Christ is the Way and the Truth and the Life. But I also believe, with St. Peter, "that God shows no partiality, but in every nation any one who fears him and does what is right is acceptable to him." (Acts 10:34–35)

Now, Jesus claimed many unique things about Himself and His Mission; but He also spoke of Himself as the great prototype for us all. He called Himself "the Son of Man," and He said, "I assure you that the man who believes in me will do the same things that I have done, yes, and he will do even greater things than these . . ." (John 14:12)

Emboldened by His identification of us with His Life and His Mission, we might want to remember how He spoke about His Life here on Earth. He put it in this context: **"I came from the Father and have come into the world; again, I am leaving the world and going to the Father."** (John 16:28)

If there is a sense in which this is, in even the faintest way, true also of our lives (and I shall say in a moment in what sense I think it is true), then instead of calling our great Creator "God" or "Father" right off, we might begin our approach to the subject of religion by referring to the One Who gave us our Mission and sent us to this planet not as "God" or "Father" but—*just to help our thinking*—as: **"The One From Whom We Came and The One To Whom We Shall Return,"** when this life is done.

If our life here on Earth is to be at all like Christ's, then this is a true way to think about the One Who gave us our Mission. We are not some kind of eternal, pre-existent *being*. We are **creatures**, who once did not exist, and then came into Being, and continue to have our Being, only at the will of our great Creator. But as creatures we are both body and soul; and although we know our body was created in our mother's womb, our soul's origin is a great mystery. Where it came from, at what moment the Lord created it, is something we cannot know. It is not unreasonable to suppose, however, that the great God created our *soul* before it entered our body, and in that sense we did indeed stand before God before we were born; and He is indeed **"The One From Whom We Came and The One To Whom We Shall Return."**

Therefore, before we go searching for "what work was I sent here to do?" we need to establish or in a truer sense *reestablish*—contact with this **"One From Whom We Came and The One To Whom We Shall Return."** Without this reaching out of the creature to the great Creator, without this reaching out of *the creature with a Mission* to *the One Who Gave Us That Mission*, the question *what is my Mission in life?* is void and null. The *what* is rooted in the *Who*; absent the Personal, one cannot meaningfully discuss The Thing. It is like the adult who cries, "I want to get married," without giving any consideration to *who* it is they want to marry.

Comment 2:
How We Might Think of Religion or Faith

In light of this larger view of our creatureliness, we can see that *religion* or *faith* is not a question of whether or not we choose to (*as it is so commonly put*) "have a relationship with God." Looking at our life in a larger context than just our life here on Earth, it becomes apparent that some sort of relationship with God is a given for us, about which we have absolutely no choice. God and we **were** and **are** related, during the time of our soul's existence before our birth and in the time of our soul's continued existence after our death. The only choice we have is what to do about **The Time In Between**, i.e., what we want the nature of our relationship with God to be during our time here on Earth and how that will affect the *nature* of the relationship, then, after death.

One of the corollaries of all this is that by the very act of being born into a human body, it is inevitable that we undergo a kind of *amnesia*—an amnesia which typically embraces not only our nine months in the womb, our baby years, and almost one-third of each day (sleeping), but more important any memory of our origin or our destiny. We wander on Earth as an amnesia victim. To seek after Faith, therefore, is to seek to climb back out of that amnesia. Religion or faith is **the hard reclaiming of knowledge we once knew as a certainty.**

Epilogue

Comment 3:
The First Obstacle to Executing This Mission

This first Mission of ours here on Earth is not the easiest of Missions, simply because it is the first. Indeed, in many ways, it is the most difficult. All can see that our life here on Earth is a very physical life. We eat, we drink, we sleep, we long to be held, and to hold. We inherit a physical body, with very physical appetites, we walk on the physical earth, and we acquire physical possessions. It is the most alluring of temptations, *in our amnesia*, to come up with just a *Physical* interpretation of this life: to think that the Universe is merely interested in the survival of species. Given this interpretation, the story of our individual life could be simply told: we are born, grow up, procreate, and die.

But we are ever recalled to do what we came here to do: that without rejecting the joy of the Physicalness of this life, such as the love of the blue sky and the green grass, we are to reach out beyond all this to **recall** and recover a *Spiritual* interpretation of our life. *Beyond* the physical and *within* the physicalness of this life, to detect a Spirit and a Person from beyond this Earth who is with us and in us—the very real and loving and awesome Presence of the great Creator from whom we came—and the One to whom we once again shall go.

Comment 4:
The Second Obstacle to Executing This Mission

It is one of the conditions of our earthly amnesia and our creatureliness that, sadly enough, some very *human* and very *rebellious* part of us *likes* the idea of living in a world where we can be our own god—and therefore loves the purely Physical interpretation of life, and finds it *anguish* to relinquish it. Traditional Christian vocabulary calls this **"sin"** and has a lot to say about the difficulty it poses for this first part of our Mission. All who live a thoughtful life know that it is true: our greatest enemy in carrying out this first Mission of ours is indeed *our own* heart and our own rebellion.

Comment 5:
Further Thoughts About
What Makes Us Special and Unique

As I said earlier, many of us come to this issue of our Mission in life, because we want to feel that we are unique. And what we mean by that, is that we hope to discover some "specialness" intrinsic to us, which is our birthright, and which no one can take from us. What we, however, discover from a thorough exploration of this topic, is that we are indeed special—but only because God thinks us so. Our specialness and uniqueness reside in Him, and His love, rather than in anything intrinsic to our own *being*. The proper appreciation of this distinction causes our feet to carry us in the end not to the City called Pride, but to the Temple called Gratitude.

> What is religion? Religion is the service of God out of grateful love for what God has done for us. The Christian religion, more particularly, is the service of God out of grateful love for what God has done for us in Christ.
> Phillips Brooks, author of
> *O Little Town of Bethlehem*

Comment 6:
The Unconscious Doing
of the Work We Came to Do

You may have *already* wrestled with this first part of your Mission here on Earth. You may not have called it that. You may have called it simply "learning to believe in God." But if you ask what your Mission is in life, this one was and is the precondition of all else that you came here to do. Absent this Mission, and it is folly to talk about the rest. So, if you have been seeking faith, or seeking to strengthen your faith, you have—willy-nilly—already been about *the doing of the Mission you were given*. Born into **This Time In Between**, you have found His hand again, and reclasped it. You are therefore ready to go on with His Spirit to tackle together what you came here to do—the other parts of your Mission.

Epilogue

Some Random Comments About Your Second Mission in Life

Your second Mission here on Earth is also one which you share with the rest of the human race, but it is no less your individual Mission for the fact that it is shared: and that is, **to do what you can moment by moment, day by day, step by step, to make this world a better place—following the leading and guidance of God's Spirit within you and around you.**

Comment 1:
The Uncomfortableness of One Step at a Time

Imagine yourself out walking in your neighborhood one night, and suddenly you find yourself surrounded by such a dense fog, that you have lost your bearings and cannot find your way. Suddenly, a friend appears out of the fog, and asks you to put your hand in theirs, and they will lead you home. And you, not being able to tell where you are going, trustingly follow them, even though you can only see one step at a time. Eventually you arrive safely home, filled with gratitude. But as you reflect upon the experience the next day, you realize how unsettling it was to have to keep walking when you could see only one step at a time, even though you had guidance in which you knew you could trust.

Now I have asked you to imagine all of this, because this is the essence of the second Mission to which *you* are called—and *I* am called—in this life. It is all very different than we had imagined. When the question, *"What is your Mission in life?"* is first broached, and we have put our hand in God's, as it were, we imagine that we will be taken up to *some mountaintop*, from which we can see far into the distance. And that we will hear a voice in our ear, saying, "Look, look, see that distant city? That is the goal of your Mission; that is where everything is leading, every step of your way."

Epilogue   **347**

But instead of the mountaintop, we find ourself in *the valley*—wandering often in a fog. And the voice in our ear says something quite different from what we thought we would hear. It says, **"Your Mission is to take one step at a time, even when you don't yet see where it all is leading, or what the Grand Plan is, or what your overall Mission in life is. Trust Me; I will lead you."**

Comment 2:
The Nature of this Step-by-Step Mission

As I said, in every situation you find yourself, you have been sent here to do whatever you can—moment by moment—that will bring more gratitude, more kindness, more forgiveness, more honesty, and more love into this world.

There are dozens of such moments every day. Moments when you stand—as it were—at a spiritual crossroads, with two ways lying before you. Such moments are typically called **"moments of decision."** It does not matter what the frame or content of each particular decision is. It all devolves, in the end, into just two roads before you, *every time*. **The one** will lead to *less* gratitude, *less* kindness, *less* forgiveness, *less* honesty, or *less* love in the world. **The other** will lead to *more* gratitude, *more* kindness, *more* forgiveness, *more* honesty, or *more* love in the world. Your Mission, each moment, is to seek to choose the latter spiritual road, rather than the former, *every time*.

Comment 3:
Some Examples of this Step-by-Step Mission

I will give a few examples, so that the nature of this part of your Mission may be unmistakably clear.

You are out on the freeway, in your car. Someone has gotten into the wrong lane, to the right of *your* lane, and needs to move over into the lane you are in. You *see* their need to cut in, ahead of you. **Decision time**. In your mind's eye you see two spiritual roads lying before you: the one leading to less kindness in the world (you speed up, to shut this driver out, and don't let them move over), the other leading to more kindness in the world (you let the driver cut in). **Since you know this is part of your Mission, part of the reason why you came to Earth, your**

calling is clear. You know which road to take, which decision to make.

You are hard at work at your desk, when suddenly an interruption comes. The phone rings, or someone is at the door. They need something from you, a question of some of your time and attention. **Decision time.** In your mind's eye you see two spiritual roads lying before you: the one leading to less love in the world (you tell them you're just too busy to be bothered), the other leading to more love in the world (you put aside your work, decide that God may have sent this person to you, and say, "Yes, what can I do to help you?"). **Since you know this is part of your Mission, part of the reason why you came to Earth, your calling is clear. You know which road to take, which decision to make.**

Your mate does something that hurts your feelings. **Decision time.** In your mind's eye you see two spiritual roads lying before you: the one leading to less forgiveness in the world (you institute an icy silence between the two of you, and think of how you can punish them or otherwise get even), the other leading to more forgiveness in the world (you go over and take them in your arms, speak the truth about your hurt feelings, and assure them of your love). **Since you know this is part of your Mission, part of the reason why you came to Earth, your calling is clear. You know which road to take, which decision to make.**

You have not behaved at your most noble, recently. And now you are face-to-face with someone who asks you a question about what happened. **Decision time.** In your mind's eye you see two spiritual roads lying before you: the one leading to less honesty in the world (you lie about what happened, or what you were feeling, because you fear losing their respect or their love), the other leading to more honesty in the world (you tell the truth, together with how you feel about it, in retrospect). **Since you know this is part of your Mission, part of the reason why you came to Earth, your calling is clear. You know which road to take, which decision to make.**

Comment 4:
The Spectacle That Makes the Angels Laugh

It is necessary to explain this part of our Mission in some detail, because so many times you will see people wringing their hands, and saying, *"I want to know what my Mission in life is,"* all the while they are cutting people off on the highway, refusing to give time to people, punishing their mate for having hurt their feelings, and lying about what they did. And it will seem to you that the angels must laugh to see this spectacle. *For these people wringing their hands*, their Mission was right there, on the freeway, in the interruption, in the hurt, and at the confrontation.

Comment 5:
The Valley versus the Mountaintop

At some point in your life your Mission may involve some grand *mountaintop experience*, where you say to yourself, "This, this, is why I came into the world. I know it. I know it." *But until then*, your Mission is here in *the valley*, and the fog, and the little callings moment by moment, day by day. More to the point, it is likely you cannot ever get to your mountaintop Mission unless you have first exercised your stewardship faithfully in the valley.

It is an ancient principle, to which Jesus alluded often, that if you don't use the information the Universe has already given you, you cannot expect it will give you any more. If you aren't being faithful in small things, how can you expect to be given charge over larger things? (Luke 16:10–12; 19:11–24) If you aren't trying to bring more gratitude, kindness, forgiveness, honesty, and love into the world each day, you can hardly expect that you will be entrusted with the Mission to help bring peace into the world or anything else large and important. If we do not live out our day-by-day Mission in the valley, we cannot expect we are yet ready for a larger *mountaintop* Mission.

Comment 6:
The Importance of Not Thinking of This Mission as "Just a Training Camp"

The valley is not just a kind of "training camp." There is in your imagination even now an invisible *spiritual* mountaintop to which you may go, if you wish to see where all this is leading. And what will you see there, in the imagination of your heart, but the goal toward which all this is pointed: **that Earth might be more like heaven. That human life might be more like God's.** That is the large achievement toward which all our day-by-day Missions *in the valley* are moving. This is a *large* order, but it is accomplished by faithful attention to the doing of our great Creator's **will** in little things as well as in large. It is much like the building of the pyramids in Egypt, which was accomplished by the dragging of a lot of individual pieces of stone by a lot of individual men.

The valley, the fog, the going step-by-step, is no mere training camp. The goal is real, however large. **"Thy Kingdom come, Thy will be done, on Earth, as it is in heaven."**

Some Random Comments
About Your Third Mission
in Life

Your third Mission here on Earth is one which is uniquely yours, and that is:

a) **to exercise that Talent which you particularly came to Earth to use—your greatest gift which you most delight to use,**

b) **in those place(s) or setting(s) which God has caused to appeal to you the most,**

c) **and for those purposes which God most needs to have done in the world.**

Comment 1:
Our Mission Is Already Written,
"in Our Members"

It is customary in trying to identify this part of our Mission, to advise that we should ask God, in prayer, to speak to us—and **tell us** plainly what our Mission is. We look for a voice in the air, a thought in our head, a dream in the night, a sign in the events of the day, to reveal this thing which is otherwise *(it is said)* completely hidden. Sometimes, from just such answered prayer, people do indeed discover what their Mission is, beyond all doubt and uncertainty.

But having to wait for the voice of God to reveal what our Mission is, is not the truest picture of our situation. St. Paul, in Romans, speaks of a law "written in our members"—and this phrase has a telling application to the question of **how** God reveals to each of us our unique Mission in life. Read again the definition of our third Mission (above) and you will see: the clear implication of the definition is that God has **already** revealed His will to us concerning our vocation and Mission, by causing it to be **"written in our members."** We are to begin deciphering our unique Mission by studying our talents and skills, and more particularly which ones (or One) we most rejoice to use.

God actually has written His will *twice* in our members: *first in the talents* which He lodged there, and second *in His guidance of our heart*, as to which talent gives us the greatest pleasure from its exercise (**it is usually the one that, when we use it, causes us to lose all sense of time**).

Even as the anthropologist can examine ancient inscriptions, and divine from them the daily life of a long lost people, so we by examining **our talents** and **our heart** can *more often than we* *dream* divine the Will of the Living God. For true it is, our Mission is not something He **will** reveal; it is something He **has already** revealed. It is not to be found written in the sky; it is to be found written in our members.

Comment 2:
Career Counseling: We Need You

Arguably, our first two Missions in life could be learned from religion alone—without any reference whatsoever to career counseling, the subject of this book. Why then should career counseling claim that this question about our Mission in life is its proper concern, *in any way?*

It is when we come to this third Mission, which hinges so crucially on the question of our Talents, skills, and gifts, that we see the answer. If you've read the body of this book, before turning to this Epilogue, you know without my even saying it, how much the identification of Talents, gifts, or skills is the province of career counseling. Its expertise, indeed its *raison d'etre*, lies precisely in the identification, classification, and (forgive me) "prioritization" of Talents, skills, and gifts. To put the matter quite simply, career counseling knows how to do this better than any other discipline—**including** traditional religion. This is not a defect of religion, but the fulfillment of something Jesus promised: "When the Spirit of truth comes, He will guide you into all truth." (John 16:12) Career counseling is part (we may hope) of that promised late-coming truth. It can therefore be of inestimable help to the pilgrim who is trying to figure out what their greatest, and most enjoyable, talent is, as a step toward identifying their unique Mission in life.

If career counseling needs religion as its helpmate in the first two stages of identifying our Mission in life, religion repays the compliment by clearly needing career counseling as **its** helpmate here in the third stage.

And this place where you are in your life right now—facing the job-hunt and all its anxiety—is the perfect time to seek the union within your own mind and heart of both career counseling (as in the pages of this book) and your faith in God.

Comment 3:
How Our Mission Got Chosen:
A Scenario for the Romantic

It is a mystery which we cannot fathom, in this life at least, as to why one of us has this talent, and the other one has that; why God chose to give one gift—and Mission—to one person, and a different gift—and Mission—to another. Since we do not know, and in some degree cannot know, we are certainly left free to speculate, and imagine.

We may imagine that before we came to Earth, our souls, *our Breath, our Light,* stood before the great Creator and volunteered for this Mission. And God and we, together, chose what that Mission would be and what particular gifts would be needed, which He then agreed to give us, after our birth. Thus, our Mission was not a command given preemptorily by an unloving Creator to a reluctant slave without a vote, but was a task jointly designed by us both, in which as fast as the great Creator said, **"I wish"** our hearts responded, **"Oh, yes."** As mentioned in an earlier Comment, it may be helpful to think of the condition of our becoming human as that we became amnesiac about any consciousness our soul had before birth—and therefore amnesiac about the nature or manner in which our Mission was designed.

Our searching for our Mission now is therefore a searching to recover the memory of something we ourselves had a part in designing.

I am admittedly a hopeless romantic, so of course I like this picture. If you also are a hopeless romantic, you may like it too. There's also the chance that it just may be true. We will not know until we see Him face-to-face.

Comment 4:
Mission as Intersection

> There are all different kinds of voices calling you to all different kinds of work, and the problem is to find out which is the voice of God rather than that of society, say, or the superego, or self-interest. By and large a good rule for finding out is this: the kind of work God usually calls you to is the kind of work a) that you need most to do and b) the world most needs to have done. If you really get a kick out of your work, you've presumably met requirement a), but if your work is writing TV deodorant commercials, the chances are you've missed requirement b). On the other hand, if your work is being a doctor in a leper colony, you have probably met b), but if most of the time you're bored and depressed by it, the chances are you haven't only bypassed a) but probably aren't helping your patients much either. Neither the hair shirt nor the soft birth will do. **The place God calls you to is the place where your deep gladness and the world's deep hunger meet.**
>
>
>
> Fred Buechner
>
> *Wishful Thinking—A Theological ABC*
>
>
>

Comment 5:
Examples of Mission as Intersection

Your unique and individual Mission will most likely turn out to be a mission of Love, acted out in one or all of three arenas: either in the Kingdom of the Mind, whose goal is to bring more Truth into the world; or in the Kingdom of the Heart, whose goal is to bring more Beauty into the world; or in the Kingdom of the Will, whose goal is to bring more Perfection into the world, through Service.

Here are some examples:

"My mission is, out of the rich reservoir of love which God seems to have given me, to nurture and show love to others—most particularly to those who are suffering from incurable diseases."

"My mission is to draw maps for people to show them how to get to God."

"My mission is to create the purest foods I can, to help people's bodies not get in the way of their spiritual growth."

"My mission is to make the finest harps I can so that people can hear the voice of God in the wind."

"My mission is to make people laugh, so that the travail of this earthly life doesn't seem quite so hard to them."

"My mission is to help people know the truth, in love, about what is happening out in the world, so that there will be more honesty in the world."

"My mission is to weep with those who weep, so that in my arms they may feel themselves in the arms of that Eternal Love which sent me and which created them."

"My mission is to create beautiful gardens, so that in the lilies of the field people may behold the Beauty of God and be reminded of the Beauty of Holiness."

Comment 6:
Life as Long as Your Mission Requires

Knowing that you came to Earth for a reason, and knowing what that Mission is, throws an entirely different light upon your life from now on. You are, generally speaking, delivered from any further fear about how long you have to live. You may settle it in your heart that you are here until God chooses to think that you have accomplished your Mission, or until God has a greater Mission for you in another Realm. You need to be a good steward of what He has given you, while you are here; but you do not need to be an anxious steward or stewardess.

You need to attend to your health, *but you do not need to constantly worry about it*. You need to meditate on your death, *but you do not need to be constantly preoccupied with it*. To paraphrase the glorious words of G. K. Chesterton: **"We now have a strong desire for living combined with a strange carelessness about dying. We desire life like water and yet are ready to drink death like wine."** We know that we are here to do what we came to do, and we need not worry about anything else.

Final Comment:
A Job-Hunt Done Well

If you approach your job-hunt as an opportunity to work on this issue as well as the issue of how you will keep body and soul together, then hopefully your job-hunt will end with your being able to say: "Life has deep meaning to me, now. I have discovered more than my ideal job; I have found my Mission, and the reason why I am here on Earth."

Epilogue

How to Choose a Career Coach or Counselor

How to Choose a Career Coach or Counselor, If You Decide You Need One

Let's start out with some simple definitions:

Career Coach. A person can be certified as a career coach after as little as three days' training.

Career Counselor. A person can call themselves a career counselor, in some parts of the U.S., without any training.

• NCCC Counselor. NCCC means "Nationally Certified Career Counselor," of which there were 850 in the U.S. at last count. However, this credential is no longer being offered; so it may not be fair to choose someone who *has* the credential over someone who does *not;* this situation may exist solely because the person without the NCCC credential came along at a later time. As noted in Appendix B, we no longer include this credential with a person's listing, for this very reason.

• NCC Counselor. NCC means "Nationally Certified Counselor." There are over 20,000 such in the U.S. This can mean general counseling expertise, not necessarily career counseling expertise.

• LPC Counselor. LPC means "Licensed Professional Counselor"—and often refers to state licensing. Again, this does not necessarily mean expertise with career counseling. There are a number of states, now, that have some sort of licensing regulation of all counselors. In some states getting this licensing is mandatory, in others getting it is optional.

I wish I could say that everyone who hangs out a sign saying they are now a career coach or counselor could be completely trusted. Nope, they can't all be. As you can see from the definitions above, the career counseling field is largely unregulated. And even where there is certification, certification doesn't tell you much.

For, as is the case in many professions, all coaches and counselors divide basically into three groups: a) those who are honest and know what they're doing; b) those who are honest but inept; and c) those who are dishonest, and merely want your money—in lump sums, and up front.

You, of course, want a list of those in the first category—those who are honest and know what they're doing. Well, unfortunately, no one (including me) has such a list. You've got to do your own homework, or research, here, and your own interviewing, in your own geographical area, or you will deserve what you get.

Why is it that *you* and only *you* can do it? You, you, and nobody else but you? Well, let's say a friend tells you to go see so-and-so. He's a wonderful coach or counselor, but unhappily he reminds you of your Uncle Harry, whom you detest. Bummer! But, no one except you knows that you've always hated your Uncle Harry. That's why no one else can do this research for you—because the real question is not "Who is best?" but "Who is best for you?" Those last two words demand that it be you who "makes the call," that it be you who does the research.

Of course, you're tempted to skip this research, aren't you? *"Well, I'll just call up one place, and if I like the sound of them, I'll sign up. I'm a pretty good judge of character."* Right. I've heard this refrain from so many job-hunters who called me, after they'd lost all their money in a bad "pay-up-front" contract, because they had been *taken*, by slicker salespeople than they had ever run into before. As they tell me their stories, they cry over the telephone. I express, of course, my sympathy and compassion (I once got *taken* myself, the same way), but then I add, "I'm terribly sorry to hear that you had such a heartbreaking experience, but—as the Scots would say—"Ya dinna do your homework." Often you could easily have discovered whether a particular counselor was competent or not, before you ever gave them any of your money, simply by doing the preliminary research that I urge upon *everybody*.

Another way people try to avoid this research is by saying, "Well, I'll just see who Bolles recommends." That's a stretch, because I never have recommended anyone. Some try to claim I do, including, over the years, some of the people listed in the following Sampler, arguing that their very listing here constitutes a recommendation from me. Nice try! Inclusion in this book does NOT constitute an endorsement or recommendation by me—as I have been at great pains to make clear for the past thirty-five years. Never has meant that. Never will. *(Anyone listed here who claims that it does, gets removed from this Sampler the following year.)* This is just a *sampler* of names *who have asked to be listed*, not a "hall of fame." With them, as with all others, you must do your own homework. You must do your own research.

Collect Three Names That You Can Research

So, how do you go about finding a good career coach or counselor? Well, you start by collecting three names of career counselors in your geographical area.

How do you find those names? Several ways:

First, you can get names from your friends: ask if any of them have ever used a career coach or counselor. And if so, did they like 'em? And if so, what is that coach's or counselor's name?

Second, you can get names from the Sampler that follows this section (beginning on page 374). See if there are any career coaches or counselors who are near you. They may know how you can find still other names in your community. But I repeat what I said above: just because they're listed in the Sampler *doesn't* mean I recommend them. It only means they asked to be listed, and professed familiarity with the contents of this book (current edition). You've still got to research these people.

Need more names? Try your telephone book's yellow pages, under such headings as: Aptitude and Employment Testing, Career and Vocational Counseling, Personnel Consultants, and (if you are a woman) Women's Organizations and Services.

Once you have three names, you need to go do some comparison shopping. You want to go talk with all three of them face-to-face, and decide which of the three (if any) you want to hook up with.

Don't try to do this over the telephone, please! There is so much more you can tell, when you're looking the person straight in the eyes.

What will this initial interview cost you, with each of the three? The answer to that is easy: when setting up an appointment, *ask*. Some, a few, will charge you nothing for the initial interview. One of the best counselors I know of makes this a part of her policy: *I don't charge for the first interview because I want to be free to tell them I can't help them, if for some reason we just don't hit it off.* In most cases, however, if it's an individual coach or counselor, you *are* going to have to pay them for this exploratory hour, or part of an hour—even if it's only five or ten minutes. Do not expect that most individual counselors can afford to give you this exploratory interview for nothing! If they did that, and got a lot of requests like yours, they would never be able to make a living. You do have the right, however, to inquire ahead of time how much they are going to have to charge you for the exploratory interview. On the other hand, if this is not an individual counselor, but a firm trying to sell you a package "up front," I guarantee you they will give you the initial interview for free. They plan to use that first interview to sell you their program.

The Questions to Ask

When you are face-to-face with the individual coach or counselor (or firm), you ask each of them the same questions, listed on the form. (Keep a little pad or notebook with you, so you can write their answers down.)

After visiting the three places you chose for your comparison shopping, you have to go home, sit down, put your feet up, look over your notes, and compare those places.

MY SEARCH FOR A GOOD CAREER COUNSELOR

Questions I Will Ask Them	Answer from counselor #1	Answer from counselor #2	Answer from counselor #3
1. What is your program?			
2. Who will be doing it with me? And how long has this person been doing it?			
3. What is your success rate?			
4. What is the cost of your services?			
5. Is there a contract up front? If so, may I see it please, and take it home with me?			

You need to decide a) whether you want none of the three, or b) one of the three (and if so, which one). Remember, you don't have to choose any of the three counselors, if you didn't really care for any of them. If that is the case, then go choose three new counselors out of the yellow pages or wherever, dust off the notebook, and go out again. It may take a few more hours to find what you want. But the wallet, the purse, the job-hunt, the life, you save will be your own.

As you look over your notes, you will realize there is no definitive way for you to determine a career counselor's expertise. It's something you'll have to *smell out*, as you go along. But here are some clues. These are primarily clues about *firms* rather than individual coaches or counselors, but many clues apply to both:

Bad Answers

If they give you the feeling that everything will be done for you, by them (including interpretation of tests, and decision making about what this means you should do, or where you should do it)—rather than asserting that you are going to have to do almost all the work, with their basically assuming the role of coach,

(Give them **15 bad points**)

You want to learn how to do this for yourself; you're going to be job-hunting again, you know.

If they say they are not the person who will be doing the program with you, but deny you any chance to meet the counselor you would be working with,

(Give them **75 bad points**)

You're talking to a salesperson. My advice after talking to job-hunters for more than thirty years, is: avoid any firm that has a salesperson.

If you do get a chance to meet the counselor, but you don't like the counselor as a person,

(Give them **150 bad points**)

I don't care what their expertise is, if you don't like them, you're going to have a rough time getting what you want. I guarantee it. Rapport is everything.

If you ask how long the counselor has been doing this, and they get huffy or give a double-barreled answer, such as: "I've had eighteen years' experience in the business and career counseling world,"

(Give them **20 bad points**)

What that may mean is: seventeen and a half years as a fertilizer salesman, and one half year doing career counseling. Persist. "How long have you been with this firm, and how long have you been doing formal career counseling, as you are here?" You might be interested to know that some executive or career counseling firms hire yesterday's clients as today's new staff. Such new staff are sometimes given training only after they're "on-the-job." They are practicing on you.

If they try to answer the question of their experience by pointing to their degrees or credentials,

(Give them **3 bad points**)

Degrees or credentials tell you they've passed certain tests of their qualifications, but often these tests bear more on their expertise at career assessment than on their knowledge of creative job-hunting techniques.

If, when you ask about their success rate, they say they have never had a client that failed to find a job, no matter what,

(Give them **5 bad points**)

They're lying. I have studied career counseling programs for more than thirty years, have attended many, have studied records at state and federal offices, and I have hardly ever seen a program that placed more than 86 percent of their clients, tops, in their best years. And it goes downhill from there. A prominent executive counseling firm was reported by the Attorney General's Office of New York State to have placed only 38 out of 550 clients (a 93 percent failure rate). If they make it clear that they have had a good success rate, but if you fail to work hard at the whole process, then there is no guarantee you are going to find a job, give them three stars.

If they show you letters from ecstatically happy former clients, but when you ask to talk to some of those clients, you get stone-walled,

(Give them **45 bad points**)

I quote from one job-hunter's letter to me: "I asked to speak to a former client or clients. You would of thought I asked to speak to Elvis. The Counselor stammered and stuttered and gave me a million excuses why I couldn't talk to some of these 'satisfied' former clients. None of the excuses sounded legitimate to me. We went back and forth for about thirty minutes. Finally, he excused himself and went to speak to his boss, the owner. The next thing I knew I was called into the owner's office for a more 'personal' sales pitch. We spoke for about forty-five minutes as he tried to convince me to use his service. When I told him I was not ready to sign up, he became angry and asked my Counselor why I had been put before 'the committee' if I wasn't ready to commit? The Counselor claimed I had given a verbal commitment at our last meeting. The owner then turned to me and said I seemed to have a problem making a decision and that he did not want to do business with me. I was shocked. They had turned the whole story around to make it look like it was my fault. I felt humiliated. In retrospect, the whole process felt like dealing with a used car salesman. They used pressure tactics and intimidation to try to get what they wanted. As you have probably gathered, more than anything else this experience made me angry."

If it is a *firm*, and they claim they only accept 5 clients out of every 100 who apply, and your name will have to be put before "The Committee" before you can be accepted,

(Give them **1,000 bad points**)

This is one of the oldest tricks in the book. You're supposed to feel "special" before they lift those thousands of dollars out of your wallet. Personally, the minute I heard this at a particular agency or service, I would run for the door and never look back.

If you ask what is the cost of their services, and they reply that it is a lump sum that must all be paid "up front" before you start or shortly after you start, either all at once or in installments,

(Give them **100 bad points**)

I have many friends among career coaches and counselors who charge one lump sum up front, and I know them to be very competent, sincere, and helpful. The trouble is, I have run into many charlatans in this field, over the years, who have also charged one lump sum up front, and were revealed to be incompetent, insincere, and (basically) crooks. And the trouble is, you won't know which one you've run into, until they have all your money. I have tried for years to think of some way around this, and I've concluded there basically is none. So now I say, if it were me, anytime I run into a coach, counselor, or executive counseling firm that charges a lump sum up front, I would go elsewhere. It's just a risk I can't afford to take. If you on the other hand can afford to gamble that much money, and lose it, then go ahead and do what you decide to do. But, I've listened to too many people who got taken, and couldn't afford to lose all that money.

If it's a firm, and they asked you to bring in your partner or spouse with you,

(Give them **45 bad points**)

This is a well-known tactic of some of the slickest salespeople and firms on the face of the earth, who want your spouse or partner there so they can manipulate them if they can't manipulate you, to reach a decision on the spot, while they have you in their "grasp."

If it is a firm, particularly an executive counseling firm, and they ask you to sign a contract "up front,"

(Give them **1,000 bad points**)

With firms that have a bad track record, there is always a written contract. And you must sign it, before they will help you. (Often, your

Appendix A

partner or spouse will be asked to sign it, too.) The fee normally ranges from $1,000 on up to $10,000 or more. You are told you can get the fee back (or some of it at least) if you are dissatisfied. Yeah, just try!! They have more ways around ever giving you your money back than you can possibly imagine, no matter what their verbal promises (or even written ones) claim.

Sometimes, for example, the written contract will claim to provide for a partial refund, at any time, until you reach a cutoff date in the program, which the contract specifies. Unfortunately, many crafty fraudulent firms bend over backwards to be extra nice, extra available, and extra helpful to you until that cutoff point is reached. So, when the cutoff point for getting a refund has been reached, you let it pass because you are very satisfied with their past services, and believe there will be many more weeks of the same. Only, there aren't. At fraudulent firms, once the cutoff point is passed, the career counselor becomes virtually impossible for you to get ahold of. Call after call will not be returned. You will say to yourself "What happened?" Well, what happened, my friend, is that you paid up in full, they have all the money they're ever going to get out of you, and now they don't want to give you any more time.

Over the last years, I have had to listen to grown men and women cry over the telephone, all because they signed a contract. Most often they were executives, or senior managers, who never had to go job-hunting before, and unknowingly signed up with some executive counseling firm that was fraudulent, or at least on the edge of legality. They thought the high fee guaranteed excellence. It didn't.

You may think I am exaggerating: I mean, can there possibly be such mean men and women, who would prey on job-hunters, when they're down and out. Yes, ma'am, and yes, sir, there are. That's why you have to do this preliminary research so thoroughly.

I quote from the late Robert Wegmann, former director of the UHCL Center for Labor Market Studies: "One high-charging career counseling firm went bankrupt a few years ago. They left many of their materials behind in their former office. A box of what they abandoned has come into my possession. Going through the contents of the box has been fascinating.

"Particularly interesting are several scripts used to train their salespeople. The goal of the sales pitch is to convince the unemployed (or unhappily employed) person that he or she can't find a good job

alone, but can do it with professional help. Hiring us, they argue, is just like hiring a lawyer. . . .

"Then, at the end of the pitch, comes the 'takeaway.' The firm may not accept your money, you are warned! There will have to be a review board meeting at which your application is considered. Only a minority of applicants are accepted. The firm only wants the right kind of clients.

"That's the pitch. But the rest of the documents tell a very different story. In fact, the firm is running a series of sales contests with all the 'professionalism' of a used car lot. . . .

"These salespeople were paid on commission. The higher the sales the higher the percentage of the customer's fee they got to keep.

"There are sales contests. The winner receives a handsome green Master's jacket. Each monthly winner qualifies for a Grand Master's Tournament, with large prizes. . . .

"So take this one piece of advice. . . . If someone offers to help you find a great job as long as you'll pay several thousand dollars in advance, do as follows:

"A. Find door

"B. Walk out same

"C. Do not return."

Good Answers

Well, those are the bad answers that may help you determine whether this is the coach, counselor, or firm that you want. How about the good answers? Yes, there are such things: career coaches or counselors or firms who charge by the hour. With them, there is no written contract. You sign nothing. You pay only for each hour as you use it, according to their set rate. Each time you keep an appointment, you pay them at the end of that hour for their help, according to that rate. Period. Finis. You never owe them any money. You can stop seeing them at any time, if you feel you are not getting the help you wish.

What will they charge? You will find, these days, that the best career coaches or counselors *(plus some of the worst)* will charge you whatever a good therapist or marriage counselor charges per hour, in your geographical area. Currently, in large metropolitan areas, that runs up to $150 an hour, sometimes more. In suburbia or rural areas, it may be much less—$40 an hour, or so.

That fee is for *individual time* with the career coach or counselor. If you can't afford the fee, ask whether they also run groups. If they do, the fee will be much less. And, in one of those delightful ironies of life, since you get a chance to listen to problems which other job-hunters in your group are having, the group will often give you more help than an individual session with a counselor would. Not always; but often. It's always ironic when *cheaper* and *more helpful* go hand in hand.

If the career counselor in question does offer groups, there should (again) never be a contract. The charge should be payable at the end of each session, and you should be able to drop out at any time, without further cost, if you decide you are not getting the help you want.

There are some career counselors who run free (or almost free) job-hunting workshops through local churches, synagogues, chambers of commerce, community colleges, adult education programs, and the like, as their community service, or *pro bonum* work (as it is technically called). I have had reports of workshops from a number of places in the U.S. and Canada. They exist in other parts of the world as well. If money is a problem for you, in getting help with your job-hunt, ask around your community to see if workshops exist in your community. Your chamber of commerce will know, or your church or synagogue.

Two are better than one;
for if they fall,
the one will lift up his fellow;

but woe to him that is alone when he falleth,
and hath not another to lift him up.
                    Ecclesiastes

370

APPENDIX B

Career
Counselors Guide:
A Sampler

This is not a complete directory of anything. It is exactly what its name implies: a Sampler. Were I to list all the career counselors out there, we would end up with an encyclopedia. Some states, in fact, have encyclopedic lists of counselors and businesses, in various books or directories, and your local bookstore or library should have these, in their Job-Hunting Section, under such titles as "How to Get a Job in ..." or "Job-Hunting in ..."

The places listed in this Sampler are listed at their own request, and I offer them to you simply as places for you to begin your investigation with—nothing more.

Many truly helpful places are not listed here. If you discover such a place, which is very good at helping people with *Parachute* and creative job-hunting or career-change, do send us the pertinent information. We will ask them, as we do all the listings here, a few intelligent questions and if they sound okay, we will add that place to next year's edition.

We do ask a few questions because our readers want counselors and places which claim some expertise in helping them finish their job-hunt, using this book. So, if they've never even heard of *Parachute,* we don't list them. On the other hand, we can't measure a place's expertise at this long distance, no matter how many questions we ask.

371

Even if listed here, you must do your own sharp questioning before you decide to go with anyone. If you don't take time to research two or three places, before choosing a counselor, you will deserve whatever you get (or, more to the point, don't get). So, please, do your research. The purse or wallet you save, will be your own.

Yearly readers of this book will notice that we do remove people from this Sampler, without warning. Specifically, we remove (without further notice or comment): places we didn't mean to remove, but a typographical error was made, somehow (it happens). We also remove: places which have moved, and don't bother to send us their new address. If you are listed here, we expect you to be a professional at communication. When you move, your first priority should be to let us know, immediately. As one exemplary counselor wrote: "You are the first person I am contacting on my updated letterhead . . . hot off the press just today!" So it should always be. A number of places get removed every year, precisely because of their poor communication skills, and their sloppiness in letting us know where they've gone to. Other causes for removal:

- Places that have disconnected their telephone, or otherwise suggest that they have gone out of business.

- Places that our readers lodge complaints against, with us, as being either unhelpful or obnoxious. The complaints may be falsified, but we can't take that chance.

- Places that change their personnel, and the new person has never even heard of *Parachute,* or creative job-search techniques.

- Places that misuse their listing here, claiming in their brochures, ads, or interviews, that they have some kind of *"Parachute* Seal of Approval"—that we feature them in *Parachute,* or recommend them or endorse them. This is a big "no-no." A listing here is no more of a recommendation than is a listing in the phone book.

- College services that we discover (belatedly) serve only "Their Own."

- Counseling firms that employ salespeople as the initial "in-take" person that a job-hunter meets.

If you discover that any of the places listed in this Sampler falls into any of the above categories, you would be doing a great service to our other readers by dropping us a line and telling us so (P.O. Box 379, Walnut Creek, CA 94597).

The listings which follow are alphabetical within each state, except that counselors listed by their name are in alphabetical order according to their last name.

What do the letters after their name mean? Well, B.A., M.A., and Ph.D. you know. However, don't assume the degree is in career counseling. Ask. NCC means "Nationally Certified Counselor." There are about 20,000 such in the U.S. This can mean general counseling expertise, not necessarily career counseling. (Sharp-eyed readers of *Parachute* will notice that "NCCC"— "Nationally Certified Career Counselor"—is no longer printed in our list, because that credential is no longer offered.) Other initials, such as LPC—"Licensed Professional Counselor"—and the like, often refer to state licensing. There are a number of states, now, that have some sort of regulation of career counselors. In some states it is mandatory, in others it is optional. But, mostly, this field is unregulated.

Some offer group career counseling, some offer testing, some offer access to job-banks, etc.

One final note: generally speaking, these places counsel anybody. A few, however, may turn out to have restrictions unknown to us ("we counsel only women," etc.). If that's the case, your time isn't wasted. They may be able to help you with a referral. So, don't be afraid to ask them "who else in the area can you tell me about, who helps with job-searches, and are there any (among them) that you think are particularly effective?"

Area Codes

Throughout the U.S. now, area codes are subdividing constantly, sometimes more than once during a short time-span. If you're calling a local counselor, you probably don't need the area code anyway (unless you live in one of the metropolitan areas in the U.S. that require ten-digit dialing). But if you call a phone number in the Sampler that is any distance away from you, and they tell you "this number cannot be completed as dialed," the most likely explanation is that the area code got changed—maybe some time ago. (We ask counselors listed here to notify us when the area code changes, but some do and some don't.) Anyway, call Information and check.

Throughout this Sampler, an asterisk before their name, in red, means they offer not only regular job-search help, but also (when you wish) counseling from a spiritual point of view; i.e., they're not afraid to talk about God if you're looking for some help, in finding your mission in life.

Readers interested in a career counselor may also check the website of the National Career Development Association at www.ncda.org. Also, you may notice that the entries of some of the counselors listed in this appendix have the designation "MCC," which indicates that this person is accredited by the NCDA as a Master Career Counselor; requirements for this designation are also on the site.

U.S.A.

ALABAMA

*Career Decisions, 638 Winwood Dr., Birmingham, AL 35226
Phone: 205-822-8662 or 205-870-2639
Contact: Carrie Pearce Hild, M.S.Ed.,
Career Counselor and Consultant

*CareerMission, 7500 Memorial Parkway S.W., Suite 215-C, Huntsville, AL 35802
Phone: 256-883-8385 Fax: 256-883-9577
www.thetrinitygrouphsv.com

Chemsak, Maureen J., NCC, LPC, Director of Counseling and Career Services, Athens State University, 300 North Beaty St., Athens, AL 35611
Phone: 256-233-8285 or 256-830-4610
e-mail: mchemsak@athens.edu

Vantage Associates, 2100-A Southbridge Pkwy., Suite 480, Birmingham, AL 35209
Phone: 205-879-0501 or 205-631-5544
Contact: Michael A. Tate

Work Matters Career Coaching,
P.O. Box 130756, Birmingham, AL 35213
Phone: 205-879-8494
Contact: Gayle H. Lantz

ALASKA

Career Transitions, 2600 Denali St., Suite 430, Anchorage, AK 99503
Phone: 907-274-4510
Contact: Deeta Lonergan, Director
e-mail: deeta@alaska.net

*Carr & Associates Consulting,
P.O. Box 233356, Anchorage, AK 99523
Phone: 907-348-0277
Contact: Diane Carr
e-mail: dcarr@gci.net
www.carrandsociates.com

ARIZONA

Boninger, Faith Gletcher, Ph.D.,
10965 E. Mary Katherine Drive,
Scottsdale, AZ 85259
Phone: 480-551-7097
e-mail: faithboninger@cox.net

DavenportFolio,
2415 E. Camelback Rd., 7th floor
Phoenix, AZ 85016
Phone: 602-553-0808
Contact: Debra B. Davenport,
Ph.D., MPM, LCC
e-mail: info@davenportfolio.com
www.debradavenport.com
(They also have a Los Angeles office;
see the California listings.)

Renaissance Career Solutions,
P.O. Box 30118, Phoenix, AZ 85046
Phone: 602-867-4202
Contact: Betty Boza, M.A., LCC
e-mail: bboza@att.net
www.rcareer-solutions.com

West Valley Career Services,
10720 W. Indian School, #19-141,
Phoenix, AZ 85037
Phone: 623-872-7303
Contact: Shell Mendelson Herman,
M.S., CRC

ARKANSAS

McKinney, Donald, Ed.D., Career Counselor,
Rt. 1, Box 351-A, DeQueen, AR 71832
Phone: 870-642-5628
e-mail: eaglnest@ipa.net

CALIFORNIA

Bauer, Lauralyn Larsen,
Career Counselor & Coach,
2180 Jefferson St., Suite 201, Napa, CA 94558
Phone: 707-363-7775
e-mail: lauralynbauer@hotmail.com

Bay Area Career Center,
Mechanics Institute Library Bldg.,
57 Post Street, Suite 804,
San Francisco, CA 94104
Phone: 415-398-4881 Fax: 415-398-4897
e-mail: info@bayareacareercenter.com
www.bayareacareercenter.com

BC Career Strategy Associates,
508 E. Chapman Ave., Fullerton, CA 92832
Phone: 714-871-2380
Contact: Brent Wood, Cassandra Clark
e-mail: bccareer@pacbell.net

Berrett & Associates, 1551 E. Shaw,
Suite 103, Fresno, CA 93710
Phone: 559-221-6543 Fax: 559-221-6540
Contact: Dwayne Berrett, M.A., RPCC
e-mail: dberrett3@fresno.com

Brown, Beverly, M.A., NCC,
809 So. Bundy Dr., #105,
Los Angeles, CA 90049
Phone: 310-447-7093
e-mail: bbcareers@aol.com

California Career Services,
6024 Wilshire Blvd., Los Angeles, CA 90036
Phone: 323-933-2900 Fax: 323-933-9929
Contact: Susan W. Miller, M.A.
e-mail: swmcareer@aol.com
www.californiacareerservices.com

Career Balance, 215 Witham Road,
Encinitas, CA 92024
Phone: 760-436-3994
Contact: Virginia Byrd, M.Ed.,
Work/Life Specialist
e-mail: Virginia@careerbalance.net
www.careerbalance.net

*Career Choices, Dublin, CA
Phone: 925-833-9994
Contact: Dana E. Ogden, M.S.Ed., CCDV,
Career & Educational Counselor,
Workshop Facilitator
e-mail: dana@careerchoices.us
www.careerchoices.us

**Career Counseling and Assessment
Associates,** 9229 West Sunset Blvd.,
Suite 502, Los Angeles, CA 90069
Phone: 310-274-3423
Contact: Dianne Y. Sundby, Ph.D.,
Director and Psychologist

A Career and Counseling Practice,
1018 E St., San Rafael, CA 94901-1860
Phone: 415-789-9113
Contact: Suzanne Lindenbaum, MSW,
LCSW, MCC
e-mail: lindenccs@aol.com
www.camft.org/therapists/
suzannelindenbaum

Career Designs, 6855 Irving Road,
Redding, CA 96001
Phone: 530-241-8570
Contact: Carla Barrett, Parachute Associate
e-mail: carla@careerdesigns.com
www.careerdesigns.com

**Career Development Center at John F.
Kennedy University,** Room 313, 100
Ellinwood Way, Pleasant Hill, CA 94523
Phone: 925-969-3542 Fax: 925-969-3541
e-mail: career@jfku.edu
www.jfku.edu/career

Career Development Life Planning,
3585 Maple St., Suite 237, Ventura, CA 93003
Phone: 805-656-6220
Contact: Norma Zuber, M.S.C., & Associates

Career Dimensions, P.O. Box 7402,
Stockton, CA 95267
Phone: 209-957-6465
Contact: Fran Abbott

Career Options, 1855 San Miguel Drive #11,
Walnut Creek, CA 94596
Phone: 925-945-0376
Contact: Joan Schippman, M.A.
e-mail: joangoforth@cs.com

**Career and Personal Development
Institute,** 690 Market St., Suite 402,
San Francisco, CA 94104
Phone: 415-982-2636
Contact: Bob Chope

**Career Planning Center/Business Action
Center,** 1623 S. La Cienega Blvd.,
Los Angeles, CA 90035
Phone: 310-273-6633

**Center for Career Growth and
Development,** P.O. Box 283,
Los Gatos, CA 95031
Phone: 408-354-7150
Contact: Steven E. Beasley
e-mail: careergrowth1@juno.com

Center for Creative Change,
3130 West Fox Run Way,
San Diego, CA 92111
Phone: 619-268-9340
Contact: Nancy Helgeson, M.A., MFCC

*Center for Life & Work Planning,
1133 Second St., Encinitas, CA 92024
Phone: 760-943-0747 Fax: 760-436-7158
Contact: Mary C. McIsaac, Executive Director

*The Center for Ministry
(an Interdenominational Church Career
Development Center), 8393 Capwell Dr.,
Suite 220, Oakland, CA 94621-2123
Phone: 510-635-4246
Contact: Robert L. Charpentier, Director

*Cheney-Rice, Stephen, M.S.
2113 Westboro Ave., Alhambra, CA 91803
Phone: 626-824-5244
Email: sccheneyrice@earthlink.net

Christen, Carol, Career Coach & Job Search
Consultant, Atascadero, CA
Phone: 805-462-8795
e-mail: parachutefirstaid@hotmail.com
(Career coaching by phone available.)

*Christian Career Center,
448 S. Marengo Ave., Pasadena, CA 91101
Phone: 626-577-2705
Contact: Kevin Brennfleck, M.A., and
Kay Marie Brennfleck, M.A., Directors
e-mail: cocareer@aol.com

The Clarity Group Inc., 244 Kearney St.,
6th Floor, San Francisco, CA 94108
Phone: 415-693-9719, ext.101
Contact: George Schofield, Ph.D.
e-mail: george.schofield@clarity-group.com
www.clarity-group.com

Cypress College, Career Planning Center,
9200 Valley View St., Cypress, CA 90630
Phone: 714-484-7000

DavenportFolio, 1800 Century Park East,
6th Floor, Los Angeles, CA 90067
Phone: 301-552-0710
Contact: Debra B. Davenport,
Ph.D., MPM, LCC
e-mail: info@davenportfolio.com
www.debradavenport.com

Dream Job Coaching, 833 Kingston Ave. #8,
Oakland, CA 94611
Phone: 510-655-2010
Contact: Joel Garfinkle
e-mail: joel@dreamjobcoaching.com

Experience Unlimited Job Club. There are
35 Experience Unlimited Clubs in Califor-
nia, found at the Employment Development
Department in the following locations:
Anaheim, Corona, El Cajon, Escondido,
Fremont, Fresno, Hemet, Hollywood,
Lancaster, Monterey, North Hollywood,
Oakland, Ontario, Pasadena, Pleasant Hill,
Redlands, Ridgecrest, Riverside, Sacramento
(Midtown and South), San Bernardino, San
Diego (also East and South), San Francisco,
San Mateo, San Rafael, Santa Ana, Santa
Cruz, Santa Maria, Simi Valley, Sunnyvale,
Torrance, Victorville, and West Covina.
Contact the club nearest you through your
local Employment Development Depart-
ment (E.D.D.) office.

Floyd, Mary Alice, M.A., Career Counselor/
Consultant, 3233 Lucinda Lane,
Santa Barbara, CA 93105
Phone: 805-687-5462 Fax: 805-898-1066
e-mail: glfloyd@sbceo.org

*Frangquist, Deborah Gavrin, M.S.,
Life Purpose & Career Consultant,
1801 Bush St., Suite 121,
San Francisco, CA 94109
Phone: 415-346-6121 Fax: 415-346-6118
e-mail: workpath@ix.netcom.com

Fritsen, Jan, Career Counseling
and Coaching,
23181 La Cadena Drive, Suite 103,
Laguna Hills, CA 92653
Phone: 949-497-4869
e-mail: janfritsen@cox.net
www.janfritsen.com

Geary & Associates, Inc.,
1100 Coddingtown Ctr., Ste. A,
P.O. Box 3774, Santa Rosa, CA 95402
Phone: 707-525-8085 Fax: 707-528-8088
Contact: Jack Geary, M.A., C.R.C.;
Edelweiss Geary, M.Ed.
e-mail: geary@gearyassociates.com
*(Career transition programs, outplacement
and spouse re-employment assistance.)*

G/S Consultants, P.O. Box 7855,
South Lake Tahoe, CA 96158
Phone: 530-541-8587 Fax: 530-541-3773
Contact: Judith Grutter, M.S.
e-mail: gstahoe@sierra.net

Hilliard, Larkin, M.A.,
Counseling Psychology,
1411 Holiday Hill Rd.,
Santa Barbara, CA 93117
Phone: 805-683-5855
e-mail: larkinhill@earthlink.net
*(Languages: English, French,
German, Russian.)*

H.R. Solutions, Human Resources
Consulting, 390 South Sepulveda Blvd.,
Suite 104, Los Angeles, CA 90049
Phone: 310-471-2536
Contact: Nancy Mann, M.B.A,
President/Career Consultant

Jewish Vocational Service,
5700 Wilshire Blvd., 2nd Floor, Suite 2303,
Los Angeles, CA 90036
Phone: 323-761-8888

The Job Forum, 235 Montgomery St.,
12th Floor, San Francisco, CA 94104
Phone: 415-392-4520

Judy Kaplan Baron Associates,
6046 Cornerstone Ct. West, Suite 208,
San Diego, CA 92121
Phone: 858-558-7400
Contact: Judy Kaplan Baron, Director

Kerwin & Associates, 3666 Arnold Ave.,
San Diego, CA 92104
Phone: 619-295-8547
Contact: Patrick Kerwin, M.B.A.
www.kerwinandassociates.com

Life's Work Center, 109 Bartlett St.,
San Francisco, CA 94110
Contact: Tom Finnegan, executive director
415-821-0930
e-mail: tom@lifesworkcenter.org

L M & A Career Coaching,
7826 W. 79th St., Playa del Rey, CA 90293
Phone: 310-301-2508
Contact: Liz Mohler, M.S.
e-mail: careeradviceliz@LizMohler.com
www.LizMohler.com

*Miller, Lizbeth, M.S., 3880 S. Bascom Ave., Suite 202, San Jose, CA 95124
Phone: 408-559-1115
(Affiliated with the Christian Counseling Center.)

Nemko, Marty, Ph.D., Career and Education Strategist, 5936 Chabolyn Terrace, Oakland, CA 94618
Phone: 510-655-2777
e-mail: mnemko@earthlink.net
www.martynemko.com

Networking Grace Career Counseling, Napa, CA 94558
Phone: 707-226-3438
Contact: Lauralyn Bauer, M.S.

Peller, Marion, 388 Market St., Suite 500, San Francisco, CA 94111
Phone: 415-296-2559

Saraf, Dilip G., Careers and Worklife Strategist
6067 Jarvis Ave. #101
Newark, CA 94560
510-477-0154
e-mail: dilip@7keys.org
www.7keys.org

*Schoenbeck, Mary Lynne, M.A., Career Counselor/Consultant/Coach, Third Age Coalition, Los Altos, CA
Phone: 650-964-8370
e-mail: schoenbeck@mindspring.com

Turning Point Career Center, University YMCA, 2600 Bancroft Way, Berkeley, CA 94704
Phone: 510-848-6370
Contact: Winnie Froehlich, M.S., Director

Wilson, Patti, P.O. Box 35633, Los Gatos, CA 95030
Phone: 408-354-1964

Zitron Career Services, 17 Skylark Drive, Suite 1, Larkspur, CA 94939
Phone: 415-924-4057
Contact: Susan Zitron-Woods, Career & Executive Coach
www.zitroncareerservices.com

COLORADO

Accelerated Job Search, 4490 Squires Circle, Boulder, CO 80303
Phone: 303-494-2467
Contact: Leigh Olsen, Counselor

Arapahoe Community College Resource Center, 2500 West College Dr., P.O. Box 9002, Littleton, CO 80160-9002
Phone: 303-797-5805

Arp, Rosemary, M.S., GCDF, Career Counselor
Boulder, CO
Phone: 303-527-1874
e-mail: rsarp@comcast.net

CRS Consulting, 425 W. Mulberry, Suite 205, Fort Collins, CO 80521
Phone: 970-484-9810
Contact: Marilyn Pultz

Gary Ringler & Associates, 1747 Washington St., #203, Denver, CO 80203
Phone: 303-863-0234 Fax: 303-863-0101
e-mail: garytringler@aol.com

Helmstaedter, Sherry, 5040 South El Camino, Englewood, CO 80111-1122
Phone: 303-794-5122

Life Work Planning, P.O. Box 81, Louisville, CO 80027
Phone: 720-890-7913
Contact: Lauren T. Griffin, Career Development Counselor

The McGee Group, 2485 W. Main, Suite 202, Old Littleton, CO 80120
Phone: 303-794-4749
Contact: Betsy C. McGee

O'Keefe, Patricia, M.A., 1550 S. Monroe St., Denver, CO 80210
Phone: 303-759-9325

*Peterson, April, M.A., NCC, LPC, Career Counselor, P.O. Box 17896, Boulder, CO 80308
Phone: 303-442-1023
e-mail: april.peterson@att.net

Strategic Career Moves, 2329 N. Glenisle Ave., Durango, CO 81301
Phone: 970-385-9597
Contact: Mary Jane Ward, M.Ed., NCC

Women's Resource Agency, 31 N. Farragut, Colorado Springs, CO 80909
Phone: 719-471-3170

YWCA of Boulder County Career Center, 2222 14th St., Boulder, CO 80302
Phone: 303-443-0419

CONNECTICUT

Accord Career Services, The Exchange, Suite 305, 270 Farmington Ave., Farmington, CT 06032
Phone: 800-922-1480 or 860-674-9654
Contact: Tod Gerardo, M.S., Director

Career Choices/RFP Associates, 141 Durham Rd., Suite 24, Madison, CT 06443
Phone: 203-245-4123

The Career Counseling Center 50 Elizabeth St., Hartford, CT 06105
Phone: 860-768-5619
Contact: Eleta Jones, Ph.D., LPC
www.CareerCounselingCenter.org

Career Directions, LLC, 115 Elm St., Suite 203, Enfield, CT 06082
Phone: 860-623-9476 Fax: 860-623-9473
Contact: Louise Garver
e-mail: careerpro@cox.net
www.ResumeImpact.com

Cohen, James S., Ph.D., Career & Voc. Rehab. Services, 8 Barbara's Way, Ellington, CT 06029
Phone: 860-871-7832

Crossroads, 30 Tower Lane, Avon, CT 06001
Phone: 860-677-2558
Contact: Carolyn A. Stigler, Psy.D.
e-mail: cstigler@earthlink.net

Fairfield Academic and Career Center,
Fairfield University, Dolan House,
Fairfield, CT 06430
Phone: 203-254-4220

The Offerjost-Westcott Group,
263 Main St., Old Saybrook, CT 06475
Phone: 860-388-6094
Contact: Russ Westcott

Pannone, Bob, M.A., Career Specialist,
768 Saw Mill Road, West Haven, CT 06516
Phone: 203-933-6383

Preis, Roger J., RPE Career Dynamics,
P.O. Box 16722, Stamford, CT 06905
Phone: 203-322-7225

**Vocational and Academic Counseling for
Adults (VOCA),** 115 Berrian Rd.,
Stamford, CT 06905
Phone: 203-322-8353
Contact: Ruth A. Polster

Your Passion Career Counseling Services,
761 Valley Road, Fairfield, CT 06432
Phone: 203-374-7649
Contact: Bob N. Olsen, M.A., NCC, LPC
www.yourpassion.com

DELAWARE

The Brandywine Center, LLC,
2500 Grubb Road, Suite 240,
Wilmington, DE 19810
Phone: 302-475-1880, ext. 7
Contact: Kris Bronson, Ph.D.
e-mail: info@brandywinecenter.com

YWCA of New Castle County,
Women's Center for Economic Options,
233 King St., Wilmington, DE 19801
Phone: 302-658-7161

FLORIDA

Center for Career Decisions
3912 S. Ocean Blvd. #1009,
Boca Raton, FL 33487
Phone: 561-276-0321
Contact: Linda Friedman, M.A., NCC

The Centre for Women,
305 S. Hyde Park Ave.,
Tampa, FL 33606
Phone: 813-251-8437
Contact: Dae C. Sheridan, M.A., CRC,
Employment Counselor

Chabon-Berger, Toby, M.Ed., NCC,
4900 Boxwood Circle,
Boynton Beach, FL 33436
Phone: 561-734-0775
e-mail: tbcareer@bellsouth.net
www.tobycareer.com

**The Challenge Program for Displaced
Homemakers,** Florida Community College
at Jacksonville, 101 W. State St.,
Jacksonville, FL 32202
Phone: 904-633-8316
Contact: Harriet Courtney,
Project Coordinator
e-mail: hcourtney@fccj.org

Crossroads, Palm Beach Community
College, 4200 Congress Ave.,
Lake Worth, FL 33461-4796
Phone: 407-433-5995
Contact: Pat Jablonski, Program Manager

**Focus on the Future: Displaced
Homemaker Program,**
Santa Fe Community College,
3000 N.W. 83rd St., Gainesville, FL 32606
Phone: 904-395-5047
Contact: Nancy Griffin, Program
Coordinator *(Classes are free.)*

Harmon, Larry, Ph.D., Career Counseling
Center, Inc., 2000 South Dixie Highway,
Suite 103, Miami, FL 33133
Phone: 305-858-8557

Jonassen, Ellen O., Ph.D.,
10785 Ulmerton Rd., Largo, FL 34648
Phone: 813-581-8526

Life Designs, Inc.,
19526 East Lake Drive, Miami, FL 33015
Phone: 305-829-9008 (Sept.–May)
Contact: Dulce Muccio Weisenborn
e-mail: dmw@qsrhelp.com

New Beginnings, Polk Community College,
Station 71, 999 Avenue H, NE, Winter
Haven, FL 33881-4299 (Lakeland Campus)
Phone: 813-297-1029

WINGS Program, Broward Community
College, 1000 Coconut Creek Blvd.,
Coconut Creek, FL 33066
Phone: 305-973-2398

The Women's Center, Valencia Community
College, 1010 N. Orlando Ave.,
Winter Park, FL 32789
Phone: 407-628-1976

GEORGIA

*****AboutYOU, Inc.,** 2526 Mt. Vernon Rd.,
Suite B #323, Dunwoody, GA 30338
Phone: 770-399-6083
Contact: Jennifer B. Kahnweiler, Ph.D.

Albea, Emmette H., Jr., M.S., LPC,
2706 Melrose Dr., Valdosta, GA 31602
Phone: 912-241-0908

Ashkin, Janis, M.Ed., NCC, 2365 Winthrope
Way Drive, Alphanetta, GA 30004
Phone: 678-319-0297
e-mail: jashkin@mindspring.com

*****Career Development Center of the
Southeast** (an Interdenominational
Church Career Development Center),
531 Kirk Rd., Decatur, GA 30030
Phone: 404-371-0336
Contact: Earl B. Stewart, D.Min., Director

Appendix B

Career Quest/Job Search Workshop,
St. Ann, 4905 Roswell Rd., N.E.,
Marietta, GA 30062-6240
Phone: 770-552-6402
Contact: Tom Chernetsky
(Focus on Internet job-hunting.)

*Center for Growth & Change, Inc.,
6991 Peachtree Ind. Blvd., Suite 310,
Norcross, GA 30092
Phone: 404-441-9580
Contact: James P. Hicks,
Ph.D., LPC, Director

*Crown Career Resources,
601 Broad St. SE, Gainesville, GA 30501
Phone: 800-722-1976
Contact: Dave Frakes, Director

D & B Consulting, 3355 Lenox Road,
Suite 750, Atlanta, GA 30326
Phone: 404-504-7079
Contact: Deborah R. Brown,
M.B.A., M.S.W.,
Career Consultant
e-mail: Debbie@DandBconsulting.com
www. dandbconsulting.com

DeLorenzo, David R., Ph.D., LPC, NCC,
431 Asbury Commons Dr., Suite E,
Dunwoody, GA 30338
Phone: 770-457-6535
e-mail: dr.d@occuas.com

Jewish Vocational Service, Inc.,
4549 Chamblee Dunwoody Road,
Dunwoody, GA 30338-6120
Phone: 770-677-9440

*St. Jude's Job Network,
St. Jude's Catholic Church,
7171 Glenridge Dr.,
Sandy Springs, GA 30328
Phone: 404-393-4578

Satterfield, Mark, 720 Rio Grand Dr.,
Alpharetta, GA 30202
Phone: 770-640-8393

William H. Waldorf, MBA, LPC, MCC
Path Unfolding Career Development
314 Maxwell Rd., Suite 400,
Alpharetta, GA 30004
Phone: 770-442-9447 ext. 14

*Hubbard Counseling Services,
94-467 Kealakaa St., Mililani, HI 96789
Phone: 808-625-2200
Contact: Dick Hubbard, MSCP, AACC
e-mail: hubbard@pixi.com

**OCM Organizational Consultants
to Management,**
720 Park Blvd., Suite 265,
Boise, ID 83712-7714
Phone: 208-338-6584
e-mail: ocm-id@rmci.net

Transitions, 1970 Parkside Dr.,
Boise, ID 83712
Phone: 208-368-0499
Contact: Elaine Simmons, M.E.

Alumni Career Center, University of Illinois
Alumni Association, 200 South Wacker Dr.,
Chicago, IL 60606
Phone: 312-996-6350
Contact: Barbara S. Hundley, Director;
Claudia M. Delestowicz, Associate Director;
Julie L. Hays, Staff

Beddoe, Marti, Career/Life Counselor
Phone: 312-281-7274

Career Path, 1240 Iroquois Ave., Suite 100,
Naperville, IL 60563
Phone: 630-369-3390
Contact: Donna Sandberg, M.S., NCC, LCPC
Owner/Counselor

Career Vision / The Ball Foundation,
800 Roosevelt Rd., E-200,
Glen Ellyn, IL 60137
Phone: 800-469-8378
Contact: Peg Hendershot, Director; Paula
Kosin, M.S., LCPC, Marketing Manager
e-mail: cv@ballfoundation.org
www.careervision.org
*(Aptitude-based career planning,
clients across U.S. & Canada.)*

Davis, Jean, Adult Career Transitions,
1405 Elmwood Ave., Evanston, IL 60201
Phone: 847-492-1002

**Dolan Career & Rehabilitation
Consulting, Ltd.,** 307 Henry Street,
Suite 407, Alton, IL 62002
Phone: 618-474-5328 Fax: 618-462-3359
Contact: J. Stephen Dolan, M.A., C.R.C.,
Career & Rehabilitation Consultant
e-mail: dolanrehab@piasanet.com

Grimard Consulting, Inc.,
Contact: Diane Wilson,
333 W. Wacker Drive, Suite 500,
Chicago, IL 60606
Phone: 312-201-1142

Harper College Career Transition Center,
Building A, Room 124, Palatine, IL 60067
Phone: 708-459-8233
Contact: Mary Ann Jirak, Coordinator

*Heartsong Consulting,
1077 Ash St., Winnetka, IL 60093
Phone: 847-441-0375
Contact: Regina Lopata Logan, Ph.D.
e-mail: gina@heartsongconsulting.com

*Lansky Career Consultants,
500 N. Michigan Ave. #1940,
Chicago, IL 60611
Phone: 312-494-0022
Contact: Judith Lansky, M.A., M.B.A.,
President; Julie Benesh, Adjunct Consultant

LeBrun, Peter, Career/Life Counselor
Phone: 312-281-7274

LifeScopes, 427 Greenwood St., Suite 3W,
Evanston, IL 60201
Phone: 847-733-1805
Contact: Barbara H. Hill, Career
Management Consultant
e-mail: LifeScopes@aol.com

*Midwest Career Development Service (an Interdenominational Church Career Development Center), 1840 Westchester Blvd., Westchester, IL 60154
Phone: 708-343-6268

Moraine Valley Community College, Job Placement Center, 10900 S. 88th Ave., Palos Hills, IL 60465
Phone: 708-974-5737

Quest Clinical Services, 1776 S. Naperville Rd., Bldg. B, Suite 205, Wheaton, IL 60187
Phone: 630-260-1933, ext. 2
Contact: Donna C. Bredrup, M.S., LPC, Career Counselor

Right Livelyhood$, 23 W. 402 Green Briar Dr., Naperville, IL 60540
Phone: 708-369-9066

The Summit Group, P.O. Box 3794, Peoria, IL 61612-3794
Phone: 309-681-1118
Contact: John R. Throop, D.Min., President

Widmer & Associates, 1510 W. Sunnyview Dr., Peoria, IL 61614
Phone: 309-691-3312
Contact: Mary F. Widmer, President

INDIANA

Jones, Sally, Program Coordinator/ Developer, Indiana University, School of Continuing Studies, Owen Hall, Room 202, Bloomington, IN 47405
Phone: 812-855-4991

KCDM Associates, 10401 N. Meridian St., Suite 300, Indianapolis, IN 46290
Phone: 317-581-6230
Contact: David A. Mueller, President

Performance Development Systems, Inc., 312 Iroquois Trail, Suite 2S, Burns Harbor, IN 46304-9702
Phone: 219-787-9216
Contact: William P. Henning, Counselor
e-mail: pdsi@netnitco.net, www.pdsiinc.com

IOWA

Beers Consulting, 5505 Boulder Dr., West Des Moines, IA 50266
Phone: 515-225-1245
Contact: Rosanne Beers

Sucher, Billie Ruth, M.S., 7177 Hickman Rd., Suite 10, Des Moines, IA 50322
Phone: 515-276-0061
e-mail: betwnjobs@aol.com

University of Iowa, Career Center, 24 Phillips Hall, Iowa City, IA 52242
Phone: 319-335-1023

Wendroff, Gloria, Secrets to Successful Job Search, 703 E. Burlington Ave., Fairfield, IA 52556
Phone: 515-472-4529

Zilber, Suzanne, 801 Crystal St., Ames, IA 50010
Phone: 515-232-9379

KANSAS

Keeping the People, Inc.
13488 W. 126th Terrace
Overland Park, KS 66213
Contact: Leigh Branham
Phone: 913-620-4645
e-mail: LB@keepingthepeople.com
www.keepingthepeople.com

*Midwest Career Development Service (an Interdenominational Church Career Development Center), 754 N. 31st St., Kansas City, KS 66110-0816
Contact: Ronald Brushwyler, Director

KENTUCKY

Career Span, 501 Darby Creek Rd., Suite 3-C, Lexington, KY 40509
Phone: 859-543-0343
Contact: Carla Ockerman-Hunter, M.A., NCC
e-mail: careerspan@aol.com
www.careerspanUSA.com

LOUISIANA

Aptitude Assessment of Louisiana, Inc.
7912 Wrenwood Boulevard, Suite C, Baton Rouge, LA 70809
Phone: 504-927-8678 Fax: 504-927-6153
Contact: Ursula B. Carmena

Career Planning and Assessment Center, Metropolitan College, University of New Orleans, New Orleans, LA 70148
Phone: 504-286-7100

MAINE

Career Perspectives, 75 Pearl St., Suite 204, Portland, ME 04101
Phone: 207-775-4487
Contact: Deborah L. Gallant

*Heart at Work, 261 Main St., Yarmouth, ME 04096
Phone: 207-846-0644
Contact: Barbara Sirois Babkirk, M.Ed., NCC, LCPC, Licensed Counselor, Presenter, and Consultant
www.barbarababkirk.com

Suit Yourself International Inc., 120 Pendleton Point, Islesboro, ME 04848
Phone: 207-734-8206
Contact: Debra Spencer, President

Women's Worth Career Counseling, 9 Village Lane, Westbrook, ME 04092
Phone: 207-856-6666
Contact: Jacqueline Murphy, Career Counselor

MARYLAND

Career Evaluation & Counseling Program, Maryland Center for Health Psychology, 21 West Rd., Suite 150, Baltimore, MD 21204
Phone: 410-825-0042 Fax: 410-825-0310
Contact: Ralph D. Raphael, Ph.D.
e-mail: ralph-raphael@erols.com

Career Perspectives, 510 Sixth St., Annapolis, MD 21403
Phone: 410-280-2299
Contact: Jeanne H. Slawson, Career Consultant

College of Notre Dame of Maryland,
Continuing Education Center,
4701 N. Charles St., Baltimore, MD 21210
Phone: 410-532-5303

CTS Consulting, Inc.,
3126 Berkshire Rd.,
Baltimore, MD 21214-3404
Phone: 410-444-5857
www.go2ctsonline.com
Contact: Michael Bryant

Friedman, Lynn, Ph.D.,
Clinical Psychologist
& Work-Life Consultant,
4401 East-West Highway, Ste. 306,
Bethesda, MD 20814
Phone: 301-656-9650
e-mail: mail@drlynnfriedman.com

Goucher College,
Goucher Center for Continuing Studies,
1021 Dulaney Valley Rd.,
Baltimore, MD 21204
Phone: 410-337-6200
Contact: Carole B. Ellin,
Career/Job-Search Counselor

*Headley, Anne S., M.A., 6510 41st Ave.,
University Park, MD 20782
Phone: 301-779-1917
e-mail: asheadley@aol.com
www.anneheadley.com

Kensington Consulting,
1001 N. Noyes Drive.,
Suite B, Silver Spring, MD 20910
Phone: 301-587-1234
Contact: David M. Reile, Ph.D., or
Barbara H. Suddarth, Ph.D.

Mendelson, Irene N., BEMW, Inc.,
Counseling and Training for the Workplace,
7984 D Old Georgetown Rd., Bethesda, MD
20814-2440
Phone: 301-657-8922

Positive Passages Life/Career Transition
Counseling and Coaching,
4702 Falstone Ave., Chevy Chase, MD 20815
Phone: 301-907-0760
Contact: Jeanette Kreiser, Ed.D.
e-mail: jkreiser@earthlink.net

Prince George's Community College,
Career Assessment and Planning Center,
301 Largo Rd., Largo, MD 20772
Phone: 301-322-0886
Contact: Margaret Taibi, Ph.D., Director

TransitionWorks, 10964 Bloomingdale Dr.,
Rockville, MD 20852-5550
Phone: 301-770-4277
Contact: Stephanie Kay, M.A., A.G.S.,
Principal; Nancy K. Schlossberg, Ed.D.,
Principal

MASSACHUSETTS
Alumni and Community Career Services,
P.O. Box 35310, Amherst, MA 01003
Phone: 413-545-0742
Contact: Karen D. Knight,
Associate Director
e-mail: kdk@acad.umass.edu

Berke & Price Associates,
Newtown Way #6, Chelmsford, MA 01824
Phone: 978-256-0482 1-800-965-0482
Contact: Judit E. Price, M.S.
email: jprice@careercampaign.com
www.careercampaign.com

Career Development Center,
Northern Essex Community Collage,
Elliott Street, Haverhill, MA 01830
Phone: 978-556-3722
Contact: M. J. Pernaa,
Director of Career Counseling

Career Link, Career Information Center,
Kingston Public Library, 6 Green St.,
Kingston, MA 02364
Phone: 781-585-0517
Contact: Sia Stewart, Library Director

*Career Management Consultants,
108 Grove St., Suite 19A,
Worcester, MA 01605
Phone: 508-756-9998
Contact: Patricia Stepanski Plouffe,
Founder/Consultant
e-mail: info@careermc.com

Career Resource Center, Worcester YWCA,
1 Salem Square, Worcester, MA 01608
Phone: 508-791-3181

Career Source, 185 Alewife Brook Pkwy.,
Cambridge, MA 02138
Phone: 617-661-7867
(Inherited the Radcliffe Career Services Office's
library, after that office closed permanently.
Also offers career counseling.)

*Center for Career Development
& Ministry,
30 Milton St., Suite 107, Dedham, MA 02026
Phone: 781-329-2100 Fax: 781-407-0955
Contact: Stephen Ott, Director
e-mail: ccdmin@aol.com

Center for Careers, Jewish Vocational
Service, 105 Chauncy St., 6th Floor,
Boston, MA 02111
Phone: 617-451-8147
Contact: Lee Ann Bennett,
Coordinator, Core Services

Changes, Career Counseling and
Job-Hunt Training,
2516 Massachusetts Ave.,
Cambridge, MA 02140
Phone: 617-868-7775
Contact: Carl J. Schneider

Jewish Vocational Service,
Mature Worker Programs,
333 Nahanton St., Newton, MA 02159
Phone: 617-965-7940

*Liebhaber, Gail, 40 Cottage St.,
Lexington, MA 02420
Phone: 781-861-9949 Fax: 781-863-5956
e-mail: gliebhaber@rcn.com
www.yourcareerdirection.com
Contact: Gail Liebhaber, M.Ed.

Miller, Wynne W., Coaching & Career
Development, 15 Cypress St., Suite 200,
Newton Center, MA 02459-2242
Phone: 617-527-4848 Fax: 617-527-2248
e-mail: wynne@win-coaching.com

Murray Associates, P.O. Box 312,
Westwood, MA 02090
Phone: 617-329-1287
Contact: Robert Murray, Ed.D.,
Licensed Psychologist

Neil Wilson Career Services,
P.O. Box 793, Newburyport, MA 01950
Phone: 978-465-1468
e-mail: info@neilwilson.com

Smith College Career Development Office,
Drew Hall, 84 Elm St.,
Northampton, MA 01063
Phone: 413-585-2570
Contact: Jane Sommer, Associate Director

Stein, Phyllis R., 59 Parker St.,
Cambridge, MA 02138
Phone: 617-354-7948
(Former director of Radcliffe Career Services.)

Wellness Center, 51 Mill St., Unit 8,
Hanover, MA 02339
Phone: 781-829-4300
Contact: Janet Barr

The Work Place, 99 Chauncey St., 2nd Floor,
Boston, MA 02111
Phone: 617-737-0093, ext. 104
Contact: Liza-Marie DiCosimo,
Coordinator of Career Services
www.theworkplace.tripod.com
*(Free workshops, free library access, free use of
twenty computer workstations, etc.; low-cost
counseling, assessment, and resume services.)*

MICHIGAN

*****C3 Circle,** Grand Rapids, MI 49544
Phone: 616-677-1952
Contact: Lois Dye, M.A., LPC

*****Career Choices Center,**
St. Paul's Episcopal Church
309 S. Jackson St.,
Jackson, MI 49201
517-787-3370

*****Career Consulting Services,**
P.O. Box 135, Union Lake, MI 48387
248-363-6233
Contact: Marybeth Robb, MA Counselor
e-mail: greatresumes@sbcglobal.net

Jewish Vocational Service,
29699 Southfield Road,
Southfield, MI 48076-2063
Phone: 248-559-5000

*****Keystone Coaching & Consulting LLC,**
22 Cherry St., Holland, MI 49423
Phone: 616-396-1517
Contact: Mark de Roo
e-mail: keystonecoaching@comcast.net
www.keystonecoach.com

Lansing Community College,
2020 Career and Employment Development
Services, P.O. Box 40010, Lansing,
MI 48901-7210
Phone: 517-483-1221 or 517-483-1172
Contact: James C. Osborn, Ph.D., LPC,
Director, Career and Employment Services

*****Life Stewardship Associates,**
6918 Glen Creek Dr. SE, Dutton, MI 49316
Phone: 616-698-3125
Contact: Ken Soper, M.Div., M.A., Director

**New Options: Counseling for Women in
Transition,** 2311 E. Stadium, Suite B-2,
Ann Arbor, MI 48104
Phone: 313-973-0003
Contact: Phyllis Perry, M.S.W.

Oakland University, Continuum Center
for Adult Counseling and Leadership
Training, Rochester, MI 48309
Phone: 313-370-3033

University of Michigan, Center for the
Education of Women, 330 East Liberty,
Ann Arbor, MI 48104
Phone: 313-998-7080

MINNESOTA

Andrea, Richard E., Ph.D.,
1014 Bartelmy Lane,
Maplewood, MN 55119-3637
Phone: 612-730-9892

Human Dynamics, 3036 Ontario Rd.,
Little Canada, MN 55117
Phone: 612-484-8299
Contact: Greg J. Cylkowski, M.A., Founder

*****North Central Ministry Development
Center** (an Interdenominational Church
Career Development Center), 516 Mission
House Lane, New Brighton, MN 55112
Phone: 651-636-5120
Contact: Kenneth J. McFayden, Ph.D.,
Director
www.ncmdc.org

Prototype Career Services, 1086 W. 7th St.,
St. Paul, MN 55102
Phone: 800-368-3197
Contact: Amy Lindgren,
Counseling Psychologist
www.prototypecareerservice.com
(Mid-life career change, recovery job search.)

Sizen, Stanley J., Vocational Services,
P.O. Box 363, Anoka, MN 55303
Phone: 612-441-8053

Southwest Family Services,
Career Planning Services,
10267 University Ave. North,
Blaine, MN 55434
Phone: 612-825-4407
Contact: Kathy Bergman, M.A., LP

MISSISSIPPI

**Mississippi Gulf Coast Community
College,** Career Development Center,
Jackson County Campus, P.O. Box 100,
Gautier, MS 39553
Phone: 601-497-9602
Contact: Rebecca Williams, Manager

Mississippi State University,
Career Services Center,
P.O. Box P, Colvard Union, Suite 316,
Mississippi State, MS 39762-5515
Phone: 601-325-3344

MISSOURI

Career Center, Community Career Services,
110 Noyes Hall, University of Missouri,
Columbia, MO 65211
Phone: 573-882-6801 Fax: 573-882-5440
Contact: Craig Benson
e-mail: umccppc@missouri.edu

Eigles, Lorrie, MSED, LPC
432 W. 62nd Terrace, Kansas City, MO 64113
phone: 816-363-4171
email: coachlor@swbell.net
www.artistsregister.com

Forest Institute of Professional Psychology,
2885 West Battlefield Rd.,
Springfield, MO 65807
Phone: 417-823-3477
Contact: Rod C. Cannedy, Ph.D.

The Job Doctor, 505 S. Ewing,
St. Louis, MO 63103
Phone: 314-863-1166
Contact: M. Rose Jonas, Ph.D.

*****Midwest Career Development Service**
(an Interdenominational Church Career
Development Center), 754 N. 31st St.,
Kansas City, KS 66110-0816
Contact: Ronald Brushwyler, Director

Women's Center, University of
Missouri–Kansas City, 5100 Rockhill Rd.,
104 Scofield Hall,
Kansas City, MO 64110
Phone: 816-235-1638

MONTANA

Career Transitions, 91 W. Southview,
P.O. Box 145, Belgrade, MT 59714
Phone: 406-388-6701
www.careertransitions.com

NEBRASKA

CMS: Career Management Services,
5000 Central Park Dr., Suite 204,
Lincoln, NE 68504
Phone: 402-466-8427
Contact: Vaughn L. Carter, President

*****Olson Counseling Services,**
8720 Frederick, Suite 105, Omaha, NE 68128
Phone: 402-390-2342
Contact: Gail A. Olson, P.A.C.

Student Success Center,
Central Community College,
Hastings Campus, Hastings, NE 68902
Phone: 402-461-2424

NEVADA

Price, Meg, M.A., NCC,
3785 Baker Lane., Suite 103, Reno, NV 89509
Phone: 775-828-9600 Fax: 775-828-9688
e-mail: worklife4U@aol.com

NEW HAMPSHIRE

Individual Employment Services,
90-A Sixth St., P.O. 917, Dover, NH 03820
Phone: 603-742-5616
Contact: James Otis, Employment Counselor

Tucker, Janet, M.Ed., Career Counselor,
10 String Bridge, Exeter, NH 03833
Phone: 603-772-8693
e-mail: jbtucker@rcn.com

NEW JERSEY

Adult Advisory Service, Kean College of
New Jersey, Administration Bldg.,
Union, NJ 07083
Phone: 908-527-2210

Adult Resource Center,
100 Horseneck Road, Montville, NJ 07045
Phone: 201-335-6910

**Arista Concepts Career Development
Service,** P.O. Box 2436, Princeton, NJ 08540
Phone: 609-921-0308
Contact: Kera Greene, M.Ed.

*****BBCS Counseling Services,**
6 Alberta Drive, Marlboro, NJ 07746
(other offices in Isleton & Princeton)
Phone: 800-300-4079
Contact: Beverly Baskin, Ed.S., M.A., CPRW,
Executive Director
e-mail: bbcs@att.net
www.bbcscounseling.com

Behavior Dynamics Associates, Inc.,
34 Cambridge Terrace, Springfield, NJ 07081
Phone: 201-912-0136
Contact: Roy Hirschfeld

Career Options Center, YWCA Tribute to
Women and Industry (TWIN) Program,
232 E. Front St., Plainfield, NJ 07060
Phone: 908-756-3836 or 908-273-4242
Contact: Janet M. Korba, Program Director

CareerQuest, 2165 Morris Ave., Suite 15,
Union, NJ 07083
Phone: 908-686-8400 Fax: 908-686-6661
Contact: Don Sutaria, Founder, President,
and Career Coach
e-mail: don@careerquestcentral.com
www. careerquestcentral.com

Center for Life Enhancement,
1156 E. Ridgewood Ave.,
Ridgewood, NJ 07450
Phone: 201-670-8443
Contact: David R. Johnson,
Director of Career Programs

Cohen, Jerry, M.A., NCC,
Chester Professional Bldg.,
P.O. Box 235, Chester, NJ 07930
Phone: 908-789-4404

Collins, Loree, 3 Beechwood Rd.,
Summit, NJ 07901
Phone: 908-273-9219

Dowd, Juditha, 440 Rosemont Ringoes
Road, Stockton, NJ 08559
Phone: 609-397-9375 Fax: 609-397-9375
e-mail: jdowd@blast.net

Grundfest, Sandra, Ed.D., Licensed
Psychologist & Certified Career Counselor,
35 Clyde Road, Suite 101,
Somerset, NJ 08873
Phone: 609-921-8401 Fax: 609-921-9430

Guarneri Associates, Career and
Job-Search Counseling, 1101 Lawrence Rd.,
Lawrenceville, NJ 08648
Phone: 609-771-1669
Contact: Susan Guarneri, LPC, CPRW, JCTC;
Jack Guarneri, M.S., NCC
e-mail: resumagic@aol.com

Job Seekers of Montclair, St. Luke's
Episcopal Church, 73 S. Fullerton Ave.,
Montclair, NJ 07042
Phone: 973-783-3442
(Meets Wednesdays 7:30-9:15 P.M.)

**JobSeekers in Princeton N.J.
Trinity Church,**
33 Mercer Street, Princeton, NJ 08542
Phone: 609-924-2277
(Meets Tuesdays, 7:30–9:30 P.M.)

Karmazsin, Pam, Ed.M., M.B.A.,
Career Strategist & Executive Coach,
19 Kershaw Court, Bridgewater, NJ 08807
Phone: 908-526-4026

Lester Minsuk & Associates,
29 Exeter Rd., East Windsor, NJ 08520
Phone: 609-448-4600

Mercer County Community College,
Career Services, 1200 Old Trenton Rd.,
Trenton, NJ 08690
Phone: 609-586-4800, ext. 304

Metro Career Services,
784 Morris Turnpike, Suite 203,
Short Hills, NJ 07078
Phone: 973-912-0106
Contact: Judy Scherer, M.A.
e-mail: metcareer@aol.com

Princeton Management Consultants, Inc.,
99 Moore St., Princeton, NJ 08540
Phone: 609-924-2411
Contact: Niels H. Nielsen, M.A.,
Job and Career Counselor

Resource Center for Women,
31 Woodland Ave., Summit, NJ 07901
Phone: 908-273-7253

Sigmon, Scott B., Ed.D.,
1945 Morris Ave., Union, NJ 07083
Phone: 908-686-7555

*W. L. Nikel & Associates,
459 Passaic Ave., Suite 171,
West Calswell, NJ 07006
Phone: 973-439-1850
Contact: William L. Nikel, M.B.A.
e-mail: wnikel@earthlink.net

Career Camp, P.O. Box 5, Taos, NM 87571
Phone: 505-751-3255
Contact: Laurel Donnellan, Director
e-mail: info@careercamp.com

Allen, Carol, Consultant, 560 West 43rd St.,
Suite 5G, New York, NY 10036
Phone: 212-268-5182

Bernstein, Alan B., CSW, PC, 122 East 82nd
St., New York, NY 10028
Phone: 212-288-4881

Career Development Center,
Long Island University,
C.W. Post Campus, Brookville, NY 11548
Phone: 516-299-2251
Contact: Pamela Lennox, Ph.D., Director

Career Resource Center,
Bethlehem Public Library,
451 Delaware Ave., Delmar, NY 12054
Phone: 518-439-9314
Contact: Denise L. Coblish,
Career Resources Librarian

CareerQuest, c/o TRS Inc.,
Professional Suite,
44 E. 32nd St., New York, NY 10016
Phone: 908-686-8400 Fax: 908-686-6661
Contact: Don Sutaria, Founder,
President, and Career Coach
e-mail: don@careerquestcentral.com
www. careerquestcentral.com

Careers by Choice, Inc.,
205 E. Main St., Huntington, NY 11743
Phone: 631-673-5432
Contact: Marjorie ("MJ") Feld

Careers In Transition,
Professional Career Services,
33 Borthwick Ave., Delmar, NY, 12054
Contact: Thomas J. Denham, Ed.M.,
Executive Director
e-mail: tdenham@siena.edu

Celia Paul Associates,
1776 Broadway, Suite 1806,
New York, NY 10019
Phone: 212-397-1020
Contact: Celia Paul, President;
Dr. Stephen Rosen, Chairman
e-mail: srosenc@ix.netcom.com
(Specializing in lawyers, doctors, and scientists.)

Center for Creativity and Work,
P.O. Box 9158, Woodstock, NY 12498
Phone: 212-490-9158 or 914-336-8318
Contact: Allie Roth, President
(Offices in Manhattan and Woodstock.)

Dent, Margaret Howe,
26 Middlesex Drive, Fredonia, NY 14063
Phone: 716-673-1490

*Judith Gerberg Associates,
250 West 57th St., New York, NY 10107
Phone: 212-315-2322

Hofstra University, Career Counseling
Center, Room 120, Saltzman Community
Center, 131 Hofstra, Hempstead, NY 11550
Phone: 516-463-6788

Appendix B

Kingsborough Community College,
Office of Career Counseling and Placement,
2001 Oriental Blvd., Room C102,
Brooklyn, NY 11235
Phone: 718-368-5115

Lewis, Laura, 101 Ives Hall,
Cornell University, Ithaca, NY 14853-3901
Phone: 607-255-2223

Livelyhood Job Search Center,
301 Madison Ave., 3rd Floor,
New York, NY 10017
Phone: 212-687-2411
Contact: John Aigner, Director

New York University, Center for Career,
Education, & Life Planning, 50 W. 4th St.,
330 Shimkin Hall, New York, NY 10012-1165
Phone: 212-998-7060
e-mail: sce.advise@nyu.edu

Onondaga County Public Library,
The Galleries of Syracuse,
447 South Salina St.,
Syracuse, NY 13202-2494
Phone: 315-435-1900
Contact: Reference Department
e-mail: reference@onlib.org.

Orange County Community College,
Counseling Center, 115 South St.,
Middletown, NY 10940
Phone: 914-341-4070

Personnel Sciences Center, Inc.,
276 Fifth Ave., Suite 401,
New York, NY 10001
Phone: 212-683-3008 Fax: 212-683-3436
Contact: Dr. Jeffrey A. Goldberg, Ph.D.,
President, Licensed Psychologist

The Prager-Bernstein Group,
122 E. 42nd St. Suite 2815,
New York, NY 10168
Phone: 212-697-0645
Contact: Leslie B. Prager, M.A., C.M.P.,
Senior Partner
e-mail: Leslie-PBG@email.msn.com

Psychological Services Center,
Career Services Unit,
University at Albany, SUNY, Husted 167,
135 Western Ave., Albany, NY 12222
Phone: 518-442-4900
Contact: George B. Litchford, Ph.D., Director
(Individual and group career counseling.)

RLS Career Center, Career Development
Specialist, 770 James Street,
Syracuse, NY 13203
Phone: 315-446-0500 Fax: 315-446-5869
Contact: Rebecca A. Livengood,
Executive Director
e-mail: rls@borg.com

Schenectady Public Library,
Job Information Center, 99 Clinton St.,
Schenectady, NY 12305
(Has weekly listings, including job-search listings of companies nationwide.)

Scientific Career Transitions,
Science & Technology Advisory Board,
1776 Broadway, Suite 1806,
New York, NY 10019
Phone: 212-397-1021
Contact: Stephen Rosen, Ph.D.
e-mail: srosenc@ix.netcom.com
(Specializes in scientists and engineers.)

Vehicles, Inc., Life Skills and Career
Training, 1832 Madison Ave., Room 202,
New York, NY 10035-2707
Phone: 212-722-1111
Contact: Janet Avery

WIN Workshops (Women in Networking),
1120 Avenue of the Americas, Fourth Floor,
New York, NY 10036
Phone: 212-333-8788
Contact: Emily Koltnow

NORTH CAROLINA

Allman & Co., Inc., 3205 Randall Pkwy.,
Suite 111, Wilmington, NC 28406
Phone: 919-395-5219
Contact: Steven Allman, LPC, NCC, MCC
e-mail: s.allman@bizec.rr.com

Career Consulting Associates of Raleigh,
P.O. Box 17653, Raleigh, NC 27619
Phone: 919-782-3252
Contact: Susan W. Simonds, President

**Career, Educational, Psychological
Evaluations,** 2915 Providence Rd., Suite 300,
Charlotte, NC 28211
Phone: 704-362-1942

Career Focus Workshops,
8301 Brittanis Field Road,
Oakridge, NC 27310
Phone: 336-643-1025
Contact: Glenn Wise, President
e-mail: glwise2@cs.com

Career Management Center,
3203 Woman's Club Dr., Suite 100,
Raleigh, NC 27612
Phone: 919-787-1222, ext. 109
Contact: Temple G. Porter, Director

***The Career and Personal Counseling
Service,** 4108 Park Rd., Suite 200,
Charlotte, NC 28209
Phone: 919-276-3162 or 704-523-7751
Fax: 704-523-7752
Contact: Sue M. Setzer, Executive Director
e-mail: career@trellis.net

Carolina Career Consulting,
1145A Executive Circle, Cary, NC 27511
Phone: 919-238-5050
Contact: Lisa Schwartz, M.A., LPC, NCC
e-mail: CareerConsulting@mindspring.com
www.careerconsulting.com

***The Intensive Life/Career Planning
Workshop,** 131 Chimney Rise Dr.,
Cary, NC 27511
Phone: 919-469-5775
Contact: Mike Thomas, Ph.D.;
Steve Mulliner Ph.D.
e-mail: mikethomas@nc.rr.com

Joyce Richman & Associates, Ltd.,
2911 Shady Lawn Dr.,
Greensboro, NC 27408
Phone: 919-288-1799

Kochendofer, Sally, Ph.D.,
Charlotte, NC 28211
Phone: 704-362-1514
e-mail: drsallyk@mindspring.com

Life Management Services, LC,
127 Chimney Ridge Dr., Cary, NC 27511
Phone: 919-481-4707
Contact: Marilyn and Hal Shook
(The Shooks originally trained with John
Crystal, though they have developed their
own program since then.)

Women's Center of Raleigh,
128 E. Hargett St., Suite 10,
Raleigh, NC 27601
Phone: 919-829-3711

OHIO

Career Point, Belden-Whipple Building,
4150 Belden Village St., NW, Suite 101,
Canton, OH 44718
Phone: 216-492-1920
Contact: Victor W. Valli, Career Consultant

Cuyahoga County Public Library
InfoPLACE Service, Career, Education
& Community Information Service,
5225 Library Lane,
Maple Heights, OH 44137-1291
Phone: 216-475-2225 or
toll-free 800-749-5560
e-mail: madams@cuyahoga.lib.oh.us
www.cuyahogalibrary.org

*Diversified Career Services, Inc.,
2675 Quarry Valley Rd.,
Columbus, OH 43204
Phone: 614-488-3359
Contact: Laura Armstrong, Executive Coach
Robert J. Armstrong, Positive Life Coach
e-mail: careers@DCScreatingfutures.com
www.DCScreatingfutures.com

Flood, Kay Reynolds,
3600 Parkhill Circle NW,
Canton, OH 44718
Phone: 330-493-1448

Human Touch
Phone: 513-772-5839
Contact: Judy R. Kroger, LPC,
Career and Human Resources Counselor
e-mail: judykroger@aol.com

J&K Associates and Success Skills
Seminars, Inc., 607 Otterbein Ave.,
Dayton, OH 45406-4507
Phone: 937-274-3630 or 937-274-4375
Contact: Pat Kenney, Ph.D., President

*KSM Careers & Consulting,
1655 W. Market St., Suite 506,
Akron, OH 44313
Phone: 330-867-0242
Contact: Kathryn Musholt, President

*Midwest Career Development Service
(an Interdenominational Church Career
Development Center),
1520 Old Henderson Rd., Suite 102B,
Columbus, OH 43221-3616
Phone: 614-442-8822

New Career, 328 Race St.,
Dover, OH 44622
Phone: 216-364-5557
Contact: Marshall Karp, M.A., NCC, LPC,
Owner

*Professional Pastoral Counseling
Institute, Inc., 8035 Hosbrook Rd.,
Suite 300, Cincinnati, OH 45236
Phone: 513-791-5990
Contact: Judy Kroger, Counselor

UA Adult Focus Career Quest,
The University of Akron,
Caroll Hall 55, Akron, OH 44325-4110
Phone: 330-972-5793
Contact: Meredith A. Kalapich, M.A., LPC,
Academic Advisor
e-mail: adultfocus@uakron.edu

Woods, Anne, 8225 Markhaven Ct.,
W. Worthington, OH 43235
Phone: 614-888-7941

OKLAHOMA

Career Development Services, Inc.,
6506 S. Lewis Ave., Suite 254,
Tulsa, OK 74136-1083
Phone: 918-293-0500 Fax: 918-293-0503
e-mail: cardevser@aol.com

Resonance and the YWCA Women's
Resource Center of Tulsa,
1608 S. Elwood, Tulsa, OK 74119
Phone: 918-587-3888
Contact: Penny Painter, Executive Director,
Resonance; Jane Vantine, Site Director,
YWCA Women's Resource Center;
Nancy Weber, M.A., Career Counselor

OREGON

*Anderson, Lisa Renee, M.A., NCC, GCDF,
Career and Life Coach
1230 Arthur St., Eugene, OR 97402
Phone: 541-484-6785
e-mail: lisaanderson_ma@hotmail.com

Career Development, P.O. Box 850,
Forest Grove, OR 97116
Phone: 503-357-9233
Contact: Edward H. Hosley, Ph.D., Director

Career Pathways, 4037 NW Elmwood Dr.,
Corvallis, OR 97330-1068
Phone: 541-754-1958
Contact: Peggy Carrick, M.A., LPC, NCC
e-mail: panda@proaxis.com

Careerful Counseling Services,
1305 NE Fremont, Portland, OR 97212
Phone: 503-997-9506
Contact: Andrea King, M.S., NCC,
Career Counselor
e-mail: aking@careerful.com
www.careerful.com

Appendix B

Verk Consultants, Inc., 1190 Olive St.,
P.O. Box 11277, Eugene, OR 97440
Phone: 541-687-9170
Contact: Larry H. Malmgren, M.S.,
President

PENNSYLVANIA

Anita's Careers, Inc., The Colonade,
100 Old York Rd., Suite E714,
Jenkintown, PA 19046
Phone: 215-517-8089 Fax: 215-517-8556
Contact: Anita Klein, President
e-mail: anitascareers@aol.com
www.anitascareers.com

Career by Design, 1011 Cathill Rd.,
Sellersville, PA 18960
Phone: 215-723-8413
Contact: Henry D. Landes,
Career Consultant

Career Development Center,
Jewish Family & Children's Service,
5743 Bartlett St., Pittsburgh, PA 15217
Phone: 412-422-5627
Contact: Linda Ehrenreich, Director

Career Strategies/JEVS, 1845 Walnut St.,
7th Floor, Philadelphia, PA 19103-4707
Phone: 215-854-1874

Center for Adults in Transition,
Bucks County Community College,
Newtown, PA 18940
Phone: 215-968-8188

Forty Plus of Philadelphia, Inc.,
1218 Chestnut St.,
Philadelphia, PA 19107-4810
Phone: 215-923-2074

Haynes, Lathe, Ph.D., 401 Shady Ave.,
Suite C107, Pittsburgh, PA 15206
Phone: 412-361-6336

Kelly, Jack, Career Counselor,
Career Pro Resume Services,
251 DeKalb Pike, Suite E608,
King of Prussia, PA 19406
Phone: 610-337-7187

Kessler, Jane E., M.A.,
Licensed Psychologist,
252 W. Swamp Rd., Suite 56,
Doylestown, PA 18901
Phone: 215-348-8218 Fax: 215-348-0329

*Mid-Atlantic Career Center,
1401 Columbia Ave., Lancaster, PA 17603
Phone: 717-397-7451
Contact: Dennis K. Hall, Executive Director
e-mail: macctr@belatlantic.org

Priority Two, P.O. Box 343,
Sewickley, PA 15143
Phone: 412-935-0252
Contact: Pat Gottschalk,
Administrative Assistant
*(Five locations in the Pittsburgh area; call for
addresses. No one is turned away for lack of
funds.)*

Taylor, Alan, M.A., M.S.,
2405 E. Swamp Rd.,
Quakertown, PA 18951
Phone: 215-536-4532
e-mail: twotaylors@comcast.net

**Vietnam Veterans Leadership Program
of Western Pennsylvania,**
1323 Forbes Ave., Suite 202,
Pittsburgh, PA 15219-4725
Phone: 412-281-8100 Fax: 412-281-3144
Contact: Michael D. Stone
e-mail: vvlp@nauticom.net
www.vvlp.org
*(Free comprehensive career advising &
job-search assistance to all era veterans.)*

SOUTH CAROLINA

Crystal-Barkley (formerly The John C.
Crystal Center), 293 East Bay St.,
Charleston, SC 29401
Phone: 800-333-9003 Fax: 800-560-5333
Contact: Nella G. Barkley, President
e-mail: crystalbarkley@careerlife.com
www.careerlife.com
*(John Crystal, the founder of the Crystal Center,
died in 1988; Nella, his business partner for
many years, now continues his work.)*

Greenville Technical College,
Career Advancement Center,
P.O. Box 5616, Greenville, SC 29606
Phone: 864-250-8281
Contact: F. M. Rogers, Director

SOUTH DAKOTA

University of Sioux Falls, The Center for
Women, 1101 W. 22nd St.,
Sioux Falls, SD 57105
Phone: 605-331-6697
Contact: Tami Haug-Davis, Director

TENNESSEE

Banks, Mary M., Career Counselor,
4536 Chickasaw Rd., Kinsport, TN 37664
Phone: 423-288-2646
e-mail: careers@chartertn.net

*Career Achievement, NiS International
Services, 1321 Murfreesboro Road,
Suite 610, Nashville, TN 37217
Phone: 615-367-5000
Contact: William (Bill) L. Karlson;
Harry McClure, Manager

*Career Resources, Inc.,
2 Brentwood Commons #150,
750 Old Hickory Blvd.,
Brentwood, TN 37027
Phone: 615-297-0404
Contact: Jane C. Hardy, Principal

*Future Solving, 3200 West End Ave.,
Suite 500, Nashville, TN 37203
Phone: 615-385-2850
Contact: Patrick Slay, M.A.
e-mail: Patrick@futuresolving.com
www.futuresolving.com

*RHM Group, P.O. Box 271135,
Nashville, TN 37227
Phone: 615-391-5000
Contact: Robert H. McKown

Career Counselors Guide   387

World Career Transition, P.O. Box 1423,
Brentwood, TN 37027-1423
Phone: 800-366-0945
Contact: Bill Karlson, Executive VP

TEXAS

Austin Career Associates,
901 Rio Grande, Austin, TX 78701
Phone: 512-474-1185
Contact: Maydelle Fason,
Licensed Career Counselor

Career Action Associates P.C.,
8350 Meadow Rd., Suite 272,
Dallas, TX 75231
Phone: 214-378-8350
Contact: Joyce Shoop, LPC;
Rebecca Hayes, M.Ed., CRC, LPC
(Office also at 1325 8th Ave., Ft. Worth, TX
76104. Phone: 817-926-9941)

Career and Recovery Resources, Inc.,
2525 San Jacinto, Houston, TX 77002
Phone: 713-754-7000
Contact: Vernal Swisher, Director

Fason, Maydelle, LCC, Employment
Consultant, 1607 Poquonock Road,
Austin, TX 78703
Phone: 512-474-1185

Life Transitions, Inc., 6800 Park Ten Blvd.,
Suite 298 West, San Antonio, TX 78213
Phone: 210-737-2100
www.life-career.com

*New Life Institute, P.O. Box 4487,
Austin, TX 78765
Phone: 512-469-9447
Contact: Bob Breihan, Director

Ragland, Chuck, Transformational
Consultancy, 2504 Briargrove Dr.,
Austin, TX 78704-2704
Phone: 512-440-1200

*Sue Cullen & Associates,
7000 Bee Caves Rd., Suite 300,
Austin, TX 78746
Phone: 512-732-1249
Contact: Sue Cullen
e-mail: sue@suecullen.com
www.suecullen.com

*Worklife Institute Consulting,
7100 Regency Square, Suite 210,
Houston, TX 77036
Phone: 713-266-2456
Contact: Diana C. Dale, Director

UTAH

Lue, Keith, P.O. Box 971482,
Orem, UT 84097-1482
Phone: 801-319-5688
e-mail: keithlue@keydiscovery.com

University of Utah, Center for Adult
Development, 1195 Annex Bldg.,
Salt Lake City, UT 84112
Phone: 801-581-3228

VERMONT

Career Networks and ProSearch,
1372 Old Stage Rd., Williston, VT 05495
Phone: 800-918-WORK or 802-872-1533

VIRGINIA

Beach Counseling & Career Center,
3070 Brickhouse Ct,,
Virginia Beach, VA 23452
Phone: 757-306-9100
Cell: 757-306-0357
Contact: Suzan Thompson, Ph.D.
www.my-career-counselor.com

The BrownMiller Group, 312 Granite Ave.,
Richmond, VA 23226
Phone: 804-288-2157
Contact: Sally Brown, Bonnie Miller

Change & Growth Consulting,
6220 Old Franconia Rd.,
Alexandria, VA 22310
Phone: 703-569-2029
Contact: Barbara S. Woods, M.Ed., NCC,
LPC, Counselor

Fairfax County Office for Women,
The Government Center,
12000 Government Center Pkwy.,
Suite 38, Fairfax, VA 22035
Phone: 703-324-5735
Contact: Elizabeth Lee McManus,
Program Manager

Hollins College, Women's Center,
P.O. Box 9628, Roanoke, VA 24020
Phone: 703-362-6269
Contact: Tina Rolen, Career Counselor

Mary Baldwin College, Rosemarie Sena
Center for Career and Life Planning,
Kable House, Staunton, VA 24401
Phone: 703-887-7221

McCarthy & Company, Career Transition
Management, 4201 South 32nd Rd.,
Arlington, VA 22206
Phone: 703-761-4300
Contact: Peter McCarthy, President

Psychological Consultants, Inc.,
6724 Patterson Ave., Richmond, VA 23226
Phone: 804-288-4125

Virginia Commonwealth University,
University Career Center, 907 Floyd Ave.,
Room 2007, Richmond, VA 23284-2007
Phone: 804-367-1645

The Women's Center, 133 Park St., NE,
Vienna, VA 22180
Phone: 703-281-2657
Contact: Conda Blackmon

WASHINGTON

Bridgeway Career Development,
3035 Island Crest Way,
Mercer Island, WA 98040
Phone: 206-375-3452
Contact: Janet Scarborough,
Ph.D., LMHC, NCC, Owner
e-mail: js@bridgewaycareer.com
www.bridgewaycareer.com

Appendix B

Career Management Institute,
8404 27th St. W., University Place, WA 98466
Phone: 253-565-8818
Contact: Ruthann Reim, M.A., NCC, LMHC
e-mail: careermi@nwrain.com

*Center for Life Decisions,
Career Counseling and Consulting,
3121 East Madison St.,
Suite 209, Seattle, WA 98112
Phone: 206-325-9093
Contact: Larry Gaffin
e-mail: lgaffin@spiritualityofwork.com
www.spiritualityofwork.com

**Centerpoint Institute for Career and Life
Renewal,** 4000 NE 41st St., Bldg D – Suite 2
Seattle, WA 98105-5428
Phone: 206-686-LIFE (5433)
e-mail: admin@centerpointonline.org
www.centerpointonline.org

Churchill, Diane, 508 W. Sixth, Suite 202,
Spokane, WA 99204
Phone: 509-458-0962

The Individual Development Center, Inc.
(I.D. Center), 1020 E. John, Seattle, WA 98102
Phone: 206-329-0600
Contact: Mary Lou Hunt, M.A., NCC,
President

*People Management Group International,
924 First St., Suite A, Snohomish, WA 98290
Phone: 206-563-0105
Contact: Arthur F. Miller, Jr., Chairman

WASHINGTON, D.C.
**Blackwell Career Management of Capitol
Hill,** 626 A St. SE, Washington, D.C. 20003
Phone: 202-546-6835
e-mail: mablack@citizen.infi.net

Community Vocational Counseling Service,
718 21st St. NW, Washington, D.C. 20052
Phone: 202-994-4860
Contact: Robert J. Wilson, M.S.,
Asst. Director for Educational Services

George Washington University,
Center for Career Education,
2020 K St., Washington, D.C. 20052
Phone: 202-994-5299
Contact: Abigail Pereira, Director

Hoppin, Prue, Career Counselor/Coach,
2632 Woodley Place NW,
Washington, D.C. 20008
Phone: 202-986-9345
e-mail: pruehoppin@ix.netcom.com

Horizons Unlimited, Inc.,
1050 17th St. NW, Suite 600,
Washington, D.C. 20036
Phone: 202-296-7224 or 301-258-9338
Contact: Marilyn Goldman, LPC
www.career-counseling.com

WEST VIRGINIA
Jepson, Ed, 2 Hazlett Court,
Wheeling, WV 26003
Phone: 304-232-2375

Ticich, Frank, M.S., MS, CRC, CVE,
Career Consultant, 153 Tartan Drive,
Follansbee, WV 26037
Phone: 304-748-1772
e-mail: freedom1@swave.net
(Free services available.)

WISCONSIN
Making Alternative Plans,
Career Development Center,
Alverno College, 3401 S. 39th St.,
P.O. Box 343922, Milwaukee, WI 53234-3922
Phone: 414-382-6010

Swanson, David, Career Seminars and
Workshops, 7235 West Wells St.,
Wauwatosa, WI 53213-3607
Phone: 414-774-4755
e-mail: dswanson@wi.rr.com
*(David was on staff at my Two-Week Workshop
twenty times.)*

WYOMING
*Gray, Barbara W., Career Consultant,
P.O. Box 9490, Jackson, WY 83002
Phone: 307-733-6544

University of Wyoming, Career
Planning and Placement Center,
P.O. Box 3195/Knight Hall 228,
Laramie, WY 82071-3195
Phone: 307-766-2398

U.S.A.—NATIONWIDE
Forty Plus Clubs: A nationwide network of
voluntary, autonomous nonprofit clubs,
manned by its unemployed members (who
must give a certain number of hours of
service per week on assigned committees),
paying no salaries, supported by initiation
fees (often around $500) and monthly dues
(often around $60). Varying reports as to
their helpfulness. However, one reader gave
a very good report on them recently: "I
would just like to let you know that 40+, for
me, has been a really big help. They provide
good job search training. . . . But even more
importantly, for me, is the professional office
environment they provide to work out of,
and the fellowship of others who are also
looking for work. . . . As they say at 40+,
'It's hell to job search alone.'"

If you have Internet access, a list of the
North American 40+ chapters is to be found
at:

www.fp.org/chapters/htm

Eleven of these chapters have their own
websites; in my opinion, the best and most
up-to-date one belongs to the Greater
Washington chapter:

www.fp.org

For those who lack Web access, at this writ-
ing there are clubs in the following cities
(listed alphabetically by state): California:
Los Angeles, Oakland, Orange, San Diego;
Colorado: Colorado Springs, Ft. Collins,
Lakewood; District of Columbia: Greater
Washington; Hawaii: Honolulu; Illinois:
Chicago; Minnesota: St. Paul; New York:

Buffalo, New York; Ohio: Columbus; Oregon: Beaverton; Pennsylvania: Philadelphia; Texas: Dallas, Houston; Utah: Salt Lake City; Washington: Bellevue; Wisconsin: Brookfield; and in Canada: Toronto.

If you live in or near any of these cities, you can check the white pages of your phone book (under "Forty Plus") for the address and phone number.

CANADA

Alberta
Work from the Heart, 8708 136 St., Edmonton, Alberta T5R 0B9
Phone: 403-484-8387
Contact: Marguerite Todd

British Columbia
CBD Network Inc., #201-2033 Gordon Dr., Kelowna, B.C. V1Y 3J2
Phone: 250-717-1821

Curtis, Susan, M.Ed., 4513 West 13th Ave., Vancouver, B.C. V6R 2V5
Phone: 604-228-9618

Find Work You Love, Inc.,
2277 West 2nd Ave., Suite 402,
Vancouver, B.C. V6K 1H8
Phone: 604-737-3955 or 888-737-3922
Fax: 604-737-3958
Contact: Marlene Haley, B.A., M.Ed.,
Career Counselor
www.findworkyoulove.com

Westcoast Vocational, Inc.,
400-1681 Chestnut St.,
Vancouver, B.C. V6J 4M6
Phone: 604-737-9884
Contact: Barbara Wilkinson, M.A.,
Career Consultant

Manitoba

Job-Finding Club, 516-294 Portage Ave., Winnipeg, Manitoba R3C 0B9
Phone: 204-947-1948

Westcoast Vocational Inc.,
400-1681 Chestnut St.,
Vancouver, B.C. V6J 4M6
604-737-9884 Vancouver
604-948-8063 Tsawwassen
Contact: Barbara Wilkinson, MA,
Career Counselor, Consultant, & Coach

Nova Scotia
Enhancing Your Horizons Consulting,
25 Birchwood Terr., Dartmouth,
Nova Scotia B3A 3W2
Phone: 902-464-9110
Contact: Sue Landry

People Plus, PLA Centre, 7001 Mumford Rd., Halifax Shopping Centre, Tower 1, Suite 101, Halifax, Nova Scotia B3L 4N9
Phone: 902-454-2809

Ontario
After Graduation Career Counseling,
73 Roxborough St. West, Toronto,
Ontario M5R 1T9
Phone: 416-923-8319
Contact: Teresa Snelgrove, Ph.D., Director

André Filion & Associates, Inc.,
151 Slater Street, Suite 500,
Ottawa, Ontario K1P 5H3
Phone: 613-230-7023
Contact: Kenneth Des Roches

Career Partners International/
Hazell & Assoc., 1220 Yonge St.,
3rd Floor, Toronto,
Ontario M4T 1W1
Phone: 416-961-3700
e-mail: mhazell@hazell.com

Career Strategy Counseling,
2 Briar Hill Place, London, Ontario N5Y 1P7
Phone: 519-455-4609
Contact: Ruth Clark, B.A., M.Ed.
e-mail: rclark4609@rogers.com

*CareersPlus Inc., 55 Village Place, Suite 203, Mississaugua, Ontario L4Z 1V9
Phone: 905-272-8258
Contact: Douglas H. Schmidt, B.A., M.Ed., Ed.D.
www.careersplusinc.com

Changes by Choice, 190 Burndale Ave., North York, Ontario M2N 1T2
Phone: 416-590-9939
Contact: Patti Davie

donnerwheeler, Career Development Consultants, Health Services Sector,
1 Belvedere Court, Suite 1270,
Brampton, Ontario L6V 4M6
Phone: 905-450-1086
Contact: Mary M. Wheeler
e-mail: info@donnerwheeler.com
www. donnerwheeler.com
(Offers workshops particularly for those in the health services sector.)

Human Achievement Associates,
22 Cottonwood Crescent, London,
Ontario N6G 2Y8
Phone: 519-657-3000
Contact: Mr. Kerry A. Hill

JVS of Greater Toronto
74 Tycos Dr., Toronto, Ontario M6B 1V9
Phone: 416-787-1151, ext. 210
Fax: 416-785-7529
e-mail: lkornberg@jvstoronto.org

Mid-Life Transitions, 2 Slade Ave.,
Toronto, Ontario M6G 3A1
Phone: 416-653-0563
Contact: Marilyn Melville

My CareerAbility.Com,
3 Embla St., Toronto, Ontario M3C 2G9
Phone: 416-444-9200
Contact: Dan Trepanier, Career Planning and Coaching Specialist
www.mycareerability.com

The Precision Group, 400 Matheson Blvd. East, Unit 18, Mississauga, Ontario L4Z 1N8
Phone: 905-507-8696
Contact: Harold Harder, B.Sc., B.Admin.St.

Puttock, Judith, B.B.A., C.H.R.P., Career Management Consultant, Strategic Career Options, Planning & Education (SCOPE), 913 Southwind Court, Newmarket, Ontario
Phone: 905-898-0180

Steinberg, Susan, M.Ed., 74 Denlow Blvd., Don Mills, Ontario M3B 1P9
Phone: 416-449-6936

YMCA Career Planning & Development, 42 Charles Street East, Toronto, Ontario M4Y 1T4
Phone: 416-928-9622.

Quebec
Jewish Vocational Service, Centre Juif D'Orientation et de L'Emploi, 5151, ch. de la Côte Ste-Catherine, Montreal, Quebec, H3W 1M6
Phone: 514-345-2625
Contact: Alta Abramowitz, Director, Employment Development Services.
(Uses both French and English versions of Parachute.*)*
(Utilise des versions françaises et anglaises de Parachute.*)*

Longpre, Jean-Marc, CRHA
Career Development Consultant
Phone: 450-883-0889
e-mail: jm.longpre@sympatico.ca

La Passerelle Career Transition Centre, 1255 Phillips Square, Suite 903
Montreal H3B 3G1
Contact: Lisa Boyle
Phone: 514 866-5982
e-mail: lapasserelle@videotron.net

Roy, Marie-Carmelle, Career Development Consultant
Phone: 514-992-5219
e-mail: mcroy20@sympatico.ca
(Marie-Carmelle was on my staff at the Two-Week Workshop for seven years.)

Saskatchewan
People Focus, 712 10th St. East, Saskatoon, Saskatchewan S7H OH1
Phone: 306-933-4956
Contact: Carol Stevenson Seller

OVERSEAS

Australia
Career Action Centre, 5 Bronte Ave., Burwood, Victoria 3125
Phone: 03 9808 5500
Contact: Jackie Rothberg
e-mail: jackie@careeractioncentre.com.au
www.careeractioncentre.com.au

Career Profilers Makeover Lounge, Suite F, 4 Railway St., Southport QLD 4215
Phone: 1300 553 903
(outside Australia: +61 7 55263918)
Contact: Danielle Rivas
e-mail: info@careerprofilers
www.careerprofilers.com

Designing Your Life, 10 Nepean Pl., Macquarie ACT 2614
Phone: 61 6 253 2231
Contact: Judith Bailey

The Growth Connection, Suite 402, 4th Floor, 56 Berry St., North Sydney, NSW 2060
Phone: 61 2 9954 3322
Contact: Imogen Wareing, Director

Life by Design, P.O. Box 50, Newport Beach, NSW 2106
Phone: 61 2 9979 4949
Contact: Ian Hutchinson, Lifestyle Strategist
e-mail: info@lifebydesign.com.au
www.lifebydesign.com.au

Milligan, Narelle, Career Consultant, 4 McLeod Place, Kambah ACT 2902
Phone: 61 2 6296 4398

Worklife, The Center for Worklife Counselling, Suite 2, 4 Bond St., Mosman, P.O. Box 407, Spit Junction NSW 2088
Phone: 612 9968 1588
Contact: Paul Stevens, Director
e-mail: worklife@ozemail.com.au
(Paul has been the dean of career counseling in Australia for many years.)

Workplace Transitions,10 Martinez Ave., Townsville, QLD 4812
Phone: 61 7 4775 4708
Contact: Gillie Johnson
e-mail: info@workplacetransitions.com.au

Brazil
Adigo Consultores, Av. Doria 164, Sao Paulo SP 04635-070
Phone: 55 11 530 0330
Contact: Alberto M. Barros, Director

Pereira, Geraldo
Av. Epitacio Passoa, 1600/402
22411-070 Lagoa, Rio de Janeiro

Far East
Byung Ju Cho, Seocho-Ku Banpo-dong 104-16 Banpo Hyundai Villa A-402, Seoul, 137-040, South Korea
Phone: 011-9084-6236
(BJ is the translator of the Korean version of Parachute.*)*

Transformation Technologies Pte Ltd. 122 Thomson Green, 574986 Singapore
Phone: 65 456 6358
Contact: Anthony Tan, Director

Germany
Career Development Seminars, offered at Westfalische Wilhelms-Universitat Muenster, Dez. 1.4 Wissenschafliche Weiterbildung, Schlossplatz 2, 48149 Munster
Phone: 0251 832 4762;
and at Universitat Bremen, Zentrum fur Weiterbildung, 28359 Bremen
Phone: 0421 Brunnenweg 10, 48153 Muenster, Germany.
For more info, contact:
Dr. Hastenrath & Partner,

An der Untertrave 96, D-23552 **Luebeck**
Phone: + 49-(0) 51-70796-0
Contact: Dr. Julia Hastenrath und
Arnulv Rudland
e-mail: info@hastenrath.de
www.hastenrath.de

Leitner, Madeleine,
Dipl. Psych. Ohmstrasse 8, 80802 **Munchen**
Phone: 089 33 04 02 03

Webb, John Carl,
Meinenkampstr. 83a, 48165 **Munster-Hiltrup**
Phone: +49 (0) 2501/ 92 16 96
e-mail: john@muenster.de
www.learnline.de/angebote/lwp

New Zealand
Career Makers, P.O. Box 277-95,
Mt. Roskill, **Auckland**
Phone: 649 817 5189
Contact: Liz Constable

Life Work Career Counselling,
P.O. Box 2223, **Christchurch**
Phone: 64 03 379 2781
Contact: Max Palmer

New Zealand Creative Career Centre, Ltd.,
4th Floor, Braemar House, 32 The Terrace,
P.O. Box 3058, **Wellington**
Phone: 64 4 499 8414
Contact: Felicity McLennan

South Africa
Andrew Bramley Career Consultants
12 Ridge Way, Proteaville, **Durbanville** 7550
Phone/Fax: 27 21 9755573
Contact: Andrew Bramley
e-mail: abramley@mweb.co.za
www.andrewbramley.co.za

Borchers, Victoir, Principal Consultant,
Deloitte & Touche Human Capital
Corporation, Recruitment &
Resourcing Division, **Capetown**
Phone: +27-21-6701731
e-mail: viborchers@deloitte.co.za

Spain
Analisi-Nic, Via Augusta,
120. Principal 1 08006 **Barcelona**
Phone: (34) 932119503,
Fax: (34) 932172128
Contact: José Arnó
e-mail: analisi@arrakis.es

Switzerland
Baumgartner, Peter, Lowen Pfaffikon,
Postfach 10, 8808 **Pfaffikon**
Phone: 055 415 66 22

Cabinet Daniel Porot,
1, rue Verdaine, CH-1204 **Geneva**
Phone: 41 22 311 04 38
Contact: Daniel Porot, Founder
*(Daniel was co-leader with me each summer at
my international Two-Week Workshop for
twenty years.)*

Hans-U. Sauser, Beratung und Ausbildung,
Rosenauweg 27, CH-5430 **Wettingen**
Phone: 056 426 64 09

Honegger Career Mgmt.,
Scheeitergasse 3, CH-8001 **Zurich**
Phone: 01 790 18 46
Contact: Urs W. Honegger

Kessler-Laufbahnberatung,
Alpenblickstr. 33, CH-8645,
Jona b. **Rapperswil**
Phone: 055 211 0977
Contact: Peter Kessler, Counselor

Lernen • Beraten • Begleiten •
Maria Bamert-Widmer,
Churerstrasse 26, CH-8852, **Altendorf**
Phone: 055 442 55 76

LifeProject, Baechlerweg 29, CH-8802,
Kilchburg/Zurich
Phone: +41 (0) 1 715 15 63
Contact: Peter A. Vollenweider, Counselor
e-mail: pvollenweider@bluewin.ch

United Kingdom
Brian McIvor & Associates, Newgrange
Mall, Unit 4B, Slane, **County Meath, Ireland**
Phone: 00 353 41 988 4035
e-mail: bmcivor@indigo.ie
www.brianmcivor.com
*(Brian was on the staff at my international
Two-Week Workshop for four years.)*

Bridgeway Associates Ltd., Career Consul-
tants, P.O. Box 16, Chipping Campden
GL55 6ZB **London and Midlands**
Phone: 01386 841840
Contact: Jane Bartlett

CareerMax Ltd., 181, Kensington High St.,
London W8 6SH
Phone: 44 207 368 4460
Contact: Steve Podmore
e-mail: steve@careermax.co.uk
www.careermax.co.uk

Career Shaman, 119 The Street, Adisham,
Canterbury, **Kent** CT3 3JS
Phone: 01304 84279
e-mail: careers@career-shaman.com

Castle Consultants International,
9 Drummond Park, Crook of Devon,
Kinross, KY13 0UX, **Scotland**
Phone: +44 1577 840122
Contact: Walt Hopkins,
Founder and Director
e-mail: Walt@Hopkins.net
www. castles.co.uk

Cavendish Associates
The Stable Courtyard, Leigh Court,
Abbots Leigh, **Bristol** BS8 3RA
Phone: +44 (0) 1275 813000
Contact: Philip Houghton
e-mail: phil.houghton@bcisgnet.co.uk

The Chaney Partnership, Hillier House,
509 Upper Richmond Rd. West,
SW14 7EE **London**
Phone: 020 8878 322
Contact: Isabel Chaney, B.A.

Appendix B

Hawkins, Dr. Peter, Mt. Pleasant,
Liverpool, L3 5TF
Phone: 0044 (0) 151 709-1760
Fax: 0044 (0) 151 709-1576
e-mail: p.Hawkins@gieu.co.uk

John Lees Associates, 37 Tatton St.,
Knutsford **Cheshire** WA16 6hauk
Phone: (UK): 01565 631625
Contact: John Lees
e-mail: johnlees@dsl.pipex.com
www.jobyoulove.co.uk

PASSPORT, 74 Blenheim Crescent,
South Croyden CR2 6BP
Phone: 020 8681 4838
Contact: Janie Wilson
e-mail: janie@passport.co.uk
www.passport.co.uk

Readers often write to ask us which of
these overseas counselors are familiar with
my approach to job-hunting and career-
changing. The answer is: all of the counselors listed above have attended my
Two-Week Workshop, and therefore know
my approach well.

Other overseas counselors not trained by
me, but who may still be quite helpful to
you, since they are experienced counselors,
and are familiar with *Parachute,* are:

Mendel, Lori, 19/6 Emanuel Haromi, 62645
Tel-Aviv, Israel
Phone: 972-3-524-1068

Transitions & Resources, Ltd.,
5a Yiftach, **Jerusalem, Israel** 93503
Phone: 02-6710673 Fax: 02-6721985
Contact: Judy Feierstein, Director
e-mail: fund@aquanet.co.il

Veeninga, Johan, Careers by Design,
Business Park "De Molenzoom,"
P.O. Box 143, NL-3990 DC,
Houten/Utrecht, **The Netherlands**
Phone: 31 (0) 3403 75153

INTERNET CONSULTING
Creative Careers Research
Principal: Carol Eikleberry
www.creativecareers.com

Piazzale, Steve, Ph.D., Career/Life Coach
Phone: 650-964-4366
e-mail: steve_piazzale@att.net
www.BayAreaCareerCoach.com

A

Accomplishments, documenting, 311
Achievements
  definition of, 184
  extracting skills from, 185–86
Ads
  answering, 26
  employer's vs. job-hunter's preference for, 38
  researching salaries through, 324
Agencies. *See* Employment agencies; Governmental agencies
Alternatives
  brain as treasure chest of, 86
  for employers vs. job-hunters, 35–37, 38
  examples of, 15
  importance of, 14, 17, 32–33, 248–49, 331
"A – B = C" method, 125–31
Answering machine messages, 272
Appearance, personal, 298–99
Area codes, 373–74
Attitude, 300–301

B

Behavioral Interviewing, 275–76, 290
Benefits, 329–30

Biofeedback, 150–51
Birkman Method, 106
Brown, Barbara, 150–51
Building-block diagram, 180

C

Calling, 337. *See also* Mission in life
Career-change. *See also* Careers
  creative approach to, 158
  frequency of, over lifetime, 4
  mastering, 11–17
  motivations for, 146–47
  paths of, 84–85
  school and, 247–48
Career counselors/coaches
  accredited, by NCDA, 374
  choosing, 359–69
  contracts for, 366–68
  definitions of, 359
  degrees for, 359–60, 364–65, 373
  distance and, 51–52
  fees for, 366–68, 369
  fraud by, 360–61, 366–68
  free workshops by, 369
  groups run by, 369
  Mission in life and, 353
  questions to ask, 362–69
  sampler of, 361, 371–93
  success rate for, 365
Careers. *See also* Career-change; Jobs

Careers (*continued*)
  best, for you, 87, 104
  choosing, 84–85, 87–89, 103–10,
    158
  hot, 103–4
  list of, with skills and job
    characteristics, 90–102
  number of different, 103
  researching, 112–14
Career tests, 105–9
Caretaking, 73
China, 52, 53. *See also* Outsourcing
Churning, 55–56
Civil service examinations, 27
Classified ads. *See* Ads
Companies. *See* Employers;
    Organizations
Compensation, 58
Competencies, 156
Competency-based interviewing.
    See Behavioral Interviewing
Considerateness, importance of,
    301
Consulting, 235
Contacts
  asking for job leads from,
    27–28
  cultivating, 271–72
  definition of, 267–68
  employer's vs. job-hunter's
    preference for, 38, 39
  identifying the person-who-
    has-the-power-to-hire-you
    through, 266–67, 268–70
  importance of, 270
  Internet and, 132
  keeping track of, 272
  for salary research, 326–27
  using, 245
Contracts
  for career counselors/coaches,
    366–68
  employment, 330
Conventions, 271
Counseling. *See* Career coun-
    selors/coaches

Co-workers, preferred, 214–17
Crystal, John, 198, 255, 338, 387
Curricula vitae (c.v.), 264. *See also*
    Resumes

D
Data, skills dealing with, 162,
    172–73
Degrees
  for career counselors, 359–60,
    364–65, 373
  without job guarantees, 110
Dictionary of Occupational Titles,
    103
Dikel, Margaret, 113
Distance-as-obstacle, death of,
    47–52, 58–59
Domestic violence, 62
Dreams, pursuing your, 105, 117,
    121, 145–47, 229

E
Education. *See* School
Employees, good vs. bad, 280
Employers. *See also* Organizations;
    Person-who-has-the-power-
    to-hire-you
  contacting interesting, 29
  differences among, 3
  fears of, 283–86, 292–95
  preferred methods to fill
    vacancies, 37–40, 42–43
  previous, 281–82, 286
  questions asked by, at
    interviews, 286–88,
    291–97
  rescuing, 272–73
  screening by, 265–66
  type of employee sought by, 280
Employment agencies
  employer's vs. job-hunter's
    preference for, 38
  success rate for, 26
  temporary, 137–38, 251–52, 325
Employment interviews. *See*
    Hiring-interviews

Enthusiasm, importance of, 229, 258
Executive search firms. *See* Search firms
Experience Unlimited Job Club, 376

F

Faith. *See* Mission in life; Religious beliefs
Family
  asking for job leads from, 27–28
  home businesses and, 118, 141
  identifying skills with, 185–86
  moving and, 67, 68–69, 81
  researching location through, 71
  support from, 68–69
Fields. *See also* Interests
  dealing with people's problems or needs, 200–204
  dealing with things, 205–7
  different jobs within, 196–97
  of fascination, 196–207
  intuitional approach to, 192–95
  using mental skills, 196–99
  vocabulary and, 193–94
50-50 rule, 278
Flower Graphic, 152–53
  example of filled-in, 154–55, 228
  geographical preferences (petal), 208–13
  interests/fields of fascination (petal), 196–207
  level and salary (petal), 223–27
  naming, 234–43
  people environments (petal), 214–17
  transferable skills (center), 181–86
  using, 229–34
  values (petal), 217–20
  working conditions (petal), 221–22
Forty Plus Clubs, 389–90
Franchises, 122–23
Fraud, 360–61, 366–68

Free-lancing. *See* Self-employment
Friends
  asking for job leads from, 27–28, 38
  career counselors/coaches used by, 361
  identifying skills with, 185–86
  moving and, 68–69
  nurturing relationships with, 243, 244
  researching location through, 71
  researching organizations through, 250, 277
  support from, 68–69
Fringe benefits, 329–30

G

Geographical preferences, 70–75, 76–77, 190–91, 208–13.
  See also Moving
God's plan. *See* Mission in life
Governmental agencies, 27, 327
Graduates, recent, 291

H

Haldane, Bernard, 184, 311, 338
Health
  employers' questions about, 294
  moving for, 62–63
Hiring-interviews. *See also* Behavioral Interviewing; Person-who-has-the-power-to-hire-you
  asking for feedback after, 309–10
  bad-mouthing previous employers during, 281–82
  bringing evidence of skills to, 276, 281, 290
  characteristics of, 256–57
  dating metaphor for, 275, 298–303
  employers' fears during, 283–86, 292–95
  ending, 276, 304–5
  50-50 rule, 278

Hiring-Interviews (*continued*)
  focus on employer during, 279–80
  importance of first two minutes of, 298–304
  length of, 276–77
  length of answers at, 278
  obtaining, 265–66, 272–73
  personal appearance and conduct at, 298–304
  preparing for, 277–78, 280–82
  questions asked by employer at, 286–88, 291–97
  questions asked by job-hunter at, 288–89, 304–5
  researching organization before, 277–78
  researching organization during, 282–83
  role-playing, 311
  salary negotiation and, 314–17
  thank-you notes after, 257, 305–7
  as a trick, 308
Holland, John, 106–7, 214–15
Holland Codes, 107, 215, 217
Home businesses
  "A – B = C" method, 125–31
  determining type of, 120–25
  fall-back strategies for, 134–40
  key to success in, 125
  problems of, 118–20
  recent popularity of, 118
  researching, 120–21, 125–34
Hope, finding, 16–17
Hurricane Katrina, 67, 69

I

Illegal immigrants, 52
Income. *See* Salary
India, 53. *See also* Outsourcing
Information
  cutting down on, 13–14
  skills dealing with (mental), 162, 172–73, 196–99
Informational Interviewing
  definition of, 194, 245

to find out about organizations, 250–51
  job offers during, 253–54
  networking vs., 243, 244–45
  PIE Method and, 255, 256–57
  questions for, 246–47
  steps in, 243, 246
  thank-you notes after, 252–53
Interests. *See also* Fields
  favorite, 192, 196–207
  measuring, 106–8
  placing on Flower Graphic, 196–207
Internet. *See also* Websites
  contacts through, 132
  job-hunting on, 25, 132
  researching on, 111, 132–34, 322–23
  testing and counseling on, 106–7, 132, 187, 189, 393
Interviews. *See* Behavioral Interviewing; Hiring-interviews; Informational Interviewing; Practice Interviewing
Inventions, 123–24

J

Jackson, Tom, 338
Job-hunting. *See also* Career-change; Life-changing job-hunt; Traditional job-hunt
  abandonment of, 16–17
  as art, not science, 2
  best methods for, 22–23, 27–32
  dating metaphor for, 3
  fishing metaphor for, 6–9
  frequency of, over lifetime, 4
  fundamental truths about, 2–3
  groups, 30, 31
  importance of alternatives in, 14, 17, 32–33, 248–49, 331
  on the Internet, 25, 132
  length of, 12
  luck and, 3, 6–7
  mastering, 2, 8–9, 11–17
  number of targets in, 331

as a reflection of job performance, 280–81
"right" vs. "wrong" ways of, 2
targeting small organizations,
332
tax deductions for, 225
as a turning point in life, 337
ultimate responsibility for, 3
using multiple methods for,
32–33
worst methods for, 22–27
Job-interviews. *See* Hiring-interviews
Job leads, 27–28, 195
Job offers
during Informational Interviewing, 253–54
at the job-interview, 276, 304
withdrawn, 331
in writing, 330
Job-postings, 132
Jobs. *See also* Careers; Fields
availability of, 18–21
creation of, 56, 264, 290–91
dream, 88–89, 105, 145–48, 229
families of, 232
mortality of, 55–56
moving to locations with, 64–65
number of, in U.S., 19
outsourcing and, 52–55
part-time, 138–40, 235, 328
philosophical approaches to,
56–58
satisfaction and, 57
screening out, while on the job,
249
stop-gap, 135–37
transforming, 57–58
trying on, 109–10, 243, 246–47,
249
Job-sharing, 139–40
Job-titles, 103, 231

L

Large organizations
hiring-interviews at, 263, 265–66

job creation at, 264
person-who-has-the-power-to-
hire-you at, 265, 266,
268–70
Level
desired, 223
salary and, 325
Life-changing job-hunt
components of, 30–31
success rate of, 31–32
LPC, 359–60, 373
Luck, 3, 6–7

M

Mail order, 122
Mannerisms, nervous, 299–300
MCC, 374
Miller, Arthur, 338
Mirror Method, 105
"Mirror Theory," 217
Mission in life
first stage, 340, 341, 342–46
second stage, 340, 341, 347–51
third stage, 340, 341–42, 351–57
career counseling and, 353
definition of, 337–38
as intersection, 355–56
job-hunting and, 337–38
secret of finding, 339–41
unlearning and learning, 341–42
Money. *See* Salary
Moving
frequency of, 61
geographical preferences and,
70–75, 76–77, 208–13
joys of, 82–83
to a location with jobs, 64–65
overseas, 73–77
reasons for, 62–67
research before, 77–78, 80–82
to rural locations, 65, 72
for survival, 67–69
to urban locations, 65
young adults and, 61–62
Myers-Briggs Type Indicator, 164,
165

N

National Career Development Association, 374
Natural disasters, 62, 67–69
NCC, 359, 373
NCCC, 359, 373
Networking, 243, 244. *See also* Contacts; Informational Interviewing
Newspaper ads. *See* Ads

O

Occupations. *See* Careers; Jobs
Offshoring. *See* Outsourcing
O*Net, 103, 187, 189
Organizations. *See also* Large organizations; Small organizations
  kinds of, 235, 238
  making list of, 238–41
  researching, 249–52, 277–78, 282–83
  size of, 263
Outsourcing, 52–55
Overseas jobs, 73–77, 391–93

P

Part-time work, 138–40, 235, 328. *See also* Temporary work
Party Exercise, 107, 215–17
Passion, importance of, 229, 258
Pay. *See* Salary
People. *See also* Contacts; Family; Friends
  favorite to work with, 214–17
  fields dealing with, 200–204
  skills dealing with (interpersonal), 162, 174–75
  as sources of job information, 241–43
  as sources of salary information, 323–25
People List exercise, 200–204
Personal traits. *See* Traits
Person-who-has-the-power-to-hire-you. *See also* Employers

  fears of, 283–86, 292–95
  identifying, 265, 266–67, 268–70
  setting up appointment with, 269
Petals. *See* Flower Graphic
Philosophy of life. *See* Mission in life
Philosophy of work, 56–58
Phone Book exercise, 206–7
PIE Method, 255–60
Pleasure interviews. *See* Practice Interviewing
Porot, Daniel, 255, 328, 392
Practice Interviewing, 255–60
Prioritizing Grid, 177–79

R

Raises, 311, 330
Religious beliefs, 338, 344. *See also* Mission in life
Research
  on careers, 112–14
  on home businesses, 120–21, 125–34
  on the Internet, 132–34
  before job-interviews, 277–78
  before moving, 77–78, 80–82
  on organizations, 249–52, 277–78, 282–83
  on salary, 321–25
Resumes
  definition of, 37
  employers' views of, 38, 39–40, 42
  example of "winning," 41
  format and style for, 40
  mailing out randomly, 25
  posting on the Internet, 132
  screening through, 265–66
Rewards, favorite, 227
RIASEC system. *See* Holland Codes
Riley Guide, 113
Rural locations, 65, 72
RVs, 72–73

S

Salary
  desired, 223–26
  fringe benefits and, 329–30
  level and, 325
  negotiating, 313–30
  ranges, 315, 325–28
  researching, 321–25
  time to discuss, 314–17
School, 63, 110, 247–48
SDS (Self-Directed Search), 106–7, 215
Search firms, 26. *See also* Employment agencies
Self-confidence/self-esteem, loss of, 300
Self-employment
  "A – B = C" method, 125–31
  determining business type, 120–25
  fall-back strategies for, 134–40
  key to success for, 125
  problems of, 118–20
  recent popularity of, 118
  researching, 120–21, 125–34
Self-knowledge, importance of, 148–50
Seven Stories exercise, 166–69
Shyness, overcoming, 255–60
Skills
  avoiding jargon and job-titles to describe, 186
  dealing with data/information (mental), 162, 172–73, 196–99
  dealing with people (interpersonal), 162, 174–75
  dealing with things (physical), 162, 170–71
  enjoyment vs. competency, 184–85
  evidence of, 276, 281, 290
  identifying, 158, 159–66, 169–76, 184–86
  levels of, 162–63

  occupations listed by, 90–102
  prioritizing, 176, 180
  traits vs., 164–65
  transferable, 159–66, 169, 176
  as verbs, 188
  writing stories about, 166–69
Small organizations
  advantages of, 264
  job creation at, 264
  person-who-has-the-power-to-hire-you at, 266
  targeting, 332
Smoking, 301–2
Stop-gap jobs, 135–37
Style. *See* Traits
Subjects Chart exercise, 197–200. *See also* Fields; Interests
Success stories, 82–83, 332–33
Support groups, 245
Survival, 67–69

T

Tax deductions, 225
Telecommuting, 122
Telephone. *See also* Yellow pages
  answering machine messages, 272
  area codes, 373–74
Temperaments. *See* Traits
Temporary work, 137–38, 235, 251–52, 325
Testimonial Dinner exercise, 217–20
Tests
  career, 105–9
  civil service, 27
  on the Internet, 106–7, 132, 187, 189
  of traits, 164, 165
  of transferable skills, 187, 189
Thank-you notes
  after hiring-interviews, 257, 305–7
  after Informational Interviewing, 252–53, 257
  after Practice Interviewing, 257

"That One Piece of Paper"
    exercise, 150–57, 228–29.
    See also Flower Graphic
Things
    fields dealing with, 205–7
    Phone Book exercise, 206–7
    skills dealing with (physical),
        162, 170–71
Traditional job-hunt
    on the Internet, 25, 132
    preferences of employers vs.
        job-hunters, 37–40
Traits, 164–65, 182
Trioing, 185–86

U
Unemployment
    benefits, 137
    by state, 64
Union hiring halls, 27
Unlearning and learning,
    341–42

V
Vacancies, existence of, 18–21, 56
Values
    determining your, 217–20
    importance of, 302–3

Vision, refining your, 88–89
Vocation, 337. *See also* Mission in
    life
Volunteer work, 235, 252

W
Wanderlust, 65, 72–73
Want ads. *See* Ads
Websites. *See also* Internet
    for career information, 104, 105,
        112–14
    for home businesses, 132–34
    with Internet tutorials, 111
    for moving, 71–72, 73
    for telecommuting, 122
"Who Am I?" exercise, 148–49
Working conditions, 221–22
Workshops, free, 369

Y
Yellow pages
    calling employers from, 30
    career counselors/coaches in,
        362
    using, to make list of fields,
        205–7
    using, to make list of organiza-
        tions, 240

Update 2007

To: PARACHUTE
   P.O. Box 379
   Walnut Creek, CA 94597

I think that the information in the 2006 edition needs to be
changed, in your next revision, regarding (or, the following
resource should be added):

_____

_____

_____

_____

_____

_____

I cannot find the following resource, listed on page _____:

_____

_____

_____

_____

_____

_____

Name _____

Address _____

Please make a copy.

Submit this so as to reach us by February 1, 2006. Thank you.

Other Resources

Additional materials by Richard N. Bolles
to help you with your job-hunt:

The What Color Is Your Parachute? Workbook
This handy workbook leads the job-seeker
through the process of determining exactly
what sort of job or career they are most
suited for, easily streamlining this potentially stressful and confusing task. $9.95

Job-Hunting on the Internet,
Fourth Edition, revised and expanded.
(with Mark Bolles)
This handy guide has quickly established
itself as the ideal resource for anyone who's
taking the logical step of job-hunting on
the Internet. $9.95

The Three Boxes of Life,
And How to Get Out of Them
An introduction to life/work planning. $18.95

How to Find Your Mission in Life
Originally created as an appendix to *What
Color Is Your Parachute?*, this book was written
to answer one of the questions most often
asked by job-hunters. $14.95

Job-Hunting for the So-Called Handicapped
(with Dale Brown)
A unique perspective on job-hunting and career-
changing, addressing the experiences of the
disabled in performing these tasks. $12.95

The Career Counselor's Handbook
(with Howard Figler)
A complete guide for practicing or aspiring
career counselors. $17.95

NOTES

- Caretaker of people's homes.
- Product photography - shoot at home, send in pics
- Researcher - outdoors
- Wildlife photographer
- Forester

⊛ Exercise on pg. 148
✪ "One Piece of Paper" - pg. 152
- Pg. 165 - online traits tests
- Pg. 167 - Story exercise ⊛
- Being outdoors - geologist, geographer
- National Parks, Hiking, taking photos

NOTES

NOTES

NOTES

NOTES

NOTES

NOTES

NOTES

NOTES

NOTES

bobbybukawski @ mac.com